Latin American Studies into the
Twenty-First Century: New Focus,
New Formats, New Challenges

SALALM Secretariat
General Library
University of New Mexico

ISBN: 0-917617-38-X

Contents

450 Years of Publishing in the Americas: What Lies Ahead?

Liberty and Justice for All: Human Rights and Democratization in Latin America

Analyzing Latin American Library Materials Price Indexes

Librarianship and Library Collections in Brazil

The ABCs of Preservation Microform Masters: Access and Bibliographic Control

The Bookdealer Connection: Access to Information

Notes from Round Tables

Preface

The choice of a very broad theme for SALALM XXXVI was conscious and deliberate. I sought to construct a program that would realistically reflect the rapidly changing context of Latin American studies and our role in it. The papers in this volume, which were prepared for presentation in June 1991, represent a wide spectrum of issues ranging from the general "state-of-the-field" presentations to focused examinations of library concerns. SALALM XXXVI saw several firsts: our first speaker from the People's Republic of China, Xu Wenyuan, and our first formal presentation via videotape (Lawrence Weschler could not be in New York and San Diego at the same time). The present volume reflects these interests and new directions for SALALM, as well as our continued attention to the issues that seem always to be with us—such as cooperative collection development.

A great deal went on at SALALM in San Diego that is not evident in this volume, however. Nowhere on these pages will you find the informal sharing of information—among librarians, bookdealers, publishers, and scholars—that is such a hallmark and highlight of our annual SALALM meeting. And as always, there was the hard work of the committees during the first two days of the conference. Numerous workshops and roundtables, though not generating formal papers, enhanced the practical and intellectual exchange: "Using New Technologies to Provide Computerized Information on Latin America to End Users"; "Electronic Imaging and Latin American Materials"; "Transborder Maps"; "Cataloging Issues and SALALM"; and "How Do You Start a Formal Bibliographic Instruction Program?" In addition, those attending were treated to a slide presentation on Rio street art, and two videos on environmental issues in Brazil. And who could forget Ariel Dorfman's dramatic reading of a chapter from his mystery novel-in-progress, *Memoria*, which features a murder during . . . a conference of Latin American librarians and bookdealers.

I hope that readers will find as much of interest among the contributions to this volume as I did when putting together the program and participating in the conference. I would like to express my sincere gratitude to all the SALALM members who lent their ideas, their talents, their humor, and their energy to building the program with me, and to the Local Arrangements Committee for their expert logistical assistance.

Deborah L. Jakubs

A New Order in the Old World: The Impact of Recent Events on Latin America

1. Latin America and the New World Order

Peter H. Smith

The title of this talk is actually a grand hypothesis. As you know, there's a longstanding debate over the whole term "Latin America," whether there is in fact some sort of cultural, political, or other kind of unity that defines the region. If memory serves, it's the French, in fact, who coined the term to further their own imperial ambitions in the late nineteenth century. And, as you'll see toward the end of these remarks, I think the very sense of the name and unity of the region might in fact be coming into question in the years ahead.

Second, there is this awful term, "the New World Order," a phrase that contains at least two oxymorons and probably three, in a fictional statement of an order that does not now exist. As we look around and ponder the significance of the end of the Cold War, we are actually witnessing the end of the Cold War. As area studies specialists, we're going to have to be very honest and look back on the formation of the field as a consequence or a product of the Cold War. My generation went to graduate school thanks to the Cold War. In the early 1960s there was a good deal of federal money available to send people to graduate school on the wistful assumption that the training of an area specialist would somehow stop revolution from occurring throughout the hemisphere. It was a generous idea. We certainly took advantage of it. One could also suggest that some of the debates that we have had in this country might in fact have reflected Cold War imperatives or at least perceived Cold War imperatives during the 1980s. The discussions over El Salvador and Nicaragua have Cold War components and even a number of significant practitioners in the field presented their arguments in Cold War terms.

Now that's changing. Or at least we can anticipate that that's going to change, and the same sorts of indications that Cole Blasier (chap. 2) sees in the Soviet Union in one way are likely to take shape to a different degree here in the United States as well.

3

There has been a great deal of discussion about the idea of a new world order. I recently visited the Soviet Union and then Japan and, prior to the outbreak of the Gulf War, the general notion of a new world order was that with the passing of the Cold War, the terms of power or the currency of power would be economic prowess and technological capability, rather than military power. This meant that the European community and Japan would achieve new positions of power. The United States was declining in its hegemony, in its economic and technological position in the world, and as a consequence of the changing definition of the currency of power we were going to see it as a rearrangement of the structure of power, which in turn would somehow shape itself into some kind of new world order. Then came the Gulf War. There came one version of the new world order from the White House early on, which was basically a kind of NATO for the Middle East, a kind of regional security apparatus that would be parallel to NATO and the U.S.-Japan security treaty, and was a limited notion of what the world order was going to mean. It also implied— one has to suggest it—stability in the world oil markets.

A second notion then came through as President Bush built up the alliance It was a grand optimistic vision of multilateral consultation that would set the rules for the game. The United Nations would become a major institution in this new world order. Decision-making would be by consultation rather than by assertion, and in this sense we would be moving toward a new and in some ways more democratic world order in which consultation, persuasion, and compliance with the U.N. rules of the game would determine international behavior. We then witnessed the war itself and what has come to be called the so-called "unipolar" moment when specialists have observed that, at least militarily, there is no longer a bipolar world. There is only a one polar world in which the United States is the only real world-class military power. Lo and behold, to all of those who suggested or thought that perhaps the passing of the Cold War would mean that military power would be less important and that economic and technological power would be more important, this seemed to be contradicted very sharply by the outcome of the war, by the political significance of the displays of not only military but technological prowess by the United States.

So some think that the new world order is in fact going to be dictated by the United States. In fact, it's no longer a Cold War bipolar world but a unipolar world, or at least a unipolar moment, and the consequences of this are still not widely determined. It is, of course, not something politicians widely discuss. You can usually tell the important topics: those that are not discussed. What *is* discussed is usually, and very frequently, the secondary consequence of that unipolarity. So we don't know what the new world is going to look like. We don't know if it's going to be a new world order. We don't know what kind of order might come to exist, and we certainly are unclear about the implications of it all for Latin America.

However abstract, and distant, and geopolitical, and grand, and world-wide and great-power-oriented these comments are, my view is that they have direct and meaningful significance, not only for the future of Latin America but also for the way we think about area studies and our place within in. Let me outline three and a half potential scenarios for Latin America in this new world, whether it's an orderly world or not.

The optimistic scenario we might think of as global development. In one scenario, peace dividends exist throughout the world and are invested in social and economic development around the world. The First World sees it as its obligation and in its interest to promote development in the Third World, including in Latin America. There's more equality. Poor people have an opportunity to move ahead in this new world order. Swords are beaten into plowshares, spears into pruning hooks, and so forth. This is the happy, optimistic idea many people had in mind as soon as the wall fell in Berlin. The notion was that somehow the end of the Cold War meant there was going to be less military spending, there would be more money for development, it would be a happier, healthier, kinder, gentler world. It's possible, but I'm not sure it's very probable.

In that first scenario, of course, Latin America would take part. We can imagine that Latin America would be an active participant in this scheme for global development, and that the atmosphere in politics in the hemisphere would also be much softer and more gentle than before. But there's a second scenario that is more likely. Or at least potentially more likely. One might think of it as a restoration of rather traditional spheres of influence by great powers, rather than a world in which everything flows freely. What we might witness is a breakup of the world into traditional-looking spheres of influence, each sphere dominated by a great power.

Indeed, there are two suggestions that we're even now moving in this direction. One is the regionalization of economic blocs. One speaks not only of the EEC and the EEC's finally coming to Great Britain to establish its own foothold in this new world order, but also of the likelihood within different spheres or regions around the world that there will be some need for security. It's going to be a new need. It's not going to be anti-Soviet, it's not Cold War security. What one can anticipate in a post-Cold War world is increasing numbers of outbreaks of regional small conflicts. Some of them will be between nations, as in the case of Kuwait and Iraq. Many of them will be actually within nations, as in the case of the ethnic strife in Yugoslavia and elsewhere in the Soviet Union. There will be a different definition of a security need in this world. It's not going to be throwing missiles back and forth; it's going to be containing small-scale conventional strife. And in this sense one could argue that rather traditional nineteenth-century style spheres of influence will develop because of the economic logic of creating regional groups, and security needs that are low level and regional. What one could imagine is that within each bloc there would be a policeman or two, whose function would be to keep down disorder within the bloc, for the good not only of the leader of the bloc but also presumably for that of the other major players.

We've seen this potentially developing in the European Community. We're now undertaking free trade discussions among the United States, Canada, and Mexico. President Bush has discussed the possibility of an enterprise for the Americas initiative, which would envision a free trade arrangement for the entire Western Hemisphere. I was in Tokyo at the time that he announced that, and the reaction of the Japanese was that it looks an awful lot like the Monroe Doctrine, folks, and we're not sure we're going to be very welcome. If you talk to Latin Americans, they're rather apprehensive as well about this otherwise benign-looking initiative to bring Latin America into what would be quite clearly a U.S.-dominated sphere of influence.

The situation in Asia is a good deal more complicated. Japan is clearly the economic leader of Asia but, for historical reasons, mainly dating back to the 1930s and of course World War II, and also because of the economic disparity between the various economies of Asia, the formation of a Pacific-Asia economic regional bloc is not as straightforward as it seems to be here in the United States or in the EEC. But it's very possible to imagine that the formation of a bloc in Europe and then in the Western Hemisphere could leave the Japanese and the Chinese with the sense that they have no other choice but to form a bloc, to ensure that we have a world in which there are at least three, and possibly four traditional spheres of influence. And what future does that leave for Latin America? Clearly it would be a subordinate partner or a subordinate member in the sphere of influence, where nineteenth-century rules of diplomacy and power politics would prevail. That we might go from the Cold War, with its own rules of the game, to a rather nineteenth-century style of rules of the game. It would be very difficult for Latin American leaders to appeal for support or help outside the Western Hemisphere, where the terms of the game would be one-sided in favor of the United States in its dealings with Latin America. There would not be the threat of communism as a rationale, but the kind of intervention we saw, for example in Panama, might be the prototype for the future. It was not justified by Cold War rhetoric but by some other kind of logic. So, one could envision the development of a scenario that is defined by the spheres of influence.

A third scenario that also leaves Latin America in a troubled position is the creation of what one might think of as a North-North axis, basically leaving out the South and the Third World, with the exception of a very small number of players. The logic here is that if you really create free-market economics in the international community, capital will go where the opportunities are. For better or worse, most of the serious opportunities and the markets exist within the North, rather than the South. So what one could imagine is the creation of a network binding together powers of the North: the United States, the European Community, Eastern Europe if it is absorbed back into the EEC, a post-perestroika Soviet Union if it manages to recover, Japan, back around to the United States again. That would be the circuit of economics, of capital, of flows of credit and political power. If that is so, it is likely that the South would simply be left out. It doesn't have much to offer, although some individual countries in the South might be able to claim membership in this North-North group. If you look at the Mexican petition for free trade, you could define it as an effort to get in the North-North circuit before countries of the South are closed out. Now we have other Latin American countries also seeking to petition to get into this free-trade arrangement. Chile and Costa Rica are the more prominent contenders now. One can anticipate that Africa for example, with the possible exception of South Africa—a post-Apartheid South Africa—would not be invited to play in the league; that Brazil would have serious trouble gaining admission; India might be left out of this game; it's not quite clear what would happen with China. But the basic point is that one could imagine a world in which the North becomes the growth center, the South, for the most part, is left out. With the South, much of Latin America would be left out. There would be a security problem. In this case, one could imagine military power in the North used to contain rebellions and discord in the South, but the economic ties might be very weak.

The half scenario is a variation on the final theme of the North-South separation or the North-North axis. In the case of Latin America, some countries might gain admission to this North-North circuit. Mexico is already petitioning for it; Chile may gain admission;

Costa Rica may gain admission; and some countries in time may get access to this North-North circuit. They will be able to offer raw materials, especially if they have oil. They will be able to offer export platforms for export somewhere else. They will be able to offer low-cost and quite skilled labor by standards of the international market. Many of them, I fear, would have to also offer, as part of the ticket of admission, very compliant foreign policies. That is, compliant with the United States. Under this set of rules of the game, it's very unlikely that Latin American countries would find it in their interests to challenge the United States on major foreign policy issues in the way that Mexico and other countries did in the 1980s. The cost would simply be too high. And the tacit price of the ticket of admission would be what will be called a mature and reasonable foreign policy. What that means in translation is a foreign policy that at least would not widely deviate far from that of the United States. What this scenario suggests—this third and a half scenario—is the fragmentation of Latin America. Some countries get into this North-North circuit, but others do not. It's hard to imagine that Peru would be a near candidate for admission. It's questionable whether, and under what circumstances, Brazil would be a candidate, or Argentina. Some countries may be able to link themselves with this North-North axis, others are left out, and what we have thought of as an intellectual and conceptual unity that is Latin America becomes divided and fragmented between two differing camps.

Clearly, it's hard to know. I don't know what's going to happen. That's why I suggested that this is a piece of fiction. But nonetheless, it's important to think about logical scenarios. My first point is: let us not blandly assume that the end of the Cold War means we're going to move into a kinder, gentler world in which the citizens and people of Latin America about whom we all care so deeply are going to live necessarily better lives. It's just not so obvious that it's going to work out that way. The second point I would make is that we really are in a critical phase of redefinition of the rules of the game for international conduct. I'm hesitant to talk of a New World Order, but the rules of the game, or what constitutes power, and what the rules of the game are for the tacit use of that power, are being redefined now. Within the next ten years, somehow the assertion or the acceptance of that set of rules is going to become clear. It will be a very important and exciting and theoretically confusing period for us all.

The last point I want to make is that we have to rethink what we mean by area studies. What I've suggested here is that the future of Latin America, or the future range of pressures on Latin America, will not be determined solely by the people in Latin America. They are going to be determined well outside of Latin America by Washington, by Tokyo, by Berlin, and by the other major capitals. As the great powers—whoever they are, whatever it is that constitutes power—establish the rules of the game for competition and consort among themselves—that's going to set the theater within which Latin America operates. What this means for us is that we should not conceive of area studies as focusing only on Latin America to the exclusion of the rest of the world. More now than was ever true for our field, we need to think about the relationship between what's going on in Latin America, or what could go on in Latin America, and what is happening in the rest of the world. It is, even if the end of the Cold War has come, not a simpler world; indeed, it's much more complex.

2. The Impact of Perestroika on Soviet Latin Americanists

Cole Blasier

In this paper I talk about the Soviet Union, what's happening there, and how that affects Latin American studies in the Soviet Union. At this writing I've just returned from six weeks in Moscow on a private visit. Many people go as tourists or with official sponsorship, but few people go on a so-called private visit. I had an apartment in Moscow, so I was able to experience at first hand some of the problems of the society.

Many people here in the United States are concerned about what's happening in the Soviet Union; about its stability, about living conditions, and so on, and I must say that I was encouraged by what I saw. Things were not as bad as I expected. In the Univermag (the grocery store that serviced the huge housing project in which I was living), there was lots of bread, huge black loaves, round white bread; there were milk, eggs, and, if you wanted to wait in line, fruit juices, a limited selection of vegetables. The store looked pretty vacant when you walked in, but there seemed to be enough for people to get by on. There was no apparent hunger. People were complaining because they could not get luxuries, and it's difficult in Moscow to get vodka or wine, but they're surviving. People could also get gas for their automobiles.

With respect to violence and security, there are demonstrations, but the situation was under fairly good control in the capital city. There are lots of troops there, and Russians for the most part don't want trouble. They've been suppressed and repressed for so many generations that they're not apt to do, or at least so it seems, something radical which would disturb the public order. There will be problems on the periphery: nationality conflicts, problems of violence, civil war, and so on. That's where the violence is most apt to occur, or has already occurred. But in the center, it's relatively quiet.

And one of the things most Americans think about is what a great figure Gorbachev has been, what he's done for Europe, what he's done for the world. He's a hero in this country. But he is not a hero in the Soviet Union. Many Soviet citizens recognize what he has done for other countries—for example, Germany—but they don't like what he has failed to do in the Soviet Union. Many of them were negative on him and positive on Yeltsin.

What is the psychological impact of these immense changes? For a long time the people had a very stable society. Too stable, in a sense. They knew that if they did certain things there would be certain results. They could count on promotions, material rewards, usually they themselves did not set patterns, somebody else set them. They were responding, and did not have to take the initiative. That's all gone now. It's not clear where the society is going; it's not clear what their institutions are supposed to do; they don't know what they're supposed to do; they're floating in a sea of uncertainty. Many of them don't like it. They don't know how to adapt to it. It's awfully hard for them to work. There are problems of getting under way, doing things day by day. People take long lunch hours. There's a breakdown in discipline and control. There was so much pressure before and suddenly it was released, so they have all these choices. And it's very hard to be productive. Of course, the economy reflects it through the declining rate of economic growth.

Moving from the USSR to a theme on Latin America, let me talk about the rationale for Latin American studies in the Soviet Union. The Soviet Union has played a big role, a public role, in events in Latin America. Or at least the U.S. leaders have cast the Soviet Union in that role since the beginning of the Cold War. Also, the Soviet Latin Americanists have become prominent considering their late arrival to the field. They have been active in many scholarly organizations. The director of the Soviet Institute of Latin America has traveled and spoken all over Latin America. They have been a force in academic life pertaining to Latin America.

The question is why have they been such a force considering not only the distance from Latin America but also the absence of important economic interests in the area. One of the explanations was that the United States was considered a military-strategic threat to the Soviet Union, waxing and waning over the years. This was taken as more or less a given. One of the ways to overcome the threat was to establish close ties with Cuba. So Cuba provided certain leverage, a strategic leverage against the United States in the event of potential conflict. The Soviet military sold the Cuban policy on that basis, and it has been a continuing consideration until recently. Of course, there was the question of potential military threat of the United States not only against the Soviet Union but also against Cuba itself. And the Cuban revolution was what got the Institute of Latin America started. Anastas Mikoyan started it after he returned from his visit to Cuba in 1960.

Another factor that justified so much Soviet interest in Latin America was the struggle between socialism and capitalism. And Cuba represented one of the best places to compete. The Soviet Union had done very poorly in expanding its influence in the Third World. For the most part the Soviet socialist model did not seem to have much future in the advanced industrialized countries either. So Cuba became an important place as a showcase. In addition, the Soviets hoped for the success of national liberation movements in Latin America. So these were the political reasons for the Soviet Union's devoting a lot of attention to Latin American studies. The fact that the Soviet Union sold very little to Latin America except to Cuba which was a captive market, that most of the trade was in imports that it bought from Latin America with hard currency, indicates how little profit, how little value economically, Latin America was to the Soviet Union.

As a result of all these political considerations the Soviets spent quite a lot on Latin America. They established the Institute of Latin America, as I mentioned. That Institute celebrated its thirtieth anniversary while I was there. It has one hundred and eleven professional researchers, maybe double that number in custodial, clerical, and technical staffs. That's a huge research group for Latin America, for one institution; in addition, there probably is an equivalent number of Latin Americanists in the other institutes in the Academy of Sciences. So it's an enormous investment and it rested on an artificial political basis: rather than serving the needs of the Soviet government and people for research, it served as a means of establishing Soviet visibility in the area and meeting certain bureaucratic targets with respect to institutes, departments, sectors, and so on, with coverage country by country, and topic by topic.

There are now some new defining trends which have wiped out the entire rationale of a big Latin America studies effort for the Soviets. In the first place, the Soviet Union has decided that the United States is not going to attack, that the United States does not pose a military threat to the Soviet Union. In fact, the United States is concerned that there might be a breakup in the Soviet Union which could pose problems for Europe, for example, nuclear problems. So it's very clear that they do not regard the United States as a military threat to the Soviet Union or, for that matter, to Cuba itself. The question of competition between socialism and capitalism is pretty much over. The Soviets themselves—not all, but many of the leading ones—say that the system, the Stalinist socialist system, doesn't work, and they are all moving toward capitalist solutions. There's not as much interest any more in national liberation movements in Latin America. Soviet sponsorship of communist parties is largely at an end. So all those political reasons which justified the support for Latin American studies in the Soviet Union are now gone.

Two major contemporary trends are shaping Latin American studies: one is that the Communist Party is no longer managing the institutes. The Academy of Science is supposed to do that, but the Academy is managing only loosely, but far more than before. The institutes are themselves planning their staff, their work. When Gorbachev moved over from the Party to the government, he took most of that power with him, and the Party was undercut. The Secretariat of the central committee used to run things. The man in charge was the general secretary, who was Gorbachev. All the various institutions like the Academy of Sciences reported to the secretary. It doesn't happen any more. They tend to run their own show, obviously within certain budgetary allocations that are made through the central planning system. In Moscow State University, for example, the university no longer consults with the Party or the ministry about routine appointments. They make their own appointments. The influence of local party cells is negligible. They weren't very great before, but they're even less now.

The second defining trend next to the decline of the Party is that the Soviet Union has a huge fiscal deficit. So that while the institutes now have great autonomy, they don't have the money to do the things that they might like to do.

Under Brezhnev for years guests were well entertained in the Soviet Union. I'd been going off and on for more than thirty years and somebody always picked up the bill. During my last trip I was invited to lunch up at the top of the Hotel Rossiia, overlooking the gardens of the Kremlin. We had a wonderful meal, but no caviar, another sign that things are getting tight. After the meal, instead of the director or his minion picking up the check, the four top people of the Institute divvied it up: fifty rubles each. They get about 700 rubles a month. That gives you an idea of the pressure.

Now, the Academy of Sciences has announced that the staffs across the board will be reduced as much as 60 percent of their present size. At the Institute of Latin America commercial consulting is part of the regular mandate. The thirtieth anniversary pamphlet lists commercial consulting as a function. Some people are going into private business. One member is becoming a painter and selling his paintings; there are all kinds of variations. Some staff will no longer be employed by the Institute, but may work on contract. So there's more flexibility. The idea is to make the Institute responsive to real needs, not simply to have a big bureaucratic structure. The whole Institute could go off and become a part of some other institute.

One wonders the extent to which the new order in the Soviet Union will affect the quality of research. In the old days, the researcher's job really was not to provide empirical challenges to policy, even less to evaluate current policy. If they did, it was classified. The job was to justify current policy, and most of the publications are in that model. Now people are going to have a chance to say what they really think and some of them will do so.

Colleagues are extremely frank in conversations, one on one, or in small groups. They often had been in the past, but five or ten years ago, when somebody was very frank with me, it made me uneasy, because I could just see them being hauled off to jail. Now the sky's the limit, they'll say almost anything. So it's wonderful. In my first thirty years of visits to the Soviet Union, I went to two or three houses, private homes. The only time you saw people socially was under approved circumstances. This time I was invited all over town to dinner night after night. Permission was no longer required.

My guess is there's going to be a lot more freedom in the Soviet Union over time. But it will come and go, in waves. Much depends on the extent to which the people exercise these freedoms. Some get great satisfaction out of saying something for which they could have been arrested a couple of years ago. And it will also depend on the extent to which the authorities permit them to speak and write freely.

3. El enfoque chino sobre los estudios latinoamericanos

Xu Wenyuan

En China existe gran interés respecto a América Latina. Los estudios latinoamericanos constituyen en China parte importante de las ciencias sociales. Así lo es porque China y los países latinoamericanos tenían un pasado parecido y hoy en día se enfrentan ante el mismo desafío: desarrollar su economía nacional, elevar el nivel de vida de sus pueblos y en fin de cuentas, modernizar sus países para alcanzar a un nivel más parecido al de los países desarrollados. Además, con la política de apertura aplicada desde hace más de diez años, el gobierno chino viene trabajando para intensificar las relaciones con todos los países extranjeros, especialmente con los países en vías de desarrollo. Los empresarios chinos ya empiezan a buscar campos de actividades fuera del país. Cada día hay más industriales y comerciantes chinos que creen que los semejantes latinoamericanos son virtuales socios y pueden cooperar tanto en el comercio como en las inversiones. Los ciudadanos chinos también muestran gran interés en saber acerca de América Latina. Todo esto lo demuestra un fenómeno: existe una demanda cada año mayor para graduados universitarios que dominan la lengua castellana.

¿Qué ubicación o qué importancia tienen los estudios latinoamericanos en China? Veamos los hechos. Los estudios latinoamericanos se desarrollan actualmente en China en las tres ramas de las instituciones académicas: las de la Academia de Ciencias Sociales de China, las de los centros de enseñanza superior y las de varios ministerios del gobierno chino. Entre estas instituciones académicas, el Instituto de América Latina es la más importante y la única que se dedica específicamente a los estudios latinoamericanos. Las otras son dependencias de alguna institución académica de carácter universal que tiene en general un grupo de investigadores que estudian respectivamente la historia, la literatura, la economía o las relaciones exteriores de América Latina.

La importancia que se da en China a los estudios latinoamericanos también la justifica el siguiente hecho: con la iniciativa de nuestro Instituto se fundó en mayo de 1984 la Asociación China de Estudios

Latinoamericanos. La Asociación tiene como objetivos coordinar los estudios latinoamericanos en China y promover los intercambios académicos tanto interinstitucionales como internacionales. Actualmente la Asociación agrupa cerca de 300 socios formales y otros tantos informales. Organiza cada año un seminario en que se discuten problemas fundamentales o coyunturales de América Latina. La secretaría de la Asociación se encuentra en el Instituto de América Latina.

El Instituto de América Latina

El Instituto de América Latina de la Academia de Ciencias Sociales de China se estableció en julio de 1961. Por la llamada revolución cultural, se interrumpieron sus trabajos académicos durante diez años, desde mayo de 1966 hasta abril de 1976. Ahora el Instituto tiene unos sesenta investigadores y traductores trabajando en cuatro divisiones de investigaciones, una división de traducciones y la redacción de la revista del Instituto, *Estudios Latinoamericanos*. Las cuatro divisiones de investigaciones son: la de la economía latinoamericana; la de la política, historia y relaciones exteriores de América Latina; la de América del Sur; y la de México, Centroamérica y el Caribe. Además, el Instituto tiene una biblioteca que cuenta con cerca de 40 mil libros especializados, en su mayoría en castellano o inglés, y más de 150 revistas y diarios en lenguas extranjeras que el Instituto recibe o en subscripción o en canje con las instituciones académicas extranjeras. Durante los últimos diez años, el Instituto ha formado 31 posgraduados. A través de convenios binacionales, por vía de la Comisión Nacional de Educación del gobierno chino o con el financiamiento de fundaciones extranjeras, la mayoría de los investigadores han estudiado o han trabajado en países latinoamericanos, los Estados Unidos, Canadá o la Unión Soviética como posgraduado o investigador visitante.

Los trabajos de los investigadores del Instituto

En los primeros cinco años del establecimiento del Instituto, los trabajos del Instituto se centraban en la recolección de materiales sobre América Latina y la selección de investigadores que empezaron a estudiar temas fundamentales o coyunturales. Se publicaron ensayos, apuntes, trabajos e informes. Salió a luz un folleto titulado *Los EE.UU. y la Organización de Estados Americanos*. Restablecido el Instituto en abril de 1976, los trabajos académicos progresaron con rapidez y vienen recorriendo un camino sano y próspero. En los últimos quince años, los investigadores han escrito centenales de ensayos, apuntes, informes y ponencias. Se han publicado un gran número de libros. Tradujeron varios trabajos o libros escritos por latinoamericanistas extranjeros. Además, los investigadores tomaron parte en la redacción de anuarios, diccionarios y enciclopedias organizados por otras instituciones académicas o editoriales. La biblioteca del Instituto redacta cada año un folleto titulado *Acontecimientos de América Latina* que ya tiene registrados los acontecimientos de América Latina desde 1492 hasta 1990.

En los primeros años después del restablecimiento del Instituto, los estudios se centraban en los temas de conocimientos básicos y de la economía de los países latinoamericanos. Como resultado, aparecieron libros como *Manual de América Latina, Partidos políticos de los países latinoamericanos, Economía de América Latina*, y trabajos sobre las economías de varios países latinoamericanos tales como Brasil, la Argentina, Venezuela, Perú, México y los de América Central y el Caribe. En la década de los 80, al mismo tiempo que se profundizaban los estudios sobre la economía latinoamericana, empezaron a dar frutos los estudios sobre la historia, la política y las relaciones exteriores de los países latinoamericanos. Se publicaron, por ejemplo, los libros *Estudios sobre las estrategias de desarrollo económico de los países latinoamericanos, Breve historia de las relaciones entre China y América Latina, La política latinoamericana en la postguerra, Historia moderna de América Latina, El desarrollo económico y la inflación: Teorías y prácticas en América Latina*. Otros estudios prontos a salir son *Relaciones económicas y comercio exterior de América Latina, América Latina en el umbral del nuevo siglo* y *Diccionario de la historia latinoamericana*. Los temas de los ensayos, apuntes y otros trabajos académicos son muy variados, tanto económicos y políticos como históricos y socioculturales, tanto regionales y subregionales como nacionales. Fueron más estudiados los problemas de la deuda externa, la estrategia de desarrollo socioeconómico, el ajuste de políticas económicas de los gobiernos latinoamericanos, las relaciones económicas y de comercio exterior y la integración económica en América Latina. En cuanto a los temas políticos y de relaciones exteriores, nuestros investigadores mostraron mayor interés en los problemas de la democratización, las corrientes ideológicas, los sistemas constitucionales y gubernamentales y el problema de América Central. A los investigadores del Instituto también les interesaban mucho los trabajos realizados por sus colegas del exterior y tradujeron al chino una apreciable cantidad de trabajos y libros escritos en castellano o inglés. Entre ellos se pueden mencionar algunos: *La economía de América Latina: Desde la conquista hasta la revolución cubana*, de Celso

Furtado; *Documentos de Simón Bolívar, Capitalismo periférico: Crisis y transformación*, de Raúl Prebisch; *Siete ensayos de interpretación de la realidad peruana*, de José Carlos Mariátegui; y *Nacionalismo económico en América Latina*, de Shoshana B. Tancer.

Temas que se están estudiando

Los investigadores del Instituto siguen profundizando sus estudios sobre América Latina. Entre los temas que se están estudiando ahora, se destacan los siguientes proyectos: "Observaciones históricas sobre las transformaciones del sistema político en el curso de la modernización mexicana", "Esbozos de la historia de relaciones entre América Latina y los EE.UU.", "Revalorización de la teoría de dependencia" y "Análisis sobre la deuda externa de América Latina". En los dos últimos años, el mundo en que vivimos ha experimentado grandes cambios. Los investigadores chinos en el campo de las ciencias internacionales los prestan mucha atención y los observan, estudian y analizan paso a paso. Los latinoamericanistas chinos no somos marginados. Mis colegas ya escribieron unos ensayos o informes a este respecto, y están preparando un estudio sistemático de los impactos de estos cambios para América Latina bajo el título "El nuevo contexto internacional y América Latina". Otros investigadores tienen el propósito de realizar estudios sobre las teorías y prácticas de la modernización latinoamericana. Los traductores del Instituto han empezado a trabajar en la versión china de los nueve tomos de *The Cambridge History of Latin America* (CHLA) y su objetivo es terminar la traducción de esta obra antes del fin de la década de los 90.

Conclusiones

Por lo arriba mencionada, los colegas aquí presentes ya pueden tener una idea general en cuanto al enfoque chino de los estudios latinoamericanos. En conclusión, los latinoamericanistas chinos persiguen en sus estudios los siguientes objetivos: divulgar conocimientos de América Latina en servicio de mejorar la calidad de conciencia internacional de nuestro pueblo; estudiar, analizar y sintetizar las experiencias con la realidad china, asimile lo positivo y evite lo negativo de ellas en servicio de las cuatro modernizaciones del país; prestar materiales de referencias y ofrecer consultas a los sectores públicos, empresariales y socioculturales del país en favor de las relaciones políticas, económicas, comerciales y culturales entre China y los países latinoamericanos. Podemos decir que todos los estudios sobre América Latina se desarrollan para alcanzar estos objetivos. De esta manera, los investigadores chinos de América Latina trabajamos directa o indirectamente por la prosperidad de nuestro país y por intensificar las relaciones entre China y América Latina en particular y entre todos los países del mundo en general.

4. Libraries *sans frontières*: REDIAL, European Bibliographic Cooperation, and 1992

Alan Biggins

This paper describes a cooperative initiative taken by a number of European libraries with an interest in Latin America.[1] Our European academic colleagues have their own well-established European associations—the European Council for Social Science Research on Latin America (CEISAL), the Association of European Latin-Americanist Historians (AHILA), the Nordic Association for Research on Latin America (NOSALF)—and there is increasing cooperation among academic libraries in general throughout Europe. The spirit of cooperation has now reached the field of Latin American librarianship.

A European Information and Documentation Network on Latin America—Red Europea de Información y Documentación sobre América Latina, REDIAL—was formed early in 1991, and is the first systematic and large-scale attempt to bring library and bibliographic cooperation to bear on Latin American materials in Europe. The network is defined as "an international association with research, educational and cultural aims." Its goal is to bring together libraries, documentation centres, non-governmental organizations, associations, and other bodies concerned with Latin America, in order "to develop cooperation, at the international and particularly at the European level, between the various centres of information and documentation on Latin America, especially in the fields of the humanities and social sciences." More specifically, it has the aim of improving access to resources by encouraging and facilitating the exchange of information and the interavailability of resources on Latin America in Europe through the compilation of bibliographic and factual databases.

Origins

In early 1988 a steering committee formed of librarians from major Latin American collections in France, West Germany (as it then was), Belgium, and the United Kingdom met to organize a symposium for the

Author's Note: I am grateful to Mona Huerta, Pat Noble, and Valerie Cooper for their helpful comments on the draft of this paper.

46th International Congress of Americanists, Amsterdam (4th-8th July, 1988). The steering committee was inspired and coordinated by Mona Huerta of the Réseau Amérique Latine, which is a research group—number GDR 26—of France's Centre National de la Recherche Scientifique (CNRS). The other members of the steering committee represented the Centre d'Etudes de l'Amérique Latine of the Institut de Sociologie, Université Libre de Bruxelles, Hamburg's Institut für Iberoamerika-Kunde, and the United Kingdom's Advisory Committee on Latin American Materials (ACOLAM).[2]

The theme of the library symposium was "Taking Stock of European Information Systems for Latin American Social Sciences and Humanities: A Framework for Cooperation."[3] Some fifty European librarians took part and thirty papers were given by specialists from seven European countries: Austria, Belgium, France, Italy, the Netherlands, Spain and the United Kingdom. The proceedings were published in 1990.[4] The papers addressed four major themes: (1) important general and special collections of Latin American library materials in Europe;[5] (2) printed sources describing Latin American collections, publications, and studies in Europe; and European online databases specializing in Latin America; (3) non-conventional library collections on Latin America in Europe (non-governmental organizations, political parties, solidarity committees, and the like); and (4) European audiovisual material on Latin America.

The symposium, a European equivalent of SALALM's annual conference, was the first of its kind and a great success. It ended with a general agreement to maintain the contacts so valuably established by the workshop, and a resolution was passed recommending that all future International Congresses of Americanists should run a similar symposium. More concretely, the meeting voted to form an independent network of European humanities and social-science libraries and documentation centres concerned with Latin America. A four-year plan of action was agreed, Mona Huerta was asked to continue as coordinator, and a first meeting of the new group was scheduled for early the following year.

Creation of REDIAL

The inaugural meeting, which took place in March 1989 at the Instituto de Información y Documentación en Ciencias Sociales y Humanidades (ISOC, a branch of the Consejo Superior de Investigaciones Científicas, Madrid), effectively brought REDIAL into being,[6] although the "Constituent Assembly" did not take place until eight months later and the first official General Assembly until January

1991. Thirty-four librarians participated from seven countries: Austria, Belgium, France, Germany, Spain, and the United Kingdom, with one delegate from Peru. It was regrettable that some librarians who had attended the Amsterdam meeting were not able to go to Madrid, most notably those from Portugal, Italy, and Sweden.

Adelaida Román (Director of Madrid's ISOC, where the meeting took place) was elected President and Mona Huerta Secretary. Serge de Ryck, a qualified Belgian lawyer, was nominated Treasurer and asked to draw up the statutes and to register REDIAL as a legal entity in the city of Brussels.[7] Brussels was chosen deliberately: an early expectation was that funds could be secured from the European Commission and that by registering REDIAL in the home of the Commission the organization might be better placed to achieve this.

REDIAL's Constituent Assembly (strictly speaking, not yet its first official General Assembly) was held in Bordeaux on November 30th, 1989, at the Institut d'Etudes Ibériques et Ibéro-Américaines, attached to Bordeaux University. The meeting of forty-one delegates from twenty-seven institutions approved the statutes, elected an Executive Committee, and set out the program of work for the future network.

General Assembly and Executive Committee

The General Assembly (*asamblea general*) is REDIAL's governing body, and is formed of all the voting and non-voting members. It meets once a year, usually in December or January.

REDIAL's administrative body is its Executive Committee (*comité ejecutivo*), responsible to the General Assembly. It is composed of the coordinators from each of the member-countries, with terms of office renewable every two years. Committee members need not be country coordinators, but they must of course represent voting institutions. They are elected by their respective countries and then approved by the General Assembly. At present, the Committee consists of the President, Secretary and Treasurer (representing Spain, France and Belgium)[8] and representatives from Austria (the delegate is from the Lateinamerika-Institut), Germany (Institut für Iberoamerika-Kunde), the Netherlands (Internationaal Instituut voor Sociale Geschiedenis)[9] and the United Kingdom (Institute of Latin American Studies, University of London). Each committee member can be deputised for at committee meetings by an alternate, or *suplente*.

The Executive Committee meets twice a year. Its first official meeting was held at the Paris Institut des Hautes Etudes de l'Amérique Latine on June 21st, 1989. Since then four further meetings have been held: Salzburg in April 1990, Paris in January 1991, London in December 1991, and Hamburg in June 1992.

Membership and Finances

There are three categories of membership: institutional (with full voting rights, representing the majority of members), individual (non-voting), and honorary (also non-voting). Some 35-40 institutions are full members of REDIAL, or have made a commitment to join, and between 80 and 90 more organizations have expressed an interest in joining the network.

REDIAL is a non-profit organization. The annual membership was originally set at US$100; this has now been changed to 100 ecus (about US$125). The subscription finances the work of the Secretariat (mainly publications and postage) and some of the activities of the working groups.

Working Groups

REDIAL's eight working groups are the equivalent of SALALM's substantive committees, performing the basic bibliographic work which REDIAL was set up to do. Each group has a committee which coordinates the work carried out in each country, where it is in turn overseen by national coordinators.

Group 1 is compiling a union catalogue of European dissertations on Latin America. The first stage has been to collect the titles of dissertations completed between 1980 and 1989. This ten-year list, containing between 3,500 and 4,000 titles from Austria, Belgium, France, Germany, the Netherlands, Spain, and the United Kingdom, will be published in Fall 1992. It is also planned to distribute the directory to REDIAL members on disk, using Micro CDS/ISIS software. (The micro version of the CDS-ISIS mini-mainframe software has been selected for REDIAL's common databases, since it is a library-based bibliographic package, developed by UNESCO, and widely used by documentation centres in Latin America; what is more, it is supplied free of charge to non-profit documentation centres in UNESCO member states.)

Group 2 is working on a union catalogue of Latin American and Latin-Americanist periodicals held by European libraries. In early 1991 it was expected that the Madrid-based Instituto de Estudios Políticos para América Latina y Africa (IEPALA), which had already compiled a union catalogue of Latin American periodicals in a number of Spanish NGO libraries, would agree to host the database; country coordinators were to send national lists of holdings to IEPALA for data entry using Micro CDS/ISIS. However, since IEPALA has decided that it cannot support the project, it is hoped that the contents of country union catalogues [10] can be merged with France's Catalogue collectif de périodiques sur l'Amérique Latine disponibles en France.

Group 3 is attempting to compile a database of early printed books, beginning with the 17th- and 18th-century imprints held by the Biblioteca Nacional (Madrid), the British Library, the Bibliothèque National (Paris), and the Ibero-Amerikanisches Institut (Berlin). The basis for this catalogue will be the early titles held by Spain's Biblioteca Nacional and already entered in the library's automated Catálogo Colectivo del Patrimonio Bibliográfico. The Biblioteca Nacional has sent magnetic tapes for testing by the other three libraries; although the records proved to be compatible—after a few adjustments had been made—with their existing database systems, no merging of holdings has yet taken place.

Group 4 is hoping to produce a census of European-produced audiovisual materials dealing with Latin America. Little progress has been made. A partial European list has been compiled, but not yet published, by the coordinator for this group, who is a member of France's Equipe de Recherche en Ethnologie Amérindienne, Paris.

Group 5 is considering the question of a multilingual macro-thesaurus for use by REDIAL members in the compilation of its cooperative databases. Originally, REDIAL thought of constructing an entirely new thesaurus in Spanish, English, French, and German. The French Réseau Amérique Latine has recently published a Latin American thesaurus for the social sciences and humanities [11] and it is not clear why REDIAL has not automatically adopted this as a ready-made tool. REDIAL could also have chosen the *HAPI Thesaurus and Name Authority, 1970-1989*, familiar to SALALM members. But REDIAL will now probably adopt the trilingual English/French/Spanish macrothesaurus produced by the Organisation for Economic Co-operation and Development (OECD), and merge the French thesaurus terms with its obviously limited vocabulary. The big advantages of the OECD thesaurus are that it is available on diskette and compatible with Micro CDS/ISIS.

Group 6 is working on a directory of European bibliographic and factual databases that deal exclusively or extensively with Latin America.

Group 7 aims to produce an inventory of documentary resources and archival material held by European non-governmental organizations. The Asociación de Investigación y Especialización sobre Temas

Iberoamericanos (AIETI, Madrid) has already published a preliminary directory of sixty-three European NGOs concerned with Latin America.[12] A revised version will be published in mid-1992 and, like the list of theses, it will be produced in printed form and also distributed on diskette to member-libraries.

Group 8 is devising a programme for the conservation of the archives of Latin American political and social movements. This implies microfilming collections on site or possibly even removing them to Europe. The group's preliminary focus is on Argentina, Bolivia, Colombia, Peru, and Uruguay, since the Bibliothèque de Documentation Internationale Contemporaine (BDIC, Paris) and AIETI already have contacts with, and appropriate archival experience in, those countries. Four projects are close to completion.

Publications

REDIAL publishes a newsletter, the *Boletín REDIAL*. A pilot number 0 was issued in June 1989. Number 1 appeared in May 1990, number 2 was dated July to September 1990, and number 3/4 was issued in March 1992. Originally it was hoped to publish the bulletin every two months but this has so far proved too optimistic. There are also more ambitious plans to publish a semi-annual *Revista Europea de Información y Documentación sobre América Latina*. The first number will be published in Fall 1992. It will carry news of REDIAL's activities, information about sources and resources in Europe, articles on member libraries, and short bibliographies. It will be free to members, or available on a separate annual subscription of (probably) 30 ecus (about $45). Both publications are edited by Mona Huerta, REDIAL's Secretary.

The *Revista* will also carry individual papers from the Amsterdam and Tulane meetings, and there are plans to publish a volume containing a selection of papers from both conferences.

International Contacts

REDIAL is planning to participate in several future international meetings concerned with Latin American documentation. In the international sphere, REDIAL is focussing on two questions: (*a*) how to make the most of limited resources for libraries on an east-west European level; and (*b*) how to develop a framework for cooperation between library systems in Europe on the one hand and North and South America on the other.

International (World) Congress of Americanists

Following its successful seminar at the 46th International Congress of Americanists (Amsterdam, 1988), REDIAL held a second symposium during the 47th Congress, Tulane University, 9th-11th July 1991. This symposium had the theme "La información científica en ciencias sociales y humanidades sobre América Latina en 1991." Librarians attended from Belgium, France, Italy, Spain, and Sweden. Invitations had been sent to a number of librarians in Latin America, but only five were able to participate, with a further two submitting their papers. The Latin American countries represented were Argentina, Bolivia, Brazil, Mexico, Peru, and Venezuela, in turn representing national, university, special, and NGO libraries. SALALM representation at the meeting was prevented by logistical difficulties.

The Tulane conference sessions were presented under three broad themes: [13]

(1) Bibliometric surveys of European publications and research on Latin America, 1980-1989: theses, journal articles, conferences, monographs and working papers, European databases relating to Latin America.

(2) The provision and handling of information on Latin America in European libraries: networks, inter-library cooperation, NGO libraries.

(3) Documentation services in Latin America: trends in information science in Latin America since 1960; the Asociación de Bibliotecas Nacionales de Iberoamérica, ABINIA; the databases produced by UNAM's Centro de Información Científica y Humanística, CICH; documentation in Peru; the Red de Información Argentina sobre Ciencias Sociales, REDICSA; and trades-union archives in Bolivia.

REDIAL hopes to hold a session on information and documentation at all future International Congresses of Americanists, and plans are already being made for the 48th Congress, to be held in Stockholm in July 1994. A resolution of the Tulane Congress was to convene a future meeting in Latin America, with the aim of strengthening cooperation between European Latin American collections and libraries in Latin America. The Latin American delegates especially welcomed, and commended to the Congress, REDIAL's working group charged with the safeguarding of the archives of certain Latin American political and social movements.

Fédération Internationale de Documentation (FID)

REDIAL will be taking part in the 46th FID congress, Madrid, in late October 1992. It will run a one-day seminar within FID's program of pre-congress *jornadas*, on 26th October, and take advantage of the venue to hold its 1992 General Assembly beforehand. The seminar will have three themes:

(1) Information for Latin American development studies

(2) European grey literature on Latin America (including bibliometric studies, similar to those presented in Tulane, which will analyse the production of grey literature since 1980)

(3) Cooperation between Europe and Latin America in the field of information and documentation.

Although this paper has talked about a "network" of European libraries, the phrase "online database networking" has been absent. Although REDIAL is for the moment purely a *human* network, many outsiders assume that it is a complete *electronic* network. Have REDIAL libraries progressed in the online searching of each other's catalogues? In the era of Open Systems Interconnection (OSI), this is technically possible, thanks mainly to the existence of EARN, the European Academic Research Network, which should eventually make it possible for computerized library catalogues to be accessed online. For the time being, though, the answer is "no." In any case, the solution is largely outside REDIAL's control. REDIAL is concentrating on producing relatively small databases as a first step—this is certainly the case of the theses and periodicals databases—and distributing the results on diskettes for local loading and searching by member-libraries who have Micro CDS/ISIS software. REDIAL members contact each other quite frequently by fax, but not yet by e-mail, although, again, this is perfectly feasible.

The two biggest obstacles to REDIAL's future are its human and financial resources. First, its membership.

At present, most of REDIAL's members are French and Spanish libraries. Since the Secretariat is based in Paris and most business meetings have been and will be held in France, the large number of French member-libraries is not surprising.[14] The number of Spanish member-libraries is also high, although Spain's Latin American network is not well developed. On the other hand, REDIAL cannot expect more than one or two members from Austria and Belgium, where there are only one or two institutions devoted to Latin American studies. Even in Germany, with a large number of Latin American collections,[15] the main commitment to REDIAL is from the Institut für Ibero-amerika-Kunde.

Perhaps it is surprising that no more than three British institutions have joined so far—these are the British Library, the University of

London Library, and the London Institute of Latin American Studies. British reluctance to join may be disappointing but is realistic and understandable, and is due to at least three factors: the high cost of travel to REDIAL meetings; what ACOLAM (now ACLAIIR) [16] member-libraries see as a rather high membership fee compared with (for example) the cost and benefits of SALALM membership; and the feeling that British libraries have already made most of their contribution to the British element in REDIAL's database projects—in other words, their contributions to the British Union Catalogue of Latin Americana, BUCLA, over the past twenty years—and are quite content for the three existing members, especially the London Institute, to get on with the work.

REDIAL cannot be a true European network until it enjoys the collaboration of important Latin American libraries in such countries as Portugal and Italy. It is also hoped that institutions from outside the European Community, from Scandinavia and in particular from Eastern Europe and the CIS, will eventually participate. It is to be expected that Sweden will become a full member after the Stockholm meeting of Americanists in 1994, at the latest. It is unfortunate that there is now no official affiliation from the Centrum voor Studie en Documentatie van Latijns Amerika (CEDLA, Netherlands); the weak position of Belgium has also been mentioned, and REDIAL considers it a high priority to restore permanent links with these two countries and use its influence to strengthen their networks.

The second obstacle is REDIAL's financial situation, which is obviously related to its membership. The question of finance dominated the discussions of the 1991 General Assembly. REDIAL has been struggling to maintain institutional support but is now in a slightly healthier position. Although only 20 libraries paid their subscriptions for 1992, at the last count REDIAL had a total of 35-40 actual or prospective members. Yet subsidies have been attracted: publication of the directories resulting from the efforts of the working groups, described earlier, will be subsidized by Spain's Sociedad Estatal del Quinto Centenario, and REDIAL's Secretariat (which has always been short of funds for such items as postage and publications) has recently won a two-year grant from the French Ministry of Education for computing equipment, underwriting of the first two numbers of the *Revista*, and clerical support.

There is also a shortage of funds at an institutional member level, especially funds for travel to meetings. The Tulane meeting went ahead only because, at the last moment, the fifteen French and Spanish delegates received grants from their respective Foreign Ministries, supplemented by their own institutions. The Organization of American States, which had at first promised to subsidize travel to Tulane by the Latin American delegates, in the end unfortunately could not do so.

In the minds of REDIAL members 1992 has been a key year. For Europeans, of course, the year 1992 is not only the occasion of the Columbus Quincentenary but also the year (strictly speaking it is the *end* of the year) of the Single European Market. The year 1992 has therefore been a strong double incentive for REDIAL to complete at least the first stage of its work by the year's end. Since REDIAL is a network conducted on the European level, it is logical that finance should be sought—and can probably only be found—also at the European level. After all, the European Community does have a Library Cooperation Plan, known as DG XIII (DG stands for Directorate-General), a programme for "innovation, the information market and telecommunications." REDIAL applied for a grant to the European Economic Commission in June 1989; unfortunately, DG XIII has made a distinct lack of progress, and the application is still pending.

This paper has tried to show that REDIAL has a modestly ambitious programme of work. There is regular contact between the members of REDIAL's executive committee. Information filters to and from the committee and the national networks. The annual general assembly provides a forum for the exchange of ideas, and the process is continued in the workshops and seminars that REDIAL stages at international meetings of other organizations. Important links have been forged with librarians in Latin America. Throughout the REDIAL membership, Micro CDS/ISIS is being used as a convenient medium of "offline" networking, for the circulation of databases and inventories on diskette. CD-ROMs and online networking will follow. REDIAL has not only brought together librarians across Europe: it has also been the catalyst for promoting cooperation between Latin-Americanist libraries *within* European countries. This has happened in Germany and Spain, where networks which were rather unstructured before have been consolidated precisely because of the example set by REDIAL. A dedicated network of European librarians—a European SALALM—is here to stay and growing in confidence.

NOTES

1. For information on European libraries see Roger Macdonald and Carole Travis, *Libraries and Special Collections on Latin America and the Caribbean: A Directory of European Resources*, University of London, Institute of Latin American Studies Monographs, no. 14 (London; Atlantic Highlands, NJ: Athlone Press, 1988), 339 pp.; Carmelo Mesa-Lago, *Latin American Studies in Europe*, Latin American Monograph and

Document Series, no. 1 (Pittsburgh, PA: University of Pittsburgh, Center for Latin American Studies, 1979), 190 pp.; *Latin American Studies in Europe: Final Report and Working Papers of the Twenty-third Seminar on the Acquisition of Latin American Library Materials. University of London, England, July 16-21, 1978*, ed. Anne H. Jordan (Austin, TX: SALALM Secretariat, 1979), 343 pp.

2. See n. 15.

3. "Los sistemas de información y documentación en ciencias sociales y humanas sobre América Latina en Europa: balance para una cooperación europea."

4. The proceedings (twenty-six of the thirty papers) were published as Congreso Internacional de Americanistas (46 : Amsterdam : 4-8 July 1988). *Simposio: Los sistemas de información en ciencias sociales y humanas sobre América Latina: balance para una cooperación europea*, Documento de trabajo (Paris [Institut des Hautes Etudes de l'Amérique Latine, 28 rue Saint Guillaume, 75007 Paris]: Réseau Amérique Latine, 1990), 354 pp.

5. Asociación de Investigación y Especialización sobre Temas Iberoamericanos (AIETI, Madrid), Bibliothèque de Documentation Internationale Contemporaine (BDIC, Nanterre), Bibliothèque Nationale (Paris), British Library, Centrum voor Studie en Documentatie van Latijns Amerika (CEDLA, Amsterdam), Instituto Italo-Latino-americano (Rome), Latinamerika-institutet i Stockholm, and the Real Academia de la Historia (Madrid).

6. The name REDIAL is a slightly strained acronym, in fact. The original name chosen was RE-I-DAL, which reflected the true order of the key terms "information and documentation," but in the end the more euphonious "REDIAL" was approved.

7. REDIAL was registered with the Belgian Ministry of Justice in January 1991, thereby obtaining civil status. The statutes were to have been published in *Le Moniteur Belge*, thus establishing REDIAL's legal status. However, Serge De Ryck soon afterwards left the Latin American field and, aware that the future of the Belgian Centre d'Etudes de l'Amérique Latine was insecure, withheld publishing the statutes. At its executive committee meeting in June 1992, REDIAL decided to publish them in Paris and at the same time to transfer REDIAL's *sede* to France.

8. In June 1992 Serge De Ryck gave notice that he could no longer continue as Treasurer (see preceding note).

9. CEDLA, represented by Jacques Van Laar, was the Netherlands' founder-member. Van Laar left CEDLA in 1991 and Rudolf de Jong, from Amsterdam's International Instituut voor Sociale Geschiedenis (International Institute of Social History), became the Dutch representative.

10. British Union Catalogue of Latin Americana (to 1988); Catálogo Colectivo de Publicaciones Periódicas en Bibliotecas Españoles; Dokumentationsdienst Lateinamerika; Nordic union catalogue of perodicals issued in developing countries.

11. *Thésaurus Amérique Latine en sciences sociales et humaines = Tesauro América Latina = Latin American thesaurus*, 2d ed. (Paris: Réseau Amérique Latine, Groupement de Recherche 26 du Centre National de la Recherche Scientifique, 1990), 344 pp.

12. *Fondos documentales sobre América Latina en ONG's* [sic] *y organizaciones afines europeas: avance de directorio*, ed. Teresa Ybarra (Madrid [Claudio Coello 86, 4° dcha, 28006 Madrid]: Asociación de Investigación y Estudios sobre Temas Iberoamericanos [AIETI] / Instituto de Estudios Políticos para América Latina y Africa [IEPALA], 1991), 56 leaves.

13. For a full list of papers see *Boletín REDIAL* (Paris) 3/4 (March 1992), 1-4; and *Alizés: revue d'information latino-américaniste* (Paris) 9 (March 1992), 21-24. The proceedings will be published at a later date.

14. See *Répertoire de bibliothèques françaises disposant de fonds sur l'Amérique Latine* ([Paris?]: Réseau Documentaire Amérique Latine, 1986), 82 pp.

15. Two recent directories are: Marion Gebhardt (comp.), *Institutionen der Lateinamerika-Forschung und -Information in der Bundesrepublik Deutschland und Berlin (West): (Stand 1990): Forschungsinstitute, Bibliotheken, Dokumentationsstellen* (Hamburg: Deutsches Übersee-Institut, Referat Lateinamerika, 1991), 161 pp., which records more than 60 research institutes and their libraries/archives; and the *Führer durch die Lateinamerika-Bestände der Hamburger Bibliotheken und Archive* (Hamburg: Institut für Iberoamerika-Kunde, 1991), 54 pp., which lists 50 libraries.

16. In June 1992 the UK's Advisory Committee on Latin American Materials (ACOLAM) took the double step of leaving its parent body, the Standing Conference of National and University Libraries, SCONUL, which was shedding its area-studies advisory committees, and of expanding its area of interest to embrace Spain and Portugal. The group is now called the Advisory Council for Latin American and Iberian Information Resources, ACLAIIR.

The Contemporary
Peruvian Crisis

5. Peru's Informal Sector: Hope in the Midst of Crisis

Raúl P. Saba

Introduction

Peru is in crisis—economically, socially, and politically. Some would contend that a state of crisis has plagued Peru for nearly a generation. Indeed, most indicators show that in its social and economic dimensions the crisis has taken on historical proportions since the onset of democratic government in 1980.

Most observers felt that Peru had reached the bottom of its economic abyss at the end of Fernando Belaúnde's second administration in 1985. Nevertheless, President Alan García's government set new records in the country's continuing saga of economic chaos and crisis. Inflation in 1989 reached a record 2,775 percent, and nearly triple that figure in 1990 at 7,650 percent. Conservative estimates indicate that cumulative inflation during Alan García's five years in office was 1 million percent! In January of this year, the minimum, legal monthly wage was raised more than 50 percent to the equivalent of 76 U.S. dollars.[1] Inflation since then, however, has increased between 6 and 9 percent a month. Government statistics show that the GDP declined by 13.6 percent in 1989 and fell another 6 percent in 1990.[2]

Terrorist incidents have kept pace with the deteriorating economy. Deaths owing to the violence reached alarming levels last year. During the first 55 days of 1990, 531 terrorism-related deaths occurred. During the same period in 1988 there were 250 deaths and, in 1989, 340 deaths.[3] Since the Shining Path or Sendero Luminoso's terrorist insurgency began eleven years ago, more than 21,000 people have been killed and more than $18 billion in economic losses have been sustained. This figure represents about 85 percent of Peru's external debt.[4] And as if "pobre Perú" has not been beaten enough while lying prostrate, a cholera epidemic hit in January and has caused the deaths of 1,300 people and untold economic losses.

According to Steve Stein and Carlos Monge in their very timely and perceptive volume titled *La crisis del estado patrimonial en el Perú* (1988), there is an increasing loss of faith by the "popular masses" in those above, a loss of loyalty and trust in the existing system and those

35

associated with it. The traditional middle classes and the state are no longer able to respond to the critical needs of the masses, who are turning more and more to popular, horizontal solutions. The multiple manifestations of this rejection of the hereditary state range from the violent response of Sendero Luminoso to the food kitchens and the informal economy of the *otro sendero*.

Given the long-lasting and deepening economic crisis over the past fifteen years—marked by underemployment, malnutrition, and overcrowding in the cities—pessimism has reached alarming heights and is being expressed in a loss of faith in the traditional institutions and governing classes. The material crisis is leading to a crisis of political culture. And because the economic crisis has been so profound and lasting, the very survival of the middle sectors has also been brought into question. This has caused many in the middle class to join the popular sectors in their rift with the state. Increasingly, the initiative for solutions is seen as something that will come from below and not from above.

Indeed, on the level of day-to-day survival, a certain resourcefulness and ingenuity *a la criolla* have prevailed among the popular masses, helping them to weather the successive storms of inflation, recession, unemployment, and ever-expanding poverty. Much of this popular creativity is embodied in the informal economic activities of the masses, developing outside or at the margin of legality. The purpose of this presentation is to discuss the pervasive presence of economic informality in contemporary Peruvian society and analyze its socio-political meaning in terms of the present crisis and Peru's future as a democracy. The discussion does not pretend to analyze the definitional and causal debate surrounding the concept of informality but rather more modestly to present an overview of the political implications surrounding this issue in its Peruvian context, where it has been subject to the deepest, most rigorous analysis and widest popular discussion.

Defining and Quantifying the Informal Economic Sector

Previously described in more disparaging terms as the underground or black market economy with its street vendors, or, as in colonial Lima, *regatones* or hagglers, informality today is more often viewed as a manifestation of "popular capitalism" and even as Peru's most practical and creative possibility for development. Marcial Rubio, the director of the Peruvian bimonthly *Qué Hacer*, recently wrote that "informality . . . constitutes a creative device of peaceful survival, an alternative to violence, crime, and subversion. Therefore, and in this sense, it is a peaceful incentive for society."[5]

The informal sector in Peru is generally defined in terms of three overlapping groups:

1.   The jobless or underemployed (in terms of the formal sector), who are forced to make ends meet in activities requiring little or no capital.

2.   Those sectors which operate partially or wholly outside the formal economy avoiding the tangle of red tape or excessive bureaucracy.

3.   Those engaged in underworld activities, especially in the cocaine-dominated illicit drugs trade—including campesinos growing the coca, market vendors selling goods brought illegally into the country, and so forth. It is estimated that currently about one millon Peruvians are engaged in the illegal narcotics trade and contribute an estimated $1 billion per year to the Peruvian economy.

Informality is basically an economy parallel to the formal one and is often in competition with it. It rests primarily on trade and services. Production is typically confined to labor-intensive goods owing to the low levels of investment capital equipment characteristic of the informal sector.   Ready-made clothing, footwear, and furniture are prime examples. According to Hernando de Soto, president of the Instituto Libertad y Democracia (a Lima-based research institute) and author of *El otro sendero*, about 60 percent of the work hours in Peru are dedicated to the informal economy, producing a little less than 35 percent of the GDP.[6] Moreover, about 52 percent of the manufacturing enterprises are informal, but their productivity is low since they contribute less than 15 percent of the manufacturing component of the GDP.[7] Although it is difficult to say precisely where the informal sector begins or ends, there is no doubt that it is large in both size and scope. This is particularly true in Lima.

It is estimated that from 50 to 60 percent of those economically active in metropolitan Lima depend on informal sector activities for all or part of their livelihoods (about 3.5 million people), generating up to 40 percent of the GDP.   Beneath the surface of the ever-present *comercio ambulatorio* or the street and market vendors lies a sophisticated network of informal wholesalers, suppliers, service and manufacturing sectors, and street vendor associations. Virtually every family has a member involved in informality. They include the policemen or teacher moonlighting as a *pirata* driving a taxi; the housewife making *marcianos* or *chupetes* to sell to the neighborhood children or the corner grocery store; the older brother replacing mufflers and tailpipes on Avenida Venezuela or buying or selling dollars as a *cambista* on Ocoña Street in downtown Lima.

The Debate: Why Is There an Informal Sector?

Since Hernando de Soto's Instituto Libertad y Democracia began its extensive study of Peru's informal economy in the early 1980s, the debate about the origins and significance of this socioeconomic reality has intensified in intellectual and political circles. Among the several interpretations of the informal sector, De Soto's is the most widely known and discussed.

De Soto essentially views the origin of the informal economy in terms of a tendency toward excessive state intervention in civil society and economic activity. This in turn generates excessive red tape and prohibitive costs, preventing or discouraging entry into the formal sector.[8] In essence, this "legalist" school "sees most informals as self-motivated people who are fleeing the excessive regulation choking the formal economy."[9] De Soto contends that the Peruvian state, regardless of what government has been in power, has usually acted in accordance with a mercantilist model, enacting laws favoring small special-interest groups in the formal sector. Hence, Peru's economic landscape has been dominated by a redistributive tradition based on centralized political decisions. The dominant characteristics of this Peruvian mercantilism have been: authoritarian law-making by executive decree; detailed, directive, and destructive regulation of the economy; poor or nonexistent access to entrepreneurial activities for those not having close ties to the government; unwieldy bureaucracies; stifling and inefficient public and private monopolies; and powerful businessmen organized into redistributive coalitions and powerful professional associations.[10]

In his now famous and widely quoted example, De Soto's investigations into the costs of access to economic activity demonstrated that to begin a small garment factory in Lima would take an individual 289 days to complete the necessary paper work and cost $1,231, or 32 times the monthly minimum wage. Of that amount, $194 would go for the actual paper work, fees, and essential bribes and $1,036 for the loss of net profits for the 10-month wait.[11] To open a small store would take 43 days and cost $491. In sum, De Soto contends that the problem is not really excessive regulation but bad regulation, bad laws. "Therefore," he says, "it is important to transform the methods for producing norms and to better distribute the power relating to their formulation."[12]

While the Instituto Libertad y Democracia's thesis might be summarized in terms of "the overbearing presence of the state," another one proposed by the anthropologist José Matos Mar can be expressed by the phrase, "the lack of state presence."[13] Matos Mar contends that population growth and migration have overwhelmed urban Peru. And that in attempting to escape the constraints of an "official" Peru, this popular outburst expresses itself in parainstitutional organizations and through its own culture. A certain Andeanization of Lima and other cities has occurred, and the new immigrants are solving their problems by drawing on their Andean traditions.

Contrasted to these theories is a third one espoused by Argentine economist and former economic advisor to President Alan García, Daniel Carbonetto. He sees informality as a structural problem arising from the normal functioning of the capitalist system, which generates a surplus or residual of labor not absorbed by the modern sector (or expelled from it). Thus he sees the problem of this informality resting exclusively on the insufficiency of, and thus the necessity for, adequate employment.[14]

The long-lived and prestigious think tank and data bank, DESCO, offers a variation of the last two conceptualizations by identifying informality as a noncapitalist form of work within a peripheral capitalist system. In turn, the informal sector fulfills and expresses itself in institutions, values, practices, and culture that give order to daily life in unique and familiar ways.[15]

Conclusion

Although De Soto's thesis on the informal sector has been the most widely published and heralded on the international scene and apparently commands a certain influence on policy with the current Fujimori administration, the conceptual and theoretical debate concerning the origins and macroeconomic significance of this popular sector of microentrepreneurs and street vendors has taken on new vigor and importance. This is particularly true in light of the Fujimori administration's inability to get a handle on the crisis and of its recent discrepancies with its principal advisor, Hernando de Soto.[16]

In the last few years a number of important books and articles have been written attempting to clarify and strengthen the varying positions analyzing the informal sector and its role in contemporary Peru.[17] Despite the intensity of the debate, and perhaps because of it, the social significance and political impact of the informal sector and all that it represents are contributing to profound changes in Peru's political culture. Alberto Fujimori, who was virtually unknown on the Peruvian political scene prior to April 1990, was elected president owing in large part to the support of the informal sector and its allies among the campesinos and the growing number of evangelicals. The increasingly delegitimized political elites and traditional parties are all seeking ways to incorporate and aggregate the now politically aware popular and informal masses into their folds. A generation of reformist programs of various ideological stripes have failed to solve the problems of Peru's poor—and indeed may have exacerbated them. Belaúnde's *cooperación popular* of the early 1960s, Velasco's military reformism of the late 1960s and early 1970s, and Alan García's invigorated *aprista* nationalism of the 1980s raised the hopes of many in the middle and poor sectors of society, only to dash them against the ever-present elitism and cronyism of Peruvian politics. Nevertheless, as suggested in the literature by various Peruvian commentators, the dynamic of survival expressed by the informal sector permits a glimmer of optimism for the new decade, which has begun under such adverse conditions. With the expansion of informal activities and the growth of *chicha* politics, a unique opportunity has been created for the development of genuine political pluralism establishing new social and economic priorities that go beyond rhetoric.[18] One Peruvian analyst, Samuel Machacuay, captures the essence of this hope in a recent article:

En un contexto de deterioro de las condiciones sociales de la población, resulta sorprendente que la violencia no se haya extendido aún más. Que tal cosa no haya ocurrido se debe en gran medida, al rol desempeñado por el sector; al brindar refugio ocupacional a virtualmente la mitad de la fuerza de trabajo, ha impedido un crecimiento explosivo e intolerable del desempleo. Pero sí debe reconocerse que la flexibilidad que ofrece al mercado—y tras ella la posibilidad de organizar la subsistencia de grandes sectores de la población—ha quedado claramente puesta a prueba en el último período. La microempresa es el seguro de desempleo de los pobres y puede ser también el seguro político de la democracia en este país.

Por último, pero ciertamente no menos importante, desde la perspectiva de la equidad distributiva y de la preservación de la democracia, las micro-empresas constituyen un sector objetivo extremadamente significativo. Debe recordarse que no sólo ocupan cerca de la mitad de la fuerza de trabajo urbano sino que, cualitativamente, concentran a la mayoría de los pobres urbanos. En un país sitiado por el terrorismo y donde la pobreza—y aún la extrema pobreza—es la regla, la significación sociopolítica del sector informal como estabilizador social es obvia.[19]

The stabilizing potential of the informal sector creates a safety valve allowing time for the solution of drug and terrorism problems. However, the clamor of the popular masses and disintegrating middle class is also witness to the need for tangible results in social, political, and economic reform. The question remains: Can the independent and eclectic Fujimori government meet the challenge?

NOTES

1. *The Times of the Americas*, Feb. 20, 1991, p. 3.

2. Inter-American Development Bank, *Annual Report 1990* (Washington, DC: IDB, 1991), p. 2.

3. *Uno Más Uno*, Feb. 26, 1990, p. 21.

4. *La Opinión*, Jan. 11, 1991, p. 6.

5. Marcial Rubio, "Perdidos en el Corto Plazo," *Qué Hacer* 69 (Jan.-Feb., 1991), 9.

6. Interview with Hernando de Soto, *Expreso*, March 5, 1989, p. 4.

7. Ibid., March 26, 1989, p. 4.

8. Hernando de Soto, *The Other Path* (New York, NY: Harper and Row, 1989).

9. Sheldon Annis and Jeffrey Franks, "The Idea, Ideology and Economics of the Informal Sector: The Case of Peru," *Grassroots Development* 13, 1 (1989), 12.

10. De Soto, *The Other Path*, pp. 208-210.

11. Ibid., p. 134.

12. Interview with Hernando de Soto, *Expreso*, March 5, 1989, p. 4.

13. See Diego Palma, *La informalidad, lo popular y el cambio social* (Lima: IEP, 1987); José Matos Mar, *Desborde popular y crisis del estado: El nuevo rostro del Perú en la década de 1980* (Lima: IEP, 1984).

14. See César Franco, *Informales: Nuevos rostros en la vieja Lima* (Lima: CEDEP, 1989), pp. 68-69; Palma, pp. 73-75; Annis and Franks, p. 10.

15. Palma, p. 38.

16. See debate Democratization of Government Decisions and controversy over De Soto's role as presidential advisor in March 4 and 11 issues of *Caretas* and *Oiga*, 1991.

17. See Enrique Ghersi, ed., *El comercio ambulatorio en Lima* (Lima: ILD, 1989); Alberto Bustamante, Eliana Chávez, et al., *De marginales a informales* (Lima: DESCO, 1990); *Debate* 62 (Nov.-Dec., 1990).

18. See Carlos Iván Degregori, "Nuestra modernidad," in *Debate*, pp. 23-27; Romeo Grompone, "Las lecturas políticas de la informalidad," in *De marginales a informales*, pp. 35-67.

19. Samuel Machacuay, "Industria Salvadora," in *Debate*, pp. 30-31.

6. Disintegration of a Culture: Peru into the 1990s

Thomas M. Davies, Jr.

During the academic year 1985-86, my family and I spent thirteen months in Peru, a time that began very auspiciously with the inauguration of Alan García as president. There was joyous optimism in the country, an optimism that infected even cynical gringos like me. Indeed, I felt more hopeful about Peru's future than I had at any time in the past thirty years.

And, García did take some extremely positive steps. He moved against the military and the police, particularly in the realm of corruption and human rights abuses, and he forcibly retired dozens of officers. He also sounded the clarion call of Peruvian nationalism by announcing in his inaugural address that henceforth Peru would pay only 10 percent of her export earnings toward the nation's horrendous external debt. People all over the hemisphere, as if one, stood and cheered.

But the United States of Ronald Reagan did not cheer. To hardline, free market Reaganites, this was not only heresy, it was a dangerously blatant invitation to other Latin American republics to do the same, thereby threatening not only the West's banking and credit structure, but also the United States's economic and political hegemony in the Western Hemisphere.

Washington's reaction was both swift and predictable. Marshaling all of its mighty resources, the United States effectively cut off all international aid to Peru and forced her to rely almost exclusively on foreign currency reserves to pay for her imports—primarily of food and medicine. Those reserves, however, were exhausted by the spring of 1988, and the country was more than $260 million in the red by August, 1988.

García reverted to the time-honored solution of turning on the printing presses, with the time-honored result that by the summer of 1988, the annual inflation rate in Peru had surpassed 1,000 percent and was climbing rapidly, headed, in the words of one of García's own advisors, "to the 5,000 percent mark by next year." In fact, it was even worse than that: inflation for the second half of 1988 was 9,000 percent and more than 20,000 percent for the last four months of that year. That inflation rate has not abated over the last three years.

But perhaps the most spectacular and most visible result of this economic malaise (apart from the millions of men, women, and children who are quite literally starving to death) is in the area of currency reform and devaluation. In 1981, the sol stood at 422 to the dollar. By 1983, however, it had dropped to 1,629 to 1, to 3,467 by 1984, and to 18,000 by 1985. The inflation rate for this same period, that is, in Fernando Belaúnde Terry's second administration, was 3,240 percent.

At this point, the Peruvian government, emulating the Argentine and the Brazilians, created a new currency—the inti—by knocking three zeros off the sol. Beginning at 18 to the dollar in 1986, the *pobre* inti dropped to 250 to 1 on September 7, 1988. By September 30, however, it was down to 427, to 516 by the end of October, 1,000 by year's end, and 2,000 by January, 1989.

From there it really got ugly. By June 1, 1989, the inti was down to 3,251; 4,777 by the end of September; 8,900 by the end of 1989. By April, 1990, the inti was over 25,000 to 1; 88,000 by July; 300,000 by August; and 547,945 by December, 1990. May I remind you that 1 inti = 1,000 soles, so the 547,945 intis are really 547,945,000 soles.

Another way to look at the enormity of the crisis is to calculate the dollar value of 1 million soles (or 1,000 intis). In 1966, when I first arrived in Peru, 1 million soles was worth $37,313.00. Ten years later, in 1976, that same million was worth only $18,000.00. Another ten years later, however, a million soles was worth only $56.00—$10.00 by 1988 and $0.11 in 1989. As if it really mattered, the value of 1 million soles during 1990 dropped from $0.08 to $0.0018 (eighteen thousandths of a dollar).

Today, on the streets of Lima, the inti is around 850,000 to 1, or $0.0012 (twelve thousandths of a dollar). On the international market, however, Peru has already dumped the inti in favor of a new currency which is currently pegged at around 1.2 to the dollar. What this new currency is, of course, is the old inti with six zeros removed. That would make it equal to 1 BILLION SOLES—that is to say 1 thousand million soles to the dollar.

The material and psychological devastation of this economic ruin has taken a terrible human toll. For example, prices and price increases always outstripped pay increases. And even if they didn't, the people of Peru faced the humiliating and psychologically damaging specter of seeing the national currency reduced in value to the extent that suitcases of it were required to buy simple, cheap items. In fact, what has happened in Peru in the 1980s is far worse than what happened in the infamous Weimar Republic in Germany after World War I.

Moreover, no socioeconomic class has been spared. The poor have become desperately poor—to the point of widespread starvation— and their numbers are growing rapidly due both to the fact that there are 18 percent more people in Peru in 1991 than in 1985, and to the fact that the middle class has all but ceased to exist in economic terms.

Indeed, among the many economic and social indicators of this catastrophe, population growth must be counted very highly. Peru's population has burgeoned from 7.6 million in 1950, to 19.7 million in 1985, to more than 24 million today. Of even greater concern, however, is the fact that 44 percent of Peru's population are currently under 15 years of age, while an additional 23 percent are between the ages of 15 and 24; THAT IS TO SAY, 67 percent of the total population are under 25 years of age.

Moreover, to this must be added the fact that more than 75 percent of all pregnant women suffer from nutritional anemia, 55 percent of all deaths are of children under 5 years of age, and of that small percentage of children who actually attend school, 60 percent of them are malnourished and therefore incapable of learning.

More than 85 percent of the population are either unemployed or underemployed, while over half of the remaining 25 percent earn the minimum wage of less than $50.00 per month. Seventy-five to eighty percent of the total population are undernourished, while as many as 65 percent are living at "high nutritional risk," that is, they do not receive the minimum amount of calories and protein needed for normal physical and mental development and activity.

Other statistics are equally grim. For example, the cost of urban transportation, particularly in Lima where more than 35 percent of the nation's population currently resides, has risen so sharply over the last 2-3 years that it has, at times, all but consumed the daily wages of most workers. Moreover, doctors in public hospitals, judges in the courts, even diplomats, have seen their salaries gyrate wildly, falling as low as $30.00 a month at several points.

Middle class professionals have become so distraught that they have been lining up at foreign embassies trying to emigrate, a situation that has forced all Latin American nations, except Haiti, to reduce drastically, or eliminate all together, the issuance of visas, tourist and otherwise, to Peruvian citizens.

Access to the United States, Canada, and Europe through a family connection is a much prized commodity. In 1988, I was in Lima for less than a week and yet five family members called to see if I could get their children out of the country. This spring I have already received more than a dozen such inquiries by mail and by phone, and this despite the fact that the children know no English and the parents cannot offer even a modicum of monetary support to the city. None of that is relevant, however, for everyone believes that it is better to simply leave for the United States than to die and rot in Peru.

During 1986-1987, I delivered papers at a number of professional meetings and my message was the same—what came to be known as "Gloom and Doom" Davies—"What I saw last year was the disintegration and near collapse of a modern society." I had mountains of data to back up my argument, but still it was hard for people to accept that an entire nation could simply collapse. But it did, and it has, to a degree never before seen in the Western Hemisphere.

For its part, the United States under Ronald Reagan was obviously much less concerned about economic diaster than it was about what it perceived to be the threat of communism from the Peruvian left, or the haunting specter of the moral debasement of United States youth through its use of Peruvian cocaine. Both problems required immediate solutions, and the solutions proposed were eminently consistent with post-1981 U.S. foreign policy—the substitution of guns and bombs for diplomacy, à la Lebanon, Grenada, Libya, Nicaragua, and El Salvador.

But neither the guns nor Reagan's policies enjoyed any more success in Peru than elsewhere in the world, because what is happening in Peru right now, while consistent with the Andean past, is almost unheard of in the twentieth century. A frighteningly large percentage of the population, in both the rural and the urban sectors, is rejecting Western culture and turning instead to some brand of Andean millenarian messianism, of which Sendero Luminoso is but one. Moreover, since the bearers of that Western culture have always been light-skinned, an ominous racial factor has been injected as well.

One example of this is the sudden resurgence of the Pishtagu. Pishtagus are very ancient and extremely important beings in Andean religious/political mythology. They are particularly prevalent in heavily Indian areas of the country, such as Ayacucho where Sendero Luminoso began, but are also increasingly important in greater Lima with its huge Serrano population, a fact not lost on the city's light-skinned middle and upper class dwellers.

The particular characteristics of the Pishtagu vary from region to region, but, in general, "He" is a mestizo or a gringo who carries a long knife and attacks solitary people, particularly women and children. He cuts their throats and then cooks the meat of their bodies into *chicharones* (or *carnitas*, if you prefer) and sells the fat. In colonial times, it was taught that the fat was used to make candles for the Christian churches; now it is charged that the fat is used to grease the modern machinery of the hated Mistis of today.

There is more, but the importance of this for our purposes is that as the socioeconomic crisis worsened, racial conflict has increased with sierran Cholos and Indians viewing all whites as being potential or real Pishtagus. In fact Sendero Luminoso has often raised the specter of Pishtagus and has charged that government officials and functionaries, including the President, the Cabinet, and the Congress, and the leaders of all political parties are evil Pishtagus who must be excised from the body politic.

Moreover, to take this one step further, it is clear that the ideology of Sendero Luminoso bears far more resemblance to the Taki Ongoy of the 1560s than it does to Mao Tse Tung. Like Sendero Luminoso some 400 years later, Taki Ongoy leaders promised their followers a millenarian upheaval which would wipe out the disastrous trends of the past. A Pan-Andean alliance of native gods, organized into two great armies, would do battle with the Christians' God, who would be defeated along with the Spaniards. Out of the destructive cataclysm would come regeneration. The revindicated Huacas (Indian Gods) would create a "New World" inhabited by "other peoples." This reborn world would be an Andean paradise—free of colonizers, materially abundant, and unplagued by disease.

But if the Cholos and Indians of the sierra have resurrected Andean racism, so have the whites and light-skinned mestizos of the coast. As early as the 1960s, one began to hear complaints from Lima's middle sectors about the "invasion of Cholos from the sierra." By 1985, however, those relatively mild complaints had become ugly, vicious epithets. Now the words Cholo and Serrano are spit out in vehement disgust and anger—now it is no longer simply Cholo, it is Cholo de Mierda. And, as the middle sectors are pushed further and further down the socioeconomic ladder, the more they are threatened by the lower class Cholos who themselves hate the middle sector Costeños.

Into this morass of societal horror one must also inject the military and paramilitary determination to defeat not only Sendero Luminoso but also the Movimiento Revolucionario de Túpac Amaru (MRTA). Apart from the heavy civilian casualties expected in any counter-insurgency operation, the current campaign could, in fact, lead to an all-out race war. After all, Sendero Luminoso began in the heavily

Indian department of Ayacucho and spread to the Indian areas of Huánuco, Puno, Cuzco, and the sprawling environs of Lima. To root out and defeat Sendero Luminoso would require that the army apply the same tactics employed by the Argentine military in the late 1970s, or the Uruguayan military a few years earlier.

Unlike Buenos Aires and Montevideo with their racially homogeneous populations, however, the overwhelming majority of Lima's 8.5 million inhabitants are largely dark-skinned migrants from the sierra. The blood bath that would ensue if an Argentine-type solution were attempted is terrifying to contemplate, and, to its credit, there is no indication that the Peruvian Comando Conjunto is even considering it.

But Lima's middle and upper classes are not only considering such a possibility, they have been openly demanding it since the mid-1980s. For centuries, Costeños have been haunted by the specter of the 1780 rebellion/race war of Túpac Amaru, an event that would occur again if "those people" ever got loose again. Now that that specter is ever closer to becoming a reality, people are terrified, so terrified that they fear "those people" even more than the terrible machine of death that would be required to defeat them. In other words, they fear the Conversos much more than they do the Inquisición. The way has been prepared, therefore, for a gigantic "Dirty War."

The final ingredient in this Andean *potaje* is the Narcotraficante. The worldwide drug traffic is now estimated to be well in excess of $300 billion a year, that is, $300 thousand million. The Narcotraficantes who control huge sectors of the Peruvian Amazonas are in league with Sendero Luminoso, and together they are probably stronger and better armed than the regular Peruvian army. Moreover, like Sendero Luminoso, the Narcotraficantes have been quick to take advantage of local hatreds for both Limeños and Mistis, and to forge alliances based on race rather than class hatreds.

If one adds all this up, one can appreciate how truly devastating life has been for Peruvians of all classes and races. For all practical purposes, the Peruvian government ceased to function years ago, but the extent of the infrastructural disintegration can best be seen in the recent cholera epidemic. The government simply has not been able to control it. Indeed, the entire health sector of the nation has all but collapsed.

Education, both public and private, has ground to a halt owing to the severity of the economic crisis. In fact, thousands of families have had to withdraw their children from private schools because they can no longer pay the monthly tuition. No greater disaster could possibly afflict middle class parents who have quite literally deprived themselves of proper food so that their children can attend the best private schools possible. But perhaps it doesn't really matter because, as I noted earlier, most of the nation's children do not receive the minimum caloric intake required to learn.

Political parties are rent with discord, the Congress meets but offers little if anything in the way of hope to the people, and the President (whether García or Fujimori) is a captive in the Palacio Nacional. The judicial system (which admittedly never worked all that well) is paralyzed and incapable of dealing with normal violence and crime, let alone with Sendero Luminoso, the MRTA, the Narcotraficantes, or the political assassinations which have become almost commonplace in the Lima of 1991.

But it is in the family, both nuclear and extended, that one really sees all the horrors of societal disintegration acted out. Whereas, what kept the United States together as a functioning, viable polity was our belief in our civic institutions and legal system, Latin American peoples have always relied upon their extended families to protect them from other citizens and, most particularly, from the state.

Now that family structure is under terrible attack. The fissures were there in 1985-86, but the ramifications were too horrible to contemplate, so most people just ignored it. They no longer can do that. I personally know of several extended families where violence has increased to unheard of levels, where many of the children are no longer in school, where relatives are stealing from one another—even one case where a child has defrauded his aged parents.

Both Reagan and Bush have responded to Peru's ills with guns and more guns, but they don't understand that guns and bombs will not kill Pishtagus, nor will they ameliorate racial tensions and violence, nor will they put families and communities back together.

Perhaps Peru is an extreme example of the economic collapse we are witnessing all over Latin America, but it also could be just the harbinger of things to come if the West in general, and the United States in particular, does not wake up quickly.

7. Origins and Trajectory of the Shining Path

Peter Stern

In May, 1980, a previously obscure guerrilla group performed the symbolic act of burning ballot boxes in the Plaza de Cangallo in Ayacucho, one of the poorest and most Indian provinces of Peru. Shortly thereafter the capital Lima awoke to find dead dogs hanging from lampposts and traffic lights, adorned with signs that read, "Deng Xiao Ping, Son of a Bitch." Thus did the self-proclaimed "fourth sword of Marxism," the Partido Comunista del Perú por el Sendero Luminoso de José Carlos Mariátegui, otherwise known as the Shining Path, make its public appearance on the national, if not the world, stage. Eleven years later, with more than 21,000 persons dead, 37 out of 127 provinces declared emergency zones under military law, and losses to the national economy in the vicinity of $18 billion, the Shining Path represents the deadliest and most intractable of all the guerrilla insurgencies of the past three decades in Latin America. The purpose of this paper is to examine Sendero a decade into its open struggle to impose a radical agrarian and collectivist vision onto a society deeply divided between European and indigenous worlds.

Before examining the texts of Sendero, a few comments about the parameters of the literature might be appropriate. Sendero Luminoso has been covered extensively in Peru, the journals *Debate* and *Quehacer* being the most cogent reporters. Not surprisingly, Peruvians, rather than Europeans or North Americans, have been the most thorough chroniclers of the movement. As of this date not one dissertation has appeared in the United States on Sendero (although there have been at least five master's theses), nor a single full-length monograph in English (the only foreseeable books will be an abridgement of Gorriti's projected three-volume work, planned by Princeton University Press and a translation of Carlos Iván Degregori's *Ayacucho, 1969-1979: El surgimiente de Sendero Luminoso* by the University of North Carolina Press). Compared with insurgencies in El Salvador or Nicaragua, this lack of attention is worthy of note. Possible explanations for the relative disinterest by outsiders may be distance, language, and the indigenous remoteness from which Sendero draws its very strength in the closed communities of the altiplano.

One common observation that runs through most of the non-Peruvian work on Sendero is that the guerrilla movement seemed to have emerged, like Athena from the head of Zeus, fully developed, both tactically and ideologically, literally from nowhere. Both the paucity of texts and the sudden appearance of Sendero represent, to internal and external observers, a radical departure from the normal curve of insurgent development, whether rural or urban in nature. Actually, as Peter Johnson has shown, both the movement and its own documentation have deep roots in the Peruvian intelligentsia, antedating the beginning of armed struggle by some fifteen years:

From the earliest positions of its founder, Abimael Guzmán, to the formal establishment of his Communist party (CP) faction and its subsequent armed engagement of government forces, the movement's objectives were enunciated and refined within a nationalist and ideological context. Much commentary characterizes it as a hermetic group and considers it difficult to discern its real intentions. A review of a cross section of the literature for the fifteen years preceding its first armed attack suggests that Sendero Luminoso leaders were open about their intentions and objectives. [1]

Sendero draws its inspiration from two sources; the first from Marxist-Leninist ideology as refined by Mao Tse-Tung and his blueprint for rural "people's war," and from the nationalist historical interpretations of José Carlos Mariátegui, founder of the Peruvian Communist Party. Most writers have emphasized the Maoist aspect of Senderista thought, wondering how such a seemingly alien doctrine can be applicable to the Andean highlands. Actually, Guzmán and his colleagues successfully rooted their ideology in an indigenous framework, combining Mariátegui's analysis of the feudal structure of Peru with a peasant-based rural insurrectionary doctrine. [2]

Mariátegui's appeal to Peruvian radicals is a natural one, for he combined a socialist outlook with an appeal to the country's indigenous past. Mariátegui's analysis of Peruvian evolution is circular: from native communalism to European feudalism, to independent capitalism, and from there, hopefully, back to socialism. He idealized an aboriginal past:

The degree to which history was severed in Peru by the conquest can be seen better on an economic than on any other level. Here the conquest most clearly appears to be a break in continuity. Until the conquest, an economy developed in Peru that sprang spontaneously and freely from the Peruvian soil and people. . . . All historical evidence agrees that the Inca people—industrious, disciplined, pantheist, and simple—lived in material comfort. With abundant food their population increased. The Malthusian problem was completely unknown to the empire. . . . Collective work and common effort were employed fruitfully for social purposes.

The Spanish conquistadors destroyed this impressive productive machine without being able to replace it. The indigenous society and the Inca economy were wholly disrupted and annihilated by the shock of the conquest. . . . Indigenous labor ceased to function as a concerted and integrated effort. The conquistadors . . . allotted land and men with no thought of their future use as forces and means of production. . . . On the ruins and remnants of a socialist economy, they established the bases of a feudal economy. [3]

Mariátegui declared that "The problem of the Indian is rooted in the land tenure system of our economy,"[4] and prescribed a return to the Pre-Hispanic communal past as a cure for the nation. Sendero has also tied the liberation of the Indian in Peru to the destruction of the capitalist economic system, but so far has failed to outline precisely what kind of nation a postcapitalist, post-Eurocentric Peru would be.

The period from 1965 to 1980 demonstrates that Sendero's ideological evolution reflected the Sino-Soviet split; Sendero placed its faith firmly in the prosecution of a Maoist "people's war." As early as the Fifth Congress of the Communist Party in 1965, the strategy for victory was enunciated: organizing the countryside, forming a popular army for armed struggle, infiltrating worker organizations, establishing a clandestine network to rally the masses, and creating links between the party and students, workers, and peasants.[5]

By the late 1960s the men and women who would form the core of Sendero had gathered in Ayacucho province at the Universidad Nacional de San Cristóbal de Huamanga. There, far from Lima, they debated and honed their strategy of *guerra popular*, building strength among the students at the university, especially the Indian students. They also fought fierce polemical battles with other leftist factions at the university, and split irrevocably from the Partido Comunista Peruano (PCP).

Ayacucho was fertile recruiting ground for Guzmán and his followers. Ayacucho is a Quechua word meaning "corner of death." The province rates among the lowest in literacy, access to services, including water, sewage, and electricity, transportation, including cars and bicycles, and even in possession of household items such as radios, televisions, refrigerators, lavatories, and sewing machines. Life expectancy is only forty-five years. Ayacucho's contribution to the GDP of the country lags far behind its proportion of national territory and population. It is overwhelmingly an agrarian department, its industry being largely of an artisan rather than of a manufacturing character. Per capita income is far below the national average (around $70);

Ayacucho is tied with Apurímac as the poorest department in all of Peru.[6] In short, Ayacucho was strongly Quechuan, agricultural, and very poor: excellent conditions for the launching of a revolutionary movement of a predominantly rural character. It even had a strong tradition of rebellion: prior to the arrival of the Spanish, Ayacucho was the scene of clashing rival ethnicities and resistance to Inca conquest.[7]

In Manuel Abimael Guzmán Reynoso the movement found its Fidel, its Mao, its Ho Chi Minh—a theorist, organizer, and inspiration, the revolutionary known as "Presidente Gonzalo." Born in Arequipa in 1934, Guzmán was first educated by the Jesuits in his home department. Said to be a brilliant student, he graduated from San Agustín University in Arequipa, having studied philosophy and law. He wrote not one but two theses: one entitled "The Kantian Theory of Space," the other, "The Bourgeois Democratic State." He arrived in Ayacucho in 1963 at the age of thirty to take over the philosophy department of the University of San Cristóbal de Huamanga. Guzmán earned wide respect as a conscientious teacher and at the same time editor of *Bandera Roja*, the official journal of the now-splintered PCP. Within five years he had almost totally gained control of the university; ironically, despite terming the government as "fascist," Guzmán adherents occupied important positions within the university itself, including those overseeing personnel and student welfare. From these crucial posts, Guzmán and his followers could recruit students and faculty to their cause and debate endlessly the nature of Peruvian society and their plans for its future. In Huamanga, the Frente Estudiantil Revolutionario (FER), a loose coalition of leftist groups, was the focus of political agitation at the university in the late 1960s and early 1970s. Gradually a division appeared between those allied with the FER and those under the influence of Guzmán over Sendero's "maximalist" line. (Senderistas called other leftist factions "parasites"; they retaliated by referring to the Senderistas as *los dogmáticos*.) Another area of contention was Sendero's refusal to participate in the many strikes and land invasions carried out in Ayacucho during this period. By 1974 the anti-Guzmán faction gained control of the university's executive council, and Guzmán resigned and withdrew from the institution that had been his most important recruiting and training grounds.[8] Three years earlier, in 1971, Guzmán planned out the path to power in five stages that reflected classic Maoist thought: mobilization, agitation, and propaganda; sabotage and rural guerrilla activity; widening of violence into general guerrilla warfare; establishment and expansion of bases and liberated zones; blockade of towns and cities by peasant armies, leading to the collapse of the government.[9]

Guzmán was also strongly influenced at Huamanga by an agronomist, Emilio Antonio Díaz Martínez, one of the leading contributors to *senderista* philosophy. Díaz Martínez was born in Cajamarca, another poor agrarian department in the Andes, but one that significantly had lost its indigenous culture, the "Indian *campesino* culture based on the Quechua language and Inca traditions of mutual help and cooperation which were still alive in some parts of rural Ayacucho."[10] Trained as an agronomist near Lima, he completed his thesis at Huamanga on the socioeconomic composition of agriculture in Ayacucho in 1959. He joined the newly formed Institute of Agrarian Reform and Colonization in 1960, and worked on colonization schemes for three years, gradually growing disillusioned with the government's technocratic approach to agrarian problems of the country, an approach that rejected restructuring landholding patterns in Peru.

He moved to the agronomy faculty at Huamanga, and in 1969 wrote *Ayacucho, hambre y esperanza*, based on his fieldwork in the department. He concluded that dominance of the *latifundio* was the greatest obstacle to progress in the countryside, and the entrapment of the *campesino* in various unfair labor practices a sign of the still-feudal nature of Ayacucho society. Díaz Martínez did not reject modern technology and training as catalysts of agricultural change; his argument with the schemes of the university were that they totally ignored the peasant himself, and his culture's traditions of self-help and coopera-tion. In his view, the agronomy specialists tried to impose rigid and narrow technical solutions on the peasantry; better if they were encouraged to rediscover their old communal and cooperative traditions, and were merely encouraged and given technical assistance by outside experts. Above all:

The worst feature of what was going on in rural Ayacucho in the mid-1960s, as far as Díaz Martínez was concerned, was the insidious introduction of values and behaviours from an alien culture, thereby destroying the emotional and ecological equilibrium which had enabled campesino communities to withstand centuries of exploitation and aggression. Teachers, engineers, government officials, bank employees, all brought in a foreign way of life which left the Indians at a disadvantage.[11]

Eventually Díaz Martínez came to believe that nothing could be changed in the countryside until the entire society was transformed as well. His book ends with the daunting challenge, "Peru will have to take the socialist road to development, the only road left to the semi-colonial and semi-feudal countries of Latin America."[12] A trip by Díaz Martínez to China in 1974 merely strengthened his view that only radical change could bring about real reform in the countryside. Two years' residence and work in China made him a confirmed Maoist and believer in the necessity of a prolonged people's war to achieve true liberation and democracy. (Díaz Martínez joined Sendero Luminoso and was captured by security forces; he died in the bloody uprising at San Pedro prison outside Lima in June, 1986.) [13]

Since the inauguration of armed struggle in 1980, Sendero has been surprisingly reticent about its goals and objectives, perhaps the only insurgency in modern times to abjure publicity, press conferences, moral aid from Western sympathizers, material aid from fraternal socialist countries, and resolutions of support at the United Nations. Sendero's isolation on the left is near total: the Soviets have been called "filthy revisionists," the Chinese "dogs who betrayed the Cultural Revolution," Fidel Castro "a puppet of social imperialism," Kim Il Sung "another Fidel Castro," and even Enver Hoxha of Albania "a betrayer of the worst kind." [14] A comparison that many observers have made is with the Khmer Rouge of Cambodia, not only for reasons of comparable ideology but also for the extremism and ruthlessness of Sendero's military actions. No doubt many analysts wish the world to draw correspondingly negative comparisons between the fate of Cambodians under Khmer Rouge and the implied fate of Peruvians should Sendero triumph.

The texts of the movement itself are few, consisting of a few manifestos: one of the first, published in 1982, was *Desarrollemos la guerra de guerrillas*, followed five years later by a lengthier document, *Desarrollar la guerra popular sirviendo a la revolución mundial*. These two papers, along with an extensive interview with "Presidente Gonzalo" in the leftist newspaper *El Diario* in 1988 and what amounts to little more than some proclamations and flyers, are all the world has to analyze the objectives of the Shining Path. [15]

Developing Guerrilla Warfare is a somewhat turgid and bombastic document, but provides insight into the mentality of Sendero. It begins by recounting 15 years of hard struggle to reconstitute itself as the organized vanguard of the proletariat which Mariátegui founded, and congratulates itself for 21 months of armed struggle, for more than 1,900 "actions" against the forces of reaction, and for being active in all but 4 departments in the country. A lengthy catalog of successful "actions" includes peasant mobilizations, sabotage of electrical lines, fire bombs in factories, bank robberies, and so forth. The blowing up of a bust of John F. Kennedy in Miraflores is mentioned as a special blow against the forces of Yankee imperialism, as are jailbreaks in Ayacucho against the reactionary state. [16]

What has been the reactionary response of the counter-revolutionary forces to Sendero's successes? "What has been the response of the self-proclaimed democratic government and the self-proclaimed respecter of constitutional order and sacred human rights?" Persecution, repression, torture, jail, and death, says Sendero; "the government of Belaúnde, falsely democratic and demagogically hypocritical, has launched its repressive forces, principally the police, to drown in its own blood the newly-born revolution."[17] The government declares the rebellion "terrorism," is aided and abetted by the Reagan administration, and is supported by the revisionist Peruvian Communists, obsequious follower of Brezhnev, servants of Russian revisionism. In fact, a good deal of invective is reserved for the "self-proclaimed" left inside Peru.[18] The military government of 1968-1980 tried, Sendero concedes, to meet its challenge by altering Peruvian society, and strengthening bureaucratic capitalism. To accomplish this the military increased spending to make the government the principal engine of the economy, and increased the "corporatist" reorganization of society, guided by "fascist" political conceptions.[19]

But whether the government is military, or civilian under Belaúnde, the real force deciding the fate of Peru is monopoly capitalism, especially international banking institutions at the behest of North American imperialism. Obsolete parliamentarism, "so-called" judicial and electoral power, are all but parts of a political reactionism masquerading as democracy, while it is the police and the army which are the real "vertebral column" of the state. And the people of Peru? They are divided into campesino, proletarian, petit bourgeois, and middle bourgeois sectors; it is the worker-peasant alliance (joined by the petit bourgeoisie), which united under the direction of the proletariat, and which will form the core of the revolutionary forces and lead the armed struggle.[20] The logic is clear, if simplistic.

Who says exploitation says State, and who says State says classes, and who says classes says struggle of the classes, and who says struggle of the classes says popular struggle . . . and who says popular struggle says rebellion, armed struggle, people's war. . . . Revolutionary violence is essential to our historical process, and if republican emancipation was gained by arms on the field of battle, it is easy to understand that the development and triumph of the Peruvian revolution, of our democratic revolution, of the emancipation of the people and of the classes will be gained only through the widest revolutionary war by our people, rising in arms *en masse* through people's war.[21]

The manifesto ends: "People of Peru! Labor, peasants, workers, women, young people, intellectuals, support the armed struggle!

Support the development of guerrilla warfare! *¡Viva el Partido Comunista Peruano! ¡Gloria al marxismo-leninismo-maoismo!"*

The same year "Sendero's 8 Basic Theses" was published in *Quehacer*. In just one page the article manages to restate the entire basis of its philosophy with remarkable brevity. Peru is a semicolonial, semifeudal, dependent country. The peasantry is its most retarded, oppressed, and exploited sector. In such a society, one cannot have democracy, and bourgeois institutions such as a parliament can exist only as caricatures. Electoral participation and bourgeois laws can only favor the exploiters. The forces of the left must choose between "parliamentary cretinism" and the view of the people, which is armed struggle. The Peruvian revolution will be democratic, nationalist, anti-imperialist, and anti-feudal. Its base will be an alliance of peasants and workers; of these two, the peasants will be the leading force while the proletariat develops and becomes the ruling class. The principal and only form of revolutionary struggle to take power and build the New Democratic State is armed struggle, "people's war," because the dominant classes will not be easily dispossessed of their power with an armed force that has converted itself into an army of occupation in its own country. Popular war is a war of the countryside, and will move into the cities: popular war is a peasant war or it is nothing. The party grows and develops in the course of armed struggle and, as a political organization, seeks during the struggle to convert itself into a true popular army.[22]

In 1987, a longer manifesto appeared, entitled *Developing the People's War, Serving the World Revolution*. Six years into the war, it posed the same questions as before: How have the forces of counter-revolution reacted to the struggle? The dictatorship of the bourgeoisie and landlords, it opines, backed by Yankee imperialism, has resorted to turning the masses against one another and has committed genocide against the people of Peru.[23] The manifesto catalogs a detailed and, unfortunately, entirely credible list of massacres in the countryside, citing villages raided and peasants killed, the discovery of mass graves, persons "disappeared," and incarceration and torture on a wide scale. Sendero charges that the government, by 1987, had killed 8,700 Peruvians.[24] Still, such tactics have not availed the government; they have, Sendero boasts, been humiliatingly defeated, and forced to abandon the countryside and take refuge in provincial and departmental capitals.[25]

In contrast with the generalities of Sendero's first manifesto, its second is quite specific in its analysis of the course of six years of people's war, going as far as to calculate the percentage of actions carried out by department (64 percent in Ayacucho, Huancavelica, and Apurímac, 28.2 percent in other areas, only 8.4 percent in metropolitan Lima), and by type of activity (military attack, sabotage, selective raid, propaganda, and armed agitation). It also analyzes in detail the voting patterns in the general elections of 1985, the economy of Peru, and agrarian reform, mocking President Alán García's early radical attempts at reform and revitalization. Not surprisingly, Sendero still finds that the ultimate aim of the civilian government is the strengthening of bureaucratic capitalism and semifeudalism within the framework of imperialism, principally Yankee imperialism.

Nowhere in these documents is any specific or concrete goal beyond the destruction of the existing order; the establishing of a workers' and peasants' democracy, it is implied, will cure all of Peru's problems. Even the celebrated interview with Guzmán in *El Diario* in 1988 (entitled *"Presidente Gonzalo rompe el silencio"*) yields few clues as to Sendero's vision of the New Democracy. The interview (for which the newspaper was closed shortly after its publication) is a long, mind-numbing Marxist polemic (a reprint is 153 pages) that nevertheless gives valuable insight into the mentality and worldview of "Presidente Gonzalo." Mariátegui would be a Maoist if he lived today, declares the president. For Guzmán, Marxism-Leninism-Maoism is the highest form of evolutionary political thought; combined with the principles Mariátegui espoused, "Gonzalo thought" (*pensamiento Gonzalo*) is a universal truth.[26] He denied that a personality cult about him existed, calling such a cult a sinister revisionist thesis: "In our Party, revolution, and people's war, the proletariat has generated a group of leaders through necessity and historical causality; in the opinion of Engels, it is a necessity that leaders and a leader emerge, but who they may be is determined by chance and specific conditions of a place and time."[27] In regard to violence, he reminded the interviewer that Mao declared violence to be a universal law without exception; only revolutionary violence permitted the resolution of the "fundamental contradictions" with an army and through people's war.

War has two aspects, one of destruction, the other of construction; construction is the principal one, and not to see this is to undermine the revolution, weaken it . . . from the moment the people take up arms in order to overthrow the old order, from this moment the reaction will seek to crush it, destroy it, annihilate it, using all means at their disposal including genocide; in our country we have seen this and are seeing it, and we will continue to see it until we demolish the decrepit Peruvian state.[28]

He denied that Sendero was practicing terrorism, insisting that terror was a tool of the forces of reaction. He called the Tupac Amaru Revolutionary Front counterrevolutionary for agreeing to a truce with Alán García. He acknowledged that the people of Peru were religious, and did not condemn this faith per se, but termed the new evangelism espoused by John Paul II as merely a prop to sustain a reactionary instrument of bourgeois domination.

Regarding the future of Peru, new relations of production, he declared, will be the outcome of a successful people's war. Land, collective work, and the reorganization of social life would constitute a "new reality," under the joint dictatorship of workers, peasants, and progressives. Asked about the confiscation of property under the New Democracy, he replied that the goals of Sendero—the smashing of imperialist domination, semifeudalism, and bureaucratic capitalism— imply redistribution of land under Mao's slogan "the land to those who work it," and the confiscation of bureaucratic capital as crucial to the economic foundation of the New Power.

In regard to the middle or national bourgeoisie, the policy would be to respect their rights. This they could rely on, but to go further would be to change the character of the revolution. The threat to confiscate all property, he said, was part of the lies and falsehoods always leveled against Communists. Furthermore, since the foreign debt was imperialist property, it would simply be confiscated. [29]

Land would be distributed principally to the poor peasantry, and later to the middle peasants, and, if there was some land left or it was convenient, to rich peasants. Even landlords could work, Mao taught, if they wanted to earn their bread with the sweat of their brow. In one area, Guzmán said, Sendero had already distributed 300,000 hectares and mobilized 150,000 peasants, undermining the APRA land reform program, which he declared a sham. [30]

It is only at the conclusion of the twelve hours of interview that Guzmán was asked some personal questions, about his early life and intellectual development. He confirmed that he had spent time in China, and that he had been trained not only in Marxist philosophy but also in guerrilla warfare, including the use of explosives. Everything in his life was related to politics, even his enjoyment of poetry and Shakespeare. Through his Marxism he was, he stated, an optimist, in an almost organic manner. Friends he had none, but he was proud of the comrades he did have. [31]

Despite his denial that any cult of personality exists in his movement, Abimael Guzmán is "more than an ideological leader; he is the guiding light, the father of a new age in Peru. The ethereal nature of his character is portrayed in Sendero propaganda. On posters, pamphlets, and wall paintings, he is depicted as a bright, soaring flame, burning with ideological passion and power."[32] Rumors abound that "Presidente Gonzalo" is suffering from a terminal illness and may be dead, but seem beside the point. Manuel Granados, who studied at Huamanga and knew many of the future senderistas, argues that the movement now has a life of its own. "Mao," he says, "has died. He's buried. But there are thirty or forty groups in the world that continue fighting for the ideas of Mao." More important than Guzmán in the flesh is the "subjective myth" that surrounds him. Senderistas declare that they are fighting for the guiding thought of President Gonzalo.[33] Another commentator declared that for Sendero's men and women, "Marxism is understood not as a scientific theory, but as a quasi-religious myth. For them, as for André Malraux, the communist myth gives creative energy to the heroic soul."[34] A final word on the role of Guzmán in Sendero Luminoso might be provided not by a sociologist or political scientist, but by the most celebrated writer of the left in this century, George Orwell. In the novel *1984*, Winston Smith asks his interrogator O'Brien, "Does Big Brother exist?" O'Brien replies, "Of course he exists. The Party exists. Big Brother is the embodiment of the Party." Smith then asks, "Will Big Brother ever die?" And O'Brien responds, "Of course not. How could he die?"

Carlos Iván Degregori is, along with Gustavo Gorriti and Raul González, a veteran Sendero observer. Midway through the decade he published *Ayacucho, raices de una crisis*, which examines in microscopic detail the province that gave birth to the rebellion. In virtually every vital indicator, Ayacucho ranks near the bottom of all Peruvian departments. But Degregori brought out other factors: Ayacucho had, in the 1970s, one of the largest rates of emigration in the country; with the notable exception of Huamanga (where the University is), females over the age of 15 outnumbered males, as the men migrated out of the department in search of work.[35] In urban areas 27 percent of the population was illiterate; in rural areas the number was 56 percent.[36] Fifty-two percent of urban households had electricity; in the country-side, scarcely 1 percent.[37] Access to potable water by household was 56 percent in cities, but only 3.4 percent in rural areas. Even worse were figures for "baños y servicios higiénicos": 20 percent in Huamanga in 1981, but bordering on 0 percent in the rest of the province. Hepatitis and internal parasites were endemic throughout Ayacucho.[38] Land concentration was just as skewed. Agricultural entities of less than 1 hectare made up 33 percent of the department's total entities, occupying only 1 percent of the available cultivated land. Units of 500

or more hectares made up 0.18 percent of the total agricultural
enterprises, but occupied more than 76 percent of the arable land. In
sum, 86 percent of the land was controlled by 0.6 percent of the
population. Agrarian reform by and large bypassed Ayacucho; a census
in 1971 found just 11 agricultural cooperatives with an average of
321 hectares apiece.[39] Degregori's conclusions are succinctly stated:
Ayacucho is an agrarian, overwhelmingly rural (meaning Indian), and
poor province. Unemployment, underemployment, infant mortality, and
illiteracy are high. The convulsion and crisis that grip Ayacucho have
their central and indisputable roots in the exploitation, backwardness,
misery, and neglect of the department.[40]

Degregori's first book on Shining Path, *Sendero Luminoso*,
appeared in 1985. Since then he has written *Que difícil es ser Dioceses:
ideología y violencia política en Sendero Luminoso* (1989) and *Ayacucho
1969-1979: El surgimiento de Sendero Luminoso* (1990). He has written
extensively on the origins of Sendero, but it is his prognosis that
engages our interest. Degregori observes that Sendero chose to launch
its people's war at a critical moment in Peruvian history: when the
armed forces left politics, weary after twelve years of military rule, a
period known as the "Peruvian military experiment," an experiment
that began progressively and ended in reaction. The military did not
want the burden of repression, and left the task of countering Sendero
to the police. Sendero's audacity, political will, capacity for organization, and decentralized structure were more than a match for the civil
authorities in the first years of the struggle.[41] (The organization, like
most modern revolutionary movements, is organized into compartmentalized "cells," a design that maintains strict security and makes
infiltration difficult.) Sendero also benefited from its appeal to
traditional Andean values; Sendero, González wrote, arrived in Indian
communities not like other factions of the left but in a distinctly nativist
manner, within the authoritarian aspect of the Andean tradition:
"Sendero appears really like a new good landlord, almost a kind of
Inkarri [a Quechua myth] which arrives *from above* to impose a new
order, or restore, perhaps, an old one, more just but not necessarily
democratic."[42] Sendero launched a "raise the harvest" movement in
zones under its control, emphasizing communal agriculture in the
manner of the old *mita* communal labor levy, a traditional (and pre-
Inca) institution. In abandoned haciendas and captured experimental
farms, hundreds of peasants were organized for collective cultivation.
Degregori believed that most of the peasants participated voluntarily in
these efforts.[43]

Sendero established "red zones," not strictly liberated zones in the classical Maoist sense but areas where "Popular Committees" ruled absolutely, and Sendero reorganized the inhabitants in functional support groups: workers, women, peasants, youth, and others. Degregori reported that "cleansing" these areas of all things not in conformity to its doctrines quickly wrecked the fragile communal equilibrium of the communities, destroying the links of *compadrazgo*, familial relationships, and participation in civic and religious institutions (such as *hermandades* and *cofradías*), which were so instrumental in the survival of Andean communities.[44]

Sendero's appeal could wear thin quickly. Summary executions of landlords (who were often not *hacendados* but small landholders), civil authorities, and "exploiters of the people" did not gain universal favor, and worse, Sendero began to impose a puritanical vision of society, beating, for example, or cutting the hair, of anyone abusing alcohol, transgressing family monogamy, and so forth. In some communities they even forbade traditional rituals of dancing and courtship.[45] Also, when Sendero tried to force communities into autarky, by cutting off all trading links with neighboring communities and cities by blockading roads, threatening to close ferries, or trying in some cases to restrict how much land was planted, peasants resisted. Community autarky fit in well with Sendero's military needs, the creation of isolated "red zones." But when Sendero closed the ferry of Lirio in Huanta province, for example, poor peasants and small merchants in Huancasancos resisted when Sendero tried to block the construction of a new road to the coast.[46]

Such stories belie the impression that Sendero's appeal is universal and unchallenged among an undifferentiated and disgruntled peasantry. Degregori's conclusions in 1986 were that Sendero could not repeat the experience of the victorious people's war in China. Nevertheless, the poverty and exploitation among some sectors of Peru, especially among the young, gave Sendero a tremendous advantage. Sendero's greatest weaknesses were its rigidity, which rejected alliance with other sectors of Peru, and its tactics, which called for a "frontal assault" upon power. This assault had caused, in Degregori's opinion, not a fragmentation of Peruvian society, but instead a drawing together of the center-left political spectrum of the country. This was demonstrated by the proliferation of worker organizations, peasant groups, barrio committees, popular organizations, women's and youth groups, organization among professionals, intellectuals, journalists, and political parties. It is these bodies, Degregori believed, and not an incapable and repressive state, that represent an obstacle to Sendero's strategy. "It is this civil society and its political and democratic manifestations, those which provide a national alternative of democratic reconstruction, which confront the violence which bloodies Ayacucho and threatens to engulf the whole country."[47]

Manuel Jesús Granados's knowledge of Sendero comes not from outside observation; he was "present at the creation." Granados is a Quechua-speaker, and attended San Cristóbal de Huamanga in the 1970s, where he befriended many who would become leaders in Sendero. As an educated Indian he is caught in a contradiction of prejudices: the *indígena* is told that education is a way to rise out of poverty and misery, but to be an educated Indian is to be suspected of being a senderista. "I am an Indian," Granados says, "but I have had access to books, to an education, so I could be a Senderista leader— there are many like me who are."[48]

Granados's bachelor's thesis at Huamanga was probably the earliest study of Sendero, based on his acquaintance with leftists at the University, and hundreds of the pamphlets with which the Guzmán faction had waged paper war. When he wrote his thesis, Sendero was about to launch its offensive, and it put pressure on many faculty members at Huamanga, who declined to read it. It was eventually approved by two foreigners and a man from Granados's hometown, after he removed all names from it, including Guzmán's. He typed three copies of the 178-page thesis himself. One was stolen by Sendero, which warned Granados that it would be used someday "for . . . adjusting accounts." Another was "borrowed" in 1983 by the government commission investigating the massacre of journalists at Uchuraccay and never returned. Granados says that it is now in the hands of the military commander of Ayacucho.[49]

A more accessible work by Granados on Sendero appeared in 1987 in the journal *Socialismo y participación*. The article shocked and alarmed many people, and came to be the topic of discussion among a wide circle of influential *limeños* as no other work on Sendero had been up to that time.[50] Granados feels impelled at the outset of the article to confront frankly and openly the suspicions that his ethnicity engenders:

I am not a member of Sendero Luminoso, and therefore not a senderista. Nor will I ever be one. In this sense trying to interpret some of their basic statements in a certain manner might indicate that I am justifying some of their violent actions. There is no intention here of making a kind of apologia; this work is pure and simple a recognition of a reality that affects Peruvian society. . . .[51]

Granados's intention is to make the world at large aware of the implications of Sendero for his country, to refute misconceptions about a group many considered mysterious and impenetrable. In the beginning, he writes, it was like a game. Some electrical towers here, some bombs there. No one took Sendero seriously. Its own systematic silence, its unknown ideology, these helped its first actions to be seen as irrational and illogical by national and international eyes. But Sendero is neither; from its first actions in 1980 it has proceeded to apply in a most practical manner a philosophy, in ideology known as "Pensamiento Gonzalo."

Being essentially an adaptation of Maoism, Sendero conceives of its struggle as a rural one. The class struggle has begun there, he writes. The representatives of the state and capitalism are the governing authorities (alcaldes, lieutenant governors, the police), the rural authorities (community presidents, traditional authorities), small merchants and bureaucrats. All of them are labeled "petty reactionaries," and they are the first victims of Sendero. Such persons are chosen selectively for punishment as easily perceived symbols. Ethical notions of good or evil do not apply in Sendero's worldview; one is either for or against the revolution. To occupy a position of authority in the countryside is to support the capitalist state. Other enemies of the people are any peasants who have wealth or power of any kind. A campesino who has five cows, a plot a little bigger than others, or a small store, is seen as a rich person, and often also has a communal or government position. This approaches *decencia*, or respectability, synonymous with wealth and *blanqueamiento* or "whitening," Europeanization, values of a feudal or semifeudal system. A senderista once explained to Granados that such people, *gente decente*, could not help but be natural allies of the existing order and the armed forces.[52]

The peasants, then, are the motor of the revolution. The working class has the role of directing the war, and the small and middle bourgeoisie are at best auxiliary forces. In the countryside poor peasants, especially the young, are the principal targets of consciousness-raising. Adults are not reliable or trustworthy; adults are an overwhelming majority in the civil patrols organized by the government called *rondas*. In urban areas, Sendero concentrates its efforts among the young poor who inhabit the barrios that now surround Lima, many of them migrants and children of migrants. Another important recruiting ground is the university. Here Sendero makes no class distinctions whatsoever; the sons and daughters of the middle and upper class are as welcome as those of the workers and the poor. The experiences of Argentina and Uruguay (not to mention

Europe and the United States) demonstrate that the most extreme of leftist ideologies can appeal powerfully to members of the privileged classes. Furthermore, these recruits are more likely to have family members occupying high positions in the government, the armed forces, political parties, industry, and commerce, and so are useful sources of information for the movement.[53]

Once recruited, the new guerrillas are tightly organized in cells, hermetically sealed one from the other for security. The main tactic of Sendero is the act of sabotage. Frontal assault on the state is to be avoided. Granados denies that Sendero engages, as the government accuses, in terrorism. Terrorism, he asserts, is the tactic of groups that lack an ideology and strike out in blind anger. Sendero acts from a design which it has clearly announced to the world. Its tactics keep the forces of order in a continual state of suspense and insecurity. They undermine the credibility of the government, the police, and the armed forces; no sooner is an announcement made that terrorism has been smashed than Sendero blacks out the capital and launches attacks all over the country. The economy of the nation is progressively bled by the war, as damaged infrastructure and revenues lost through inactivity contribute to the worsening of the economic situation. The tactics of guerrilla warfare are appropriate to the semifeudal and semicolonial condition of the country, to the arms at hand (dynamite hurled from *huaracas*, Indian slings), and to the theory of people's war. Sophisticated arms, Granados writes, have no correlation to the Moist dialectic of Sendero. The link between Sendero and *narcotraficantes* should, in theory, yield enormous sums of money to Sendero, with which it can buy whatever arms it wishes. But in 1987, Granados found no evidence of any change in Sendero's tactics or armaments, although he conceded that this may change in the future.[54]

Granados, unlike other observers of Sendero, is able to confront directly the ethnic dimension of the rebellion. Historically, the Indian has been crushed, brutalized by five hundred years of domination. Because of this, many peasants have a fatalistic and resigned view of their place in society, accepting domination as natural. Sendero, he believes, understands this reality and presents itself as a "we," a defender of the *indígena* against "them," the exploiters. In communities where the peasants have not been receptive to Sendero, the choice is simple: cooperate in silence or die; permit your sons to be enrolled in the Popular Guerrilla Army or die. Neutrality, to Sendero, is impossible. Reeducation is a gigantic task; to eliminate the reluctant is more convenient.[55]

Terror, however, has its limits, especially when it is applied by those fighting subversion. When the peasants are under such pressure, some flee for other areas, some ally themselves with one side or the other, but the majority try to maintain a neutrality in which they suffer from both sides. Granados, in the end, is unequivocal about where he stands in his judgment of Sendero Luminoso. On the one hand, he quotes the bishop of Ayacucho, who explains that infant mortality in the province is high not because of a lack of food but because people do not know how to balance their diet properly from the foods they have on hand, and they must be taught proper nutrition.[56] He also quotes a general who states that it matters little that to kill two or three senderistas it is necessary to kill eighty innocents.[57] But on the other hand, he believes that Sendero's triumph would utterly devastate Peru:

From the massacres of the ancient Assyrians, Persians, Romans, Huns, we pass to the massacres of the civilized world, which had one of its maximum expressions in that of Nazi Germany. In the realm of socialist revolutions, we see that with Stalin there were more than thirty million deaths; in the Cultural Revolution of Mao, the figure is almost forty million; the Vietnamese achieved six million; but it is Pol Pot where almost half of the population of the country was annihilated. In our country, up to now, the deaths numerically are still not many. If Sendero Luminoso triumphs, how many Peruvians will be left to tell the story? A million, half a million? For Sendero, in the Marxist conception, these "cleansing operations" are necessarily indispensable in order to adequately secure their aims.[58]

Virtually all Peruvian intellectuals have attacked Sendero Luminoso from the left, condemning its violence while simultaneously decrying the social and economic conditions that have permitted Sendero to flourish, and accusing the government of indecision, ineptitude, and brutality in fighting the insurgency. It is, possibly, the only attitude they can adopt safely today in Peru under the circumstances. Henri Favre, who wrote *Perú—Sendero Luminoso y horizontes ocultos* in 1987, believes Sendero is merely the most violent manifestation of a crisis gripping all of Latin America. To begin with, Sendero could have begun in any number of departments in Peru. The fact that Ayacucho is among the poorest is incidental. Favre argues that poverty and backwardness have never spurred a people to rebel; in fact they tend to be powerful forces for conservatism.

The forces Sendero has tapped are not local but national and even transnational. Modernization and the multiple shocks of the modern capitalist state have created landless peasants, uprooted peoples, cities swarming with the under- and unemployed: "Day labor yesterday in Chanchamayo, porters today in Huancayo, tomorrow they will be in

Lima washing . . . the windshields of cars waiting for a green light at the corners on Arequipa Avenue."[59]   Since the 1970s, Favre asserts, many migrants and children of migrants have returned to their ancestral homes in the sierra, carrying all the frustrations of their failed urban experiences, which is manifested in senderista violence.   To such people, whom Favre describes as "not campesinos, nor workers, nor rural nor urban, neither *andinos* nor *criollos*, who have little social or cultural identity and who are adrift in anonymity, Sendero offers structure, norms, values, for their frustrations, action. To their useless life, a purpose."[60]

Sendero knows that the only victory it can win will be a political one, with Lima, as the center of power, the ultimate prize. Its purpose now is to make life in Lima unlivable, to show *limeños* that the government cannot function.   In ten, twenty, or thirty years the inhabitants will take control of the metropolis for themselves and for Sendero.   Urban terrorism is not even an exclusive prerogative of Sendero: the Túpac Amaru Revolutionary Movement (MRTA) and other fringe groups have entered the fray.   Sendero's more fearsome legacy may be that it has legitimized recourse to the bomb and the machine gun in the pursuit of political objectives. Favre calls this the "senderization" of society. But, like Granados, he cannot identify with either MRTA or Sendero Luminoso. He calls Túpac Amaru a terrorist group without a social base, and Sendero an insurrectional movement that values terrorism as part of a more general scheme of armed popular revolt.[61]

Favre nevertheless sees only a grim outcome for Peruvian society. Sendero, in classic guerrilla manner, does not seek military victory. It weakens the economy, destabilizes the government, and prevents the real problems of society from being effectively addressed. In 1986 the military was absorbing 26 percent of the total government budget; to continue to fight inflation the government must raise taxes, alienating the middle class, or cut social spending, alienating the popular classes. Finally, Favre sees Sendero as part of a larger pattern of social and economic change marginalizing large portions of the continent's people. The model of capitalist development to which Latin America has subscribed is responsible for Sendero. He concludes an interview in *Quehacer* by pointing out that in 1937 the per capita income of Argentina was equal to that of France, and in 1950 Peru's surpassed that of Japan. What remains of this today [1986]? It would be, Favre says, cruel to answer.[62]

Analysis of Sendero from outside Peru comes from a less politically engaged but no less sympathetic viewpoint. Often it has focused on a particular aspect of the problem. Cynthia McClintock, for example, differs from many observers in that she actually did field research in rural Peru. In her 1984 article "Why Peasants Rebel" she analyzed the rural structure of Ayacucho and its relevance to the origins of Sendero there. What distinguishes Sendero from other rural revolutionary movements is that it arose *after* a major agrarian reform. The southern highlands of Peru, McClintock notes, are mainly agricultural, in an area particularly unsuitable for agriculture: the terrain is stony, arid, and windswept; altitudes often surpass 12,000 feet. Pasture for cattle is meager, and little beyond potatoes will grow there. Ayacucho is not only poor, but poorer than other rural departments, and poorer now than it was twenty years ago.[63] Throughout the 1970s, food consumption actually fell in many parts of Peru. In 1980 families in the central sierra consumed 92 percent of daily caloric requirements specified by the FAO, while families in the northern highlands consumed only 72 percent. McClintock presumes that figures for the southern highlands, which are worse off, were probably actually below 70 percent. In a government study, daily caloric intake among lower class people throughout the entire country fell from 1,934 calories per capita in 1972 to 1,486 in 1979, 63 percent of FAO requirements.[64] Population density in Ayacucho increased by more than 25 percent since 1961, and by almost 50 percent since 1940. Land is scarcer in Peru than in any other country in Latin America except El Salvador,[65] and is eroding rapidly under population growth and the decline of traditional soil management mechanisms.

Land reform under the Velasco government transformed the land tenure in Peru. Most hacendados were dispossessed, their haciendas turned into cooperatives. Nevertheless, only about one-quarter to one-third of farm families benefited from the reform, and Ayacucho as a province benefited the least of all; although 30,000–35,000 families gained property, the average value of the property they gained was less than $150 (4,900 soles).[66] In addition, agricultural terms of trade worsened over the last two decades. Prices for agricultural staples increased much more slowly than consumer prices. Fertilizer prices were low until the 1980s, when they rose at almost twice the rate of inflation. Real credit availability increased until 1975, when it declined precipitously, and, in any case, it has always been more readily accessible to large-scale estates on the coast than to highland communities. Half the agricultural investment budget of the Belaúnde government went to just three high-tech coastal irrigation projects. According to the World Bank, between 1975 and 1982 Ayacucho received less than 2 percent of the Bank's annual credit, and in 1981-82 only 1.1 percent.[67]

All these factors, plus increasing Peruvian imports of U.S. wheat, high interest rates for agricultural credit, the withdrawal of subsidies for fertilizers, and the reduction of agricultural tariffs on imports (mandated in large measure by agencies such as the World Bank and International Monetary Fund), contributed to the marginalization and alienation of highland peasants. McClintock adds two geopolitical elements: Ayacucho is the only one of five southern highland departments without a main road from the coast, and has a prominent university where the sons and daughters of traditional communities could be educated. All these combined to turn Ayacucho into an isolated area of misery, fertile soil for the seeds of revolution. McClintock points out that the reverse of the very factors that aided revolution in Ayacucho—effective land reform, access to credit, government financial backing—improved the lot of coastal peasants, and probably accounts for their resistance to Sendero. In fact, in a certain sense, Ayacucho validates the revolutionary theory known as the "j-curve" of rising expectations: "Although the agrarian reform did not significantly improve the lot of the highland peasants, it set the stage for their politicization and radicalization. The military government had promised even more strongly than previous administrations that it would provide help; when it failed to do so, intense disillusionment was the predictable result."[68]

By 1989 McClintock believed that Sendero's early success in Ayacucho, up to 1983, was attributable to an absolute economic decline and a real threat to subsistence, a politicization of society during the 1970s, shrewd strategies on the part of the guerrillas, and a weak and disorganized response by the government. The Belaúnde government at first ignored Sendero, and then dispatched to Ayacucho special counterinsurgency police called *sinchis*, purportedly trained in counter-insurgency techniques. Most were from the coast and found the highland environment alien. The *sinchis* were reported to be not only ineffective but also abusive of the people they were supposed to be protecting. Even after the rebellion had begun, the government made no special economic or political initiatives to improve conditions in the highlands. More than 90 percent of all agricultural investment went to the coast or the jungle. Total planned public investment for Ayacucho in 1982 was 1 percent of the national public investment.[69]

Indians in the highlands were angry, and Sendero appealed powerfully to their anger. Many observers have placed "Presidente Gonzalo" and the fourth sword of Marxism in the context of a messianic revival tradition familiar to highland communities.[70] Still, if "Indianness" were the only basis of Sendero's appeal, Cuzco, not Ayacucho, would be the center of the rebellion. It is not; McClintock suggests that Cuzco had been more prosperous and had benefited more substantially from agrarian reform and peasant organized activity. *Cuzqueños* were therefore more oriented toward participatory politics than toward revolution, and Izquierda Unida, a coalition of Marxist parties seeking power through elections, had garnered much of their support.[71]

If both Peruvian and outside social scientists have traced the origins of Sendero Luminoso in the generalized problems of Peruvian society and the localized conditions of Ayacucho province, what prognosis do they offer as to the continued viability of the guerrilla war? Most observers believed that, by the middle of the decade, Sendero had seriously eroded its own base of support outside Ayacucho through harsh and alienating tactics. But when the Peruvian army finally awoke to the seriousness of the guerrilla threat, it flooded the troubled areas with troops whose own repressive measures quickly alienated in turn the very people whose support was essential for counterinsurgency. During 1985 between five and seven thousand army, air force, civil guard, republican guard, and police personnel were deployed in the highlands, along with helicopters. In many cases senderistas fled from the army, leaving the people defenseless in the face of repressive countermeasures by the military. Various Americas Watch reports chronicled the increasing toll of human rights violations by the security forces of the state.[72]

The military also established civil defense patrols among the peasant communities, a classic counterinsurgency tactic that had only questionable success in Vietnam, and less in Guatemala. These patrols, known as *rondas campesinas*, have proved to be little more than litmus tests of loyalty; if you refuse to join, you are a senderista and the army kills you. Many armed peasants in fact took advantage of the chaotic situation in the sierra to wreak vengeance upon traditional enemies.[73] The García government also attempted to improve the social and economic conditions that gave rise to revolt. Agricultural credit was dramatically increased, by some 68 percent. The total of hectares worked in the highlands with this credit rose by 141 percent between 1985 and 1986, and the amount of revenue loaned went up by 17 percent. In the "Andean trapezoid" the García government's name for the poorest areas of the highland (Ayacucho, Apurímac, Huancavelica, Cuzco, and Puno), a majority of the loans were made at zero interest. The prices for fertilizers were cut, and sales tripled in the same period. Government subsidies for food crops were increased; the price paid for corn, sugar, and rice was $110 million by 1987. [74] Deliberate economic policies under García stimulated a national growth rate in 1986 of 8.5 percent nationally, and 7 percent in 1987, the best since the early 1970s. [75]

Yet it may be a case of too little, too late. By the end of the García administration, public confidence had shrunk to almost nothing (less than 4 percent, and the disastrous state of Peru's economy undid most of the benefits of the mid-1980s (inflation ran at over 20,000 percent). Ayacucho remains the fiercely loyal heart of the rebellion: one military officer estimated that 80 percent of the people were committed to Sendero. When Edith Lagos, a 19-year-old guerrilla commander, died in police custody in Ayacucho in 1982, an estimated 10,000 to 30,000 people turned out for her funeral, in a city of only 70,000. The Lurigancho prison uprising (at the conclusion of which the government massacred 279 Sendero prisoners, 100 of them after surrendering) demonstrates that Sendero's strategic and tactical errors have been more than matched by those of the government at every turn. The ominous rise of a Sendero-*narcotraficante* alliance has opened a whole new arena of opportunity for Sendero, and an immense military and economic headache for the government. The new alliance demonstrates that whenever Sendero is counted out, it astutely adapts its tactics to an evolving situation. An analysis for RAND ventured that Sendero is really waging four campaigns simultaneously: the battle for the emergency zones, the campaign for the coca-producing Upper Huallaga Valley, a struggle to bring the rebellion to areas not yet affected, and the battle for the cities. Each has required a different set of tactics and strategy; that Sendero has been able to do so in the face of strong government opposition is a testament to its viability after a decade of war. [76]

One of a seemingly endless series of articles analyzing Sendero Luminoso and its people's war offered the following prescription for defeating the rebellion: a more sophisticated counterinsurgency strategy and extensive military and economic aid for Peru, an analysis about as astute as saying that America's underclass problem can be solved with better education and more jobs. Sendero's ideological extremism, and the ethnic dimension of the conflict, are elements that distinguish Peru's war from other revolutionary movements, but they do not essentially alter the parameters of guerrilla warfare, the "war of the flea." The numerous insurgencies in colonial or neocolonial societies since the end of World War II have given Britain, France, the United States, and other nations many opportunities to analyze and try to address the social and economic roots of popular insurrection. More than thirty years ago, as America started on its road to disaster in Vietnam, the following words were written:

To bring about some degree of social, economic, and political justice or at the very least to ameliorate the worst causes of discontent and redress the most flagrant inequities, will invariably require positive action by the local government. In some cases only radical reforms will obtain the necessary results. yet the measures we advocate may strike at the very foundation of those aspects of a country's social structure and domestic economy on which rests the basis of a government's control. [77]

Peru has the advantage over South Vietnam, Guatemala, El Salvador, and other countries in that successive governments have tried, however, feebly, to take that positive action. But the present cholera epidemic in Peru reveals that the scale of reform necessary, both urban and rural, is staggering, and may be beyond the power of any government to bring about. To effect those changes in the midst of epidemic, economic disintegration, and world recession may be impossible.

The Peruvian journal *Quehacer* has covered Sendero Luminoso in many articles since the early 1980s. In one, an editor inserted a photograph, more to fill up space than for any real purpose of illustration. The picture was that of a peasant sitting in the back of a truck, cloaked in a poncho, with a hat pulled down over his eyes, the very embodiment of the mystery and remoteness of the altiplano. But it was the photo's caption that summed up neatly the frustrating challenge of *senderismo* in Peru. It read: "It is probable that they do not understand the programs nor the ideology but they feel their poverty."

NOTES

1. Peter T. Johnson, "The Consistency of a Revolutionary Movement: Peru's Sendero Luminoso and its Texts, 1965–1986," in *Studies of Development and Change in the Modern World*, ed. Michael T. Martin and Terry R. Kendal (New York, NY: Oxford University Press, 1989), pp. 268-269.

2. Ibid.

3. José Carlos Mariátegui, "Outline of the Economic Revolution," in *Seven Interpretive Essays on Peruvian Reality*, trans. Marjory Urquidi (Austin: University of Texas Press, 1971), pp. 3-4.

4. Ibid., p. 22.

5. Partido Comunista Peruano (PCP), Conferencia nacional, *Resoluciones y conclusiones*, Peru, pp. 1-4; cited in Johnson, p. 272.

6. See Carlos Iván Degregori, *Sendero Luminoso: los hondos y mortales desencuentros* (Lima: Instituto de Estudios Peruanos, 1986), pp. 9-17.

7. Ibid., pp. 19-20.

8. See ibid., pp. 24-35; also James Anderson, *Sendero Luminoso: A New Revolutionary Model?* (London: Institute for the Study of Terrorism, 1987), pp. 22-24, and Raymond Bonner, "Peru's War," *The New Yorker*, January 4, 1988, p. 34.

9. Cited in Anderson, p. 40.

10. Colin Harding, "Antonio Díaz Martínez and the Ideology of Sendero Luminoso," *Bulletin of Latin American Research* 7:1 (1988), 66.

11. Ibid., p. 69.

12. Antonio Díaz Martínez, *Ayacucho: hambre y esperanza* (Ayacucho: Ediciones Waman Puma, 1969), p. 275; cited in Harding, p. 69. A second edition of *Ayacucho* published in 1985 concluded that "the road of the people, the democratic road in the years between 1964 and 1975" lay with that taken by the indisputable chief of the revolution, Presidente Gonzalo.

13. Harding, pp. 72-73. Díaz Martínez wrote *China: la revolución agraria* out of his experiences overseas, a work that wholeheartedly praised Mao Tse-Tung and the radical collectivization of rural China.

14. Ibid., pp. 28-29.

15. Other publications include *Nuevo gobierno y la perspectiva económica, política, y de la lucha de clases en general* (n.p., 1981); *¡A nuestra heróica pueblo combatiente!* (n.p.: Comité Central, 1981); *¡Si votar! Sino, ¡Generalizar la guerra de guerrillas para conquistar el poder para el pueblo!* (n.p.: Ediciones Bandera Roja, 1985); *¡Combatir y resistir, repudiar las elecciones del régimen genocida y desarrollar más la lucha armada!* (n.p.: Bases, 1985); *Día de la heroicidad* (Peru, 1986); *Nada ni nadie podrá derrotarnos* (Peru, 1986).

16. Partido Comunista del Perú, *¡Desarrollemos la guerra de guerrillas* (n.p.: Comité Central, 1981), pp. 2-6.

17. Ibid., p. 7.

18. Ibid., pp. 10-11.

19. Ibid., p. 16.

20. Ibid., pp. 20-21.

21. Ibid., pp. 21-22.

22. "Tres tesis más que las de Mao," *Quehacer* 19 (October, 1982), 40.

23. Partido Comunista del Perú, *Desarrollar la guerra popular sirviendo a la revolución mundial* ([Sweden]: Ediciones Bandera Roja, 1987), pp. 4-7.

24. Ibid., p. 17.

25. Ibid., p. 5.

26. "La entrevista: habla Presidente Gonzalo," *El Diario* (Lima), June 24, 1988, p. 5.

27. Ibid., p. 11.

28. Ibid., p. 15.

29. Ibid., pp. 36-37.

30. Ibid., p. 37.

31. Ibid., pp. 46-47. The interview, originally published in *El Diario*, has been reprinted in English as *Interview to [sic] Chairman Gonzalo* (n.p.: Red Banner Editorial House, 1989). The translation is exceedingly literal, making the dialectic at times incomprehensible.

32. Gabriela Tarazona-Sevillano, *Sendero Luminoso and the Threat of Narco-Terrorism*, with John B. Reuter (New York, NY: Praeger/Center for Strategic and International Studies, Washington, DC, 1990), p. 22.

33. Bonner, p. 37.

34. Eugenio Chang-Rodríguez, "Origin and Diffusion of the Shining Path in Peru," in *APRA and the Democratic Challenge in Peru*, ed. Eugenio Chang-Rodríguez and Ronald G. Hellman (New York, NY: The Graduate School and University Center of the City University of New York, 1988), p. 85.

35. Carlos Iván Degregori, *Ayacucho, raices de un crisis* (Lima, PROPACEB, 1986), p. 44.

36. Ibid., p. 52.

37. Ibid., p. 56.

38. Ibid., pp. 57-58.

39. Ibid., pp. 78-79.

40. Degregori, *Ayacucho*, p. 115. The author backs up his conclusions with 106 pages of tables of vital statistics on economic activity in Ayacucho.

41. Carlos Iván Degregori, *Sendero Luminoso*, Part I, *Los hondos y mortales desencuentros* (Lima: Instituto de Estudios Peruanos, 1986), pp. 40-41.

42. Ibid., pp. 42-43.

43. Ibid., p. 45.

44. Ibid.

45. Ibid., p. 43.

46. Ibid., pp. 45-46.

47. Ibid., pp. 49-50.

48. Bonner, p. 36.

49. Ibid.

50. Ibid.

51. Manuel Jesús Granados, "El PCP Sendero Luminoso: aproximaciones a su ideología," *Socialismo y Participación* 37 (March, 1987), 16.

52. Ibid., pp. 16-17.

53. Ibid., pp. 20-21.

54. Ibid., pp. 21-22.

55. Ibid., p. 17.

56. Ibid., p. 19.

57. Ibid., p. 33.

58. Ibid., p. 18.

59. Henri Favre, "La dialéctica de la toma del poder de Sendero Luminoso, entrevista con Henri Favre," in *Peru: una luz en el sendero* (Mexico: Distribuciones Fontamara, 1988), p. 212.

60. Ibid., p. 213.

61. Ibid.

62. Ibid., p. 216.

63. Cynthia McClintock, "Why Peasants Rebel: The Case of Peru's Sendero Luminoso," *World Politics* 37:1 (October, 1984), 59.

64. See World Bank, *Peru: Major Development Policy Issues and Recommendations* (Washington, DC: World Bank, 1981), p. 35; also Jorge Fernández Baca, "La producción de alimentos en el Perú," *Quehacer* 17 (June, 1982), 89-90, both cited in ibid., pp. 60-61.

65. Daniel Martínez and Armando Tealdo, *El agro peruano 1970-1980: análisis y perspectivas* (Lima: CEDEP, 1982), p. 39, cited in ibid., p. 63.

66. McClintock, "Peasants," pp. 66-67.

67. See ibid., n. 61.

68. Ibid., p. 83.

69. Cynthia McClintock, "Peru's Sendero Luminoso Rebellion: Origins and Trajectory," in *Power and the Popular Protest: Latin American Social Movements*, ed. Susan Eckstein (Berkeley: University of California Press, 1989), pp. 65, 79-80.

70. See Felipe Regatero, "'Sendero Luminoso' ¿Nuevo mesianismo andino?" *Indigenismo, Boletín del Seminario Español de Estudios Indigenistas*, Instituto de Cooperación Iberoamericana 3 (3d ser.), January, 1984, pp. 12-15.

71. McClintock, "Peru's Sendero Luminoso," p. 32.

72. See *Abdicating Democratic Authority: Human Rights in Peru* (New York, NY: Americas Watch, 1984); *A New Opportunity for Democratic Authority* (New York, NY: Americas Watch, 1985); *A Certain Passivity* (New York, NY: Americas Watch, 1987).

73. McClintock, "Peru's Sendero Luminoso," p. 90; see also Billie Jean Isbell, "The Emerging Patterns of Peasants' Responses to Sendero Luminoso," a paper presented at "Patterns of Social Change in the Andes," NYU and Columbia University LAS Consortium Conference, 1988, p. 15.

74. Banco Agrario del Perú, *Memoria* (Lima: Banco Agrario, 1987), pp. 19, 33, 38; cited in McClintock, "Peru's Sendero Luminoso," p. 92.

75. See David Scott Palmer, "Terrorism as a Revolutionary Strategy: Peru's *Sendero Luminoso*," in *The Politics of Terrorism: Terror as a State and Revolutionary Strategy*, ed. Barry Rubin (Washington, DC: Foreign Policy Institute, Johns Hopkins School of Advanced International Studies, 1989), p. 151.

76. Gordon H. McCormick, *The Shining Path and the Future of Peru* (Santa Monica, CA: RAND Corporation, 1990), p. 48.

77. U. Alexis Johnson, "Internal Defense and the Foreign Service," *Foreign Service Journal* (July, 1962), 23, cited in Douglas Blaufarb, *The Counterinsurgency Era: U.S. Doctrine and Performance* (New York, NY: Free Press, 1977), p. 65.

Man and Environment:
A Battle for Survival
in Latin America

8. Poisoning the Garden: Costa Rica's Ecological Crisis

Fred G. Morgner

Underlying Costa Rica's reputation as a regional leader in conservation are seriously environmental problems that have brought the nation to an unprecedented crisis and threaten its varied but limited natural resources. Four decades of accelerated exploitation of forests and irrational land use have brought Costa Ricans to a crucial point in their country's development. A massive effort must soon be made to conserve the natural environment and reverse the slide toward further contamination. If this is not undertaken, destructive patterns will irreparably damage ecosystems, cripple economic development, and breed health problems beyond the capacity of the country's medical care system to control.

Environmental abuses have been clearly defined in a body of literature which has grown steadily since the early 1970s. It is probable that more monographs have been published by *tico* conservationists since 1970 than in the entire national period prior to that date. Authors are united in defining two problems that stand out above all others: the incredibly fast rate of deforestation and the overuse of pesticides in agricultural production.

Deforestation

Costa Rica is well known for its system of national parks and beaches, biological reserves and protected forests. Eleven percent of the country's 51,000 square kilometers has absolute protection from development and another 15 percent has some protection, insuring that one-fourth of national territory is legally protected from despoilment.[1] Owing to these protected resources the tourism industry has soared to third place as a source of revenue, expanding at a rate of 15 percent per year since 1987.[2]

Contrasting with popular images of forest sanctuaries and threatening the growing *industria sin chimineas* is the reality of deforestation, at a rate among the highest in Latin America. Estimates vary of when the nation's remaining 5,000 square km of commercial forests will be exhausted, but there is agreement that it will occur between 1995 and 2001. Costa Rica will then be faced with the importation of lumber at the rate of between $290 and $350 million per year. A 1990 ecological report by the Ministry of Natural Resources, Energy and Mines describes the process as "accelerated, inefficient and without control," and links deforestation to soil erosion, meteorological cycles of drought and flooding, wildlife extinction, and the destruction of vital watersheds.[3] Books on the subject invariably show the dramatic stages of deforestation in a series of maps that illustrate the rate at which Costa Rica's dense forest cover declined from 80 percent to about 30 percent in fifty years. Predictions of exhausted supplies are based upon the present estimated rate of cutting of from 30,000 to 50,000 hectares per year. About one-half of that rate is reportedly illegal cutting from protected reserves.[4]

Current and past deforestation is related only marginally to the export of lumber as a source of revenue. During the period of rampant exploitation, when 18,000 square km were cleared, between 1957 and 1985, the value of lumber products rose from only 2.5 to less than 4 percent of agricultural production. Of the trees cut, about half are lost as residual "waste." Other minor factors in the disappearance of Costa Rican forests are the activities of squatters and miners.[5]

The largest single cause of the decline of *tico* woodlands has been the conversion of forests to pastures for the production of cattle. One author described this process as the *potrerización de* Costa Rica" while another authority has branded it the "hamburger connection." It fits the pattern of subordinating long-term Third World interests and resources in order to satisfy markets in the industrial West.[6] Conversion to pasture was a clear response to the rise of fast food chain restaurants beginning in the late 1950s and the ensuing insatiable American appetite for the cheap fast hamburger. Pasture conversion and beef production were stimulated by the *tico* government, and U.S. aid programs benefited primarily a small group of Costa Rica's landed elite and sacrificed valuable resources at the expense of relatively minor short-term economic gains.

The United States imports about 10 percent of its beef, of which 90 percent comes from Central and Latin America. Costa Rican Brahma steers, not known for their tender cuts, are ideal for grinding into burger. Almost all Latin American beef imported to the United States ends up as the fast cheap burger, which led to a boycott of Burger King by the Rainforest Action Network during the 1980s. Undeterred, Burger King established its first stand in San José, Costa Rica in 1989, joining the already entrenched McDonald's units. One ecologist commented that "in every Big Mac there is a piece of the tropical rainforests."[7]   But judging from the volume of business in Third World burger palaces, the consumers in Central America are as unconcerned about this as U.S. consumers, and as undiscerning in their choice of food. It is indeed difficult to conceive a similar circumstance when such valuable resources were sacrificed on such a major scale to produce so mediocre a product.

From 1960 to 1980 beef production in all of Central America increased 16 percent. During that time the amount of pasture in Nicaragua and Panama doubled while their humid forests shrank by half. In Costa Rica, land use for traditional agricultural products increased from only 10 to 12 percent from 1950 to 1985, while pasture expanded from 17 to 43 percent. With vast expanses of forests converted to pasture, Costa Rica's meat production tripled between 1959 and 1978, while the percentage of meat exported jumped from 20 to 56 percent. Despite these significant increases, meat exports never grew to represent more than 8.6 percent of the nation's total exports in any year.[8] By 1983 the tourist industry, dependent upon the maintenance of the diminishing natural environment, was bringing in more than four times the amount of revenue of the cattle industry, which was systematically raping the environment.[9]

Requiring relatively little labor to sustain, beef production created a new form of "cattle baron." Throughout the 1960s and 1970s the *tico* government subsidized this elite through bonuses for converting to cattle production. By 1981 government grants to landholders of 100 hectares or more represented 97 percent of the territory deforested.[10]

Recent studies have argued that about 60 percent of Costa Rica's predominantly mountainous topography is suitable only for forest growth.[11] The conversion of such land to pasture has set in motion a chain of ecological calamities. According to the Ministry of Resources report, of the 1,650,000 hectares of pastureland in Costa Rica, about 1,100,000 "lack the capacity to sustain an economically profitable cattle industry."[12] Once cleared of its trees and foliage, such land is quickly impacted by grazing, compaction, and patterns of heavy rain, and begins to undergo erosion, which in turn leads to a demand for new pastures. It is estimated that about 40 percent of Costa Rican land is subject to erosion and that 725 million tons of soil are lost every year. It is further projected that 84 percent of this total is lost from pasturelands. Translated into the cheap fast burger quotient, about 2.5 tons of *tico* soil are blown or washed away from every kilo of meat exported.[13] As erosion worsens, a pattern of drought and flooding ensues, which in turn fills hydroelectric facilities and river estuaries with sedimentation.

Costa Rica has paid a heavy price for its rise to the number one place among meat exporting nations of Central America. Despite this example, other economic interests are deforesting new areas, as shown by the cutting frenzy around Puerto Viejo and the Tortuguero Canal region to expand banana plantations and independent deforestation in the Corcovado Park region of Oso Peninsula.[14] If rational cutting is not quickly defined and strictly enforced and reforestation drastically escalated, what future?

Poisoning the Garden

As the principal buyer of Costa Rican beef, the United States rejected more *tico* meat during the early 1980s than from any other nation . . . more than one half million kilos in 1981 alone. The tissues were found to be so contaminated with DDT that the flesh was deemed unsuitable even for the cheap, fast burger. The periodic American rejection of contaminated *tico* fruits and vegetables has also increased sharply during the 1980s.[15] This phenomenon has been called the *efecto de boomerang* by one *tico* author and among many conservationists is known as the "circle of poison." *El efecto de boomerang* operates with a perversely destructive simplicity: chemical companies of the industrial West sell tons of toxic products, in the form of pesticides, to Third World nations, which then use the product on their crops and export them to the same country from which they had purchased the pesticides. That country then rejects the crops as they are heavily contaminated with the pesticides they had sold.[16]

A brutally cynical element is added with the realization that pesticide companies in the "developed West" have for years exported tons of toxic materials that have been banned or restricted, or are unlicensed for domestic use. Responsible government agencies had deemed these poisons dangerous to humans, yet they are produced and freely exported to Third World nations for use on their crops.

This practice is finally receiving international attention and, in most quarters, an appropriate level of revulsion. Yet the tide continues to flow. Chemical companies flooded the Third World with almost 4 million pounds of "outlaw pesticides" during one three-month period alone in 1990. A recent British study revealed that although the industrial West uses 80 percent of all chemicals for agriculture, 99 percent of the 220,000 annual deaths from accidental pesticide poisoning occur in Third World countries.[17]

With Costa Rica's tropical climate and biological diversity, agriculture is faced with a staggering insect and fungus problem. During the past four decades production has been guided by the assumption that the key to combating these plagues was to apply pesticides more often and vigorously. Throughout the 1970s and most of the 1980s dozens of toxins were imported by Costa Rica, many on conservationist "hit lists" such as the Pesticide Action Network's "Dirty Dozen" or the U.N.'s "Lista Consolidada."[18] During the same period a number of domestic reports began to document spreading toxicity.[19] There were deaths among agricultural workers using paraquat, the Nixon administration's antimarijuana placebo. With Drug Enforcement Agency influence, the poison continues to be sprayed on pot plantations in the Petén and Belize.[20] Of the 279 pesticide deaths between 1980 and 1986, 161 involved paraquat, which has also become one of the preferred methods of suicide in Costa Rica.[21]

Improved laboratory techniques and record keeping have helped to build a body of literature that contradicts the "pesticide-as-panacea" belief. During the 1980s more than 400 people per year were hospitalized for pesticide poisoning, believed to be only the "tip of the iceberg." Toxic deaths were also increasingly found among livestock. Ministry of Agriculture investigators estimated that 12 percent of the national honey production was lost in the late 1980s because hives died from contact with bees extracting pollen from recently treated fields. A German research institute found residues of pesticides above FAO tolerance levels in *tico* cabbage, lettuce, celery, potatoes, wheat, and beans.[22] The DDT pesticide has surfaced in substances from the eggshells of Guanacaste's birds to mothers' milk. Soil tests from coffee and banana regions have revealed high levels of paraquat and copper. In such areas the level of productivity also declined sharply. Rivers and estuaries near such areas have also revealed higher toxic levels.[23] Effects on humans are inevitable.

Symbols of toxicity may be immediate or chronic, and include skin diseases, nervous disorders, respiratory problems, sterility, birth defects, mental deterioration, and blood disorders. The ministry of health found a greater accumulation of pesticides in the fat tissues of patients with leukemia, nervous disorders, and hepatitis, with the highest levels among rural campesinos. Costa Rica also ranks third in per capita deaths from gastric cancer among the nations of the world.[24]

Despite the tons of chemicals applied to *tico* fields, the number of insect species resistant to pesticides grew from 182 in 1965 to 364 in 1977. This has been attributed in part to the elimination of the predators of harmful insects. Plagues of bananas have also risen, from 2 in 1950 to 11 in 1960. Banana transnationals used a toxin known as DBCP throughout the 1970s, and within a few years cases of sterility among workers began to appear. With about 1,000 employees now affected, a landmark case has been brought by *tico* unions against Dow Chemical and Shell Oil, now in the courts of Texas.[25] The companies deny shipment or shift responsibility to Chiquita Banana's supervision of the application. Rolando Rojas, a 33-year-old sterile worker, claims that the effects of DBCP were known to the companies "and they just sent it to us as if we were animals."[26]

The Response

A small group of energetic and motivated scientists, naturalists, health officials, journalists, and government employees comprise the vanguard of the *tico* conservation movement. The pluralistic nature of their political system provides some guarantee that their views will be heard and weighed in making decisions and establishing priorities. Powerful transnationals and local vested interests, however, also enjoy the same guarantees.

During the 1980s more than fifty major monographs on ecological issues were published, more than twenty conservation groups were formed, and newspaper columns or other segments of the media were regularly devoted to environmental issues. During the year 1990 alone, new groups were formed to protect rivers, provide an ecology hotline, halt deforestation, and supply conservation news.[27] During the past several years national and international conferences were held on deforestation and pesticides, university programs were initiated on the environment, and a major TV network declared itself *el canal ecológico* with its own hotline. Another promising trend was the appearance of three organic grower groups, formed to offer limited quantities of produce and herbs and to teach pesticide-free farming methods.[28]

Another trend emerging in the 1980s has been compromise or legal confrontation between developers and conservationists to resolve disputes. Plans for Costa Rica's new highway from San José to Limón were secured by support for the new Braulio Carrillo park, which the highway dissects. Two proposed hydroelectric dams on the undeveloped Pecuare River have met with organized legal opposition and "float-ins" by river guides.[29] Accelerated cutting along Tortuguero Canal's delicate boundaries has led to a movement to expand the park into an international facility with Nicaragua. A typical countermeasure was the formation of the Committee in Defense of the Farmers of Tortuguero to halt the expansion. A recent "catch and release" measure, designed to protect recreational fishing and curb the taking of 20 to 30 tons of marlin and sailfish each day by commercial vessels, was on the point of being decreed law. A last minute injunction by the commercial fishing association, however, has stymied the measure.[30] Despite the slowness of the *tico* system, its openness provides a forum for education, opposition, and challenge unavailable in much of Latin America.

Government challenges to environmental abuses have become more common, adding another level on which to guard resources. Such cases include prosecution of a subsidiary of Chiquita Banana corporation for dumping boiling palm oil residue in the Río Colorado. Further north, six small farmers have filed a joint suit against a company that washes chemical containers, claiming that dumping of residue into the Coris River has ruined their crops.[31]   It should also be noted that environmentalists have complained that fines and penalties for such violations are almost laughable.

Elements within the hierarchy of the *tico* Church, not known for its liberalism, have recently added their voice to the call for the preservation of resources.   In a recent publication the Vicarage of Limón expressed opposition to the expansion of banana transnationals along the Atlantic coast, at times sounding more like liberation theologists than members of Archbishop Ramón Arrieta's flock.   Their recommendations included halting land sales to transnationals in the region, working condition reforms, a halt to environmental abuses, and an environmental impact study on the expansion of the banana empire.[32]

Given the groundswell of grassroots opinion and activity, no *tico* politician can ignore the conservation issue.   At the end of the Arias administration, an extremely promising program known as "Ecodes" (La Estrategia de Conservación para el Desarrollo Sostenible de Costa Rica) was formulated in a lengthy document published by the Ministry of Natural Resources.   The sharp analysis and logical, progressive proposals found in this study were soon overshadowed by the Calderón government's heralded declaration of a "new world ecological order." One conservationist has not been heartened by progress under the new order, however, commenting that it had not progressed beyond rhetoric and that promising past efforts such as Ecodes appeared to be lost in the archives.[33]   Legislation and a bureaucracy have never been lacking, with 152 public institutions to enforce Costa Rica's large number of environmental laws.   The 1990 Ecodes report claimed such a vast bureaucracy often created more confusion than advantages.   Political will, centralized planning, and efficient administration were needed, Ecodes proclaimed, to combat the "vested interests which continue to feast at the expense of the national patrimony for their own personal gain."[34]

Recent Trends in Reforestation

The Arias administration claimed that in 1990 it had cut deforestation to 30,000 hectares per year, down from 60,000 in 1986. Although Rafael Calderón has assigned the Rural Guard to police illegal cutting, it is too early to tell if this has further stemmed the tide. Government subsidies have proved to be a promising stimulus during the past two years. Between 1950 and 1980 reforestation was hardly known, existing at the rate of 300 hectares per year. In 1981 the figure reached 1,000 hectares, in 1986 it rose to 3,600 per year, and in 1987 to 5,000. Respectable numbers were finally achieved with 15,000 reforested hectares in 1989 and 19,000 in 1990, about two-thirds of which were accomplished with government aid. It has been estimated that in order to maintain minimal commercial production and to continue to preserve existing forests, more than 50,000 hectares must be reforested each year over the next 20 years. Whether the next generation of *ticos* will have forests is being decided.

Recent Trends in Pesticide Restriction

During the past half decade advances have been made in regulating pesticides in Costa Rica. More than twenty-five pesticides have been prohibited or restricted during the past two years, many on the "Dirty Dozen" list. The highly damaging DBCP was added to the list of prohibited toxins. Moreover, the Ministry of Agriculture announced that in February of 1990 it would adopt U.S. EPA standards regarding pesticide residue on fruits and vegetables, and that it had acquired German aid to establish a testing program of products destined for both export and domestic consumption. Germany is also the second largest exporter of pesticides to the Third World, although it lags far behind the United States in the amount. [35]

Despite gains in the restriction of the more notorious pesticides, toxic materials continue to flow into Costa Rica. The world's largest producer of paraquat is ICI, a Delaware-based subsidiary of a British multinational. Paraquat's reputation as killer of workers is so noxious that another pesticide firm, American Cyanamid of Wayne, NJ, refuses to market it. Its use has become so standard in Costa Rica that the nation's leading paper has cheerfully described it as "an all-purpose herbicide for use on nearly all crops." An ICI official defended it as "useful, beneficial and which can be managed properly. So why should we take it off the market?" [36]

Lest American Cyanamid appear a high model of corporate consciousness, its production of an organophosphate known as Counter should be considered. This pesticide represents a new and unrestricted breed known as "nonpersistents" since they disappear soon after application, sometimes within hours. "The trade-off," reports the Richmond *Times-Dispatch*, "is that these legal pesticides . . . are generally much more toxic and can bring immediate harm to farm workers." Cyanamid officials profess a clear conscience, passing the responsibility for poisonings to local distributors. Examples of pesticides not licensed by the EPA that are exported to Central America are Aldicarb of the Rhone-Poulenc Ag. Co. of North Carolina and Galant of the Dow and Eli Lilly Co.

The case of DBCP has major implications regarding the legal responsibility that corporations may be forced to face because of their exportation of toxins. It is also the first case brought by foreign workers in a U.S. court against American corporations for damages received through handling a dangerous product. As early as 1958 laboratory tests showed that the substance disrupted the reproductive system of mice. In 1977 American workers manufacturing DBCP became sterile. Several hundred thousand gallons were still shipped to Standard Fruit in Costa Rica after these revelations.[37]

Chemical companies in the United States export almost one half of the world's pesticide products to the Third World. Germany, Holland, and France follow with a combined 29 percent of expects, and Guatemala and El Salvador are next with a total of 9 percent.[38] There is no doubt that these companies will continue to export their wares as long as there is a profit to be made. Therefore, Oklahoma Representative Michael Synar's current bill designed to break the "circle of poison" and prohibit U.S. companies from exporting unlicensed pesticides should be supported. To do less would be to acquiesce to a macabre and destructive practice.

The image of magnificent forests stripped so that Americans may indulge their passion for cheap fast burgers is troubling. The pattern of U.S. corporations selling products deemed dangerous in their own country to Third World nations is well beyond troubling, producing shame and anger. Costa Rica has begun to set limits on how much it will sacrifice for the U.S. market and what poisons it will continue to accept. There exist organic fungicides in Costa Rica which have proved to be effective. The hope is that more of them will be developed and utilized. Within the land of the cheap, fast burger there is always the hope that Americans will some day begin to assess the consequences of their patterns of consumption. On a more short term basis, it is clearly time to draw limits and impose responsibilities on mendacious corporate leaders who knowingly profit from a deeply sinister commerce.

NOTES

1. Carlos A. Quesada Mateo, *Estrategia de conservación para el desarrollo sostenible de Costa Rica* (San José: Ministerio de Recursos Naturales, Energía y Minas), p. 73.

2. Alonso Ramírez Solera, ed., *Desarrollo socioeconómico y el ambiente natural de Costa Rica: situación actual y perspectivas* (San José: Fundación Neotrópica, 1988), p. 9; Quesada Mateo, *Estrategia*, pp. 19-21.

3. Quesada Mateo, *Estrategia*, p. 103.

4. Ibid., p. 114.

5. Ibid., p. 1.

6. Ingemar Hedstrom, *Somos parte de un gran equilibrio: la crisis ecológica en centroamérica*, 3d ed. (San José: Departamento Ecuménico de Investigaciones, 1988), pp. 41, 46.

7. Luis A. Fournier O., *Desarrollo y perspectiva del movimiento conservacionista costarricense* (San José: Editorial de la Universidad de Costa Rica, 1991), p. 15.

8. Ramírez Solera, *Desarrollo socioeconómico*, p. 51.

9. Ibid, p. 17.

10. Roxana Salazar Cambronero, *Legislación y ecología en Costa Rica* (San José: Asociación Libro Libre, 1991), p. 153.

11. Quesada Mateo, *Estrategia*, p. 36; Hedstrom, *Somos parte*, p. 46.

12. Fournier, *Desarrollo y perspectiva*, p. 92.

13. Quesada Mateo, *Estrategia*, pp. 60-61.

14. Isabel M. Chacón, *Introducción a la problemática ambiental costarricense: principios básicos y posibles soluciones* (San José: Editorial Universidad Estatal a Distancia, 1990), p. 46; Salazar Cambronero, *Legislación y ecología*, pp. 149-150.

15. Ramírez Solera, *Desarrollo socioeconómico*, p. 96.

16. Salazar Cambronero, *Legislación y ecología*, p. 85.

17. *Richmond Times Dispatch*, May 27, 1991, p. 2.

18. Ramírez Solera, *Desarrollo socioeconómico*, p. 57.

19. Salazar Cambronero, *Legislación y ecología*, pp. 92-93.

20. Alexander Bonilla Durán, *Crisis ecológica de América Central* (San José: Ediciones Guayacan, 1988). pp. 16-17.

21. Ramírez Solera, *Desarrollo socioeconómico*, p. 94; Luisa Castillo, "Uso e impacto de las plaguicidas en tres países centroamericanos," *Estudios Sociales Centro-americanos* 49 (Jan.-April, 1989), p. 135.

22. Ramírez Solera, *Desarrollo socioeconómico*, p. 93; Castillo, "Uso e impacto," pp. 25, 127, 130.

23. Hedstrom, *Somos parte*, pp. 62-66; Bonilla, *Crisis ecológica*, p. 52; Ramírez Solera, *Desarrollo socioeconómico*, pp. 92, 95, 115.

24. Chacón, *Introducción a la problemática*, p. 118; Salazar Cambronero, *Legislación y ecología*, pp. 90-91; Hedstrom, *Somos parte*, pp. 68-70.

25. Hedstrom, *Somos parte*, p. 71; Bonilla, *Crisis ecológica*, pp. 53; Chacón, *Introducción a la problemática*, p. 120.

26. *Richmond Times Dispatch*, May 27, 1991, p. 2.

27. Fournier, *Desarrollo y perspectiva*, pp. 70-80, 85; *Tico Times 1990 Year in Review*, December, 1990, p. 4.

28. Chacón, *Introducción a la problemática*, pp. 113-114, 116; Castillo, "Uso y impacto," p. 119.

29. *Aportes* 72 (Nov., 1990) 12-13; *Primera Plana* 5, 83 (June, 1990), 8; *Tico Times*, May 4, 1990, p. 11.

30. *Tico Times*, Jan. 18, 1991, p. 8; Jan. 25, 1991, p. 13; May 4, 1990, pp. 20-21.

31. *La Nación* (April 17, 1991), p. 6A.

32. *Carta pastoral del Obispo y Presbiteros del Vicario Apostólico de Limón* (San José: Litografía Cosmos, 1989), pp. 6-22.

33. *Aportes* 72 (Nov., 1990), p. 13.

34. Salazar Cambronero, *Legislación y ecología*, pp. 107-108; *La Nación*, May 5, 1991, p. 6A; Fournier, *Desarrollo y perspectiva*, p. 93.

35. Chacón, *Introducción a la problemática*, pp. 148-149; *Tico Times 1990 Year in Review*, p. 5; *Tico Times*, Feb. 8, 1991, p. 24.

36. *La Nación*, April 12, 1991, p. 4C; *Richmond Times Dispatch*, May 27, 1991, pp. 2, 3.

37. *Richmond Times Dispatch*, May 27, 1991, pp. 2, 3.

38. Castillo, "Uso y impacto," p. 124.

9. Environment in Brazil: A Checklist of Current Serials

Carmen M. Muricy

This is a selective list of serials published in Brazil by government and nongovernment organizations concerned with environmental issues. It was compiled based on the publications acquired by the Library of Congress, Rio de Janeiro Office. Most of the titles listed will be included in the next edition of the Library of Congress microfilm collection titled "Brazil Popular Groups Collection," supplement 1990-1992. The list is arranged in alphabetical order by title. The titles marked with an asterisk are found in the regular collection of the Library of Congress. The government organizations are identified as "G" and the nongovernment as "NG." Information on first issue published and frequency is given whenever possible as well as the latest issue received as of June 1991. A few important serials that have ceased publication are also mentioned.

ABES-DF
a. 1– n° 01– fev. 1990– Irregular
Associação Brasileira de Engenharia Sanitária e Ambiental—ABES
Seção Distrito Federal   NG
SCS Q. 6, Ed. José Severo, 4° andar
70.300 – Brasília, Distrito Federal

ABES-RJ
Associação Brasileira de Engenharia Sanitária e Ambiental—ABES
Seção Rio de Janeiro   NG
Av. Beira Mar, 216 – 11° andar
20.021 – Rio de Janeiro, Rio de Janeiro
Latest issue received: 5:19 (February 1991)

Alerta Amazônia: ecologia
v. 1–   n° 1–   nov. 1987–   Monthly
INFORMAN–Sistema de Informação Científica e Tecnológica da Amazônia
   Brasileira   G
Universidade Federal do Pará
Biblioteca Central
Campus Universitário do Guamá
66.059 – Belém, Pará
Latest issue received: 4:1/2 (January/February 1991)

Amazônia: informação e debate*
v. 1–   n° 1–   jan. 1988–   Irregular
Campanha Nacional de Defesa e pelo Desenvolvimento da Amazônia—
   CNDDA   NG
Rua Araújo Porto Alegre, 71 – 10° andar
20.002 – Rio de Janeiro, Rio de Janeiro
Latest issue published: 1/2:3/1-3 (September/December 1988 – January/
   December 1989)

Amazônia brasileira em foco*
n° 1–   1967–   Irregular
Campanha Nacional de Defesa e pelo Desenvolvimento da Amazônia—
   CNDDA   NG
Rua Araújo Porto Alegre, 71 – 10° andar
20.002 – Rio de Janeiro, Rio de Janeiro
Latest issue published: 18 (1989/1990)

Ambiente: revista CETESB de tecnologia*   ISSN 0102-8685
Companhia de Tecnologia de Saneamento—CETESB   G
Av. Prof. Frederico Hermann Jr., 345, prédio 1, 1° andar, s. 100
05.489 – São Paulo, São Paulo
Latest issue received: 5:1 (January 1991)

Ambiente hoje
a. 1–   nov./dez. 1988–   Irregular
Associação Mineira de Defesa do Ambiente—AMDA   NG
Rua Viçosa, 542-A
30.330 – Belo Horizonte, Minas Gerais
Latest issue received: 2:6 (March/April 1991)

Antes que seja tarde
Grupo Ecológico Queremos Gente   NG
Av. Tiradentes, 1067
94.800 – Alvorada, Rio Grande do Sul
Latest issue received: 5:4 (November 1990)

Bio*   ISSN 0103-5134
a. 1–   n° 1–   set./out. 1989– Quarterly
Associação Brasileira de Engenharia Sanitária e Ambiental—ABES   NG
Av. Beira Mar, 216 – 13° andar
20.021 – Rio de Janeiro, Rio de Janeiro
Latest issue received: 2:4 (October/December 1990)
Supersedes *Engenharia sanitária*

Biodiversidade em notícias
n° 0–   dez.–   1990–
Fundação Biodiversitas para Conservação da Diversidade Biológica   NG
Rua Bueno Brandão, 372 – Santa Teresa
Caixa Postal 2462
31.010 – Belo Horizonte, Minas Gerais
Latest issue received: 1 (March 1991)

Boletim (Grupo Seiva de Ecologia)
Grupo Seiva de Ecologia   NG
Caixa Postal 55.190
04.799 – São Paulo, São Paulo
Latest issue received: 31 (July/August 1989)

Boletim ANAÍ-Ba
Associação Nacional de Apoio ao Índio   NG
Rua dos Algibebes, 4 – s. 806
40.015 – Salvador, Bahia
Latest issue received: 4/5 (January/August 1990)

Boletim ecológico
a. 1–   n° 1–   jan. 1991–   Monthly
Associação dos Moradores da Praça Cte. Xavier de Brito e Adjacências—
   AMPRA   NG
Departamento de Ecologia
Rua Oliveira da Silva, 11
20.530 – Rio de Janeiro, Rio de Janeiro

Boletim FBCN*   ISSN 0101-249
v. 1–   1966–   Irregular
Fundação Brasileira para a Conservação da Natureza—FBCN   NG
Rua Miranda Valverde, 103 – Botafogo
22.281 – Rio de Janeiro, Rio de Janeiro
Latest issue received: 24 (1989)

Boletim FUNATURA
a. 1–   n° 1–   1986–
Fundação Pró-Natureza   NG
SCLN 107 – Bloco B – salas 201/13
70.743 – Brasília, Distrito Federal
Latest issue received: 2:2 (June 1988)

Boletim informativo (ACAPRENA)
Associação Catarinense de Preservação da Natureza—ACAPRENA   NG
Rua Antônio da Veiga, 140
Caixa Postal 1507
89.010 – Blumenau, Santa Catarina
Latest issue received: 4:28 (November/December 1990)

Boletim informativo (Movimento Ecológico Mater Natura)
a. 1–   n° 001–   1987–
Movimento Ecológico Mater Natura   NG
Caixa Postal 81
80.001 – Curitiba, Paraná

Boletim informativo (Sociedade para Estudos de Defesa Ambiental)
Sociedade para Estudos de Defesa Ambiental—SEDA   NG
Centro de Ciências Biológicas da Saúde
Universidade Federal de Mato Grosso do Sul—UFMS
Caixa Postal 306
79.100 – Campo Grande, Mato Grosso do Sul
Latest issue received: 1:2 (1986)

Boletim S.O.S. Mata Atlântica
Fundação S.O.S. Mata Atlântica   NG
Rua Manoel da Nóbrega, 456
04.001 – São Paulo, São Paulo
Latest issue received: 3 (1989)

Brasil X fome: movimento em busca de soluções
n° 1–   jan. 1990–
Escola Libre de Agricultura Ecológica—ELAE   NG
Caixa Postal 343
11.900 – Registro, São Paulo
Latest issue received: 4 (July 1990)

Brasil florestal*   ISSN 0045-270X
1970– Quarterly
Instituto Brasileiro do Meio Ambiente e dos Recursos Naturais Renováveis—
   IBAMA   G
SAIN – Lote 4 – Ed. Sede IBAMA
70.800 – Brasília, Distrito Federal
Latest issue received: 17:69 (1st semester 1990)

Brasil meio ambiente
a. 1–   n° 1–   jan. 1991–   Monthly
Secretaria de Imprensa da Presidência da República
Palácio do Planalto, 2° andar
Praça dos Três Poderes
10.150 – Brasília, Distrito Federal
Latest issue received: 1:4 (April 1991)

Bulletin (Preparatory Forum of Brazilian NGOs for UNCED–92)
Executive Secretariat
CEDI—Centro Ecumênico de Documentação e Informação
Rua Santo Amara, 129 – Glória
22.211 – Rio de Janeiro, Rio de Janeiro
Latest issue received: 4 (March 12, 1991)

Cadastro nacional das instituições que atuam na área do meio ambiente*
Irregular
Instituto Brasileiro do Meio Ambiente e dos Recursos Naturais Renováveis—
   IBAMA   G
SAIN – Lote 4 – Ed. Sede IBAMA
70.800 – Brasília, Distrito Federal
Latest issue received: 4th edition, 1990. 2 vols.

Canto da terra
Associação Pernambucana de Defesa da Natureza—ASPAN   NG
Caixa Postal 7862
50.000 – Recife, Pernambuco

Carta verde: boletim informativo do mandato Carlos Minc—PT
Gabinete Carlos Minc   NG
Praça XV, Palácio 23 de Julho, s. 207
20.010 – Rio de Janeiro, Rio de Janeiro
Latest issue received: 14 (March 1991)

Catálogo brasileiro de engenharia sanitária ambiental—CABES*
1st ed. – dez. 1975–   Annual
Associação Brasileira de Engenharia Sanitária e Ambiental—ABES   N
Av. Beira Mar, 216 – 13° andar
20.021 – Rio de Janeiro, Rio de Janeiro
Latest issue received: 11/14 (1986/89)

CEACON informativo
Monthly
Centro de Estudos e Atividades de Conservação da Natureza—
    CEACON   NG
Caixa Postal 20684
01.498 — São Paulo, São Paulo
Latest issue received: January/February 1991

O Charão
Twice a year
Clube de Observadores de Aves—COA   NG
Rua Sara Vilela, 83
22.460 – Rio de Janeiro, Rio de Janeiro
Latest issue received: 16 (July 1990)

Correio ecológico
a. 1–   n° 1–   abr. 1991–
Fundação Pró-Natureza   NG
SCLN 107 – Bloco B, salas 201/13
70.743, Brasília, Distrito Federal

CPPA informa
a. 1–   n° 0–   1989–
Empresa Brasileira de Pesquisa Agropecuária—EMBRAPA
Centro de Pesquisa Agroflorestal da Amazônia   G
Rodovia AM-010, km 28
Caixa Postal 319
69.000 – Manaus, Amazonas
Latest issue received: 2:2 (November 1990)

Desafio
1989– Bimonthly
Associação Interamericana de Engenharia Sanitária e Ambiental—
    AIDIS   NG
Rua Nicolau Gagliardi, 354
05.429 – São Paulo, São Paulo
Latest issue received: 2:3 (July/September 1990)

Ecologia e ação
Grupo Ação Ecológica   NG
Estrada do Capenha, 275/801 – Bl. 2
22.743 – Rio de Janeiro, Rio de Janeiro
Latest issue received: 1:4 (March/April 1991)

*Ecologia e desenvolvimento**
a. 1–   n° 1–   mar. 1991–   Monthly
Editora Terceiro Mundo
Rua da Glória, 122/105-106
20.241 – Rio de Janeiro, Rio de Janeiro
Latest issue received: 1:2 (April 1991)

Ecologizando; boletim informativo
a. 1–   n° 1–   jan./mar.–   1989–
Federação de Entidades Ecologistas Catarinenses—FEEC   NG
Rua Almirante Tamandaré, 208
89.140 – Ibirama, Santa Catarina
Latest issue received: 3:9 (March 1991)

Ecopaulista
n° 1–   1989–   Irregular
Assembléia Permanente de Entidades em Defesa do Meio Ambiente do
    Estado de São Paulo—APEDEMA   NG
Caixa Postal 6866
01.064 – São Paulo, São Paulo

Ecopress (International Edition)
n° 0–   Oct. 1989–   Monthly
Ecopress News Agency   NG
Rua Sampaio Viana, 72
04.004 – São Paulo, São Paulo
Latest issue received: 3 (February 1991)

EcoRio
a. 1–   n° 1–   maio 1991–   Monthly
Andina Cultural Ltda.
Av. Rio Branco, 156 – grupo 3103
20.040 – Rio de Janeiro, Rio de Janeiro

Em nome do amor à Natureza
Irregular
Associação Ecologista em Nome do Amor à Natureza   NG
Rua Otávio Corrêa, 62
90.040 – Porto Alegre, Rio Grande do Sul
Latest issue received: 8 (1985)

Espaço, ambiente e planejamento
v. 1–   n° 1–   jan. 1986–   Irregular
Companhia Vale do Rio Doce—CVRD   G
Superintendência do Meio Ambiente
Av. Graça Aranha, 26 - 14° andar
20.005 – Rio de Janeiro, Rio de Janeiro
Latest issue received: 2:12 (September 1990)

Floresser
Irregular
Associação Mineira de Defesa do Meio Ambiente—AMDA   NG
Rua Viçosa, 542-A
30.330 – Belo Horizonte, Minas Gerais
Latest issue received: 4:13 (1987)

FMV Newsletter
Fundação Mata Virgem   NG
SCS – Ed. Palácio do Comércio, s. 1103
70.300 – Brasília, Distrito Federal
Latest issue received: 3d ed. (1990)
Former title: *Newsletter da FMV*

Folha ambiental
Irregular
Grupo Ambientalista da Bahia—GAMBÁ   NG
Rua Guedes Cabral, 05 – s. 106
41.910 - Salvador, Bahia
Latest issue received: 2:6 (November/December 1990)

A Folha da Frente Verde
Sociedade Grupo Ecológico Frente Verde   NG
Rua Álvaro Alvim, 24/1001 – Cinelândia
Caixa Postal 62522
20.031 – Rio de Janeiro, Rio de Janeiro
Latest issue received: 4:1 (February/March 1991)

Folha do meio ambiente
a. 1–   n° 1–   mar. 1990–   Bimonthly
Forest Cultura Viva Ltda.
SCS, Q. 08, Ed. Venâncio 2000, Bl. B-60, s. 224/225
70.333 – Brasília, Distrito Federal
Latest issue received: 2:5 (March/April 1991)

Folha verde
Secretaria de Estado para Assuntos do Meio Ambiente—SEAMA   G
Av. Princesa Isabel, 629 – 6° andar
29.010 – Vitória, Espírito Santo
Latest issue received: 1:4 (February/March 1991)

Folhinha da UVA
a. 1–   n° 1–   fev. 1991–   Monthly
União Veleparaibana de Ambientalistas   NG
Rua Dr. Emílio Winther, 40
12.030 – Taubaté, São Paulo
Latest issue received: 1:2 (March 1991)

Fórum
a. 1–   n° 1–   abr. 1991–
Fórum de ONGs Brasileiras Preparatório para 92   NG
Secretaria Executiva
CEDI—Centro Ecumênico de Documentação e Informação
Rua Santo Amara, 129 – Glória
22.211 – Rio de Janeiro, Rio de Janeiro

Gaia: informativo mensal de movimentos ecológicos
Monthly
Caixa Postal 68029
Cidade Universitária
21.944 – Rio de Janeiro, Rio de Janeiro
Latest issue received: 1:2 (December 1990)

O Geca
Grupo de Estudo Ecológico e Controle Ambiental   NG
Av. Tiradentes, 161
12.030 – Taubaté, São Paulo
Latest issue received: 2:8 (December 1990)

GRUMIN
a. 1–   n° 1–   fev. 1989–   Irregular
Grupo Mulher – Educação Indígena – GRUMIN   NG
Rua da Quitanda, 185 – s. 503
20.091 – Rio de Janeiro, Rio de Janeiro
Latest issue received: 3:4 (April/May 1991)

Habitat
a. 1–   n° 1–   jan. 89– Monthly
Associação Brasileira de Caça e Conservação—ABC   NG
Rua Mourato Coelho, 1371
05.417 – São Paulo, São Paulo
Latest issue received: 2:5 (June 1990)

Informativo (ADFG)
Monthly
Ação Democrática Feminina Gaúcha—ADFG   NG
  Amigos da Terra   NG
Rua Miguel Tostes, 694
90.420 – Porto Alegre, Rio Grande do Sul
Latest issue received: 1 (January 1991)

Informativo ABES
Associação Brasileira de Engenharia Sanitária e Ambiental—ABES
Seção São Paulo   NG
Rua Costa Carvalho, 234
05.429 – São Paulo, São Paulo
Latest issue received: 26 (1990)

Informativo da FBCN
Irregular
Fundação Brasileira para a Conservação da Natureza   NG
Rua Miranda Valverde, 103 – Botafogo
22.218 – Rio de Janeiro, Rio de Janeiro
Latest issue received: 13:51 (July/September 1989)

Informativo SBE
Sociedade Brasileira de Espeleologia—SBE   NG
Av. Brigadeiro Luís Antônio, 4442
01.041 – São Paulo, São Paulo
Latest issue received: 5:2/29 (July/October 1989)

Informativo SEMAX
Sociedade Ecológica e Meio Ambiente de Xaxim—SEMAX   NG
Rua do Comércio, 1619
89.810 – Xaxim, Santa Catarina
Latest issue received: November 1988

Ingeniería sanitaria*
1948– Quarterly
Asociación Interamericana de Ingeniería Sanitaria y Ambiental—AIDIS   NG
Rua Nicolau Gagliardi, 354
05.429 – São Paulo, São Paulo
Latest issue received: 44:1/2 (January/May 1990)
Previously published by AIDIS in United States, Mexico, and Argentina

O Ipê
Associação Anapolina de Proteção ao Meio Ambiente—AAPMA   NG
Rua Calixto, 76
Caixa Postal 676
77.100 – Anápolis, Goiás
Latest issue received: 3:5 (Autumn 1991)

Jornal ABES
Jan. 1975–   Monthly
Associação Brasileira de Engenharia Sanitária e Ambiental—ABES
Diretoria Nacional   NG
Av. Beira Mar, 216 – 13° andar
20.021 – Rio de Janeiro, Rio de Janeiro
Latest issue received: 17:1/2 (January/February 1991)

Jornal da ecologia
Rua Prudente de Morais, 554 – apto. 144
14.100 Ribeirão, São Paulo
Latest issue received: 1:5 (April 1990)

Jornal do Pró-Natura
a. 1–   n° 1–   verão 1990–   Irregular
Instituto Brasileiro de Pesquisas e Estudos Ambientais – Pró-Natura   NG
Rua da Quitanda, 20 – 4° andar
20.011 – Rio de Janeiro, Rio de Janeiro

Jornal Pró-Rio
a. 1–   n° 1–   abr. 1991–
Pró-Rio   NG
Rua Uruguaiana, 10 – 2° andar
20.050 – Rio de Janeiro, Rio de Janeiro

Jornal SODEPAN
n° 01– 1991
Sociedade de Defesa do Pantanal—SODEPAN   NG
Av. Américo Carlos da Costa, 320 – Parque Laucídio Coelho
79.100 – Campo Grande, Mato Grosso do Sul

Jornal verde: a ecologia levada a série
a. 1–   n° 1–
Jornal Verde Comunicação Ecológica Ltda.
Rua Manuel Maria Tourinho, 880
01.236 – São Paulo, São Paulo
Latest issue received: 11 (1990?)

JornalECO
a. 1–   n° 1–   nov. 1988–   Monthly
Secretaria de Estado do Meio Ambiente   G
Rua Tabapuã, 81 – 13° andar
04.533 – São Paulo, São Paulo
Latest issue received: 2:12 (March 1991)

Meio ambiente*
a. 1–   2ª série, n° 1–   jun./jul. 1989–
Thesaurus Editora
SIG – Quadra 8, Lote 2356
70.610 – Brasília, Distrito Federal

Mensageiro
Abr. 1979–   Bimonthly
Conselho Indigenista Missionário—CIMI   NG
Caixa Postal 2080
66.050 – Belém, Pará
Latest issue received: 68 (March/April 1991)

Movimento ecológico
Associação Brasileira de Ecologia—ABE   NG
Av. Nilo Peçanha, 12 – gr. 801/3
20.020 – Rio de Janeiro, Rio de Janeiro
Latest issue received: 9 (October/November 1989)

Natureza viva
Instituto Brasileiro do Meio Ambiente e dos Recursos Naturais Renováveis—
    IBAMA   G
Assessoria de Comunicação Social e Imprensa
SAIN – Lote 4 – Ed. Sede IBAMA
70.800 – Brasília, Distrito Federal
Latest issue received: 1:8 (January/February 1990)

Nova terra
Quarterly
Centro de Estudos e Preservação da Natureza Nova Terra—
  HIPPOKAMPUS   NG
Caixa Postal 11461
05.499 – São Paulo, São Paulo
Latest issue received: 10

Pau Brasil*
a. 1–3   nº 1–16   jul./ago. 1984–jan./fev. 1987   Bimonthly
Departamento de Águas e Energia Elétrica—DAEE   G
Rua Riachuelo, 115
01.007 – São Paulo, São Paulo

Pólo agora
a. 1–   nº 1–   set. 1990–   Monthly
PetroRio—Petroquímica do Rio de Janeiro   G
Av. Rio Branco, 80 – 6º/7º andar
20.040 – Rio de Janeiro, Rio de Janeiro
Latest issue received: 2:1 (January 1991)

População & desenvolvimento*   ISSN 0102-8332
a. 1–   nº 1–   mar. 1967–   Bimonthly
Sociedade Civil Bem-Estar Familiar—BEMFAM   NG
Av. República do Chile, 230 – 17º andar
20.031 – Rio de Janeiro, Rio de Janeiro
Beginning with nº 159, 1990, coedition with Fundação Brasileira para
  Conservação da Natureza
Latest issue received: 24:159 (1990)

Porantim: em defesa da causa indígena*
Monthly
Conselho Indigenista Missionário—CIMI   NG
Caixa Postal 11-1159
70.084 – Brasília, Distrito Federal
Latest issue received: 13:137 (April 1991)

Quero-Quero
a. 1–   nº 1–   mar. 1990–   Bimonthly
Secretaria de Estado da Educação
Grupo de Trabalho em Educação Ambiental—GTEA
Rua Antônio Luz, 101 – s. 605
88.010 – Florianópolis, Santa Catarina
Latest issue received: 1:4 (October/November 1990)

Resenha ambiental
Secretaria de Estado de Meio Ambiente—SEMAN   G
Av. 13 de Maio, 33 – 24° andar
20.031 – Rio de Janeiro, Rio de Janeiro
Latest issue received: December 1990

Saneamento ambiental*
a. 1– n° 1–   jan. 1990–   Monthly
Signus Editora
Rua Eugênio de Medeiros, 499/507
05.425 – São Paulo, São Paulo
Latest issue received: 2:11 (December 1990/January 1991)

Saúde e meio ambiente*
Secretaria da Saúde e do Meio Ambiente   G
Sistema Unificado de Saúde—SUS-RS
Av. A. J. Renner, 10
90.250 – Porto Alegre, Rio Grande do Sul
Latest issue received: January/March 1990

Sinal verde: green light for Latin American rivers
Irregular
União Protetora do Ambiente Natural—UPAN   NG
Rua Lindolfo Collor, 560
Caixa Postal 189
93.001 – São Leopoldo, Rio Grande do Sul
Latest issue received: 3 (1989)

Sobrevivência
Irregular
Associação Gaúcha de Proteção ao Ambiente Natural—AGAPAN   NG
Rua João Telles, 439
Caixa Postal 1996
90.050 – Porto Alegre, Rio Grande do Sul
Latest issue received: 6 (1988)

SobreViver: jornal de ecologia e meio ambiente da Ilha do Governador
Rua Crundiúba, 71/101 – Ilha do Governador
21.931 – Rio de Janeiro, Rio de Janeiro

Sociedade de Preservação dos Recursos Naturais e Culturais da Amazônia—
  SOPREN
Sociedade de Preservação dos Recursos Naturais e Culturais da Amazônia—
  SOPREN NG
Alameda Lúcio Amaral, 193 – Jardim Independência
66.040 – Belém, Pará
Latest issue published: 16:55 (January/December 1990)

SOS Terra
a. 1– n° 1– jan. 1991–   Monthly
Movimento Conservacionista Teresopolitano—MCT NG
Rua Francisco de Luze, 66
25.965 – Teresópolis, Rio de Janeiro
Latest issue received: 1:4 (April 1991)

Terra indígena*   ISSN 0103-2437
Quarterly
Centro de Estudos Indígenas G
Faculdade de Ciências e Letras – UNESP
Rodovia Araraquara/Jaú, km 1
Caixa Postal 174
14.800 – Araraquara, São Paulo
Latest issue received: 8:55 (April/June 1990)

Tupari
Monthly
Grupo de Trabalho Missionário Evangélico—GTME NG
Av. João Gomes Sobrinho, 3149
Caixa Postal 642
78.00 – Cuiabá, Mato Grosso
Latest issue received: 9:30 (August 1989)
Continues *Boletim de GTME*

Um mais
Ação Democrática Feminina Gaúcha—ADFG
  Amigos da Terra NG
Rua Miguel Tostes 694
90.420 – Porto Alegre, Rio Grande do Sul
Latest issue received: 3:11 (October 1985)

Uniambiente
a. 1– n° 0–   dez. 1990–   Bimonthly
Comissão Interinstitucional sobre Meio Ambiente e Educação Universitária—
  CIMAEU NG
Av. Prof. Frederico Herman Jr., 345
05.459 – São Paulo, São Paulo
Latest issue published: 1:0 (December 1990)

Urihi
Irregular
Comissão pela Criação do Parque Yanomami—CCPY NG
Rua Manoel da Nóbrega, 11 – conjunto 32
04.001 – São Paulo, São Paulo
Latest issue received: 13 (March 1991)
English edition

Urtiga
Associação Ituana de Proteção Ambiental—AIPA NG
Caixa Postal 83
13.300 – Itu, São Paulo
Latest issue received: 4:44 (February 1991)

O Verde
Irregular
Associação para Proteção Ambiental de São Carlos—APASC NG
Praça Coronel Paulino Carlos, s/n
Caixa Postal 596
13.560 – São Carlos, São Paulo
Latest issue received: 5:19 (December 1990)

n° 1– 1990–   Biweekly
Associação Brasileira de Engenharia Sanitária e Ambiental
Diretoria Nacional NG
Av. Beira Mar, 216 – 13° andar
20.021 – Rio de Janeiro, Rio de Janeiro
Latest issue received: 5 (March 1991)

Viva alternativa: porta-voz das entidades ambientalistas autônomas
n° 0– maio 1989– Bimonthly
Esquadrão da Vida Produções Culturais NG
Caixa Postal 04/081
70.312 – Brasília, Distrito Federal
Latest issue received: 16/17 (December/January 1990/91)

Yanomami urgente
nº 1– 20 de abr. 1988– Irregular
Comissão pela Criação do Parque Yanomami—CCPY NG
Rua Manoel da Nóbrega, 111 – conjunto 32
04.001 – São Paulo, São Paulo
Latest issue received: 13 (December 1991)
English edition

10. Areas naturales protegidas y desarrollo: Perspectivas y restricciones para el manejo de parques y reservas en la Argentina

Alejandro Winograd

Las relaciones entre las sociedades humanas y el ambiente se han modificado de forma acelerada en los tiempos recientes. Se han realizado distintos ensayos de ordenar esas modificaciones y establecer tendencias en la percepción social de los beneficios esperables del ambiente y sus recursos y de los sistemas adecuados para obtenerlos. Las caracterizaciones de Myers (1988) y Colby (1990) reflejan un proceso en el cual la atención se ha desviado desde la expansión de las fronteras económicas y las tasas de extracción de recursos hacia la búsqueda de sistemas sostenibles de manejo de los recursos naturales. En el presente, los esfuerzos están orientados a la integración entre los temas ambientales y los problemas vinculados con el crecimiento económico y el bienestar de las sociedades humanas (Goodland y Ledec, 1987; BID, 1988).

La sostenibilidad es un concepto antropocéntrico vinculado con el compromiso de garantizar que un sistema dado de uso no disminuya—o lo haga en la mínima medida posible—la viabilidad de sistemas diferentes, eventualmente deseables para otras sociedades o para generaciones futuras (IUCN et al., 1980; Repetto, 1985; Myers, 1988). Los sistemas sostenibles configuran una respuesta que intenta satisfacer, simultáneamente, las aspiraciones sociales y ambientales de largo plazo y las necesidades materiales inmediatas de la sociedad que los adopte. Desde la perspectiva de la sostenibilidad, estas aspiraciones y necesidades no configuran términos opuestos sino componentes de sistemas sociales, económicos y políticos para el establecimiento de los cuales se puede acceder, en el presente, a los conocimientos científicos y técnicos necesarios (Gallopin y Winograd, 1991).

La integración de distintos sistemas sostenibles, aplicados a los recursos naturales, la energía y la organización social o económica, ha conformado los modelos sostenibles de desarrollo (IUCN et al., 1980; WRI-IIED, 1988; Comisión de Desarrollo, 1990). Los mismos han sido discutidos por la falta de un encuadre temporal y espacial estricto (Brown et al., 1987) y a la dificultad de aplicar las definiciones teóricas a los distintos contextos sociales y ambientales para los que fueron concebidas (Caldwell, 1984; Leonard, 1989). Una corriente de pensamiento con expresión particularmente significativa en el campo económico discute la base misma de estos modelos a partir de la noción de que el crecimiento económico es un proceso de límites abiertos y que las únicas restricciones al mismo son aquellas que derivan de las leyes del mercado (Kwong Echard, 1990).

Se ha discutido extensamente cuáles son las nuevas funciones que deben asignarse, como contribución al establecimiento de modelos sostenibles, a las áreas naturales protegidas (McNeely y Miller, 1984; Ledec y Goodland, 1988). Se han identificado objetivos vinculados con ellas y se han establecido nuevos parques y reservas en distintos países enfocados a la consecución de los mismos. Paralelamente, se ha tomado conciencia de que, a escala planetaria, son pocas las perspectivas de establecer grandes áreas protegidas nuevas en el futuro (Harrison et al., 1984). En ese contexto, son prioritarios los estudios orientados a identificar el equilibrio entre la preservación de sistemas ecológicos cada vez más amenazados y la obtención de los beneficios que los mismos pueden ofrecer, en plazos relativamente cortos, a las poblaciones vinculadas con ellos (Ledec y Goodland, 1988; Bianciotto et al., 1989). En los países en desarrollo, donde la pobreza se traduce en fuertes presiones sobre el ambiente (World Bank, 1990a; Foy y Daly, 1989; Pulley, 1989), es necesario discutir las funciones cubiertas por los sistemas de áreas protegidas si se pretende garantizar su existencia. Finalmente, un sistema de áreas protegidas acorde con las necesidades de las sociedades contemporáneas constituye una fuente de experiencia valiosa para el establecimiento de un modelo sostenible de relación entre el hombre y la biosfera.

Areas naturales protegidas

En el presente, los sistemas nacionales de parques nacionales y los programas vinculados conceptual y metodológicamente a los mismos, conforman el modelo más general en el cual se encuadran las áreas naturales protegidas del mundo. Si bien existen diferencias importantes en la forma adoptada por estos sistemas en distintas regiones, hay elementos comunes que permiten asignar funciones análogas a los sistemas de parques nacionales y reservas afines en casi todos los países del mundo (Machlis y Tichnell, 1985).

De las 5289 áreas protegidas reconocidas en 1989 (WRI, 1990), más de 1000 son, formalmente, Parques Nacionales. Si se consideran las áreas protegidas adscritas a otras categorías u otras formas de administración, pero sometidas a un sistema de manejo similar, y se excluyen del total las 786 áreas correspondientes a los sistemas internacionales de protección—ya que, normalmente, están parcialmente superpuestas con parques nacionales si se tratan de Reservas de la Biosfera o Humedales de Importancia Internacionales y son poco extensas si corresponden al Programa de Sitios Naturales del Patrimonio de la Humanidad (MAB, 1989)—se alcanza una visión de la significación de este sistema de manejo a escala mundial.

En 1967, la IUCN publicó la primera lista de parques nacionales y reservas equivalentes (IUCN, 1975). La inclusión de áreas protegidas en esta lista se basó en tres criterios: status de protección, área mínima y control efectivo.

La definición considerada en este primer intento de globalizar la entidad de los parques nacionales fue modificada en 1969 y, nuevamente, en 1972, para alcanzar mayor precisión y abarcar también aquellas áreas donde la protección del patrimonio cultural era el principal objetivo (MAB, 1989).

Entre los principios comunes de los parques y reservas equivalentes figura, como objetivo esencial, la satisfacción de necesidades humanas (Miller, 1980; McNeely y Miller, 1984; Ormazábal, 1988). Los criterios en juego en la selección de las áreas a transformar en parques y reservas y en la determinación de pautas concretas de manejo son esencialmente antropocéntricos. La consideración de que el fin último de los parques se vincula con necesidades y aspiraciones humanas es la diferencia más importante entre éstos y un área natural considerada desde una perspectiva estrictamente ecológica.

Pero si los valores de inspiración, educativos, culturales y recreativos de las áreas naturales protegidas en general están disponibles para la humanidad, el uso concreto se inscribe en un sistema mucho más acotado formado por cada una de un grupo humano determinado. Se han discutido los problemas de escala y las formas de interdependencia entre las relaciones de los parques y la humanidad, globalmente considerados, y cada parque y sus usuarios específicos (Cahn, 1985; Machlis y Tichnell, 1985; Thelen, 1990; Winograd, 1990).

Entre las funciones ambientales y simbólicas vinculadas a las áreas protegidas en su conjunto pueden mencionarse:

1. Contribución al mantenimiento de la diversidad de ecosistemas planetarios;
2. Mantenimiento de la diversidad de la vida animal y vegetal, permitiendo la supervivencia de especies amenazadas por la extinción bajo otra condiciones;

3. Conservación del germoplasma, fuente eventual de recursos alimentarios, farmacológicos o de otra aplicación futura;
4. Externalización de servicios ambientales, tales como la preservación de la calidad del agua y del aire, preservación de la cobertura vegetal de suelos amenazados, mantenimiento de masas boscosas y otros;
5. Satisfacción de aspiraciones de contenido simbólico vinculadas con la existencia de áreas libres de modificaciones antropogénicas significativas.

Si las funciones citadas derivan de propiedades emergentes de un sistema—nacional, regional o mundial—de áreas protegidas cabe preguntarse cuáles son las que les corresponden de forma individual y a qué objetivos debe propender el manejo que haga de los mismos cada región o país. La respuesta trivial a este interrogante se basa en el compromiso, que cada sociedad tiene, de contribuir a la preservación y al manejo del patrimonio mundial. Pese a ello, no existen motivos para restringir de ese modo el alcance de una política pública de áreas protegidas. El Programa acerca del Hombre y la Biosfera, llevado adelante por la UNESCO, pone énfasis en el potencial de los sistemas de manejo que, sin descuidar las funciones globales mencionadas, contribuyan de forma efectiva a satisfacer las necesidades y mejorar las condiciones de vida de las poblaciones de áreas incluidas o adyacentes a las reservas. El desarrollo de esos sistemas de manejo cobra particular importancia en las regiones del mundo que enfrentan dificultades para satisfacer las necesidades básicas de sus habitantes.

Las formas de interacción entre cada parque o reserva y la comunidad que vive en las adyacencias del mismo son de índole cualitativamente distinta de las mencionadas. Normalmente, o bien implican usos controversiales del área protegida, sus recursos y las tierras adyacentes, o son consideradas detrimentales. Previa consideración de las características del sistema de áreas protegidas de la Argentina, pero de validez en la mayor parte de los países en desarrollo, pueden destacarse (Koremblit et al., 1990; Quesada Mateo, 1990; Thelen, 1990):

1. Extracción de recursos efectuada por pobladores asentados en el área con anterioridad al establecimiento del área protegida;
2. Explotación comercial, frecuentemente ilegal, de recursos parcial o totalmente incluidos en las normas de protección (caza y pesca furtiva, pastoreo de ganado, extracción de madera, etc.);
3. Expansión de la actividad turística regional a partir de los atractivos naturales y simbólicos del área protegida;

4. Sistemas de uso de las tierras adyacentes generadores de impactos o amenazas sobre el área protegida;
5. Presiones sociales y políticas tendientes al levantamiento de ciertas restricciones al uso de los recursos protegidos;
6. Conflictos entre las autoridades del parque o la reserva y autoridades locales u otros actores sociales en relación con las potestades de manejo del área afectada y sus adyacencias.

Este esquema puede justificar, paradójicamente, el debilitamiento de los sistemas nacionales de áreas protegidas. Existen antecedentes, especialmente en los países más pobres, respecto del bajo grado de consenso que alcanzan los parques y reservas en virtud de su escasa o nula contribución al bienestar de las poblaciones locales (Machlis y Tichnell, 1985; Sobral y Winograd, 1984; White y Savina, 1987; Kwong Echard, 1990).

El éxito de un programa de manejo tendiente a la conservación de un ecosistema tiene escasas posibilidades de éxito sin el apoyo de la población local (Cernea, 1989; Quiroga, 1990). Sin embargo, ese apoyo no va necesariamente acompañado por una distribución equitativa de los beneficios producidos. Los usos recreativos, los eventuales réditos económicos y las funciones educativas aparecen fuertemente restringidos para los sectores más pobres. El turismo, la actividad económica por excelencia vinculada a los parques, distribuye sus costos sociales, ambientales y económicos, de forma más generalizada que las ganancias generadas (Boo, 1985; Brailovsky, 1988).

Un contexto regional: América Latina

Entre los factores esenciales que afectaron, durante la década pasada, a la mayoría de los países no desarrollados, pueden citarse los cambios en el escenario económico internacional, la profundización de ciertas tendencias en los modelos de desarrollo predominantes, el alcance y éxito relativos de las políticas de reducción de la pobreza y el conjunto de procesos antropogénicos genéricamente reunidos bajo la denominación de crisis ambiental global (WRI, 1989; Maihold y Urquidi, 1990; World Bank, 1990). Las consecuencias de los mismos en cuanto al crecimiento económico en América Latina han justificado el uso de la expresión de "década perdida" para los años 80. La satisfacción de las necesidades de amplios sectores de la población, el establecimiento de un modelo de desarrollo apropiado apropiado para generar un crecimiento económico sostenible y la definición de políticas ambientales congruentes con los dos objetivos anteriores y aptas para detener y, eventualmente, revertir los procesos de degradación ambiental en curso son los desafíos que la última década ha planteado a las sociedades de América Latina.

Existe un número creciente de propuestas que vinculan la superación de esos desafíos al establecimiento de modelos de desarrollo más profundamente vinculados con las características ambientales de la región. A escala global se ha definido el desarrollo sostenible como "el manejo del uso humano de la biosfera de forma tal que produzca el máximo beneficio sostenible a las generaciones presentes manteniendo su potencial para satisfacer las necesidades y aspiraciones de las generaciones futuras" (IUCN et al., 1980). Las derivaciones de la misma basadas en el contexto latinoamericano reflejan las urgencias inmediatas de comunidades pobres asentadas en un ambiente potencialmente rico.

Winograd (1989) ha caracterizado un escenario sostenible para América Latina. Este "corporiza el énfasis en la satisfacción de las necesidades humanas, la mejor distribución de la riqueza y una aproximación participativa y descentralizada". En este escenario se asume la implementación de una serie de políticas vinculadas con temas ambientales, científicos, tecnológicos, económicos y sociales. Se hace referencia a la necesidad de políticas de regulación en relación con el uso de la tierra, el estímulo de ciertos sectores industriales y comerciales y el desarrollo de fuentes locales de energía. Esta y otras caracterizaciones apuntan a resolver la "inevitable" contradicción entre la lucha contra la pobreza y el establecimiento de sistemas de protección ambiental (Leonard, 1989). Los proyectos de intercambio de deuda externa por naturaleza (Sevilla Larrea, 1990) constituyen ejemplos de la aplicación de sistemas originales de financiación de un desarrollo sostenible. Sin embargo, la controversia respecto de la oportunidad de algunos de ellos y su condición marginal en términos económicos los presentan más como una opción de interés que como una solución inmediata. Del mismo modo, numerosas soluciones tecnológicas pueden ser insuficientes sin una serie de cambios vinculados con el contexto sociocultural en que desean aplicarse (Lele y Stone, 1989; Burger, 1990).

Pese a las particularidades sociales y ambientales de la Argentina en relación con la región en su conjunto, existe una visión similar acerca de la vinculación entre los problemas ambientales y las dificultades sociales, económicas y políticas del país (Balderiote, 1990; Catoggio, 1990; WRI, 1990). Sin embargo el análisis de las relaciones entre la comunidad y el ambiente y sus consecuencias sobre el sistema nacional de áreas naturales protegidas en la Argentina debe considerar esas particularidades.

Argentina es uno de los países de América Latina—como Chile y Uruguay—en los cuales los ecosistemas tropicales ocupan sólo áreas de poca significación espacial, demográfica y económica (Udvardy, 1975; Cabrera, 1989; IGM, 1989; INDEC, 1991).

Los ambientes más representativas están determinados por los extremos australes de grandes ecosistemas sudamericanos—bosque húmedo brasileño, sabana del gran Chaco, Andes meridionales, yungas y puna—y por ecosistemas endémicos de las latitudes medias australes—desierto patagónico, bosque de *nothofagus*, bosque valdiviano, pampas (Udvardy, 1978).

Argentina y Uruguay sufrieron un proceso de artificialización relativamente tardío pero de velocidad y alcance significativos (Brailovsky, 1991). La determinación de la proporción de la superficie argentina que se ha mantenido en estado natural varía según los criterios que se utilicen. Algunas cuantificaciones dan cuenta de un 24,7% de la superficie del país ocupada por bosques y montes materiales (IGM, 1989). El sistema de evaluación de uso del suelo utilizado en ese análisis no distingue claramente ecosistemas naturales y alterados cuando éstos no están sujetos a un sistema de uso agropecuario. Otros estudios reducen esa superficie a sólo el 5% de la superficie de Argentina (WRI, 1990). Resulta significativo que la estimación de la superficie del sistema nacional de áreas protegidas presentada por la misma fuente, es de un 4% de la superficie del país.

La tasa de crecimiento poblacional es, junto a la de Uruguay, la más baja de la región. En las últimas dos décadas se ha reducido de 1,76% anual a 1,34% anual (INDEC, 1991).

La densidad de población es de 11,8 hab x km^2, la segunda más baja de América Latina. Más del 85% de la población es urbana y casi el 39% vive en la provincia de Buenos Aires (WRI, 1990; INDEC, 1991). Este patrón de ocupación determina que, a diferencia de la mayor parte de los países en desarrollo de la región tropical, hay pocas áreas de alta densidad de población campesina (World Bank, 1989) y que, incluso la producción generada en minifundios, se canaliza a través de mecanismos tradicionales de mercado capitalista (Winograd, 1989*b*).

El sistema de áreas protegidas de la Argentina

El sistema de áreas naturales protegidas argentino es de origen relativamente temprano. México, Chile y Argentina establecieron las primeras reservas de tierras específicamente destinadas a la preservación del ambiente entre 1876 y 1907 (Ormazábal, 1988). La selección de áreas siguió, originalmente, criterios de belleza escénica apoyados en cánones que privilegiaron los paisajes glaciarios y los bosques de ladera de la precordillera patagónica. Si parte del bosque húmedo brasileño (Udvardy, 1975 y 1978) presente en el nordeste del país fue protegido a través de la creación de un parque nacional desde 1934 (Giúdice, 1985) fue, presumiblemente, como consecuencia de la presencia de las cataratas del Iguazú más que por una temprana conciencia de la fragilidad de los ecosistemas forestales tropicales.

Los criterios escénicos fueron reemplazados por prioridades de raíz ecológica, vinculadas con la noción de que los sistemas nacionales de áreas protegidas constituían un instrumento de preservación de bienes sociales. En 1986 se estableció, para los organismos nacionales de veinte países latinoamericanos, el orden de prioridades de los criterios de incorporación de nuevas áreas protegidas al sistema nacional. La diversidad biológica, la presencia de comunidades particulares de fauna y la protección de cuencas hidrográficas resultaron los más difundidos aunque, en el caso de la Argentina, este último fue relegado por la presencia de valores naturales geomorfológicos o paisajísticos (Ormazábal, 1988).

La extensión precisa del sistema de áreas protegidas de la Argentina y el conjunto de áreas y categorías que los componen son datos de difícil precisión. La existencia, al menos legal, de áreas protegidas de distintas jurisdicciones y dominios—nacional, provincial, municipal, privado, otras instituciones públicas u ONGs—dificulta el uso de inventarios, que no siempre están basados en criterios comunes. Las reservas "de papel" y el uso de denominaciones equivalentes— aplicadas a áreas de distintos usos (cotos de caza, recreación u otros)— implican diferencias significativas en el recuento de las áreas involucradas. Estas divergencias quedan reflejadas en la comparación de los inventarios publicados en dos ediciones sucesivas del reporte bianual del World Resources Institute (Tabla 1) así como en el análisis de distintas publicaciones y mapas nacionales y provinciales.

Aún los datos correspondientes a 1988, si pueden haber soslayado áreas efectivamente protegidas, incluyen otras donde la falta de fondos, personal o las fallas en las definiciones jurisdicciones implican, eventualmente, amenazas al ambiente que se pretende conservar (Machlis y Tichnell, 1985; Bianciotto et al., 1990; Quesada Mateo, 1990). Un ejemplo claro lo conforma el área costera protegida citada. La misma corresponde al Parque Nacional de Tierra del Fuego, único parque nacional de la Argentina que llega hasta el litoral marítimo. Sin embargo, la protección del ambiente marítimo y el manejo de sus recursos son ajenos a la jurisdicción y funciones del mismo (Koremblit et al., 1990). La misma restricción es válida para las seis áreas costeras incluidas en la serie de datos de 1989, a las cuales les corresponden status de protección menores que los de un Parque Nacional.

Tabla 1. Protección nacional e internacional
de áreas naturales en la Argentina

Total de áreas protegidas			Marinas y cost			Res. de la Biosfera	
Año	N°	Superficie (ha)	N°	Superficie (ha)	% ª	N°	Superficie (ha)
1988	33	4.571.871	1	63.000	1,7	4	2.004.980
1989	69	10.974.795	7	1.498.648	4,0	4	2.004.980

a. Porcentaje de la superficie del país comprendido por las áreas protegidas.
Fuente: WRI-IIED, 1988; WRI, 1990.

De las diez provincias biogeográficas (Udvardy, 1975 y 1978) presentes en la Argentina (Tabla 2), al menos dos, el desierto patagónico y las pampas, pueden considerarse claramente subrepresentadas en el sistema.   Esta subrepresentación tiene particular importancia tanto desde una perspectiva nacional como desde el punto de vista global de conservación de los ecosistemas mundiales.   Las pampas constituyen un ecosistema endémico de la Argentina y el desierto patagónico, aún presente también en Chile presenta diferencias ecológicas a uno y otro lado de la cordillera de los Andes y en sus áreas litorales Atlántica y Pacífica (Morello, 1985).   Por otra parte, ambos ecosistemas presentan un alto grado de artificialización en la casi totalidad de su extensión y los sistemas agropecuarios predominantes en ellos han provocado fenómenos de erosión, extinción local de especies y desaparición de microambientes (Bondel, 1985; Cattalano y Fernández, 1986; Darwich, 1990; Glave, 1990; Senigagliesi, 1990; Soriano y Paruelo, 1990; Viglizzo, 1990). El estudio de la dinámica de ese proceso de degradación y su reversión estaría facilitado por la disponibilidad de áreas representativas del estado original de los mismos.

Tabla 2. Provincias biogeográficas presentes en la Argentina

1.	Bosque húmedo brasileño	6.	Desierto Patagónico
2.	Bosque Valdiviano	7.	Pampas Argentinas
3.	Bosque de Nothofagus Chilenos	8.	Montañesa de los Yungas
4.	Sabana del Gran Chaco	9.	Puna
5.	Desierto Monte	10.	Andina meridional

Fuente: Según la clasificación de Udvardy.

El monte es la otra provincia biogeográfica endémica de la Argentina (Udvardy, 1975). Al no contar con un mínimo de 100.000 hectáreas y cinco áreas protegidas (Giudice, 1986) debe considerarse prioritaria la creación de nuevas áreas protegidas en base a los criterios definidos por el Proyecto FAO-PNUMA sobre manejo de áreas silvestres. La provincia incluye una serie de reservas provinciales aunque la variación entre los límites impuestos al monte por distintos autores (Udvardy, 1975; Cabrera, 1989) implica diferencias significativas en la cantidad y superficie de las mismas.

Las provincias restantes se extienden más allá de las fronteras y se ha destacado que los sistemas de protección ambiental de las mismas deben coordinarse entre los gobiernos involucrados (Thelen, 1985; Ormazábal, 1988). Sin embargo, el análisis de algunos casos indica que no es fácil superar las restricciones institucionales de los organismos involucrados (Koremblit et al., 1990).

Entre los factores ecológicos emergentes de la posición relativa de la Argentina pueden mencionarse:

1. Ambientes de transición entre áreas tropicales, subtropicales, templadas y frías;
2. Intensidad creciente de los pulsos estacionales en los límites australes de los grandes ecosistemas subtropicales;
3. Estrategias de adaptación vinculadas con la colonización de espacios marginales en términos ecológicos y espaciales a la vez, i.e., Patagonia austral y Tierra del Fuego;
4. Presencia de ecosistemas caracterizados por su juventud derivada del corto tiempo transcurrido desde la retirada de los hielos, sumada, en algunos casos a la condición insular.

Los objetivos del sistema nacional de áreas protegidas de la Argentina fueron explicitados en el proyecto de Ley de Parques Nacionales y Areas Protegidas redactado en 1985. Los objetivos expresados pueden agruparse como vinculados a la conservación, a la investigación, a la recreación y a la educación. La comparación de los mismos con aquellos definidos por Miller (1980) teniendo como meta la integración de las áreas naturales en el desarrollo económico y social refleja algunas diferencias dignas de atención.

El proyecto argentino no considera entre los objetivos principales de las áreas protegidas:

1. La conservación y manejo de los recursos pesqueros y de la fauna silvestre como fuente de proteínas, o base de actitudes económicas;

2. El manejo y mejoramiento de los recursos forestales incluyendo, entre sus funciones, la disponibilidad de madera para construcción u otros usos "de importancia para el país" (Miller, 1980);
3. La organización de todas las acciones en función del desarrollo rural integral.

Una investigación orientada a comparar la actitud pública respecto del ambiente en quince países reveló que la reducción de los riesgos ambientales es un objetivo más relevante que el acceso a un *standard* de vida más elevado (Harris et al., en WRI, 1990).   Sin embargo Argentina fue el único país donde el público no se declaró dispuesto a pagar impuestos específicamente orientados al mejoramiento del ambiente.   No se han llevado a cabo estudios que permitan determinar el conjunto de causas que han determinado la relativa debilidad de la conciencia ambiental en la Argentina.   Puede presumirse que, al menos en parte, está vinculada con las dificultades económicas que atraviesan la población, con la existencia de fuertes barreras entre las culturas urbana y rural, con el proceso temprano de artificialización mencionada y con dificultades de participación y organización comunitaria vinculadas con la historia política reciente (Quiroga, 1990).   Esta debilidad no ha impedido el surgimiento de fuertes movimientos espontáneos en relación con modificaciones en el status o la jurisdicción de distintas áreas protegidas (Sobral y Winograd, 1985; Winograd, 1988).   Tópicos tales como la federalización de los parques nacionales o proyectos de canje de deuda externa por naturaleza han sido objeto de atención por parte de las comunidades próximas a las áreas involucradas pero, en cambio, no están suficientemente desarrollados los mecanismos permanentes que permitan que los pobladores locales en particular y el resto de la población en general se involucren en la toma de decisiones de largo alcance respecto de las áreas protegidas.

Según se ha mencionado, los objetivos asignados al sistema nacional de áreas protegidas están poco vinculados con los problemas concretos del desarrollo rural.   La ausencia de las categorías V, Paisajes protegidos; VI, Reserva de recursos; VII, Reservas antropológicas; y VIII, Areas manejadas de uso múltiple, descritas por la IUCN (1985) en el sistema argentino, da cuenta del énfasis puesto sobre las funciones científicas o recreacionales sobre aquellas vinculadas al desarrollo rural, la preservación de sistemas culturales o tecnológicos locales o la integración de actividades de protección y aprovechamiento de recursos. Es cierto que existen otros organismos específicamente orientados a algunas de estas actividades pero las concepciones actuales respecto de los sistemas de manejo adecuados tienden a articular los parques y reservas tradicionales con algún grado de control sobre el uso de las tierras adyacentes (Shafer, 1990). Este control puede ser:

1. Tan solo con el objeto de disminuir las fuentes de *stress* sobre el área protegida (Machlis y Tichnell, 1985);
2. De escala experimental y enfocado al conocimiento de alternativas de manejo, regeneración o extracción de recursos (MAB, 1989), o, normalmente frente a la presencia de poblaciones aborígenes;
3. Orientado al aprovechamiento sostenible de recursos.

Conclusiones

La Argentina cuenta con una red de áreas naturales protegidas relativamente amplia. Los bosques andinopatagónicos son el sistema mejor representado con una serie de parques naturales que se extiende entre los 39 y casi 55 grados de latitud S (IGM, 1974 y 1989).

Los ecosistemas presentes en las provincias biogeográficas del monte, del desierto patagónico y de las pampas están subrepresentados en el sistema. La condición endémica del monte y de las pampas y las características que permiten diferenciar el desierto patagónico a uno y otro lado de la cordillera de los Andes (Bondel, 1985 y 1988; Morello, 1985) asignan un alto grado de prioridad a la protección de áreas naturales en esas regiones. Por otra parte los sistemas vigentes de uso agrícola han generado procesos de erosión y disminución de la diversidad significativos, especialmente en el desierto patagónico (Méndez Casariego, 1990; Soriano y Paruelo, 1990) y las pampas (Darwich, 1990; Glave, 1990; Senigagliesi, 1990; Viglizzo, 1990). El estudio de la dinámica y de los mecanismos de reversión de esos procesos, así como el ensayo de alternativas sostenibles de producción (Winograd, 1986), estarán facilitados por la existencia de áreas protegidas sometidas a un manejo controlado.

Existen datos contradictorios respecto de la extensión y el grado de cobertura efectivo del sistema nacional de áreas protegidas. Las reservas de papel y la combinación de áreas protegidas de distintas jurisdicciones implican divergencias en los resultados dependiendo de los criterios que se utilicen. Una derivación alarmante de algunas evaluaciones es que habría una superficie menor a 2.750.000 hectáreas en estado natural ajenas al sistema. Existen los conocimientos para iniciar un proceso de recuperación y los fondos necesarios no son exorbitantes (Gallopin y Winograd, 1991). El amplio rango de variación entre las distintas estimaciones sugiere la necesidad de determinar con precisión la superficie de las distintas categorías de uso del suelo.

Las áreas naturales protegidas, en la Argentina, están orientadas principalmente a las funciones de conservación, investigación, recreación y educación. El grado de cumplimiento de estas funciones es variable y se vincula con la facilidad de acceso y con la infraestructura disponible en cada una. Las restricciones de presupuesto y personal son un mal ampliamente generalizado en las áreas protegidas y la Argentina no es ajena a esa realidad. Sin embargo, la falta de participación por parte de las comunidades locales, una atmósfera de desconfianza entre los pobladores y los administradores del parque, la existencia de presiones por el uso de ciertos recursos por parte de pobladores, empresarios y autoridades locales y la caza y extracción ilegales son riesgos cuya eliminación no depende exclusivamente del fortalecimiento de las estructuras de vigilancia. Los avances en la búsqueda de sistemas de administración y manejo que armonicen las funciones mencionadas y una contribución efectiva al desarrollo económico de la región y al bienestar de sus habitantes son indispensables para la disminución de esos riesgos. Si los modelos sostenibles de desarrollo deben adecuarse al contexto ambiental y cultural de cada región, es indudable que las áreas protegidas tienen un alto potencial como sitios de experimentación.

La estabilidad de los sistemas económicos agrícolas y la preservación de la calidad de los suelos imponen al aumento de la diversidad de opciones productivas (Sunkel, 1990; Goodland y Ledec, 1987). En el marco de los modelos sostenibles de desarrollo se considera necesario la búsqueda de nuevos mercados para productos agrícolas poco difundidos y la oportunidad de desarrollar tecnologías plurales que combinen tecnologías tradicionales y modernas (Winograd, 1989a; Gallopin y Winograd, 1991). Estos procesos no están estrictamente vinculados con la protección de áreas silvestres pero se basan, en buena medida, en la investigación y puesta en valor de los recursos que éstas contienen (Ledec y Goodland, 1988; World Bank, 1990b). Buena parte de los esfuerzos y los fondos orientados a la investigación de sistemas agrícolas sostenibles se concentran en las áreas tropicales (Radulovich, 1991). Por lo tanto, la extensión de los resultados a los distintos contextos socioambientales de la Argentina y, eventualmente, de los demás países del extremo sur americano, requiere un proceso de adaptación importante. Las áreas naturales protegidas brindan un espacio adecuado para la fase experimental del mismo y su uso contribuirá a extender la conciencia del valor potencial de las mismas facilitando la consecución de sus objetivos primarios (Bianciotto et al., 1990; Winograd, 1990).

Las áreas naturales funcionan como reservorio de un patrimonio genético eventualmente valioso (WRI, 1989). Los análisis referidos a los problemas de desarrollo de las regiones tropicales destacan los posibles usos industriales, principalmente en las industrias farmacéutica y de cosméticos, de numerosos derivados de plantas y animales así como el potencial de variedades endémicas en el desarrollo de nuevas variedades (McNeely et al., 1990). Existen ejemplos alentadores y, sin embargo, se asume que las perspectivas de aprovechamiento del germoplasma latinoamericano permanecen hasta ahora casi totalmente inexploradas (Comisión de Desarrollo, 1990). Si bien es cierto que la enorme diversidad biológica de las áreas tropicales implica que allí se concentran los esfuerzos de investigación respecto del potencial genético, no pueden descuidarse las perspectivas de los ecosistemas de transición. De hecho, hay una serie de factores ecológicos relevantes en la parte austral del continente que imponen presiones de selección cuyos resultados merecen particular atención.

En síntesis, puede decirse que la toma de conciencia de la responsabilidad ambiental y las nuevas formas de relación entre el hombre y su entorno implican la asignación de nuevas funciones a los sistemas de áreas protegidas. En la Argentina se ha establecido una serie de parques y reservas que satisficieron, razonablemente, las aspiraciones de conservación de áreas naturales según eran concebidas hasta hace poco tiempo. Los cambios ambientales, culturales y políticos operados a escala global en las últimas décadas hacen necesario el diseño y puesta en vigencia de nuevos y más amplios sistemas de manejo si se pretende asegurar la existencia de áreas naturales para el futuro. El manejo de las áreas protegidas debe incluir, entre sus objetivos, la contribución al establecimiento de nuevas formas de uso de las tierras adyacentes y al bienestar de la población. A la protección de paisajes, comunidades animales y vegetales y procesos ecológicos, debe agregarse la búsqueda de nuevas y más ricas formas de interacción de las comunidades urbanas y rurales, entre sí y con el ambiente que ocupan. En la Argentina, como en muchos otros países en desarrollo, se discute la oportunidad de ampliar y revalorizar los sistemas de protección ambiental en un contexto socioeconómico crítico. Quizás, el primer paso sea destacar que no es a pesar sino como consecuencia de las carencias de los modelos de desarrollo predominantes, que los seres humanos vuelven a fijar su atención en la naturaleza.

BIBLIOGRAFIA

Balderiote, Marta. 1990. "Las consideraciones de la política ambiental para los años '90". En *Seminario Latinoamericano sobre Medio Ambiente y Desarrollo*. San Carlos de Bariloche, Argentina, octubre 15-21.

BID (Banco Interamericano de Desarrollo), ed. 1988. *Marco conceptual para la acción del Banco en protección y mejoramiento del medio ambiente y conservación de recursos naturales*. Washington, D.C.: BID, Comité del Medio Ambiente.

Bandeira Ryff, Tito. 1990. "Algunas consideraciones sobre el caso de Brasil". En Gunther Maihold y Víctor Urquidi, eds., *Diálogo con Nuestro Futuro Común: Perspectivas latinoamericanas del Informe Bruntland*. Caracas: Nueva Sociedad.

Bianciotto, Oscar, Hernán Vidal y Alejandro Winograd. 1989. "Pautas preliminares para la elaboración de un plan de manejo del oriente fueguino". *Informe elevado a la Subsecretaría de Planeamiento. Gobernación de Tierra del Fuego*. Ushuaia.

_____. 1990. "Proyecto Fuegia: Diseño de una estrategia de manejo aplicable al oriente fueguino (R.A.)". *Working Paper*. Ushuaia: FIDER Foundation.

Bondel, Santiago C. 1985. *Tierra del Fuego: la organización de su espacio*. Ushuaia: CADIC.

_____. 1988. *Geografía de Tierra del Fuego*. Ushuaia: Gob. de Tierra del Fuego.

Boo, Elizabeth. 1985. *Ecotourism: The Potential and Pitfalls*. Vol. 1. Baltimore: World Wildlife Fund.

Brailovsky, Antonio. 1988. "El impacto ambiental del turismo". *Ambiente y recursos naturales* 1:34-43.

Brailovsky, Antonio, y Dina Foguelman. 1991. *Memoria Verde: Historia ecológica de la Argentina*. Buenos Aires: Editorial Sudamericana.

Brown, Becky, Mark Hanson, Diana Liverman y Roberto Merideth. 1987. "Global Sustainability: Toward Definition". *Environmental Management* 11(6): 713-719.

Burger, Julian. 1990. *The Gaia Atlas of First Peoples: A Future for the Indigenous World*. London: Gaia Books Ltd. y Anchor Books.

Cabrera, Angel. 1988. *Mapa fitogeográfico de la República Argentina*. Buenos Aires: IGM.

Cahn, Robert, ed. 1985. *An Environmental Agenda for the Future*. Washington, D.C. y Covelo: Island Press.

Caldwell, Linton. 1984. "Integración de la política ambiental y el desarrollo económico: Prioridad para el accionar político nacional e internacional. Algunos ejemplos latinoamericanos." *Ambiente y Recursos Naturales* 1(3): 22-35.

Cattalano, Alejandro, y Edgardo Fernández. 1986. "Aspectos de la producción pecuaria en las regiones agroecológicas de Tierra del Fuego". En *Memorias del INTA*. Rio Grande: INTA.

Catoggio, José. 1990. "Los problemas ambientales regionales de América Latina". En *Seminario Latinoamericano sobre Medio Ambiente y Desarrollo*. San Carlos de Bariloche, Argentina, octubre 15-21.

Cernea, Michael. 1989. *Organizaciones no gubernamentales y desarrollo local*. World Bank Discussion Papers 40S. Washington, D.C.: The World Bank.

Colby, Michael. 1990. *Environmental Management and Development: The Evolution of Paradigms*. World Bank Discussion Papers 80. Washington, D.C.: The World Bank.

Comisión de Desarrollo y Medio Ambiente de América Latina y el Caribe, ed. 1990. *Nuestra propia agenda*. Washington, New York, y Santiago de Chile: BID y PNUD.

Darwich, Nestor. 1990. "Estado actual y manejo de los recursos naturales en la región pampeana húmeda sur". En INTA, ed., *Juicio a nuestra agricultura: Hacia el desarrollo de una agricultura sostenible.* II Recursos Naturales. Buenos Aires: INTA.

Foy, George, y Herman Daly. 1989. *Allocation, Distribution and Scale as Determinants of Environmental Degradation: Case Studies of Haiti, El Salvador and Costa Rica.* Environment Department Working Paper 19. Washington, D.C.: The World Bank.

Gallopin, Gilberto, y Manuel Winograd. 1991. "Obstáculos y oportunidades para el desarrollo sustentable en América Latina". En *Seminario: Problemática futura del medio ambiente en América Latina.* Buenos Aires, Argentina, mayo 13-15.

Giudice, Luis. 1985. *Estrategia de gestión planificada de los parques nacionales.* Serie del Cincuentenario. Buenos Aires: Administración de Parques Nacionales.

_____. 1986. "Documento sobre el Sistema Nacional de Areas Naturales Protegidas". En *Taller sobre planificación de sistemas nacionales de áreas silvestres protegidas.* Caracas, Venezuela, julio 9-13.

Glave, Adolfo. 1990. "Agricultura conservacionista para la región subhúmeda y semiárida pampeano". En INTA, ed., *Juicio a nuestra agricultura: Hacia el desarrollo de una agricultura sostenible.* II Recursos Naturales. Buenos Aires: INTA.

Goodland, Robert, y George Ledec. 1987. "Neoclassical Economics and Principles of Sustainable Development". *Ecological Modelling* 38: 19-46.

Harrison, Jeremy, Kenton Miller y Jeffrey McNeely. 1984. "The World Coverage of Protected Areas: Development Goals and Environmental Needs". En *Proceedings of the World Congress on National Parks.* Bali, Indonesia, octubre 11-22, 1982.

IGM (Instituto Geográfico Militar), ed. 1974. *Carta Topográfica. Hoja 5569. Ushuaia: 1:500.00.* Buenos Aires: IGM.

_____. 1989. *Atlas de la República Argentina.* Buenos Aires: IGM.

INDEC (Instituto Nacional de Estadística y Censos). 1991. "Censo de población 1991". En *El Cronista Comercial*, mayo 18.

IUCN, ed. 1975. *World Directory of National Parks and Other Protected Areas.* Gland: IUCN.

IUCN, WWF y UNEP, eds. 1980. *World Conservation Strategy: Living Resource Conservation for Sustainable Development.* Gland: IUCN.

Koremblit, Gabriel, Hernán Vidal y Alejandro Winograd. 1990. "Nuevos pasos sobre un viejo camino: Recursos ambientales y desarrollo en la cordillera fueguina". En *Seminario Latinoamericano sobre Medio Ambiente y Desarrollo.* San Carlos de Bariloche, Argentina, octubre 15-21.

Kwong Echard, John. 1990. "Protecting the Environment: Old Rhetoric, New Imperatives". En William Poole, ed., *Studies in Organization Trends 5.* Washington, D.C.: Capital Research Center.

Ledec, George, y Robert Goodland. 1990. *Wildlands: Their Protection and Management in Economic Development.* Washington, D.C.: The World Bank.

Lele, Uma, y Steven Stone. 1989. *Population Pressure, the Environment and Agricultural Intensification: Variations on the Boserup Hypothesis.* MADIA Discussion Paper 4. Washington, D.C.: The World Bank.

Leonard, Jeffrey. 1989. *Environment and the Poor: Development Strategies for a Common Agenda.* New Brunswick, NJ: Transaction Books.

MAB, ed. 1989. *El hombre pertenece a la tierra: La cooperación internacional en la investigación ambiental.* Montevideo: MAB, UNESCO, ORCYT.

Machlis, Gary, y David Tichnell. 1985. *The State of the World's Parks: An International Assessment for Resource Management, Policy and Research*. Boulder y London: Westview Press.

McNeely, Jeffrey, y Kenton Miller. 1984. *National Parks: Conservation and Development: The Role of Protected Areas in Sustaining Society*. Washington, D.C.: IUCN y Smithsonian Institution Press.

McNeely, Jeffrey, Kenton Miller, Walter Reid, Russell Mittermeier y Timothy Werner. 1990. *Conserving the World's Biological Diversity*. Gland and Washington, D.C.: IUCN, WRI, CI, WWF y The World Bank.

Maihold, Gunther, y Víctor Urquidi, eds. 1990. *Diálogo con nuestro futuro común: Perspectivas latinoamericanas del Informe Bruntland*. Caracas: Nueva Sociedad.

Méndez Casariego, Hugo. 1990. "Hacia una producción ovina sostenible en Patagonia". En INTA, ed., *Juicio a nuestra agricultura: Hacia el desarrollo de una agricultura sostenible*. II Recursos Naturales. Buenos Aires: INTA.

Miller, Kenton. 1980. *Planificación de parques nacionales para el ecodesarrollo en Latinoamérica*. Madrid: FEPMA.

Morello, Jorge. 1985. *Perfil ecológico de Sudamérica: Características estructurales de Sudamérica y su relación con espacios semejantes del planeta*. Vol. 1. Madrid: Ediciones Cultura Hispánica, ICI.

Myers, Norman. 1988. *Natural Resource Systems and Human Exploitation Systems: Physiobiotic and Ecological Linkages*. Environment Department Working Paper 12. Washington, D.C.: The World Bank.

Ormazábal, César, ed. 1988. *Sistemas nacionales de áreas silvestres protegidas en América Latina*. Santiago de Chile: FAO-UNEP.

Pulley, Robert. 1989. *Making the Poor Creditworthy: A Case Study of the Integrated Rural Development Program in India*. World Bank Discussion Papers 58. Washington, D.C.: The World Bank.

Quesada Mateo, Carlos. 1990. *Estrategias de conservación para el desarrollo sostenible de Costa Rica*. San José: Servicios Litográficos.

Quiroga, Pablo. 1990. "El caso de Argentina". En Gunther Maihold y Víctor Urquidi, eds., *Diálogo con nuestro futuro común: Perspectivas latinoamericanas del Informe Bruntland*. Caracas: Nueva Sociedad. Pp. 73-91.

Radulovich, Ricardo. 1991. "Desarrollo agrícola en el trópico latinoamericano: El caso del pequeño agricultor vs. la economía nacional". *Interciencia* 16(3): 125-130.

Repetto, Robert, ed. 1985. *The Global Possible*. New Haven, CT: Yale University Press.

Senigagliesi, Carlos. 1990. "Estado actual y manejo de los recursos naturales particularmente el suelo, en el sector norte de la pampa húmeda". En INTA, ed., *Juicio a nuestra agricultura: Hacia el desarrollo de una agricultura sostenible*. II Recursos Naturales. Buenos Aires: INTA.

Sevilla Larrea, Roque. 1990. "El canje de la deuda por conservación: Los casos de Bolivia, Ecuador y Costa Rica". En Gunther Maihold y Víctor Urquidi, eds., *Diálogo con nuestro futuro común: Perspectivas latinoamericanas del Informe Bruntland*. Caracas: Nueva Sociedad. Pp. 139-161.

Shafer, Craig. 1990. *Nature Reserves*. Washington, D.C., y London: Smithsonian Institution Press.

Sobral, Alvar, y Alejandro Winograd. 1985. "Antecedentes para el desarrollo de la Isla de los Estados". *Boletín de Medio Ambiente y Urbanización* 3:12 (1984), 36-39.

Soriano, Alberto, y José Paruelo. 1990. "El pastoreo ovino: Principios ecológicos para el manejo de los campesinos". *Ciencia Hoy* 2(7): 44-53.

Sunkel, Osvaldo. 1990. "El difícil contexto internacional para un desarrollo sustentable". En Gunther Maihold y Víctor Urquidi, eds., *Diálogo con nuestro futuro común: Perspectivas latinoamericanas del Informe Bruntland*. Caracas: Nueva Sociedad. Pp. 35-51.

Thelen, Kyran, ed. 1985. *Un sistema de áreas silvestres protegidas para el Gran Chaco*. Documento Técnico 1. Asunción y Santiago de Chile: FAO-UNEP.

_____. 1990. *Informe del Taller Internacional sobre Areas Silvestres Protegidas y Comunidades Locales*. Monte Verde y Santiago de Chile: FAO-UNEP.

Udvardy, Miklos. 1975. *A Classification of the Biogeographical Provinces of the World*. IUCN Occasional Paper 18. Morges: IUCN.

_____. 1978. *World Biogeographical Provinces*. Sausalito: Co-evolution Quarterly.

Viglizzo, Ernesto. 1990. "Pampa Semiárida". En INTA, ed., *Juicio a nuestra agricultura: Hacia el desarrollo de una agricultura sostenible*. II Recursos Naturales. Buenos Aires: INTA.

White, Alan, y Gail Savina. 1987. "Community-Based Marine Reserves: A Philippine First". In *Coastal Zone '87*. Seattle, Washington, mayo.

Winograd, Alejandro. 1988. "Recomendaciones respecto del poblamiento, recuperación y manejo del oriente fueguino". *Informes del Programa del Extremo Oriental del Archipiélago Fueguino*. Ushuaia: PEOAF, Museo Territorial.

_____. 1990. *Environmental Public Policy and Development Contribution of National Parks and Equivalent Areas*. Working Document. Buenos Aires: CEPPA.

Winograd, Manuel. 1986. "Comportamiento de los grandes ecosistemas suramericanos: Ensayo de elaboración de los modelos cualitativos". *Textos para discusión: Proyecto prospectiva tecnológica para América Latina*. San Carlos de Bariloche: Fundación Bariloche.

_____. 1989a. "Simulación del uso de tierras: escenarios tendencial y sostenible". In Gilberto Gallopin, Isabel Gómez y Manuel Winograd, eds., *El futuro ecológico de un continente: Una visión prospectiva de América Latina*. San Carlos de Bariloche: Fundación Bariloche.

_____. 1989b. *Subsistema frutihortícola: Perfiles de estrategias de desarrollo*. Documento preliminar. Buenos Aires: Banco Mundial.

World Bank, ed. 1989. *Renewable Resource Management in Agriculture*. A World Bank Operations Evaluation Study. Washington, D.C.: The World Bank.

_____. 1990a. *Informe sobre el desarrollo mundial 1990: La pobreza*. Washington, D.C.: The World Bank.

_____. 1990b. *The World Bank and the Environment: First Annual Report. Fiscal 1990*. Washington, D.C.: The World Bank.

WRI-IIED (World Resources Institute–International Institute for Environment and Development), eds. 1988. *World Resources 1988–89: An Assessment of the Resource Base That Supports the Global Economy*. New York: Basic Books.

WRI (World Resources Institute). 1989. *Las riquezas naturales: El financiamiento de la conservación de recursos para el desarrollo*. Washington, D.C.: WRI.

_____. 1990. *1990–91. World Resources: A Guide to the Global Environment*. New York y Oxford: Oxford University Press.

11. Mexico's Environmental and Ecological Organizations and Movements

George F. Elmendorf and Joan A. Quillen

Ecology in Mexico is a large and complicated subject. This paper can only attempt to present an overview and to make available to research librarians some sources of information on the topic.

The following bibliographic sources, available from the authors, can be consulted for additional information.

1. A printout of titles held by the Library of Congress, located through subject headings and key word title searches. This list in no way shows all of the holdings in the field, as many titles would not be located by the search techniques and numerous newer titles are not yet cataloged.
2. A list from the *Boletín Bibliográfico Mexicano*, Año 51, enero-febrero 1991, published by Porrúa Hermanos, México, D.F. Thirty-nine titles are shown, mostly from well-known commercial publishers.
3. A pamphlet published by the World Wildlife Fund. It includes a bibliography, as well as the addresses of ecological organizations and projects in Mexico.
4. A copy of List 14, issued by Mexico Sur, on Ecology and Human Rights. One hundred thirty-seven titles are cited, perhaps half on ecology. Most of the titles are from smaller ecological organizations.

Fortunately, and perhaps strangely, there is little duplication among these four sources.

The first thing I would like to note about ecology in Mexico is the predominant position of the Mexican government both in causing ecological problems and in attempting to solve those problems. The Mexican government still means PRI, the Partido Revolucional Instititucional, and the president of Mexico has made ecology a basic part of his program. It is certainly an advantage for ecological pressure groups and organizations that the PRI has serious political competition and has had to appeal to different pressure groups. Formerly PRI had such a political monopoly that the pressures were more internal to the party.

A second important, if obvious, factor is that Mexico is a developing country. This means that the development/ecological trade-offs are more difficult than in the United States, for example.

A third important factor is the large indigenous population, primarily in southern Mexico. The dependence of these people on natural resources is important in ecological considerations. A segment of this population practices slash-and-burn agriculture, many of them are farming marginal land with difficult erosion problems, and most of them have serious health and nutritional problems. These factors complicate the ecological situation.

Although there are ecological organizations and projects in every Mexican state, ecological awareness and ecological pressure groups are primarily an urban phenomenon. Mexico City predominates, as would be expected, but there are numerous organizations in other large urban centers, such as Guadalajara, Monterrey, Puebla, and Tijuana. The Mexican government has two *secretarías* that deal with ecology; they are SEDUE, the Secretaría de Desarrollo Urbano e Ecología, and SARH, the Secretaría de Agricultura y Recursos Hidráulicos. Both SEDUE and SARH have offices and projects in every state of Mexico.

The opposition parties in Mexico exert ecological pressure on the PRI and the Mexican government through denunciations, demonstrations, newspaper articles, and political campaigns. The Partido de la Revolución Democrático (PRD), Partido Auténtico de la Revolución Mexicana (PARM), and Partido Popular Socialística (PPS) are the most aggressive. This pressure has probably resulted in more ecological sensitivity and ecologically positive actions and positions than would have been the case if the opposition did not exist. There is even a "Green" party, the Partido Ecológico Mexicano. In addition, there are numerous ecological organizations in Mexico such as INAINE, the Autonomous Institute of Ecological Research; MEN, the Mexican Ecological Movement; the Centro de Alternativas Ecologistas; the Group of 100; and the Mexican Public Health Association. A number of other organizations are mentioned below.

Mexican ecology has been much in the U.S. news lately in connection with the proposed Free Trade Agreement and the visit of the Mexican president, Carlos Salinas de Gortari. I believe this news may have given the impression that Mexican ecology is driven by U.S. pressure. Although ecology is an international concern and many U.S. and European ecology professionals are working in Mexico, ecological concerns and organizations in Mexico are internally driven and may well have a beneficial effect on U.S. ecology that is greater than the reverse.

It is certainly the case that Mexico City newspapers print much more ecological news than their U.S. counterparts, though most rural state newspapers do not print much ecological news beyond the president's speeches. An interesting phenomenon is the predominance of ecology in *The News*, an English-language newspaper published in Mexico City. Twenty-five years ago it was a wretched gossip rag, but for the last few years it has published ecological articles in almost every daily issue and is read by a number of ecologically oriented Mexicans.

As an example of what is taking place in Mexico, I would like to point to air pollution in Mexico City. Mexico City air is so badly polluted that at some times of the year it very seriously threatens the health and even lives of the residents. The Mexican government has taken several serious steps over the last few years to alleviate the pollution. A policy was initiated to forbid cars with Mexican license plates ending in a given number from driving on certain days in Mexico City. This resulted in fewer cars on any given day, though it must be noted that car ownership is rising and more cars are on the road.

The availability of lead-free or at least better quality gasoline has increased dramatically. Several years ago I bought a Mexican car that used regular gasoline, partly because I could not be sure I could get lead-free gasoline in many rural cities in Mexico. Now Magna Sin is widely available throughout Mexico. Pemex stations that carry it have been painted green for identification, and there are signs on every highway that indicate how far it is to the next Magna Sin station. This allows the mandating of catalytic converters on Mexican-built cars.

There is a plan to retrofit 40,000 taxis and 15,000 *combis* in Mexico City with catalytic converters, with an emphasis on pre-1984 models. In addition, *peseros* and other types of public auto transportation are being prohibited in certain sections of Mexico City.

The Air Quantity Index (IMECA) is reported each day in the newspapers. This index has been widely criticized as inadequate and inaccurate. In March 1991, the index underwent a number of changes in answer to pressure from ecological groups and health and science organizations. An environmental contingency plan was introduced by SEDUE to warn inhabitants of extreme pollution and to tell the population what to do in certain pollution circumstances. It is also reported that a Borderline Environmental Program will be launched in July 1991 to prevent polluting industry from coming into Mexico.

Another major step was the closing of the largest refinery in Mexico. This probably would not have been politically possible if the government had not previously prosecuted and jailed several high officials of the oil company union. The 18th of March refinery, located in the northern part of Mexico City, was closed and all its refining activities were shut down. The president of Mexico called on the city government to turn most of its 435 acres into green areas by planting trees. It should be noted that the storage facilities were not shut down, and this was criticized by environmentalists. This has been a general pattern. The government does something the ecological groups want; they applaud it but at the same time say it is not enough, and demand more.

SEDUE has been shutting down certain plants or parts of plants recently because they pollute. Ecologists applaud these moves but demand more stringent applications of the rules and, in fact, more stringent rules. Some of the difficult trade-offs are the loss of jobs and, in the case of the refinery, the need to import some petroleum products until a new refinery can be built. The newspapers carried information that a replacement refinery might be built near Monterrey. Immediate opposition arose and a "not-in-my-backyard" stance was taken by regional ecologists, state officials, and party leaders in Nuevo León.

Although earlier laws have addressed the environment in Mexico, the Ley General del Equilibrio Ecológico y Protección del Ambiente of March 1988 is the major environmental law in Mexico now in effect. It has been criticized in various ways by environmentalists, and there is pressure to amend it, to tighten it up, and to pass supplementary laws.

The First National Congress of Ecological Law took place May 28-31 in Guadalajara, Jalisco. This meeting was hosted by SEDUE and PROTEMA (Professionals and Technicians for the Improvement of the Environment). This meeting discussed the state of environmental law in Mexico and made recommendations for improvements.

One of the major international ecological groups working in Mexico is the World Wildlife Fund. This organization is headquartered in Washington, D.C., but has 26 regional offices in Mexico and is currently supporting 33 ecological projects in that country. Some of the most important projects supported by WWF are:

1. Biological and Institutional Overview of Oaxaca
2. Conservation and Natural Resource Management in Chiapas
3. Conservation of Monarch Butterfly Overwintering Habitats
4. Support to the Sian Ka'an Biosphere Reserve
5. Conservation of El Triunfo Tropical Rain Forest in Chiapas
6. Education, Training, Research, Conservation and Sustainable Use of the Selva Lancandona

7. Diagnostic Study and Evaluation of El Ocote Ecological Reserve
8. Support for the Preparation of a Conservation and Development Plan for the Chimalapas Region of Oaxaca
9. General Plan for the Conservation and Management of the Wildlife in the Revillagigedo Islands.

The WWF offers a useful pamphlet on Mexico, available from its office (1250 Twenty-Fourth Street NW, Washington, DC 20037). This pamphlet lists the offices in Mexico and provides addresses, phones, and names of people to contact. It also includes 19 bibliographic references. Finally, this pamphlet has a list of 79 priority areas in Mexico for the conservation of biological diversity.

An important group mentioned in the WWF pamphlet is Cultura Ecológica (CEAC). This group worked with the government of Querétaro to establish Mexico's first state environmental law and set of regulations. They are also working with the states of Oaxaca and Tlaxcala to establish their state ecological laws.

There are a number of problems of an ecological nature at border areas between the United States and Mexico. These problems are well discussed in a number of books, many of them published by the Colegio de la Frontera Norte. *El medio ambiente como fuente de conflicto en la región binacional México-Estados Unidos*, by Roberto Sánchez (Tijuana, Baja Central America, Mexico: Colegio de la Frontera Norte, 1990) is one of them. He discusses sewage and water pollution and the problem of air pollution caused by copper smelters both in Arizona and Sonora. He particularly emphasizes binational negotiations. It includes an ample bibliography.

Several other problems that have been in the news focus on the hawkbill turtles and tuna. Turtles are taken by poachers primarily at their breeding grounds. The turtles are doubly endangered, as the eggs are taken for local consumption. Many of the turtle shells are sold to Japan, which has an artisan industry working the shells into combs and other items. Japan has recently agreed to phase out the importation over a number of years. Mexico has put troops at the breeding areas during breeding periods to discourage the poachers. The U.S. tuna industry has imposed a boycott on Mexican tuna owing to their manner of netting the fish, which kills dolphins and/or porpoises. Mexico is working to change the fishing methods of its tuna fleets to end the boycott.

There is a serious problem of dumping of toxic chemicals in Mexico by U.S. companies. It is a grave health risk that is difficult to avoid in view of the porosity of the U.S.-Mexican border. Another serious problem is well discussed in the book *Naturaleza muerta. Los plaguicidas en México*, by Iván Restrepo. Many pesticides and herbicides that are prohibited in the United States are sold in Mexico, primarily by U.S. companies or their Mexican subsidiaries. The field-workers suffer sickness and perhaps even death owing to the use of these chemicals, and groundwater supplies are contaminated. The solution would seem to be strengthening of Mexican laws to prohibit dangerous pesticides, fertilizers, and herbicides. Restrepo's book also has an ample bibliography.

There is also an active antinuclear movement in Mexico that centers on the Laguna Verde facility in the state of Veracruz. Several groups are involved, including La Campaña de la Población en Contra de Laguna Verde Nuclear (CCLAVE) and Comité Antinuclear de Madres Veracruzanas. They publish pamphlets and attempt to educate the general public to protest Laguna Verde.

The institution that publishes the most is the Instituto Nacional sobre Investigaciones sobre Recursos Bióticos (INIREB), located in Xalapa, Veracruz. This organization's publications date back at least to 1980 and include both serials and monographs. It offers a two-year masters degree program, and has a staff of more than 150 people and a library of more than 16,000 volumes. The World Wildlife Fund pamphlet claims that it was disbanded by the Mexican government in 1988. The WWF pamphlet also mentions that a number of the members of INIREB formed ECOSFERA, A.C. in 1989. There is some bibliographic evidence that its publishing program has been taken over by the Instituto de Ecología, which has long shared an address with INIREB. In any case, the physical plant is still in Xalapa and was visited recently by Joan Quillen as part of the research for this paper.

Another major source of publications is the Centro de Ecodesar-rollo in Mexico City. It is a large organization with good facilities and has been the recipient of numerous international awards.

A third major organization is the Centro de Ecología associated with UNAM, whose only publication is a serial called *OIKOS*. It is the major ecological think-tank in Mexico. It is in part from international funds.

Various other states have important ecological centers. Among them are two especially worthy of mention. The Centro de Investi-gaciones Ecológicas del Sureste in San Cristóbal de las Casas is a fairly large research center that has been publishing for at least ten years. It has a large library and is open to the public. The Centro Ecológico de Sonora is outside Hermosillo. It does not publish much, but concentrates on educational work. It has a library and is open to the public.

I would like to end this paper with a personal story that, perhaps, is illustrative of the peculiar ecological problems that are common to developing countries.

In the fall of 1988, Joan Quillen and I crossed the border at Tapachula, Chiapas on our first exploratory trip to southern Mexico. We ran into the most violent rainstorm either of us had ever seen, the tail end of hurricane Gilbert. This hurricane did a tremendous amount of damage to buildings, roads, and bridges in Campeche, Yucatan, and Quintana Roo. Six months or so later, we drove through the Yucatan Peninsula and could still see a great deal of damage, including standing water in low places, many thatch houses, destroyed, and a large number of downed trees. We could not see or know the great damage done to forests in Quintana Roo that were not on any road. During the Yucatan Peninsula trip, we met an American forester who had married a woman from Quintana Roo and was working for SARH in Quintana Roo. He told us of a number of interesting forestry projects on which he was working in Quintana Roo. Shortly thereafter we began to read about a fire in the forests of Quintana Roo. It went on for the better part of a year, with increasing criticism from ecologists concerning why it was not put out. The governor of Quintana Roo spoke in the newspapers about the difficulty of the terrain, the lack of equipment such as airplanes to bomb the fire with retardant chemicals, and the like. It finally burned itself out, mostly, it seems, in the new rainy season and because of the fact that on one side it ran into the ocean.

A few months later I made another trip which took me through Quintana Roo, and I stopped to see my forester friend. He had been a member of the investigating team that the intense criticism had made necessary. He was very circumspect, as he wanted to continue living and working in Quintana Roo, but he did tell me it was a series of fires rather than one fire. The causes were also multiple and included lightning and slash-and-burn that got out of control. Two other probable causes were deliberate arson to clear land for cattle raising rather than peasant agriculture and deliberate arson to clear land for a possible tourist development on an isolated beach in Quintana Roo.

I hope this brief survey of ecology in Mexico has been helpful in the sense of indicating the richness of the environmental movement and its publications.

12. El medio ambiente en Chile hoy: Informe y bibliografía

Marta Domínguez Díaz

En octubre de 1559, Pedro de Valdivia, refiriéndose al Reino de Chile, escribía al Emperador Carlos V: "Certifico a vuestra Majestad que, después que las Indias se comenzaron a descubrir, hasta hoy, no se ha descubierto tal tierra a vuestra Majestad; es más poblada que la Nueva España, muy sana, fertilísima e apacible, de muy lindo temple, riquísima de minas de oro sobre la tierra y en ella no hay otra falla, si no es de españoles y caballos . . .".

Lejos está Chile ahora de tales elogios, pues en este momento responde a todas las catástrofes derivadas de los cambios tecnológicos ocurridos en las últimas décadas en el país, los cuales han venido acompañados de la mayor producción de contaminantes y de degradación de los recursos naturales. Y si la tecnología es producto de la transformación de los recursos naturales en instrumentos que tienen como fin el mejoramiento de la calidad de vida de la población, transformación que no ocurre sin la participación del hombre, es sólo responsabilidad del hombre, que dicho objetivo se cumpla. De aquí la necesidad de crear en él una conciencia ecológica profunda.

La constitución chilena le asigna al estado un rol insustituible en el adecuado manejo de las políticas ambientales: "La aplicación de los instrumentos de regulación de la política nacional ambiental, resulta inoperante en la gran mayoría de los casos o genera conflictos. El caso típico lo constituye el establecimiento de prohibiciones administrativas o legales para explotar un recurso (caso del loco, el erizo, el choro zapato, el ostión), lo que provoca la transformación del carácter abierto de la actividad, en actividad clandestina. Fiscalizar se hace muy dificultoso por lo extenso del litoral chileno" (*Ambiente y Desarrollo*, Número Especial, 1990, pp. 111-115).

El desarrollo industrial, minero y agrícola se ha llevado a cabo prácticamente sin ninguna restricción ambiental, ni de conservación de los recursos naturales. Ninguno de los proyectos realizados tuvo una evaluación del impacto ambiental, ni se han impuesto restricciones a las empresas extranjeras o chilenas que llevan a cabo sus proyectos.

El estilo de desarrollo y el modelo de diversificación de las exportaciones implantados ha sido el de construir una estructura gigante de desgaste de la naturaleza que ha traído consigo la contaminación atmosférica, la sobre-explotación marina, la desertificación, la degradación de recursos, la marginalidad, la erosión de suelos, la sobrepoblación urbana, la contaminación química, la basura, la destrucción de la flora y fauna, la contaminación acústica y la pérdida de identidad cultural de los pueblos precolombinos (Informe RENACE, 1989). Se dio mayor valorización al intento de salir del subdesarrollo, sin pensar que la calidad ambiental juega un rol importante en la calidad de vida (Mires, 1990).

Sin embargo, la cultura y grado de civilización de Chile no han estado ajenos del todo a la temática ambiental. Los primeros escritos acerca de las repercusiones que tuvo la explotación minera en la destrucción de la naturaleza humana provinieron de los cronistas de la Conquista, particularmente aquellos del Padre Bartolomé de Las Casas (1559), quien decía que los indios no sólo morían a consecuencia del trabajo a que eran sometidos, sino porque la actividad minera destruía rápidamente sus fundamentos naturales de existencia, por el deterioro provocado en la naturaleza por la actividad extractiva, y porque catalizaba en su entorno una serie de actividades económicas que los indios desconocían, como por ejemplo la utilización de medios de transporte, el desarrollo de centros urbanos en territorios que antes estaban dedicados a la agricultura, a la pesca o a la recolección. Coincide con el Padre Las Casas el geógrafo chileno Pedro Cunill (*La América Andina*, 1979), que relata como fue destruida la vegetación en el norte de Chile por los propios animales dedicados al transporte, en vastas áreas que conformaban, tanto para las poblaciones indígenas como para la propia autorreproducción de la naturaleza, amplias reservas de biomasa. Otra actividad económica relevante, la agroganadería, completó la obra devastadora de las reservas ecológicas, iniciada por la minería. La incorporación de numerosas cabezas de ganado vacuno y equino, pero sobre todo de cabras y ovejas, alteró absolutamente las relaciones ecológicas que habían contraído los indígenas. Claudio Gay en sus 24 tomos de estudios sobre Chile (1830-1842), ya advertía sobre el avance de las dunas, cuando se elimina el bosque nativo (Huneeus, 1991).

A la luz de la bibliografía existente, se descubre que desde hace casi dos décadas, investigadores rigurosos como Gastó, Grau, Geisse, Stutzin, Hayek, Max-Neef, Sunkel, Saavedra, Hoffmann y muchos otros, cada uno desde su centro de estudios, agota horas en investigación y escritos destinados a ir creando una cultura sobre el medio ambiente, en Chile. Corresponde destacar entre los centros de estudios, al CIPMA (Centro de Investigación y Planificación del Medio Ambiente), creado en 1979, cuya difusión la realiza a través de una amplia gama de materiales bibliográficos, y a través de la organización de congresos, encuentros y seminarios periódicos. También destacan el PNUMA (Programa de Naciones Unidas para el Medio Ambiente), REDMA (Red Regional de Información sobre Medio Ambiente en Chile), cuyo nodo central funciona en CIPMA, y al que están integrados importantes estamentos académicos y gubernamentales. También en forma especial destacamos a RENACE (Red Nacional de Acción Ecológica), cuyo Informe del Primer Encuentro en Santiago, en abril de 1989, es un documento básico de diagnóstico de los problemas ambientales de la I a la XII Regiones de Chile, inclusive Isla de Pascua. Es interesante conocer los acuerdos a que arrivó este Primer Encuentro, pues reflejan claramente el deterioro ambiental de Chile y porque participaron en él organizaciones de acción ecológica de todo el país. Se acuerda realizar un segundo encuentro; establecer coordinaciones regionales; solicitar una Carta Pastoral en defensa del medio ambiente a la Conferencia Episcopal de Chile; solidarizar con las reivindicaciones ecológicas y culturales de la Ley de Pesca que va al congreso, pues representa un serio peligro para la economía de los pescadores artesanales e industrias nacionales y un deterioro de la fuente de recursos para generaciones futuras; solicitar la creación de un Programa Nacional de Educación Ambiental; poner término a la contaminación ambiental producida por la basura, contaminación del aire, emanaciones industriales de empresas químicas, pesqueras, mineras y forestales, sobre todo éstas últimas, en el Golfo de Arauco; poner fin a la explotación del bosque nativo y reemplazarlo por monocultivos forestales; denunciar el uso de pesticidas y anabólicas en la producción de alimentos, que están afectando el equilibrio ecológico y la salud de la población; prohibición del uso de aerosoles elaborados con clorofluorocarbonos que destruyen la capa de ozono. Se realizó un diagnóstico de los problemas ambientales a partir de la información de los grupos participantes; se crearon comisiones regionales para llevar a cabo los acuerdos tomados. El material recogido permitió la elaboración del Mapa del Descalabro Ecológico de Chile, que se dio a conocer en un número especial de la revista *APSI*, de julio de 1990.

Por su parte el gobierno, de acuerdo a lo señalado en sus bases programáticas, definió que su política ambiental concentraría sus esfuerzos en dos áreas gruesas de acción: por una parte, lograr un uso y explotación racional de los recursos naturales renovables, particularmente los hidrobiológicos, bosques nativos y suelos y, por otra parte, reducir los niveles de contaminación del aire, agua y suelo en aquellas áreas en que ello ha alcanzado magnitudes tan críticas que afectan la calidad de vida y salud de la población. Para cumplir estos fines, se ha nominado al Ministerio de Bienes, Tierras y Colonización, que por su rol de preservador de los recursos naturales del país, actúe de coordinador, junto a los ministerios de economía, transporte, salud, educación, agricultura, vivienda y municipalidades, para los estudios, diagnósticos y políticas que se implementarán en relación con el deterioro del medio ambiente, a través de CONAMA (Comisión Nacional de Medio Ambiente), COLMA (Comisión de Legislación Ambiental) y la Comisión Especial de Descontaminación de la Región Metropolitana, creadas recientemente, además de los servicios y unidades del medio ambiente que funcionan a nivel de universidades e instancias privadas y cuyos programas de acción ya están preparados.

Debemos agregar que actualmente existen en Chile más de 200 cuerpos dedicados a estudios ecológicos, según lo registra el DIRPER (1990) y el DIRINS (1989), directorios ambos, realizados por el Centro de Documentación del CIPMA.

Evidentemente Chile carece de técnicos en estudios de impacto ambiental en cantidad y calidad, de manera que se está promoviendo el intercambio de experiencias de los ambientalistas europeos con las personas e instituciones vinculadas al problema en Chile. CIPMA prepara el IV Encuentro Científico del Medio Ambiente para 1992.

Si tomamos como punto de referencia el Mapa del Descalabro Ecológico de Chile (1990) y el Informe de RENACE, observaremos que Chile presenta 4.200 km de litoral expuesto y más o menos 3.000 km de litoral interno en la zona patagónica, lo que lo pone en alto riesgo para la contaminación por el mar.

La I, II y III regiones son dañadas por los procesos de salinización y alcalinización del suelo, por agentes minerales. Los relaves mineros que se vierten en los ríos y mar, han ocasionado grandes colapsos. Es conocido el caso de Chañaral en cuya costa no existe vida de ningún tipo hasta 15 km mar adentro, producto del vaciado de desechos de los minerales de cobre del Salvador y Potrerillos. A raíz de un fallo de la Corte Suprema, la Corporación del Sobre (CODELCO), habilitó un tranque como vaciadero artificial que soluciona el problema sólo en parte (*APSI*, 1990). Un informe del Colegio Médico apunta que, en Chuquicamata, el mineral de cobre más grande de Chile, en el día en que no hay viento, los escolares no pueden salir a la calle, por la contaminación del aire con dióxido de azufre y arsénico. En 1980, el 21% de las muertes en la zona se debió a enfermedades broncopulmonares.

En la IV región, como en las anteriores, la actividad minera afecta el aire y amenaza con monopolizar el agua y devolverla a sus cursos, contaminada. Sufre la sobreexplotación de peces, mariscos y algas, y la fetidez por industrias de harina de pescado en Coquimbo. Fuerte erosión y degradación de los vegetales por tala, sobrepastoreo e intensa explotación minera (Informe RENACE, 1989).

En la región Central, el mayor descalabro se advierte en la contaminación del litoral de la V región, ya que en el país el 98% de las aguas servidas no tiene tratamiento. Esto ocasiona que se vacíen al mar, a los ríos y lagos, altas cantidades de bacterias, pesticidas, hidrocarburos y desechos minerales y tóxicos que van aniquilando la vida acuática. Estudios señalan que la fundición de Chagres en Catemu, zona central, lanza al aire de 2 a 5 toneladas de azufre por hora. Otro tanto ocurre con las fundiciones de ventanas y caletones, en la zona.

El presidente del Consejo de Ancianos de Isla de Pascua, Alberto Hotus, expresó en el Encuentro RENACE, que la isla ha enfrentado serios problemas ecológicos, a raíz de la construcción, y luego la ampliación del aeropuerto de Mataveri, que seccionó en dos partes la Isla, aislando el sector de Rano Kau de la población humana ubicada en Hanga Roa, alterando seriamente las costumbres de la población pascuense. Los caminos de la isla se observan bastante erosionados con la maquinaria pesada, y continuamente los están rellenando con escoria roja sacada de los cerros. La lluvia arrastra dicha escoria que va a caer al mar, causando la muerte de fauna y flora marina, por la contaminación de la escoria. En las canteras han producido hoyos de 15 a 20 metros de profundidad, que luego se convierten en basurales. Lo que fue el cerro Tararaina, de 130 metros de altura, y que fuera ocupado como material de relleno para la ampliación de Mataveri, quedó convertido en una depresión que hoy es también un basural. Además agrega que sufren de una enorme contaminación acústica por el ruido de los aviones y la pérdida de su vida apacible por el ir y venir de los turistas.

En lo que respecta a la región metropolitana, el aire de Santiago se cuenta entre los tres más contaminados del mundo, junto a São Paulo y Ciudad de México. Alrededor de 480 mil vehículos motorizados circulan en Santiago, y los indices de contaminación son la causa de un 20% de niños con afecciones respiratorias que llenan los servicios de urgencia. La situación geográfica de Santiago es particularmente inconveniente para la lucha contra la contaminación, toda vez que las estribaciones de la cordillera de los Andes dificulta la circulación de los vientos que desde el sur y el sureste, soplan sobre la ciudad

(Alessandri, 1989). Pero no sólo el aire es problema ecológico en la región metropolitana. La ciudad produce más de un millón de toneladas de desechos sólidos al año, que se depositan en "rellenos sanitarios" ubicados en medio de poblaciones marginales. Ellos producen gases y fetidez que emanan de la tierra en los patios y en los pisos de las casas.

El río Mapocho, el Zanjón de la Aguada y el Canal San Carlos, que cruzan la ciudad a lo largo y ancho, son vertederos de aguas servidas sin tratamiento, de 4.365.481 habitantes (cifra de junio 1990), lo que desemboca en altos niveles de hepatitis, tifoidea, parasitosis y, ahora, de alto riesgo por el cólera. La contaminación acústica de unos 80 decibeles provoca daños fisiológicos y psicosociológicos y afecta el sueño, el rendimiento laboral y la comunicación.

La contaminación de los alimentos por riego con aguas servidas y pesticidas en el caso de las frutas y las carnes es amenazante. Investigadores de la Universidad Austral de Chile detectaron residuos tóxicos en la leche y en la carne proveniente de la X y XI regiones debido al uso de pesticidas permitidos, y/o prohibidos, en las empastadas. De ahí al hombre, hay un paso. Se calcula un gasto de 50 millones de dólares anuales en importación de plaguicidas para la actividad hortofrutícola (Mires, 1990).

Entre Linares y Llanquihue donde hay 6 millones de hectáreas agrícolas, el proceso de erosión abarca el 73,7% de los suelos. Se sostiene que 40.000 hectáreas de suelo fértil se destruyen en un año en Chile. Un estudio acabado de esta debacle lo han presentado los profesores Juan Gasto, ingeniero agrónomo de la Universidad Católica, y Mario Peralta, especialista de la Universidad de Chile, quien en su Mapa Preliminar (1978), demuestra que Chile se está convirtiendo en un desierto, lo que ratifica en un texto didáctico, "Uso, clasificación y conservación de los suelos" (1986), cuando prueba que el 50% de la superficie total de Chile está afectada por procesos de desertificación.

Las características ambientales de los ecosistemas del país presentan diferencias marcadas de un lugar a otro del territorio. Las estadísticas indican que una ínfima proporción de un 0,12% de las tierras son de óptima calidad. Un 13% son sólo arables, sin uso agrícola y un 65,1% corresponden a desiertos, cordilleras, glaciares, playas y roqueríos (Gasto y Schmidt, 1990). El clima templado secoestival o mediterráneo del centro del país donde se conjugan las noches frías y los cielos luminosos, presenta las condiciones favorables para la producción agrícola y para los asentamientos humanos. Las condiciones climáticas varían entre rangos muy amplios. Las capacidades de uso de la atmósfera en cada caso son muy diferentes.

La cordillera de los Andes localizada en el lado oriente del país, a pesar de su baja productividad vegetal y animal, se comporta como una cuenca de captación de agua que da origen a numerosos ríos, que permiten el riego, el desarrollo de industrias, ciudades, generadores eléctricos y minería.

Los recursos vegetales y animales del país obedecen a condicionantes ambientales del suelo, atmósfera, agua y clima. Sobre el uso del espacio, la tendencia de las últimas décadas es a agruparse en centros urbanos, lo que se estima en un 83% urbano y un 17% rural. El uso industrial del espacio ha carecido absolutamente de restricción ecológica. Santiago cuenta con unas 100 industrias contaminantes.

El uso agrícola y ganadero de la tierra ha desencadenado problemas de erosión, desertificación y deterioro de la pradera de extensas áreas del país, en sectores del altiplano, precordillera y estepa patagónica, incluyendo la destrucción de algunos parques nacionales. Según CONAF, Chile posee 30 parques nacionales, 37 reservas nacionales y 10 monumentos nacionales, abarcando 13.650.626 hectáreas, que corresponden a un 18,05% del territorio nacional (Gastó, 1989).

En el área forestal, que se divide en 1.300.000 hectáreas de cultivos forestales, especialmente *Pinus radiata*, 7.616.500 hectáreas de bosque nativo con valor maderero, y 13.604.088 hectáreas de montes de protección y monte abierto-pradera de escaso valor maderero (Chile Forestal, 1988), también hay terrenos devastados y mediocremente habilitados.

La minería (minas, tranques de relave y refinerías) se ha localizado principalmente en la zona norte, en terrenos de montaña y ondulados, donde la actividad agrícola, urbana e industrial es insignificante. La faena minera provoca la destrucción de la cubierta vegetal de los recursos mineros y de sus alrededores, quedando extensas áreas desprotegidas, lo cual no se reemplaza una vez concluida la faena (Gastó y Schmidt, 1990). En los últimos 400 años en el territorio Chile, ha desaparecido el 75% de la superficie forestal. Hoy existen 12 especies arbóreas-arbustivas en peligro de extinción y 26 en carácter de vulnerables, entre las que se cuentan la araucaria y el alerce. Hasta hace cuatro años el 87,9% de la superficie forestal era autóctona. Hoy el pino insigne foráneo es el monocultivo mayor de Chile y eso acarrea daños ecológicos como disminución de los cursos hídricos, procesos de aridez, pérdida de agua mayor que lo normal y disminución de la fauna (Aaron Caviedes, CONAF). La tala de bosque nativo para convertirlo en astillas es un asunto muy serio en la IX y X regiones. Una empresa suiza ha comenzado a hacer astillas 100.000 hectáreas de bosque de

lenga, único árbol de tamaño en una zona muy erosionada. Afortuna-
damente el nuevo gobierno volvió a prohibir la tala de la araucaria,
para felicidad del pueblo pehuenche que depende vitalmente de dicho
árbol, al que venera como sagrado. En el boletín *INFORMA CODEFF*,
de abril 1990, se transcribe una carta del presidente Aylwin a la
comunidad de Quinquén en que les expresa su gran preocupación por
la grave situación que los afecta a raíz del corte de los bosques de
araucaria, de cuyo fruto los indígenas se alimentan, así como por la
amenaza que están sufriendo de ser expulsado de las tierras que han
habitado por cientos de años. Les expresa su voluntad de adoptar
medidas para proteger a los comunidades indígenas en lo que respecta
a sus tierras ancestrales y a la preservación de los bosques que los
rodean. Ya se encuentra en vigencia el decreto que declara a la
araucaria "Monumento Nacional", de acuerdo al espíritu de la
Convención para la Protección de la Flora y Fauna y las Bellezas
Escénicas Naturales de América, así como al del Protocolo de
Montréal, a los que Chile está suscrito. La protección de su medio
forestal que decretan los países desarrollados para respetar el hábitat
de algunas especies en peligro de extinción, aumenta el interés y la
presión sobre el bosque nativo chileno (Mires, 1990).

En los relativo a la preservación forestal, destaca el visionario
estudio "La Sobrevivencia de Chile" (Elizalde, 1970), y las innume-
rables investigaciones científicas de especies y bosques realizadas por
investigadores de la Universidad de Chile, Universidad Austral de Chile
y del Instituto Forestal (INFOR). En el año 1989 se vendieron al
exterior, 1 millón doscientos mil metros cúbicos de madera. El 84,6%
de los productos forestales que se exportan y la casi totalidad de las
astillas provienen del bosque nativo. La depredación y desertificación
de la zona de bosques es dramática, pues a la sobreexplotación de los
bosques, hay que agregar la denominada "quema controlada" del
bosque nativo. Nadie puede cultivar estas tierras erosionadas, lo que
significa empujar a miles de familias a la ciudad y aumentar así las
poblaciones callampas.

"Lo que ocurre con los bosques de araucarias, arrayanes, pataguas,
alerces, coigües y canelos, es capítulo aparte: la maquinaria los voltea,
los transporta y tritura hasta dejarlos convertidos en las renombradas
astillas que alimentan las plantas de celulosa de Suecia y Japón"
(Huneeus, 1991).

En lo que a fauna se refiere, fuera del peligro de extinción de
algunas especies como el huemul, el lobo de dos pelos, la langosta, el
calibú y otras vulnerables a la extinción, como los camélidos (alpaca,
llama, guanaco), y la ballena de la Antártica, la sobreexplotación

marina es el deterioro de mayor magnitud a lo largo de todo el litoral, y alcanza a todas las especies, tanto de flora como de fauna. El 90% de la captura es para la producción de harina de pescado; el resto se divide para conserva y para el consumo de los chilenos. Las zonas críticas de devastación marina son Chiloé, Magallanes, algunas del norte de Chile y la Antártica, cuyos jóvenes pingüinos están siendo exportados a Japón.

La instalación de la industria de harina de pescado ha significado la aniquilación de toneladas de peces, sin importar cuáles. Los buques-factoría que se instalan arrasan todo tipo de especímenes, además de envilecer la belleza de la zona. El escritor chileno Pablo Huneeus en sus *Crónicas ecológicas* (1991) destaca la diferencia con que el pescador ribereño realiza su actividad, sin afectar el medio ambiente, ni poner en riesgo la subsistencia de los bancos de peces. Las empresas pesqueras, con 45 plantas de harina de pescado, que procesan diariamente 60 mil toneladas de fauna marina, han despoblado el mar de anchoveta o de merluza, que agregamos, era el alimento popular básico en Chile, de muy bajo costo. El mar olor que despiden los buques-factoría se sufre en Arica, Iquique, Coquimbo, Talcahuano, Puerto Montt y Chiloé. Serios estudios sobre la situación del mar son realizados por el Instituto de Fomento Pesquero (IFOP), la Subsecretaría de Pesca, la Escuela de Ciencias del Mar de la Universidad Católica de Valparaíso y el Instituto Oceanográfico de la Aramada. La dictación de la nueva Ley de Pesca, enviada recientemente al congreso, dispondrá del futuro de la variada vida marina de Chile.

En 1985, científicos ingleses descubrieron una destrucción del 40% del ozono sobre la Antártica. Sus efectos son aún impredecibles, pero sin duda, es un problema que atañe a todo el planeta. La Antártica chilena soporta además la extracción indiscriminada del crustáceo krill para la exportación.

Agregaremos que el gobierno chileno muestra gran preocupación y realiza las averiguaciones pertinentes, porque habría en la zona de la patagonia argentina, un proyecto de instalar un basurero nuclear, de grave repercusión para Chile. Ya en ocasión anterior la comunidad chilena del norte, mediante acciones varias, logró desbaratar un intento de instalar basureros tóxicos en tierra del desierto.

En este momento el gobierno prepara una legislación apropiada a un desarrollo sustentable, más solidario y menos reduccionista. El problema, dice el ministro de tierras, Luis Alvarado, requiere un alto consenso, pues hay que poner de acuerdo a inversionistas, empresas públicas y privadas, organismos científicos y académicos y a la población toda. El gobierno de Chile, agrega Alvarado, tiene una propuesta de creación de un fondo mundial para disponer recursos que sirvan para la reconversión tecnológica de las industrias que emiten clorofluorcarbono, que es el que destruye la capa de ozono.

Por otro lado, a ciudadanía consciente de la debacle ecológica que afecta Chile genera desde todos los ámbitos proposiciones para implementar una política ecológica nacional, que parta desde los programas escolares y universitarios y se extienda con campañas a lo largo y ancho del país. La corte suprema ha fijado un caudal de jurisprudencia ecológica, comenzando por las fábricas de harina de pescado por la fetidez que despiden, siguiendo con los vertederos de basuras, y las empresas del cobre por la contaminación del aire con dióxido de azufre y arsénico. El movimiento de jóvenes, Alianza Humanista-Verde, desarrolla una actividad programada año a año de protesta pública, con afiches, por la contaminación nuclear que de una manera u otra, amenaza a Chile. Las radios desarrollan programas dominicales, como el muy conocido "La Manzana", y a su vez la televisión realiza constantes foros y spots publicitarios, llamando a la conciencia de los chilenos sobre el problema de nuestro medio ambiente tan deteriorado.

Terminaré este informe repitiendo como muy oportuna la aseveración de Manfred Max-Neef, Premio Nobel Alternativo de Economía 1983, actual director de CEPAUR (Centro de Estudios y Promoción de Alternativas Urbano Rurales), en su obra *Ecodesarrollo y estilos de desarrollo* (1989): "o habrá sociedad ecológica, o no habrá sociedad, porque ahora es una cuestión de sobrevivencia".

BIBLIOGRAFIA

Abalos Koning, José A., y Francisco Sabatini D. *Contribuciones de los organismos no gubernamentales a esquemas de desarrollo sustentable.* Documento Trabajo, 8. Santiago: CIPMA, 1989. 35 pp.

Aguilera, J. A., J. A. Guzmán y M. Rutman. *Recursos renovables chilenos.* Santiago: Ediciones Universidad Católica de Chile, 1984.

Alessandri, Gustavo. *Santiago agoniza: La contaminación.* Santiago: Editorial Ver, 1989. 190 pp.

Alianza Humanista Verde. *Política del Partido para el Medio Ambiente.* Santiago, 1991.

Almeyda, E., y F. Sáez. *Recopilación de datos climáticos de Chile y mapas sinópticos respectivos.* Santiago: Ministerio de Agricultura, 1958.

Altieri, M. A., y J. A. Rodríguez. *Acción ecológica del fuego en el matorral mediterráneo de Chile, en Rinconada de Maipú.* Santiago: Facultad de Agronomía, Universidad de Chile, 1975. Tesis.

Arana Espina, Patricio M. *Análisis de pesquerías chilenas.* Valparaíso: Escuela de Ciencias del Mar, Universidad Católica de Valparaíso, 1983. 247 pp., mapas, gráficos. Medidas para la racionalización de la pesquería chilena. Contiene la Conferencia del Mar.

_____. *Recursos marinos del Pacífico. Marine Resources of the Pacific.* Santiago: Oregon State University; U.S. International Sea Grant Program; Escuela de Ciencias del Mar; Instituto de Estudios Internacionales, 1983. 608 pp., apendia, mapas, gráficos. Trabajos presentados a la Conferencia Internacional sobre Recursos Naturales, Viña del Mar, Chile, mayo 1983.

Aranda, R., A. Bergquist y S. González. "Intoxicación crónica por cobre de origen industrial en bovinos de carne". *Archivos de Medicina Veterinaria* (Santiago de Chile), vol. 17, no. 1, 1985.

Araya, Leonardo. "Centralismo: Deterioro ambiental social y humano". *Eco Tribuna* (Santiago de Chile, CODEFF), enero 1991, pp. 28-30.

Armanet Armanet, Pilar, y Daniel Asenjo. *La regulación de las principales pesquerías chilenas y la Convención sobre Derechos del Mar.* Serie Estudios Especiales, 60. Santiago: Instituto de Estudios Internacionales, 1983.

Arnzt, J. C., et al. *Influencia de un rodal de "Pinus radiata" D Don sobre algunos factores ecológicos en comparación al campo abierto.* Valdivia: Facultad de Ingeniería Forestal, Universidad Austral de Chile, 1969. Tesis.

Astorga, Eduardo. "Fundamentos de una política nacional ambiental". *Eco Tribuna* (Santiago de Chile, CODEFF), agosto 1990, pp. 18-21.

Baer von Lochow, Heinrich von. *Gestión del medio ambiente y desarrollo regional: Algunas ideas para estimular la acción.* Documento Trabajo, 9. Santiago: CIPMA, 1989. 29 pp.

Bahamonde N., Nibaldo. *Posible contribución de la ciencia y de la tecnología a desarrollar en Chile para el sector pesquero, con miras a un desarrollo ambientalmente sustentable.* Documento Trabajo, 2. Santiago: CIPMA, 1989. 30 pp.

Baquedano, Manuel. *La seguridad ecológica en América del Sur.* Documento de Estudio, 2. Comisión Sudamericana de Paz, 1988. 84 pp., notas, bibliografía. Autor, director del Instituto de Ecología Política. El documento incluye un directorio de organizaciones sudamericanas de ecología y medio ambiente.

Beas, Josefina, et al. *Diario de un explorador ecológico.* Santiago: TELEDUC, 1988. 88 pp. Material didáctico.

_____, et al. *La ecología: Un desafío educacional. Estrategia metodológica para la educación ambiental.* Santiago: Facultad de Educación, Universidad Católica de Chile, TELEDUC, 1988. 253 pp.

Borcosque Díaz, José L. *Proyecto de reducción de riesgos e impacto ambiental del Zanjón de la Aquada.* Santiago: Universidad de Santiago, 1987.

Bráñez, Raúl. *Seguridad ambiental en América del Sur: Los principales problemas y los nuevo desafíos a la soberanía.* Santiago: Comisión Sudamericana de Paz, 1990.

Brigagão, Clovis. *Amazonia y Antártica: Diagnóstico de seguridad ecológica.* Documento Trabajo, 3. Santiago: Comisión Sudamericana de Paz, 1990.

Brown González, Gerardo R. *Medio ambiente en Chile: Proyecto subregional educacional no formal sobre medio ambiente y desarrollo social.* La Serena: SECAB, 1989.

Bustos, M. *Vulnerabilidad de sitios geográficos frente a incendios forestales.* Santiago: Instituto de Geografía, Universidad Católica de Chile, 1985. 162 pp.

Campos, L. "Pesticidas: Frutales, área de mayor consumo". *Revista del Campo,* Edición Especial, El Mercurio, Santiago de Chile, 1990.

Cárdenas, Juan Carlos. "La pesquería de centolla en la región de Magallanes: Crónica de un colapso anunciado". *Eco Tribuna* (Santiago de Chile), enero 1991, pp. 4-9. Bibliografía. Programa de Ecología Oceánica, Greenpeace América Latina.

Castilla, Juan Carlos, y Francisco Orrego Vicuña. *La coordinación de políticas pesqueras dentro de las zonas económicas exclusivas.* Serie Publicaciones Especiales, 59. Santiago: Instituto de Estudios Internacionales, 1983.

Caviedes, A., y A. Lara. "La destrucción del bosque nativo para efectuar plantaciones de pino insigne en la cuenca del río Canicura, provincia de Bio Bio, VIII región". *Informe Técnico* (Comisión de Investigación Forestal, Santiago de Chile), no. 1, 1983.

Centro de Estudios del Desarrollo. *Santiago dos ciudades: Análisis de la estructura socio-económica espacial del Gran Santiago.* Santiago: CED, 1990. 235 pp.

Centro de Investigaciones y Planificación del Medio Ambiente. *DIRPER, Directorio de personas vinculadas al tema del medio ambiente en Chile.* Serie Directorios, 1. Santiago: CIPMA, 1990. 210 pp. Agrega índices de temática de la especialidad y de instituciones.

_____. *Encuentro Científico sobre el Medio Ambiente, 1° La Serena, Chile, agosto 1983.* 2 vols. Santiago: CIPMA, 1983. Anexo: Informe y conclusiones.

_____. *Encuentro Científico sobre el Medio Ambiente, 2° Talca, Chile, agosto 1986.* 3 vols. Santiago: CIPMA, 1986. Anexo: Informe y conclusiones.

_____. *Encuentro Científico sobre el Medio Ambiente, 3° Concepción, Chile, agosto 1989.* 4 vols. Santiago: CIPMA, 1989. Anexo: Informe y conclusiones.

_____. *Medio ambiente en Chile y planificación desde la comunidad: Ampliando el campo de lo posible.* Santiago: CIPMA, s.f.

_____. *Seminario Sector Agrícola. Ciclo: Acción Ambiental. ¿Obstáculo o impulso al desarrollo?* Serie Documentos de Seminario. Santiago: CIPMA, 1989.

_____. *Seminario Sector Forestal (6-7 julio 1990). Ciclo: Acción Ambiental. ¿Obstáculo o impulso al desarrollo?* Serie Documentos de Seminario. Santiago: CIPMA, 1990. 211 pp.

_____. *Seminario Sector Industrial Urbano (enero 1990).* Serie Documentos de Seminario. Santiago: CIPMA, 1990.

_____. *Seminario Sector Minero (11-12 mayo 1990). Ciclo: Acción Ambiental. ¿Obstáculo o impulso al desarrollo?* Serie Documentos de Seminario. Santiago: CIPMA, 1990. 189 pp.

_____. *Seminario Sector Pesquero (septiembre 1990). Ciclo: Acción Ambiental. ¿Obstáculo o impulso al desarrollo?* Serie Documentos de Seminario. Santiago: CIPMA, 1990. 193 pp.

Cepeda Pizarro, Jorge. *El hombre en el contexto de la teoría ecológica.* Notas Científicas, no. 3. Departamento de Biología Química, Universidad de La Serena, Chile, 1989. 31 pp.

Cerda, Rodrigo. "Area metropolitana: Elementos para un diagnóstico". *Informe RENACE* (Santiago de Chile).

_____. "VI y VII regiones: Problemas ambientales". *Informe RENACE* (Santiago de Chile).

Comisión Especial de Descontaminación de la Región Metropolitana. *Programa de descontaminación ambiental del área metropolitana de Santiago.* Santiago: Comisión Especial de Descontaminación de la Región Metropolitana, 1990. 43 pp.

Comisión Nacional de Investigación Científica y Tecnológica. *Catálogo colectivo de publicaciones periódicas en ingeniería sanitaria existentes en Chile.* Serie Directorios, 18. Santiago: CONICYT, 1984. 113 pp.

_____. *Principios para una política ambiental.* Santiago: CONICYT, 1988.

Comité Nacional Pro Defensa de la Fauna y Flora. *Lo ambiental: Una preocupación de hoy y para siempre. Carta de CODEFF a los partidos políticos, 21 de abril 1989.* Santiago: CODEFF, 1989. 9 pp.

_____. *Informe del Encuentro sobre Medio Ambiente en Chile: Diagnóstico y propuestas ambientales para la democracia.* Santiago: CODEFF, 1989.

Comité de Higiene Ambiental y Desarrollo Local de Villa O'Higgins. *Primer Encuentro Metropolitano: Los pobladores y su medio ambiente. Resoluciones.* Santiago: Sur, 1989.

Concha, Claudia. "Areas marinas y costeras protegidas". *Eco Tribuna* (Santiago de Chile, CODEFF), septiembre 1990, pp. 7-16. Bibliografía.

Contreras, D., Juan Gastó, y Fernando Cosío González. *Ecosistemas pastorales de la zona mediterránea árida de Chile.* Santiago: UNESCO/MAB-3, Chile/Montevideo, 1986.

Convocatoria Segundo Encuentro Científico sobre el Medio Ambiente, Talca, Chile, 4-8 de agosto, 1986. Organiza CIPMA y auspicia Academia Chilena de Ciencias, Sede Regional Universidad de Talca. Santiago: CIPMA, 1986. 47 pp.

Cornejo, R., I. López, y S. Romero. *Determinación de contaminantes de origen industrial en sedimentero atmosférico en la zona de Quintero, V región.* Valparaíso: Universidad de Valparaíso, 1985. Tesis.

Cortés, Marco, Susan Smith y Aaron Caviedes. *Informe acerca de la explotación de los bosques de Araucaria en Quinquén.* Santiago: CODEFF, 1990.

Cosío González, Fernando A., y R. Demanet. *Ecosistemas pastorales de la zona mediterránea árida y semiárida de Chile.* Valparaíso: Escuela de Agronomía de Quillota, Universidad Católica de Valparaíso, 1984.

Díaz, P., y R. Abeliuk. *Calidad del agua y del aire.* Santiago: Escuela de Ingeniería, Universidad Católica de Chile, 1984.

Di Castri, Francesco. *Esbozo ecológico de Chile.* Santiago: Centro de Perfeccionamiento, MINEDUC, 1975.

Donoso Zegers, Claudio. *Ecología forestal: El bosque y su medio ambiente.* Santiago: Universidad Austral de Chile/Universitaria, 1990. 368 pp. Bibliografía, gráficos, láminas, mapas.

Ducci, María Eugenia, U. Fernández P. y Daisila Aguero. *Evaluación de las variaciones de la calidad de vida de la población erradicada en el área metropolitana de Santiago: Un estudio de casos para el período 1979-1985.* Documento de Trabajo, 161. Santiago: Instituto de Estudios Urbanos, Universidad Católica de Chile, 1989. 133 pp.

Duhart, Solange, y Jacqueline Weinstein. *Pesca industrial: Sector estratégico y de alto riesgo.* Colección Estudios Sectoriales, 5. Santiago: PET, 1988.

"Ecología". *Indice General de la Revista Hoy* (Santiago de Chile), vol. 1 (1981), pp. 88-89.

"Ecología." "Cristianos y Ecología". *Mensaje,* no. 391 (agosto 1990).

Elizalde, R. *La sobrevivencia de Chile.* Santiago: Servicio Agrícola Ganadero, Ministerio de Agricultura, 1970. 493 pp.

Escudero, José Carlos. "Salud-Ecología-Política". *Salud y Cambio* (Santiago de Chile), año 2, no. 3 (primavera 1991), pp. 8-20. Debate.

Fernández, Silvia. "Basural lo Errázuriz". *El Canelo* (Santiago de Chile), no. 4, junio-julio 1987.

Fierro, M. "Lluvia ácida: Muerte con progreso". *CODEFF* (Santiago de Chile), no. 20 (1988), p. 3.

Figari, Andrea M. "Antártida frente al nuevo escenario ambiental: Un desafío hacia el tercer milenio". *Eco Tribuna* (Santiago de Chile), octubre 1990, pp. 9-16. Greenpeace América Latina.

Frid, Alex. "Los bosques magallánicos: ¿Cuál será su futuro?" *Eco Tribuna* (Santiago de Chile), julio 1990, pp. 22-27.

————. "Diversidad biológica y los proyectos astillas de Magallanes". *Eco Tribuna* (Santiago de Chile), diciembre 1990, pp. 22-24.

Fuentes, Eduardo, y Sergio Prenafeta, eds. *Ecología del paisaje en Chile central: Estudios sobre sus espacios montañosos.* Santiago: Ediciones Universidad Católica de Chile, 1988. 125 pp. Bibliografía, láminas, gráficos, notas, fotografías.

Fuenzalida, P. H. *Geografía económica de Chile.* Tomo I: Clima. Los suelos. Biogeografía. Santiago: CORFO/Editorial Universitaria, 1950.

Gallardo, V., y A. Augsburger. *Bases para el manejo de la contaminación de origen terrestre en Chile.* Santiago: CIPMA, 1982.

García Naranjo, Juan. *El desarrollo sustentable: Una opción a considerar para la agricultura chilena en la frontera del siglo XXI.* Santiago: CODEFF, Comisión de Pesticidas, 1990. Bibliografía.

————. "Plaguicidas: Una interrogante conflictiva e inquietante". *Eco Tribuna* (Santiago de Chile, CODEFF), septiembre 1990, pp. 16-20. Bibliografía.

Garrido Ruiz, Samuel. *Asentamientos humanos y calidad de vida: Regiones IV y IX.* Documento Trabajo, 16. Santiago: CIPMA, 1990. 41 pp.

Gastó C., Juan y D. Contreras. "Un caso de desertificación en el norte de Chile: El ecosistema y su fitocenosis." *Boletín Técnico* (Facultad de Agronomía, Universidad de Chile), no. 42 (1977).

Gastó C., Juan, R. Nava y R. Armijo. *Ecosistema: La unidad de la naturaleza y el hombre.* México, 1979.

Gastó C., Juan, Eduardo Schmidt y Mario Trivelli. *Medio ambiente: ¿Realidad o moda?* Documento Trabajo, 143. Santiago: CEP, 1990. 87 pp.

Gastó C., Juan, Mario Trivelli y Cristina Contzen. *Ciencia y tecnología para un desarrollo sostenible en la agricultura desde una perspectiva ambiental.* Documento Trabajo, 6. Santiago: CIPMA, 1989. 41 pp.

Gilchrist, L. J. *Estudio forestal de la Isla de Chiloé.* Santiago, 1968.

Gómez, Andrés, y Juan Capella. "Conservación marina y la nueva Ley de Pesca." *Eco Tribuna* (Santiago de Chile), julio 1990, pp. 14-21.

González, Claudia. "VII y IX regiones: Elementos para un diagnóstico." *Informe RENACE* (Santiago de Chile), 1989, pp. 55-57.

González Tagle, Sergio. "El impacto de fundiciones de minerales sobre las actividades agropecuarias." *La Platina* (Santiago de Chile, Estación La Platina), no. 39 (1987).

————. "Transporte vehicular en Santiago: Anarquía, contaminación, congestión." *Creces* (Santiago de Chile, CONIN), junio 1990, pp. 6-13, 49.

González Tagle, Sergio, y E. Bergquist. "Alteraciones cualitativas y cuantitativas en especies vegetales cultivadas en suelos contaminados." *Simiente* (Santiago de Chile), no. 54 (1984).

_____. "Evidencias de contaminación con metales pesados en un sector del secano costero de la V región." *Agricultura Técnica* (Santiago de Chile), julio-septiembre 1986.

_____. "Metales pesados: Indicadores de contaminación ambiental en Puchuncavi, V región." *Simiente* (Santiago de Chile), no. 54 (1984), pp. 1-2.

Grau, Juan. *Cómo y por qué dejar de fumar.* Santiago: Ediciones Oikos, 1983.

_____. *Ecología y ecologismo.* Santiago: Ediciones Oikos, 1985. 504 pp. Fotografías, glosario ecológico, índice analítico.

Gross, Patricio, et al. *Análisis de los componentes de un modelo de gestión ambiental para el área metropolitana de Santiago.* Documento Trabajo, 113. Santiago: Instituto de Estudios Urbanos, Universidad Católica de Chile, 1980. 69 pp.

_____. *Diseño de indicadores para medir la calidad del medio ambiente físico en el área metropolitana de Santiago y su aplicación a nivel comunal.* Documento Trabajo, 102. Documento Trabajo, 113. Santiago: Instituto de Estudios Urbanos, Universidad Católica de Chile, 1977. 187 pp.

Gross, Patricio, y Armando de Ramón. *Santiago en el período 1891-1918: Desarrollo urbano y medio ambiente (Versión preliminar), Vol. I.* Documento Trabajo, 131. Santiago: Instituto de Estudios Urbanos, Universidad Católica de Chile, 1983.

Guerra, G. "Los incendios forestales: Catástrofes artificiales periódicas." *RENARES*, no. 6, 1986, pp. 16-17.

Guerrero Cossío, Víctor. "Principales impactos ambientales urbanos e industriales en Tarapacá". *Informe 1er Encuentro RENACE*, 1989, pp. 18-23.

Gutiérrez Bermedo, Hernán. "Legislación ambiental: Lo deseable versus lo factible". *Occidente*, año 46, no. 334, marzo-agosto 1990, pp. 29-36.

Hajek, Ernst R., Patricio Gross y Guillermo A. Espinoza. *Problemas ambientales de Chile.* 2 vols. Santiago: Pontificia Universidad Católica de Chile, Comisión Nacional del Medio Ambiente, 1990.

Hartman, Peter, et al. "Agricultura orgánica y su aporte al desarrollo sustentable." *Informe 1er Encuentro RENACE*, 1989, pp. 86-87.

_____. "X y XI regiones: Diagnóstico de la situación ecológica." *Informe 1er Encuentro RENACE*, 1989, pp. 63-80. Cuadros, tablas.

Henríquez Valásquez, Víctor Hugo. *La aevología y el reemplazo de las leyes naturales.* Santiago: Editorial Universitaria, 1983.

Hermosilla, A., y H. Rojas. *Cuantificación de niveles de arsénico en individuos expuestos a altos índices de contaminación.* Valparaíso: Universidad de Valparaíso, Escuela de Química y Farmacia, 1988.

Hoffmann, Adriana, y Marcelo Mendoza. *De como Margarita Flores puede cuidar su salud y ayudar a salvar al planeta.* Santiago: Editorial La Puerta Abierta, 1990.

Hotus, Alberto. "Isla de Pascua." *Informe 1ᵉʳ Encuentro RENACE* (Santiago de Chile), 1989, pp. 96-98.

Huneeus, Pablo. *En defensa de los senos: Crónicas ecológicas.* Santiago: Nueva Generación, 1991. 239 pp.

Instituto de Economía, Universidad Católica de Chile. *Proyecto: Algunas medidas para la descontaminación atmosférica de Santiago.* Santiago: CIAPEP, U.C., 1989. x, 311 pp.

Instituto de Fomento Pesquero. *Diagnóstico de la contaminación marina en Chile.* 2 vols. Santiago: IFOP, 1986. Anexos, bibliografía.

Instituto de Ingenieros de Chile. *Consideraciones conceptuales para un proyecto de ley: Uso, protección y desarrollo del medio ambiente.* Santiago: Instituto de Ingenieros de Chile, 1990. 13 pp.

_____. *La contaminación en Chile.* Santiago: Instituto de Ingenieros de Chile, 1990.

Instituto de Investigaciones del Patrimonio Territorial de Chile. "Ozono y territorio." *Boletín Inpater* (Universidad de Chile), no. 3, 1989.

Intendencia Región Metropolitana. *Estudio para la definición de un programa de control de la contaminación hídrica.* Santiago, 1989.

Lagos Cruz-Coke, Gustavo. *Preservación de un equilibrio ambiental en la explotación de recursos renovables.* Documento Trabajo, 3. Santiago: CIPMA, 1989. 18 pp.

_____. *Preservación de un equilibrio ambiental en la explotación de recursos no renovables. Tercer Encuentro Científico sobre el Medio Ambiente.* Ponencias centrales II. Chile piensa en Chile. Concepción: CIPMA, 1989.

Lara, Antonio, et al. *Consideraciones para una política forestal en el gobierno de transición, 1990-1994.* Documento Serie Forestal 89/11. Santiago: CODEFF, 1989. 17 pp.

_____. "Los ecosistemas forestales en el desarrollo de Chile." *Ambiente y Desarrollo* (Santiago de Chile), no. 1, 1986.

Lladser Llull, María Teresa. *Conclusiones del Seminario Red Regional de Información sobre Medio Ambiente en Chile.* Documento Trabajo, 17. Santiago: CIPMA, 1990. 36 pp.

_____. *DIRINS. Directorio de instituciones privadas de investigación en ciencias sociales y promoción del desarrollo.* Santiago: CIPMA/FLACSO, 1989. 66 pp.

Lladser Llull, María Teresa, et al. *Seminario Red Regional de Información sobre Medio Ambiente en Chile.* Documento Trabajo, 14. Santiago: CIPMA, 1990. 51 pp.

_____. *Una propuesta de desarrollo: Red de información ambiental de CIPMA.* Documento Trabajo, 19. Santiago: CIPMA, 1990. 15 pp.

Marfan R., Octavio, Antonio Marino R. y Jorge Vargas O. *Experiencia internacional en la lucha contra la contaminación ambiental: Los casos de Gran Bretaña y Japón.* Documento Trabajo, 153. Santiago: CEP, 1991.

Martínez A., José. *Educación ambiental: Hacia el desarrollo de una conducta ecológica en Chile.* Santiago, 1986.

Matas, Jaime. *Hacia una conceptualización del medio ambiente urbano.* Documento Trabajo, 103. Santiago: Instituto de Estudios Urbanos, Universidad Católica de Chile, 1978. 57 pp.

Matas, Jaime, Patricio Gross, y Humberto Molina. *Los problemas ambientales del sistema de transporte urbano.* Documento Trabajo, 123. Santiago: Instituto de Estudios Urbanos, Universidad Católica de Chile, 1981. 33 pp.

Matas, Jaime, y Ricardo Jordán. *Expansión urbana en Santiago.* Documento Trabajo, 160. Santiago: Instituto de Estudios Urbanos, Universidad Católica de Chile, 1988. 60 pp.

Matas, Jaime, Fernando Riveros, y Patricio de la Puente. *El espacio público en el habitat residencial de menores ingresos: Realismo y percepción. El caso de Conchali.* Documento Trabajo, 159. Santiago: Instituto de Estudios Urbanos, Universidad Católica de Chile, 1988. 76 pp.

Max-Neef, Manfred. *Ecodesarrollo y estilos de desarrollo.* Santiago: CEPAUR, Centro de Estudios y Promoción de Alternativas Urbano Rurales, s.f.

_____. "Economía política y salud: Una síntesis ineludible". *Revista Universitaria* (Santiago de Chile, Universidad Católica), s.f.

Mendoza Prado, Marcelo y Guillo, pseud. *Mapa del descalabro ecológico en Chile.* Santiago: Ediciones Revista APSI, 1990. 4 pp. Doblada.

Menke-Glukert, Peter. *Economía de mercado y ecología: Mesa redonda.* Documento Trabajo, 7. Santiago: Corporación Nacional Forestal, 1989. 30 pp.

Mifsud, Tony, S.J. "La ecología: Una preocupación eclesial". *Mensaje* (Santiago de Chile), no. 391, 1990, p. 273.

Ministerio de Planificación y Cooperación, División de Planificación, Estudios e Inversión. *La situación del medio ambiente en Chile: Informe.* Santiago: MIDEPLAN, 1990. 29 pp.

Ministerio de Salud. *Manual de toxicología ocupacional.* Santiago, 1979.

_____. *Política del ambiente: Informe final. Proposiciones anexos, I y II.* Santiago, 1983. 83 pp. Anexos.

Mires, Fernando. *El discurso de la naturaleza: Ecología y política en América Latina. Para una nueva radicalidad social 1.* Amerinda Estudios. Santiago: Editorial Amerinda, 1990.

Montaldo, P. *Estudios ecológicos en la provincia de Valdivia.* Valdivia: Universidad Austral de Chile, 1966.

Morande C., Pedro. "Medio ambiente: Hacia una ética de la gratuidad". *Revista Universitaria,* no. 30, 1990, pp. 53-58.

Muñoz Pizarro, Carlos. *Sinopsis de la flora chilena.* Santiago: Ediciones Universidad de Chile, 1969.

Muñoz, E., y E. Pizarro. *Estudio de incidencia de enfermedades respiratorias agudas en la comuna de Puchuncaví.* Santiago: Consultorio Médico de Cochali, 1989.

Naciones Unidas. CEPAL. *Agua potable y saneamiento ambiental en América Latina 1981-1990.* Estudios e Informes, CEPAL, 25. Santiago: CEPAL, 1983. 140 pp.

_____. *Información para la gestión ambiental: Directorio de especialistas latinoamericanos (versión preliminar).* Santiago: CEPAL, CLADES, 1990. 246 pp. (LC/L.538)

_____. *Información para la gestión ambiental: Directorio de instituciones latinoamericanas (versión preliminar).* Santiago: CEPAL, CLADES, s.f.

_____. *Información para la gestión ambiental: Directorio de especialistas latinoamericanos de Brasil y Chile (versión preliminar).* Santiago: CEPAL, CLADES, 1990. Proyecto CEPAL-PNUMA.

_____. *Información para la gestión ambiental: Directorio de instituciones latinoamericanas para la cooperación horizontal (versión preliminar).* Santiago: CEPAL, CLADES, 1990. 194 pp. (LC/L.539)

_____. *Resúmenes de documentos sobre planificación y medio ambiente.* Serie INFOPLAN: Temas Especiales de Desarrollo, 4. Santiago: CEPAL, CLADES, 1987. 111 pp. (LC/G.1462-P)

Necochea V., Andrés. *Santiago poniente: Un caso de deterioro urbano y dinámico social.* Documento Trabajo, 152. Santiago: Instituto de Estudios Urbanos, Universidad Católica de Chile, 1986. 73 pp.

Odanzit, Sajor. *El silabario de la naturaleza.* Santiago, 1983. Texto dirigido a los niños y jóvenes.

Oficina Promotora de Desarrollo Chilote. "Primer Seminario Internacional sobre la Situación de los Recursos del Mar en el Sur Chileno". *Quepuca* (Ancud, Chile), 1990.

Ortiz S., Gilberto. "El concepto y las condiciones de seguridad ambiental". *Eco Tribuna* (Santiago de Chile, CODEFF), agosto 1990, pp. 10-17. Bibliografía.

Peralta, M. "El avance de los desiertos". *Revista Naturaleza* (Santiago de Chile), 18, 1986, pp. 4-6.

Los Plaguicidas: Otra amenaza para la vida. Santiago: AGRA Ltda., Departamento de Asistencia Técnica, s.f.

Plaguicidas y salud: Primeros auxilios. Santiago: AGRA Ltda., s.f.

Pozo, Hernán. *La ciudad como espacio de segregación social.* Material de Discusión, 47. Trabajo presentado al Primer Encuentro Científico sobre Medio Ambiente Chileno, La Serena, 1983. Santiago: FLACSO, 1983. 20 pp.

Programa de Naciones Unidas para el Medio Ambiente. *El estado del medio ambiente.* Santiago: PNUMA, 1985. 47 pp.

_____, FAO. *La fauna silvestre chilena: Estado actual, políticas, conservación y aprovechamiento de la flora, fauna y áreas silvestres.* Santiago: PNUMA, 1986.

Puente, Patricio de la. *Valores socioculturales y hábitat residencial urbano.* Documento Trabajo, 156. Santiago: Instituto de Estudios Urbanos, Universidad Católica de Chile, 1987. 25 pp.

"Recursos forestales de Chile." *Chile Forestal,* Edición Especial, Centro de Documentación, no. 4, 1988.

Riveros, Fernando, Jaime Matas y Patricio de la Puente. *Los valores del espacio público en la percepción del habitante urbano.* Documento Trabajo, 158. Santiago: Instituto de Estudios Urbanos, Universidad Católica de Chile, 1988. 80 pp.

Rodrigo, P. *Desarrollo de un planeamiento metodológico clínico de ecosistemas para el ecodesarrollo.* Santiago: Universidad Católica de Chile, 1980. Tesis Magister.

Rodríguez, Alfredo. *Desastres naturales, causas no-naturales.* Documento Trabajo, 84. Santiago: SUR, 1987.

Rodríguez, M. "Regiones naturales de Chile y su capacidad de uso". *Agricultura Técnica* (Santiago de Chile, Ministerio de Agricultura), vols. 19-20, 1959-1961.

Rodríguez Seeger, Claudia. *Diagnóstico físico ambiental del crecimiento urbano de Puerto Montt entre 1960 y 1989: Lineamientos de acción para un desarrollo sustentable.* Santiago: Instituto de Estudios Urbanos, Universidad Católica de Chile, 1990. Tesis.

Rojas, Roberto. "Elementos para evaluar la crisis ambiental". *Informe 1er Encuentro RENACE,* 1989, pp. 15-18.

Rompczyk, Elmar. "¿Cuánta economía de mercado ecológica es posible?" *Eco Tribuna,* enero, 1991, pp. 23-27. Autor, director Consultora Friedrich Ebert.

Ruiz, C. *Geología y yacimientos metalíferos de Chile.* Santiago: Instituto de Investigaciones Geológicas, 1965.

Sabatini, Francisco. *Alternativas de acceso al suelo urbano para familias de bajos ingresos.* Documento Trabajo, 142. Santiago: Instituto de Estudios Urbanos, Universidad Católica de Chile, 1984. 130 pp.

Sabatini, Francisco, y Patricio Vergara Rojas. *Centralismo, medio ambiente y organización social regional.* Documento Trabajo, 11. Santiago: CIPMA, 1989. 28 pp.

Saborido, María Soledad. *El allegamiento: Una forma de habitar popular.* Documento Trabajo, 148. Santiago: Instituto de Estudios Urbanos, Universidad Católica de Chile, 1985. 40 pp.

Sancha, A., y C. Assar. *Proyecto: Calidad de las aguas del Zanjón de la Aguada y su impacto en el ambiente: Antecedentes y parámetros de contaminación orgánica.* Santiago: Universidad de Chile, Ingeniería Sanitaria, 1982.

Sánchez, Vicente. *La problemática del medio ambiente: Mitos, dilemas y proposiciones.* Documento Trabajo, 155. Santiago: Instituto de Estudios Urbanos, Universidad Católica de Chile, 1987. 32 pp.

Sanhueza Suárez, Gabriel. "El efecto invernadero en Chile". *Eco Tribuna* (Santiago de Chile), diciembre 1990, pp. 17-20.

_____. "El programa de descontaminación de Santiago". *Eco Tribuna* (Santiago, CODEFF), agosto 1990, pp. 3-9. Política Global de Descontaminación de Santiago.

Schmidt, E. *Los efectos económicos y sociales producidos por la contaminación ambiental en las zonas agrícolas.* Antofagasta: Rotary Internacional, 1989.

Secretaría Regional de Planificación y Coordinación. *Contaminación atmosférica en el área metropolitana de Santiago.* Santiago: SERPLAC, 1984. 19 pp.

Soler Rioseco, Fernando. *Medio ambiente en Chile.* Santiago: Universidad Católica de Chile/CIPMA, 1985. 413 pp. Contiene entre otros capítulos: "Ecosistema terrestre", de Juan Gastó; "Ambiente oceánico", de Patricio Bernal; "Contaminación atmosférica", de Baldomero Sáez; "Entorno cultural", de Hernán Godoy.

Stutzin, Godofredo. *Ausencia de San Francisco.* Santiago, 1989. 443 pp.

_____. *Cuando los animales tenían voz . . .* Santiago: Salesiana, 1991[?].

_____. *Presencia de San Francisco.* 2 partes. Santiago: Salesiana, 1989. 346 pp.

Stutzin, Miguel. "La conservación de la fauna silvestre en Chile". *Eco Tribuna* (Santiago, CODEFF), enero 1991, pp. 10-13.

Sunkel, Osvaldo. *Desarrollo, subdesarrollo, dependencia, marginación y desigualdades espaciales: Hacia un enfoque totalizante.* Documento Trabajo, 21. Santiago: Instituto de Estudios Urbanos, Universidad Católica de Chile, 1970. 66 pp.

_____, et al. "El desarrollo sustentable". *Ambiente y Desarrollo* (Santiago de Chile), Edición Aniversario, vol. 6, no. 3, diciembre 1990, pp. 21-38.

Susaeta S., Pedro. *Apoyo de la ciencia y la tecnología a un desarrollo forestal sustentable.* Documento Trabajo, 4. Santiago: CIPMA, 1989. 24 pp.

Susaeta, Eladio, y Susana Benedetti. *El sector forestal y la conservación ambiente.* Documento Trabajo, 18. Santiago: CIPMA, 1990. 83 pp.

Tovarias Marimón, José. "Disposiciones legales que permiten vivir en un medio ambiente libre de contaminación". *Eco Tribuna* (Santiago, CODEFF), diciembre 1990, pp. 21-22.

Tsakoumagkos, Pedro. *Indicadores económico-ambientales para las cuentas nacionales.* Santiago: CEPAL, 1990. 90 pp. (LC/R.876 [Sem. 545])

Undurraga Matta, Jaime. "Medio ambiente, poder, ética". *Ambiente y Desarrollo* (Santiago de Chile), Edición Aniversario, vol. 6, no. 3, diciembre 1990, pp. 14-50.

Universidad Austral de Chile. *Aplicaciones biotecnológicas para el tratamiento de aguas residuales y descontaminación de los ríos Calle Calle y Valdivia.* Valdivia: Universidad Austral/ODEPLAN, 1986. 86 pp.

Universidad de Chile. *Tercer Encuentro Nacional Universitario sobre el Medio Ambiente: Contaminación Urbano-Arquitectónica, Santiago, 19 al 22 de noviembre de 1984.* Santiago: Departamento de Investigación y Bibliotecas, Facultad de Arquitectura, Universidad de Chile, 1986. 90 pp.

_____. *Contaminación: Las aguas servidas. Tratamiento.* Santiago: Facultad de Ciencias Agrarias y Forestales, Centro Experimental Melipilla, Universidad de Chile, s.f.

Uribe Velásquez, Mario C. *Manejo de recursos del mar en Chiloé: 1968-1983.* (Versión periodística resumida.) Ancud, mayo, Mes del Mar, 1989. s.p.

Urquiza, Alberto. "De la destrucción a la construcción ambiental". *Informe RENACE*, 1989, pp. 30-33. Referido a la III y IV regiones de Chile.

Valle, Alfredo del. *Un gobierno metropolitano para el Gran Santiago: Presenta y futuro para una ciudad a la deriva.* Documento Trabajo, 12. Santiago: CIPMA, 1989. 10 pp.

Van Gerwen, Jef, S.J. "Mensaje papal sobre ecología: Comentarios ético-teológicos". *Mensaje* (Santiago de Chile), no. 391, 1990, p. 276.

Vergara Rojas, Patricio. *Movimiento regionalista, medio ambiente y política en el Chile de los ochenta.* Documento Trabajo, 15. Santiago: CIPMA, 1990. 27 pp.

Verscheure, Hernán. "El sistema nacional de áreas silvestres protegidas del Estado: ¿Parques nacionales o parques minerales?" *Eco Tribuna* (Santiago, CODEFF), septiembre 1990, pp. 3-7. Bibliografía.

Viel, Benjamín. *Crecimiento de la población y dignidad humana.* Viña del Mar, Chile, 1985. III Seminario Nacional.

Villarroel, Tania. "V Región: Problemática ambiental". *Informe RENACE*, 1989, pp. 39-41.

Wrobel, Andrzej. *El crecimiento de Santiago y el proceso de concentración.* Documento Trabajo, 52. Santiago: Instituto de Estudios Urbanos, Universidad Católica de Chile, 1972. 26 pp.

Yáñez V., José. "La Convención para la Reglamentación de Actividades de Recursos Minerales Antárticos". *Eco Tribuna* (Santiago, CODEFF), julio 1990, pp. 8-14.

Yáñez, V., José, y María C. Zañartu. "Incierto futuro de la Antártica: ¿Protección medio ambiental o explotación minera?" *Eco Tribuna* (Santiago, CODEFF), Comisión Antártica, enero 1991, pp. 19-22.

Publicaciones periódicas

Agricultura Técnica. Santiago de Chile, Ministerio de Agricultura.

Ambiente Ahora. Informativo mensual. Santiago de Chile, CIPMA.

Ambiente y Desarrollo. Edición aniversario. Santiago de Chile, CIPMA.

Boletín ELAN-FLEA. Boletín del Encuentro Latinoamericano Antinuclear. Santiago de Chile.

Bosque. Valdivia, Chile, Facultad de Ciencias Forestales, Universidad Austral de Chile.

Chile Forestal. Santiago de Chile, Instituto Forestal.

Chile Pesquero. Santiago de Chile, Instituto de Fomento Pesquero.

Ecoprensa. Santiago de Chile, Red Nacional de Acción Ecológica (RENACE).

Eco Tribuna. Santiago de Chile, Comité Nacional Pro Defensa de la Fauna y Flora (CODEFF).

Informativo Pesquero. Santiago de Chile, Sociedad Nacional de Pesca.

Naturaleza. Santiago de Chile. Publicación bimensual de ecología y conservación.

Revista Chilena de Historia Natural. Museo Nacional de Historia Natural.

Revista del Instituto de Ecología de Chile. Santiago de Chile.

Serie Bibliográfica Ambiental. Santiago de Chile, CIPMA. 250 registros por volumen.

Serie Encuentros. Santiago de Chile, CIPMA.

Serie Publicaciones. Santiago de Chile, CIPMA. Contiene el análisis bibliográfico de las publicaciones editadas por CIPMA desde 1979 hasta 1989: Revista *Ambiente y Desarrollo*, vol. I, 1984 al vol. V, 1989; Documento Trabajo, no. 1 al no. 13 y libros.

Fuentes para estudios del medio ambiente

Asociación Chilena de Derecho Ambiental, ACHIDAM, Santiago de Chile.

Asociación Ecológica Chilena, Santiago de Chile.

Biblioteca Pública de Ecología, Santiago de Chile.

Casa Andrómeda, La Serena, Chile.

Centro de Alternativas del Desarrollo, CEPAUR, Santiago de Chile.

Centro de Información de Recursos Naturales, IREN, Santiago de Chile.

Centro de Investigación y Planificación del Medio Ambiente, CIPMA, Santiago de Chile.

Colectivo de Ecología, Política y Autogestión, Santiago de Chile.

Club Ecológico, Peumo, Chile.

Colegio de Biólogos Marinos y Oceanólogos, A.G., Santiago de Chile.

Comisión de Ecología, Sociedad Chilena de Salud Pública, Santiago de Chile.

Comisión de Estudios de la Problemática Ambiental, Cámara de Diputados, Chile.

Comisión de Legislación Ambiental, COLMA, Chile.

Comisión de Medio Ambiente y Bienes Nacionales del Senado, Congreso, Chile.

Comisiones Municipales del Medio Ambiente, Chile.

Comisión Especial de Descontaminación de la Región Metropolitana, Santiago de Chile.

Comisión Nacional de Investigación Científica y Tecnológica, CONICYT.

Comisión Nacional del Medio Ambiente, CONAMA, Ministerio de Bienes Nacionales.

Comisión Sudamericana de Paz, Santiago de Chile.

Comité Chileno por el Desarme y la Desnuclearización, CODD, XI Región, Chile.

Comité de Defensa de las Aguas, I Región, Chile.

Comité de Defensa de los Recursos del Mar, XI Región, Chile.

Comité Ecológico de Talcahuano, Chile.

Comité Nacional Pro Defensa de la Flora y Fauna, CODEFF, Chile.

Comunidad Agrícola "Hierba Loca", Choapa, Chile.

Comunidad Cultural Aymara para el Desarrollo Andino, "Pacha-Aru", I Región, Chile.

Comunidad de Turi, Area de Pastoral Social, Obispado de Calama, Chile.

Consejo de Ancianos, Instituto Isla de Pascua, Isla de Pascua, Chile.

Coordinación de Organizaciones Aymara, I Región, Chile.

Corporación de Fomento de la Producción, CORFO, Chile.

Corporación de Investigaciones para el Desarrollo, CINDES, Santiago de Chile.

Corporación Nacional Forestal, CONAF, Chile.

Departamento de Areas Silvestres Protegidas, CONAF, Chile.

Departamento de Programas sobre el Medio Ambiente, Ministerio de Salud Pública.

División de Recursos Naturales y Energía, CEPAL, Santiago de Chile.

Fundación Crate, Talca, Chile.

GAIA, Centro de Difusión Ecológica, Santiago de Chile.

Grupo de Acción Ecológica Universitaria, Santiago de Chile, Concepción, Chile.

Impacto Ambiental Minorías Etnicas, GIA, Santiago de Chile.

Instituto de Ecología Política, Santiago de Chile.

Instituto de Fomento Pesquero, IFOP, Chile.

Instituto de Investigaciones Pesqueras, VIII Región, Chile.

Instituto de Investigación y Extensión en Ecología y Medio Ambiente, Santiago de Chile.

Instituto de la Mujer, Santiago de Chile.

Instituto Geográfico Militar, Santiago de Chile.

Instituto Nacional de Capacitación, INACAP, Gestión Ambiental, Santiago de Chile.

Instituto Oceanográfico de la Aramada, Valparaíso, Chile.

Instituto para la Paz y el Desarrollo Alternativo, Valparaíso, Chile.

Kiosko, Sistemas de Información, Santiago de Chile.

Lif Mapu, Facultad de Ciencias Biológicas y Recursos Naturales, VIII Región.

Ministerio de Bienes Nacionales, Tierras y Colonización, Coordinación, Chile.

Ministerio de Economía, Fomento y Reconstrucción, Chile.

Ministerio de Educación, Chile.

Ministerio de Salud, Chile.

Ministerio de Transportes y Telecomunicaciones, Chile.

Ministerio de Vivienda y Urbanismo, Chile.

Movimiento Pro Eliminación de Malos Olores de Talcahuano, Chile.

Oficina de Planificación Nacional, ODEPLAN, actualmente Ministerio de Planificación, MIDEPLAN-Departamento de Apoyo Regional.

Oficina para el Desarrollo de Chiloé, OPDECH, Ancud, Chiloé, Chile.

Organización de Mujeres por el Desarrollo, OMIDES, Chile.

Partido Humanista-Verde, Chile.

Pehuenche Alto Bio Bio, VIII Región, Chile.

Programa Conversando de Ecología, XI Región, Chile.

Punto Verde, XI Región, Chile.

Red Nacional de Acción Ecológica, RENACE, Chile.

Red Regional de Información sobre Medio Ambiente en Chile, CIPMA, Chile.

Secretarías Ministeriales Regionales, Chile.

Servicio Agrícola y Ganadero, SAG, Chile.

Sistema Nacional de Areas Silvestres Protegidas del Estado, SNASPE, Chile.

Sociedad de Vida Silvestre de Chile, Temuco, Chile.

Sociedad Mapuche Lonco Kilapán, Temuco, Chile.

Taller de Educación y Capacitación Ambiental, TECA, Santiago de Chile.

Taller de Estudios Aymara, I Región, Chile.

Universidad Austral de Chile: Instituto de Botánica, Desastres Naturales; Instituto de Ecología, Facultad de Ingeniería Forestal; Instituto de Ecología y Evolución, Valdivia, Chile.

Universidad Católica de Chile, Pontificia: Departamento de Ecología; Instituto de Estudios Urbanos, IEUR; Instituto de Geografía, Santiago de Chile.

Universidad Católica de Talcahuano: Departamento de Pesquerías, Talcahuano, Chile.

Universidad Católica de Valparaíso: Facultad de Recursos Naturales; Instituto de Oceanología, Valparaíso, Chile.

Universidad Central: Departamento de Ecología y Paisaje, Santiago Bernardo, Santiago de Chile.

Universidad de Concepción: Departamento de Oceanología y Biología Marina; Facultad de Ciencias y Recursos Naturales; Proyecto EULA, Gestión Ambiental, Concepción, Chile.

Universidad de Chile; Departamento de Geografía; Escuela de Ingeniería Forestal; Facultad de Ciencias Forestales; Facultad de Arquitectura y Urbanismo, Santiago de Chile.

Universidad del Norte: Oceanografía y Pesca, Antofagasta, Chile.

Universidad de Magallanes: Instituto de Flora y Fauna Marina, Medio Ambiente Físico, Punta Arenas, Chile.

Universidad de Talca: Instituto de Medio Ambiente, Talca, Chile.

Universidad de Tarapacá: Facultad de Estudios Andinos, Recursos Naturales, Medio Ambiente Físico, Arica, Chile.

Algunos eventos en torno al tema del medio ambiente en Chile

1er Encuentro Científico sobre el Medio Ambiente, La Serena, Chile, agosto 1983.

2° Encuentro Científico sobre el Medio Ambiente, Talca, agosto 1986.

3er Encuentro Científico sobre el Medio Ambiente, Concepción, agosto 1989.

1er Encuentro de Acción Ecológica, RENACE, Santiago de Chile, 1989.

Mesa Redonda: "Economía de Mercado y Ecología", CONAF, Santiago de Chile, 1989.

Primer Seminario Internacional sobre la Situación de los Recursos del Mar en el Sur Chileno, OPDECH, Ancud, Chile, 1990.

Seminario "Arbolado Urbano", Grupo de Investigadores del Paisaje, GIP, Santiago de Chile, noviembre 1985.

Seminario "Acción Ambiental: ¿Obstáculo o Impulso al Desarrollo?": Sector Industrial Urbano, enero 1990; Sector Minero, mayo 1990; Sector Forestal, julio 1990; Sector Pesquero, septiembre 1990; Sector Agrícola, noviembre 1990, CIPMA, Santiago de Chile.

Seminario Red Regional de Información sobre Medio Ambiente en Chile, CIPMA, Santiago de Chile, 1990.

Seminario: "Santiago, Economía y Futuro", Instituto Río Colorado, Santiago de Chile, 1985.

5 de Junio, Día Mundial del Medio Ambiente.

Acciones

Acción de Denuncia Pública sobre el Smog, 1988. Comisión Justicia, Paz y Ecología, Orden Franciscana de Santiago de Chile.

Cadena Humana alrededor del Basural "Lo Errázuriz", Comité Ecológico Estación Central, Santiago de Chile.

Conferencias en Semana Internacional del Ambiente, Universidad de Concepción, Chile.

Brigadas Escolares de Ecología, Universidad de Concepción, Chile.

Charlas de Difusión Ambiental, Centro de Alumnos INACAP, Santiago de Chile.

Campaña Publicitaria: "Santiago Descontamina Santiago", I. Municipalidad de Santiago de Chile.

Campaña Publicitaria en Defensa del Medio Ambiente: Folletos distribuidos por KARU MAPU (Tierra Verde, en lengua mapuche), Santiago de Chile.

Denuncias a Atentados Ecológicos, CODEFF, Aysén, Chile.

Encuentro "El Desarrollo Sustentable, Desafíos para la Equidad". Organizan ILADES y PET, 4 y 5 de abril, 1991.

Encuentro Minorías Etnicas, CODEFF, Aysén, Coyhaique, Chile.

Entrevista con Relator de Naciones Unidas para los Derechos Humanos en Chile, de los convocantes al Encuentro "Propuestas y Demandas de Pueblos Indígenas", Jacha Marka Aru, aymaras residentes en Santiago de Chile.

Jornadas de Educación Callejera, Institución de Educación para la Paz, IDEPA, Valparaíso, Chile.

Otros

Libretos radiales, Radio UMBRAL, Iglesia Metodista de Chile, Santiago de Chile.

Afiches, panfletos, boletines, cartillas didácticas, actos por la vida, ciclos, documentos, informes, proyectos, apoyo, talleres, monitores.

Programas de televisión "Al Sur del Mundo" y "La Tierra en que Vivimos".

450 Years of Publishing in the Americas: What Lies Ahead?

13. Is the Sky Falling? Scholarly Publishing in the 1990s

Lynne Rienner

I'm going to be gloomy, because I think that we have a problem. In fact, I think that we are in, or are approaching, a state of crisis. "Crisis" is one of those overused words that I've come to hate—along with terms in book titles like "perspectives on" and "the political economy of"—but I don't know of anything else that will serve as well right now.

Simply stated, there are too many books. That is not, I suppose, a clever thing for a publisher to say, but I think that it is the crux of the problem. There are way too many books. Even assuming that there were enough money for you to buy them all, there is not enough room to put them all, and too many of them are too little needed, if circulation records are any indication. As a result of this excess, fewer copies are sold of each title—and our sales figures confirm exactly what Grant Barnes has been saying. Unfortunately, though we are selling fewer copies, we still have the same overheads to cover. So what do we do? We raise the prices of the books. Then you, with your fixed budgets, buy fewer copies. Then we raise the prices of the books further. This goes on and on and on.

To make matters worse, some publishers are producing more titles to try to make up for this shortfall, because again, the rent is not going down, the staff is not getting smaller, the overheads have to be covered by the sales of fewer copies of each title. Which leaves you with a budget that has to be spread across more choices. So we sell still fewer copies of each title. And the prices go up again. And this cycle seems to be never ending.

This is the first problem I've encountered in this business that I don't have a clue how to solve. I do know, though, that there are three places that we have to look to try to find an answer.

First there is the university, where the quest for tenure—a reasonable thing—and for promotion fuels to some degree the enormous amount of material that is being published. And it seems to me sometimes that it matters a great deal more that someone *is* publishing than it does *what* he or she is publishing. It has been suggested at one major research university, and I realize that the concerns that inspired the suggestion are different from mine, that faculty be permitted to submit only a limited number of articles and books when they are being considered for tenure or promotion. That might help stem the flood of material, but I doubt it. People don't stop publishing when they get tenure, and full professors don't stop publishing either. The dissemination of information is what this business, the pursuit of scholarship, is about. People want to learn things, and then they want to share that knowledge.

There is a very important issue here. It is to my advantage that people want to publish, that they need to publish, but it seems very wrong to me that a commercial decision (and whether you are Stanford University Press or Lynne Rienner Publishers, you have to sell the books that you are publishing, so there is some degree of commercialness entering into any publishing decision) should be determining who gets a job in a university, who keeps a job in the university, and, to some degree, the very nature of the whole scholarly endeavor.

Recently I received a phone call from the head of a tenure committee at a major research university, asking: were we going to publish a book, a manuscript we had in house that was going through our review process? A few weeks later, there was another call from the dean at that school, again wanting to know whether a decision had been made yet. And what I want to say to these people is, "read it." *You* are equipped to know if it's any good. *You* know if you think this person is doing good work. If he is, give him tenure. Why are you waiting to find out whether we can *afford* to publish this book?

More money for libraries would be the easiest solution. I'd like that. But it doesn't seem to be forthcoming, especially not for books on Latin America. To the contrary, if what I'm hearing everywhere is true, libraries are buying little this year.

Of course, if you never bought a bad book, that would help. But that's no more likely than publishers never publishing a bad book. Besides, how can you tell whether a book is good or not? If you wait for the reviews, which seem to take two years (when we are lucky), you are going to have a very out-of-date collection. You can buy to some extent, I assume, on the basis of requests from faculty, but that has its own problems. For example, a friend of mine writes on the welfare state, and he wants his library to purchase every single thing that comes out on the welfare state, good, bad, indifferent, because he wants to know what is being done on the subject; but he thinks it would be great if his library only bought exceptionally good books on Latin American politics!

One way that libraries try to extend the reach of their financial resources is through interlibrary loan programs. I can understand the motivation for that, but it simply contributes to the cycle. It still means that you are buying fewer copies of each title. And we are therefore raising our prices. And you are ending up with the same—well, actually, you are ending up with fewer books, not more. You are trying to find a way to deal with the fact that you have less money to spend; but the cycle just continues to go round and round and round.

So what can a publisher do? To return to my starting point, publishing fewer books might, on the surface of things, help, but in the present system that means less income for us, and ultimately that means we go out of business. We should certainly try to publish better books, but that raises the whole question of quality and what part it plays in this enterprise. We know that it is possible for some publishers, operating, I guess, on an economy of scale, to publish very small print runs—very small editions—of an enormous number of very high-priced books of less than certain value. And who doesn't want his or her dissertation published? I know of one editor who visited the campus of a state university and knocked on doors asking professors, do you still have your dissertation lying around, from twenty years ago, fifteen years ago, it doesn't matter. I don't think this kind of approach is doing any of us any good.

What causes a book-buying decision to be made? If Grant Barnes's list were exactly the same as it is now, only the press were called Palo Alto Publishing Partnership instead of Stanford University Press . . . I don't know, would there be fewer units of each book sold? Is the label what makes the thing work? Luck? I don't know.

I've touched on the topic of price a number of times, so I put together some numbers for you, and I found the results interesting. This is a book that we published in August of '89. It is by Carlos Vilas and it's called *State, Class, and Ethnicity in Nicaragua*, with a very long subtitle and a $30.00 retail price. We ordered 900 copies, we received 949. The manuscript went out to two reviewers before we decided to publish it, both of whom thought it was very good. And the journal reviews we've gotten so far, including one in *Choice*, confirm that. So we have a good book here.

Through April of this year, we sold 469 copies, which again follows Grant's average-sales-for-two-years' figures. In fact, I guess I should feel we're doing great; it hasn't been two years yet. The actual sales receipts for those 469 copies were about $10,600. The cost to us of producing the books—just the typesetting, the paper, printing, and binding, and the freight to ship 949 books to our warehouse—was about

$4,500. This was a book that was translated from Spanish, and we were very fortunate: the translation cost us only $750, which was a pittance, a present. (We are unable to publish more translations because usually many thousands of dollars are needed to pay for them.) We spent about $900 on copy editing, a little bit higher than usual because it was a translation, but not much, maybe $50. About $300 for proofreading. The author received a royalty of 7.5 percent of our sales receipts—that was $795—and we paid about $1,000 to process orders and returns and to the service that warehouses our books. That left us after almost two years with about $2,300 with which to cover all of our marketing costs: the catalogs that we mail out, the exhibits that we attend, the review copies that we send to journals, the ads that we do. Then there are eight people in my company who like to be paid on a regular basis. There is the rent, the utilities . . . all those normal things. And there is me, traveling here to attend this meeting. It all has to be paid for.

Obviously, it is not being paid for by the Vilas book! Obviously, too, we didn't price this book high enough—and the prices of books are increasing not because our cost of producing books has gone up significantly; salaries have not risen that much, the cost of typesetting has held, and manufacturing has seen only modest increases every year—maybe 4 percent, 5 percent, and paper prices sometimes even go down. What is happening is that all of the overheads must be covered by the sale of fewer copies. And in order to do that we've got to raise our prices.

Perhaps to survive we will have to publish something other than social science scholarship! (Romance novels?) We don't only publish on Latin America, but also on Africa, the Middle East, Asia, Europe, and what I've found over the years is that sometimes certain regions are up, sometimes they are down, and we are not going to try and decipher which is going to happen when. We are just going to try to publish good books on these areas. There was a time when nobody knew where El Salvador was; and then all of a sudden you could sell anything on El Salvador. Sadly, a famine in Ethiopia does wonders for the sales of books on Ethiopia. Recently, we brought out a book on oil security in the Gulf, right when everything was happening, so we sold 600 copies in two months. But all of our books are in the "soft areas"—area studies, development, international relations, women's studies—so it looks like I should go back to the office and, before we issue the next catalog, raise the prices on everything.

It is often remarked that if we'd publish our books in paperback, we'd sell a lot more copies and wouldn't have this problem. So I did a little exercise. I calculated what would have happened if we had published the Vilas book in paperback. Let's price it at $15.95, print twice as many copies, and assume that in the same period we will sell twice as many copies—938—which again would bear out Grant's figures. As you can see, most of the costs remain the same, so we end up selling twice as many books but with less income. Well, maybe I don't have to print 1,800 copies, I am smarter now, I know I won't sell them, so I'll only print 1,100 copies. That raises the amount that we are left with from $2,300 to $2,600. And the fact is that we *won't* sell twice as many copies. We've done this as a real experiment before: if a book is intended for courses, we publish it in paperback and intend to sell it not just in the year it comes out, but also in the second year and the third year. And that way the economics work. But if a book is not really right for a course and we bring out a paperback, we end up selling, instead of 800-1,200 hardcover books, 400-500 hardcover copies and maybe 600 paperbacks. So the total number out there may be at best 200 more than it would have been otherwise, and we end up with less revenue. The books are specialized books. That's why we do them the way that we do them.

Back to the crisis. Since the day I was invited to come to this conference, I have been trying to think of some positive conclusion that I could offer. And I've failed. I don't know if there are any solutions, but if there are, whatever solutions there are can be found only through a tripartite effort on the part of librarians, scholars, and publishers. And I would really like to see an organization like SALALM take the lead in seeking foundation funding, a really serious effort to start up some kind of commission to sort out what we can—and cannot—do to protect ourselves if the sky is indeed falling.

I attend a lot of meetings, of political scientists, of anthropologists, of publishers (this is my first meeting of librarians, and it's long overdue), and everybody talks about the problems. But the response has too often been to try to figure out who is to blame, and it's always the other guy. After all these years, it still surprises me how much antagonism and distrust there is between publishers and librarians, between publishers and authors, between authors—well, I don't know about authors and librarians to tell you the truth. But this doesn't seem to me to be a very productive approach. We have resources. We don't have financial resources, that's true. But there are other kinds of resources. Just yesterday when I was talking with Jim Breedlove about resource sharing, I realized I didn't really understand all the ramifications of it and what it meant; I only took it as something that meant we would sell fewer copies of a book. And I understand it a lot differently now. There are many issues like this where, if we understood each other's problems, we could all be lobbying, all be working toward this program that would benefit libraries, or that program that would benefit scholars, or publishers, or what have you—to our mutual benefit. But I don't think we've really looked at it in a serious way involving the three players. I do believe that we need to do this to see whether the system of producing and disseminating scholarly material—books, journals, electronic resources—can be made to work, not just to *improve* our mutual lot, but so that we can carry on at all.

14. Acerca de la inexistencia de América Latina como uno de los inconvenientes para adquirir material literario a su respecto

Daniel Divinsky

En primer lugar les debo una aclaración para evitar ser ubicado equivocadamente dentro del espectro político y consecuentemente para que lo que diga no sea interpretado equivocadamente. El título de esto que no me atrevería nunca a calificar de ponencia fue improvisado a partir de la presión de Jim y Deborah Jakubs que necesitaban un título para el programa y no implica en absoluto una afirmación metafísica. Quería advertir el hecho de que tras más de ciento cincuenta años de historia compartida, los diversos países que integran lo que se considera América Latina son precisamente eso, diversos. Diversos en casi todo excepto en la herencia cultural compartida, desarrollada a partir de una historia común. Por eso, todo intento de abordarlos como unidad editorial, y todo intento de proveerse de esa producción editorial que no tenga en cuenta esa diversidad y esa ausencia absoluta de centralización, está destinado al fracaso.

Esto lo saben bien los bibliotecarios como ustedes, que desde hace años vienen tropezando con los inconvenientes derivados de este hecho. Pero debía decirlo para evitar que el título que figura en el programa tuviera otro sentido. Ya que estoy entre declaraciones, aquí va otra: no soy un académico, ya lo habrán notado, sino un abogado en retiro dedicado a la actividad editorial en Argentina desde hace veinticuatro años. Por diversos motivos profesionales y conexos con los profesionales, he recorrido en estos años casi toda América Latina. Por eso, si puedo hacer algún aporte a este seminario, ese aporte derivará de la experiencia y no de un saber científico.

Para que sepan desde dónde les hablo, un poco de autobiografía—autobiografía editorial para suministrarles alguna información. Con dos socios y un capital de trescientos dólares, fundé en 1966 Ediciones de la Flor, cuya dirección literaria ejerzo desde entonces. Esos trescientos dólares se gastaron en anticipos de derechos de autor sobre tres libros, dos de autores franceses: *Adén Arabia* de Paul Nizan y una antología poética de Georges Brassens que no habían sido nunca publicadas en español. El tercero, una novela de Bernardo Verbitsky, un escritor

argentino por entonces bastante conocido, era una forma de incluir en
el catálogo un nombre famoso con una novela poco famosa del autor,
una novela de juventud. Y agotado así el capital, los libros se editaron
a base de crédito. Los dos primeros títulos que aparecieron, antologías
de cuentos para las que conseguimos el aporte gratuito y benevolente
de Cortázar, Borges y Sábato entre otros, aparecieron en 1967. Mi
medio de vida seguía siendo la abogacía. En 1970, con treinta títulos
publicados y algunos éxitos de venta como los libros de Vinicius de
Moraes, el poeta y cantante brasileño que no había sido, curiosamente,
publicado en castellano antes, la editorial empezó a prosperar.
Entonces, me casé con Kuki Miler y juntos compramos la parte de
mis socios. Mi mujer era economista y comenzó a convertirse en
profesional de la edición.

Desde entonces hasta hoy, se desarrolló una historia empresaria
muy típicamente latinoamericana y sólo posible para una actividad
marginal en la vida capitalista como es la actividad editorial. La
publicación de los libros de Mafalda, una tira cómica de autor
argentino que muchos de ustedes tal vez conozcan, que se edita con un
suceso increíble en todo el mundo latino, pero también en Finlandia,
Alemania, Grecia e Israel, para dar sólo unos ejemplos, abrió una línea
inusual. La editorial sofisticada que había publicado a pérdida total
poemas de Le Roi Jones y Tennessee Williams, que pretendía estar a la
vanguardia con Nizan y con Brassens, que ofrecía un lugar para
publicar a jóvenes autores inéditos argentinos, peruanos, colombianos,
ecuatorianos, etc., tenía por fin un *best-seller* que le permitía ser más
profesional y al mismo tiempo lanzar más colecciones.

En un país como la Argentina muchos grandes éxitos editoriales
son promovidos por los libreros. No por los premios literarios ni por la
publicidad ni por las buenas críticas bibliográficas. Es un caso típico de
un *self-fulfilling prophecy*. Cuando un librero cree que un libro se va a
vender, ordena más ejemplares con los que arma pilas grandes junto a
la caja de la librería; como consecuencia el libro se vende y el librero se
felicita por su clarividencia: es un profeta que sabe qué va a pasar con
cada libro. Cuando una editorial tiene un éxito, un best-seller como
fue el caso nuestro con Mafalda, es posible que el librero, que es
exitista en el buen sentido de la palabra— apuesta al éxito— preste
mayor atención a los siguientes títulos de la misma editorial y eso
provoca un cambio de actitud que se traduce luego en la venta de los
títulos sucesivos.

Esta nueva situación permitió inaugurar nuevas colecciones, dos de
libros infantiles y una de autores de Puerto Rico que tuvo su origen en
un hecho fortuito que fue el conocer *La guaracha del Macho Camacho*

de Luis Rafael Sánchez. Esta novela, que publicamos en 1975, fue reeditada constantemente desde entonces y provocó un gran interés nuestro por la literatura de Puerto Rico, y se ha traducido en una colección con doce títulos publicados ya y más todavía por publicar en adelante.

Así tengo una selección de títulos con la que funciona una editorial de medianas dimensiones, profesional, pero absolutamente artesanal. Funciona lo que Della Volpe, crítico italiano, llamaba la crítica del gusto. Mi idea es que por lo menos hay tres mil personas a las que les gustan los mismos libros que me gustan a mí. Y entonces eso es una base para un mercado posible. Y Ediciones de la Flor creció con el humor gráfico a partir del éxito internacional de Mafalda y los demás libros de Quino (que es el dibujante autor de Mafalda, un seudónimo de Joaquín Lavado). La introducción de Mafalda en toda América Latina permitió penetrar el mercado para el resto del catálogo, algo que generalmente no es fácil. Eso me obligó a viajar personalmente por el continente, una obligación placentera, que implicaba conocer países con cuyas culturas me sentía ligado, convertido en vendedor de mis propios libros. Atendíamos directamente a las librerías del exterior, lo que significa mayores costos por el envío de pedidos pequeños, pero da presencia al catálogo, porque el librero no puede tener el mismo stock que un distribuidor mayorista. Y para el bibliotecario que desde fuera del país necesita proveerse de títulos, implica en muchos casos proveerse obligadamente con cada editorial. Esto significa, y ustedes lo saben bien, múltiples cuentas, órdenes pequeñas, cartas que no responden, correo que no funciona, y el uso del fax que ha proporcionado la prueba más evidente de que las únicas cartas que no se contestan son las que no se reciben porque el fax realmente se contesta. Y en muchos casos, se deja de dar respuesta por las editoriales, a las que no se les justifican los gastos de enviar pedidos de muy pocos libros. A veces personal no muy eficaz a cargo de la recepción de las órdenes genera incidentes divertidos. Un amigo mío, Rogelio García Lupo, fue director de la Editorial Universitaria de Buenos Aires en 1973-1974. Visitando la sección de ventas de la editorial, descubrió una cantidad de paquetes que provenían de universidades y bibliotecas donde les devolvían un ejemplar de un libro que, según decían en cada caso había sido incluido por error, y era la *Introducción a la Lógica* de Irving Copi, que los empleados de la sección de ventas habían incluido en los pedidos cuando decían "one copy": ponían un ejemplar del libro de Irving Copi que no había sido solicitado.

Ediciones de la Flor tuvo todo tipo de choques con el poder político y la censura, algo que en América Latina es parte inseparable del trabajo editorial o periodístico. Durante las dictaduras militares de 1966-1973 y 1976-1983, hemos tenido libros prohibidos por decreto presidencial, por ordenanzas del Municipio de Buenos Aires, por disposición del correo que podía prohibir la circulación de libros por este medio y por procesos judiciales en los tribunales. A veces por invocación de supuestas causas, como obscenidad, oposición a la moral y buenas costumbres, infracción a diversas leyes dictatoriales que prohibían la difusión del pensamiento progresista; y a veces simplemente como expresión del poder dictatorial durante la vigencia del llamado "Estado de Sitio" durante el cual las garantías constitucionales se suspenden y el Poder Ejecutivo puede decretar prohibiciones y prisiones, sin expresión de causa y sobre las cuales no se puede recurrir a los tribunales. No se puede apelarlas.

En 1977, con el General Videla en el poder, sucede el hecho más grave: un decreto presidencial prohibe un libro infantil que habíamos publicado, titulado *Cinco dedos*, editado en Berlín, el Berlín "occidental" para ser más preciso, cuyos derechos había comprado yo en la Feria de Frankfurt un año antes. El libro era una simple versión de la fábula de que la unión hace la fuerza. Se trata de una mano cuyos dedos están peleados entre sí y están perseguidos cada uno por separado por otra mano que los torturaba, los encarcelaba, los aislaba, hasta que finalmente los dedos perseguidos descubren que juntos forman un buen puño y se defienden. Esto fue interpretado como una incitación a la subversión para los niños y el hecho de que los colores fueran el verde y el rojo fue leído por algún coronel (y lo supe después) como que el verde representaba el uniforme de las fuerzas armadas. Es decir, el tipo de sutileza a que puede llegar el sargento García cuando ejerce la censura, es francamente inimaginable para los intelectuales. Esto determinó que intentara un recurso de apelación. Allí, el abogado que había en mí apareció: presenté un recurso jerárquico pidiendo se levantara la prohibición y la respuesta del gobierno fue dictar un decreto ordenando mi prisión, la de mi mujer que es socia de la editorial y directora de la colección infantil y de Amelia Hannois que era la co-directora de la colección y en aquel entonces la esposa de Augusto Roa Bastos el laureado narrador paraguayo que, prudentemente, ya estaba viviendo en París con ella por entonces. Esto implicó ciento veintisiete días de prisión a disposición del Poder Ejecutivo, una campaña internacional de los colegas en todo el mundo empezada por los editores franceses que se tradujo finalmente en nuestra libertad y en el exilio de siete años en Venezuela. En el ínterin la editorial siguió funcionando dirigida por teléfono y por carta, con una mínima estructura de emergencia. En Venezuela me dediqué a trabajar en la Biblioteca Ayacucho, una editorial del Estado que publica ediciones muy hermosas de los clásicos latinoamericanos precisamente a cargo de la distribución y difusión. También haciendo unos libros para *El Diario de Caracas*, un matutino por entonces nuevo que decidió, en vez de editar un *magazine* dominical, repartir con el periódico del domingo un libro de 64 a 100 páginas, lo cual fue una experiencia fascinante y el ideal de todo editor: publicar libros que no hubiera que vender, que directamente fueran regalados. Esto creo que es el desideratum de todos los editores: hacer libros que se regalen, que la gente los reciba de todas maneras.

Y eso implicó un paréntesis en Ediciones de la Flor. La editorial, como dije, siguió funcionando en Buenos Aires, y a fines de 1983 con la vuelta a la democracia, regresamos a la Argentina donde le dimos un nuevo impulso a la editorial. Celebramos acuerdos españoles de coedición con la editorial española Lumen y sin pagar ni un dólar de anticipo sobre los derechos de autor, sólo por amistad y solidaridad, no concedieron los derechos para coeditar para América del Sur *El nombre de la rosa* de Umberto Eco, que tuvo un éxito enorme en todos los idiomas. Este es un hecho que cuento para que se vea que ésta es una actividad, la de la edición, en América Latina y aún en España, en la que factores no económicos pesan en las decisiones, incluso elementos afectivos, de gustos, de simpatía en una solidaridad que no existe en otras actividades. Este carácter *amateur* aun dentro de los profesionales se presenta incluso en las editoriales grandes de España que se relacionan en mi opinión por cualidades personales independientemente de quién es el capitalista. Algo muy diferente a la actitud mercantil que se encuentra en la actividad editorial anglosajona, siempre hablando en general. La mayoría de las editoriales de libros en español no hacen *marketing* y toman sus decisiones según opciones subjetivas de sus directores literarios. Hay una cuestión de olfato, una cuestión de decisión sentimental, que no tiene nada que ver con el mercado posible para los libros que se decida publicar.

Todo esto, por supuesto, determina la vulnerabilidad económica, cosa que por lo visto no es patrimonio exclusivo de las editoriales en español. Una tras otra sufren crisis económicas que hacen que muchas editoriales desaparezcan al cabo de un tiempo o entren en bancarrota, porque no son proyectos empresariales sino producto de las inquietudes intelectuales de sus propietarios, que no tienen mucho capital para soportar y a veces no realizan su distribución con la profesionalidad necesaria.

Hay un pequeño restaurante en París que en su menú de pocos y muy exquisitos platos tiene una referencia que dice "la casa por el momento no tiene *freezer*", como para demostrar que no sirve comidas congeladas y luego calentadas. La editorial, no lo digo por orgullo, es un dato de la realidad. Mi editorial tiene veinticuatro años, más de quinientos títulos publicados y todavía no tenemos una computadora.

Esto va a originar buena parte de las dificultades con las que ustedes se encuentran para informarse de lo que se publica en América Latina, y para, una vez obtenida esta información, conseguir los libros que interesan a sus departamentos. Todo es producto de una actividad que, en vísperas del siglo XXI, se desarrolla casi como en el siglo XIX. Que a pesar de todo esto ustedes consigan mantener al día sus bibliotecas es producto de vuestro esfuerzo y dedicación. Como decía el escritor colombiano Juan Gustavo Cobo Borda de los poetas, "todos los bibliotecarios son santos e irán al cielo".

15. La situación de la producción bibliográfica nicaragüense

Conny Méndez Rojas

Antecedentes

La producción editorial nicaragüense no ha tenido la suerte de escaparse de los desastres naturales, guerras y crisis económicas que ha vivido Nicaragua en su historia. En el pasado que corresponde a la etapa de gobierno previa a 1979 (distintos gobiernos hasta culminar con el de la familia Somoza, en julio de este año), la actividad de producción bibliográfica se encuentra de forma incipiente y dado en el ejercicio de un conjunto estructurado como editorial-producción gráfica-distribución de libros. Se puede decir que esta actividad inicia en nuestro país a principios del siglo XIX.

En su primera etapa, la producción bibliográfica se inicia con las características de que en su mayoría eran folletos, papelería de oficina, panfletos que contenían información religiosa, otras de carácter político, editados por imprentas que publicaban sin contar con criterios editoriales, pero que pretendían llenar esta necesidad. La mayor parte de estos materiales se perdieron debido a las guerras, huracanes y terremotos sucedidos durante esa época. Es más o menos a partir de 1930 que aparecen otros movimientos culturales, donde los diarios del país juegan un rol importante en la publicación de información cultural nacional haciendo el papel de instituciones editoras, y algunos centros que son únicamente talleres de impresiones, entre ellos la Tipografía El Correo, los Talleres Gráficos Pérez, Editorial La Nueva Prensa, etc.

Un poco después nacen grupos que prácticamente dan a conocer y definen el desarrollo de las letras nacionales, lo que llaman nueva expresión de "gustos literarios".[1] Cuenta entre estos la formación del Movimiento de Vanguardia, que se caracterizó por concentrar a un buen grupo de escritores nacionales cuya creación poética debería marcar una nueva corriente literaria y cultural, teniendo como influencia la poesía realista norteamericana de esa época. Se considera que este movimiento fue iniciado por José Coronel Urtecho con la aparición de su obra "Oda a Rubén". Otro fuerte impacto en esta época fue el trabajo de Pablo Antonio Cuadra con sus *Cuadernos del Taller San Lucas*, cuyo sentido fue formar una "cofradía de escritores y artistas católicos nicaragüenses". Esta iniciativa se fundó con el objeto de difundir en Nicaragua "una actitud humanista, civilizada".[2] Además de que también fuera uno de los integrantes del Movimiento de Vanguardia, Pablo Antonio Cuadra es también impulsor de las ediciones de la revista literaria *El Pez y la Serpiente*, la que actualmente circula.

Al inicio de los años 40 la Editorial Nuevos Horizontes, dirigida por María Teresa Sánchez, publica una revista literaria con el mismo nombre, y unos veinte títulos de libros del círculo de escritores amigos que ella también forma. Un esfuerzo más fue el de Ernesto Cardenal, que inicia una colección de publicaciones, a las que le da el nombre El Hilo Azul. La Universidad Nacional en León funda la editorial universitaria, en la cual se publican alguno que otro texto científico, y obras literarias nacionales. Allí mismo nace también la revista *Ventana*, con cuyo nombre se funda también un movimiento literario, dirigido por Sergio Ramírez y Fernando Gordillo, en su época de estudiantes universitarios.

De vez en cuando el gobierno hizo algunas publicaciones a través del Ministerio de Educación, sacando algún texto de educación primaria, o patrocinando algún autor nacional. También se editaron algunas veces memorias o anuarios, apoyados por otros ministerios o alguno de los bancos existentes en esa época.

Están además otros esfuerzos como las Ediciones de Librería Cardenal, la Editorial Nicaragüense, la Librería y Editorial Recalde, la Distribuidora Cultural y el Fondo de Promoción Cultural del Banco de América. Este último publicó cuarenta libros, de buena calidad, pero de escaso acceso al pueblo lector por sus altos costos. Hay muchos más esfuerzos privados, yendo desde librerías hasta conocidos escritores nicaragüenses que financiaban sus propios tirajes a través de préstamos bancarios u otros. Ellos mismos se encargaban de la edición de sus libros y contrataban la imprenta de mayor conveniencia. Hacían tirajes muy pequeños (hasta un máximo de 500 ejemplares), y establecían sus propios contactos para distribuirlos en librerías e instituciones afines.

Acercándonos al final de la década de los años 70, la situación de la producción editorial no mejora. A pesar de que Nicaragua tiene una gran riqueza de escritores, particularmente literarios, el gobierno no parece reconocer la necesidad de apoyar este movimiento. Por el contrario, en ningún momento se da la oportunidad de desarrollar la producción bibliográfica. Muchos de los esfuerzos empíricos que surgen fracasan, y los que sobreviven no logran desarrollarse. Esto crea en el ámbito literario la sensación de un desprecio por la cultura y el libro nacional de parte del gobierno. De la misma manera, por las mismas características de gobierno de Somoza, durante su última etapa, hay libros de autores nacionales que no se permiten circular en el país, y algunos escritores viven prácticamente en el exilio.

No obstante, considerando que una buena parte de este patrimonio histórico-cultural se perdió por razones políticas, económicas, desastres naturales y guerras, hay actualmente algunos vestigios de estos esfuerzos en algunas bibliotecas, otros en manos particulares, y posiblemente una buena parte de ellos están por lo menos citados en la *Bibliografía Nacional Nicaragüense, 1800-1978.*

Situación entre 1979 y 1990

Es así que llegamos al final de la década de los 70 y empieza para Nicaragua una etapa completamente diferente. Nos encontramos en esta época con que Nicaragua vive un cambio político-económico en forma radical. Se da el triunfo de la revolución popular sandinista, que origina un nuevo gobierno y pone fin a una guerra de varios años. Como consecuencia, esto deja al país en una situación económica muy delicada. Sin embargo, a partir de 1980 se impulsan fuertes incrementos en el consumo y la inversión del sector público, lo que permite una evolución favorable de la economía, pero que no se llega a superar.

Como parte de la política del nuevo gobierno, se pretende apoyar los valores nacionales y todo lo que se refiera al conocimiento y desarrollo de la cultura nicaragüense. Fue este uno de los objetivos de la creación del Ministerio de Cultura, a partir de julio de 1979. Como también se trata de mejorar el nivel de vida, se da una serie de esfuerzos para extender los servicios de salud, se monta un programa nacional de educación de adultos, un programa de desarrollo cultural, y una campaña nacional de alfabetización que reduce el nivel de analfabetismo a un 12%.

Junto con la creación del Ministerio de Cultura se funda además una dependencia llamada Dirección Nacional de Bibliotecas y Archivos, que ha de integrar un sistema bibliotecario con doce bibliotecas públicas que existen desde el gobierno anterior, y se da a la tarea de ampliar este sistema, fundando 27 bibliotecas más a lo largo del país.

Asimismo, el Ministerio de Educación impulsa su red de bibliotecas escolares a nivel nacional. Esta situación crea un hermoso auge en la literatura nacional, y un interés por las letras nicaragüenses. Todo este conjunto de desarrollo social y cultural hace sentir la necesidad de afrontar la demanda creciente de libros y textos, así como de información política y social. Nos encontramos entonces, a partir de aquí, con que la producción bibliográfica nicaragüense presenta nuevas características y un giro totalmente diferente.

Teniendo como precedente que es casi nulo el desarrollo editorial del país, a pesar de su gran riqueza literaria, se inicia un proceso que permita el impulso de este aspecto. Se trata entonces de fomentar los componentes de la industria editorial, "estimulando al máximo la actividad de cada uno de ellos y al mismo tiempo establecer las relaciones recíprocas entre ellos con el fin de articular un todo armónico y coherente: El estímulo y la protección del autor, el financiamiento y la formación del editor, el equipamiento y el rendimiento óptimo del impresor, la fluidez de una red de distribución, la eficacia de los servicios bibliotecarios y la capacidad de adquisición de libros y de comprensión de su lectura por parte del lector, constituyen la totalidad del proceso LIBRO".[3]

Esta labor de apoyo y estímulo permitiría entonces tanto el desarrollo de la bibliografía nacional como la protección de los autores nicaragüenses. Unido a estas intenciones es que se ejecuta el nacimiento y desarrollo de casas editoras nacionales, mientras se mantienen de forma particular los pocos esfuerzos privados e institucionales que lograron sobrevivir la etapa anterior.

De esta manera se puede expresar cuales fueron algunas de las más sobresalientes iniciativas en lo que se refiere a la producción bibliográfica que se dieron en la época de la revolución sandinista.

Casas editoras
Editorial Nueva Nicaragua

Esta editorial fue fundada por decreto del gobierno en enero de 1981. Inicialmente el gobierno financió los gastos de su presupuesto administrativo. Después, hasta 1987, recibió un subsidio parcial para este rubro. Su objetivo fundamental es "publicar libros, revistas, folletos, panfletos, discos y cassettes de carácter científico, educativo y cultural para promover las ideas, la ciencia y la cultura".[4] Estableció como política de publicación la "edición de los grandes clásicos de la literatura universal, y promover la divulgación de lo más representativo de la creación literaria nacional".[5] Cuenta esta institución con un consejo editorial y de acuerdo a la opinión de escritores y quienes se desenvuelven en campos similares, esta tiene las características de una auténtica editorial. La impresión de sus obras la hacen a través de contratos con imprentas nacionales.

Entre 1981 y 1990 llegó a publicar 260 títulos, de los cuales 89 corresponden a la literatura clásica universal. El resto corresponde a literatura nacional, libros sobre Nicaragua, literatura testimonial y otros. La mayoría de sus libros han sido publicados en formatos sencillos, pero generalmente buenos, y han tenido precios muy económicos. Sus tirajes de libros alcanzaron inicialmente entre 10,000 y hasta 50,000 ejemplares. Actualmente, los tirajes de sus últimos títulos sólo han alcanzado un cifra de 3,000 ejemplares.

Editorial Vanguardia

Nació como iniciativa de un grupo de intelectuales después del triunfo de la revolución sandinista, aunque se inicia oficialmente como empresa a partir de 1985. Su fin primordial es "la difusión del pensamiento nicaragüense en todas las esferas del pensamiento humano",[6] como también contribuir a la labor de información y orientación que las transformaciones económicas, sociales y políticas que la sociedad nicaragüense estaba viviendo.

La Vanguardia es una editorial seria, independiente, y tiene como característica que la empresa está integrada por socios, que se identifican con la revolución sandinista. Han contado con apoyo de algunos organismos de solidaridad internacional y sindicatos gráficos de Europa.

En la última etapa de esta década ha tratado de establecer contratos especiales para encontrar la forma de importar y exportar libros. La dirección de la editorial considera que en efecto han logrado desarrollar una política de comercialización nacional e internacional. Al igual que la Editorial Nueva Nicaragua, utiliza servicios privados para la impresión de sus obras.

Fondo Editorial del CIRA

El CIRA es una institución no gubernamental, sin fines de lucro, dedicada al trabajo de investigación en las ciencias sociales, a la promoción de la organización popular, así como la labor de divulgación y capacitación. El Fondo Editorial del CIRA tiene el objetivo de divulgar los resultados de las investigaciones del Centro y otras que se producen en Nicaragua, así como contribuir a la divulgación de la cultura y alternativas del conocimiento. No cuenta con ningún tipo de financiamiento y se apoya en sus propios recursos. Sin embargo, dentro del programa de esta institución se está apoyando actualmente a la Asociación Nicaragüense de Literatura Infantil y Juvenil, que tiene como objetivo básico el estimular la cultura y la recreación de niños y jóvenes, buscando con esto contribuir al desarrollo integral de la niñez y la juventud. Esta asociación nació con carácter autónomo en 1986, y su meta es publicar los cuentos nacionales inéditos e incentivar a los autores para que escriban para niños y jóvenes, y estimular el hábito lector en la niñez. Se financia a través de las donaciones y solidaridad de pueblos y organizaciones gubernamentales y no gubernamentales.

En su primer concurso de literatura infantil tuvo la participación de 219 cuentos y de 113 autores. Actualmente tienen en imprenta tres obras.

Editorial Nicarao

Es esta una editorial que nació a finales de 1990, con un espíritu ecuménico, humanista y social. Su fundación es producto del esfuerzo de iglesias protestantes de Alemania, así como de grupos solidarios. Se considera que está en su fase de consolidación; hasta la fecha ha publicado cuatro títulos, y para agosto de 1991 espera haber completado un total de 12.

La Editorial Nicarao llena todas las características de una editorial seria y está estructurada para hacer exclusivamente el papel de una compañía editorial. A pesar de que nació en los momentos más críticos, particularmente en relación al problema económico de Nicaragua, parece un proyecto lleno de optimismo y con seguridad de que va a cumplir las metas que se ha fijado. En cuanto a su trabajo de editor, considera fundamentalmente tres criterios para la publicación de libros: que sean de buena calidad, que tengan atractividad, y que sean vendibles. Los tirajes de sus obras oscilan entre 1,000 y 5,000 ejemplares.

Editorial Universitaria, Universidad Nacional Autónoma de Nicaragua, León

Esta empresa fue creada como parte integral de los servicios estudiantiles de la universidad. Tiene como objetivos fundamentales la publicación o impresión de libros de textos más necesarios para los estudiantes de la educación superior, dando prioridad a las facultades donde el material bibliográfico es demasiado escaso o de difícil acceso económico para el estudiante, y la publicación de revistas culturales.

La Editorial Universitaria tiene su personal financiado por el presupuesto de la universidad. Para la edición de materiales, han contado con alguna ayuda externa, particularmente de organismos de Alemania, el Servicio Universitario Mundial. El material que produce para uso de los estudiantes es usualmente vendido en la librería de la universidad.

Durante los últimos diez años sólo logró publicar 9 libros, y edita la revista *Cuadernos Universitarios*, que contiene generalmente artículos literarios, críticos, científicos, etc. Hace la labor de impresión de toda la papelería que requiere la universidad para su funcionamiento, y a veces hace trabajos para instituciones de beneficio social y cultural.

Editorial y Publicaciones, Universidad Centroamericana

La Universidad Centroamericana tiene una imprenta establecida, que fue fundada a finales de los años 60. La imprenta está en capacidad de desarrollar un proceso completo de publicaciones. Gracias a la cooperación de instituciones europeas, otros tipos de financiamiento y asesoría externa, ha logrado formar un equipo completo.

La imprenta prepara todos los materiales que la universidad necesita, y muy pocas veces hace trabajos externos. En la rama editorial no hay un programa de ediciones, ni hay un formato definido o único para los materiales. Sin embargo, se editan libros de textos a solicitud de las escuelas y/o facultades, siendo los mismos solicitantes los que hacen la labor de editores de sus libros.

La Universidad Centroamericana maneja a modo de proyecto la creación de la editorial universitaria; sin embargo, edita la *Revista Encuentro*, su publicación oficial. Esta revista abarca todos los campos científicos, pero pone especial énfasis en las ciencias sociales. Publica también la revista *Diakonia*, que es del orden de la Teología Espiritual; la revista *Envío*, definida en el orden social y coyuntural del país; la revista *Cuadernos de Sociología*, que responde a las necesidades de la escuela de sociología de la universidad.

La universidad financia el presupuesto de salarios y servicios básicos. Los libros que son publicados a través de la imprenta se venden únicamente a través de la librería universitaria, y los tirajes son pequeños en general. El costo de los libros a los estudiantes es muy bajo, pero la mayor parte de los materiales han sido conseguidos a través de donaciones, al igual que la maquinaria que se utiliza.

Distribuidora Cultural

Esta institución de carácter privado nació como importadora-distribuidora-editora en el año 1973. Ha actuado como principal distribuidora de la Editorial Oveja Negra de Colombia, Siglo XXI Editores de México, Editorial Universitaria Centroamericana (EDUCA), Editorial Trillas de México, la Editorial Nueva Nicaragua, etc. Su actividad comercializadora de libros ha sido relevante en el mercado nacional, pero también la labor de editora principalmente de textos básicos no es de menor importancia. La Distribuidora Cultural llegó a publicar 21 títulos en el año 1984, con tirajes promedios de 3,000 a 5,000 ejemplares, y la excepción del tiraje de un diccionario básico de la lengua castellana (para estudiantes de primaria y secundaria), con 50,000 unidades. La mayoría de las obras editadas en esta época eran de autores nacionales y de la literatura clásica, que estaban siendo requeridos por los programas escolares de ese momento. Sus impresiones las hace generalmente en Costa Rica. Por diversas razones, entre ellas el factor económico, esta institución cerró operaciones entre 1987 y 1990.

IMELSA

IMELSA: Importaciones y Exportaciones Literarias, S.A., fue fundada en 1980 por un grupo de empresarios de librerías de Managua, al que se integraron algunos accionistas. Nació con la característica de apoyo incondicional a la revolución sandinista, con criterio político e ideológico. Esta empresa se convirtió en poco tiempo en una fuerte distribuidora-comercializadora a nivel nacional. Estableció relaciones de trueque y compensación, convenios comerciales y líneas de créditos con países amigos, para la importación de bibliografía técnica, juvenil, infantil, política, literaria, etc. Sus principales proveedores han sido la Unión Soviética (editoriales Progreso, Ciencias Sociales, MIR, Rauda, Malich); Cuba (Pueblo y Educación, Ciencias Sociales, Editorial Oriente, Ciencias Técnicas, etc.); México (Editorial Cártago, Siglo XXI Editores, Porrúa, Nueva Imagen); España (Editorial Fontamara y Alianza Editorial); Costa Rica (EDUCA); y otros países europeos. IMELSA es también una distribuidora de material nacional, particularmente del fondo de la Editorial Nueva Nicaragua. Actualmente mantiene su actividad de comercio con el libro, aunque también su intensidad de trabajo ha bajado, como consecuencia de la crisis económica. La labor de esta institución en cuanto a exportaciones no ha sido tan intensa, sobre todo por problemas de legislación.

No se debe obviar que existen muchas más instituciones dedicadas a la edición y distribución de bibliografía nacional (y extranjera) que no fueron entrevistadas para este trabajo. Están entre estas la Distribuidora Ramírez, varios centros que funcionan como librería-café, algunas recién fundadas imprentas-editoriales de las universidades más jóvenes del país, organismos no gubernamentales, supermercados, organismos religiosos, tipografías, autores individuales, que harían una lista interminable, pero que de alguna manera han tenido participación en la labor de publicación y distribución de las obras nacionales.

Problemas que se dieron en esta etapa (1979-1990)

Fue esta, sin lugar a dudas, una gran época para Nicaragua en cuanto a que hubo un asombroso auge de difusión de la información nacional. Pero eso no significa que no hayan habido problemas, algunos de los cuales presentan las mismas características de las etapas anteriores. Como característica común se dio el caso de que surgieron nuevas instituciones, se modificaron algunas, y murieron otras. En muchos casos, en esas instituciones que sobrevivieron, hubo problemas comunes, y otros distintos, originados por sus propios particularidades.

En la primera parte de la etapa de gobierno sandinista hubo un entusiasmo contagiante que hizo volcar los esfuerzos, quizás no muy bien organizados, hacia un objetivo común que era el desarrollo de una política de estímulo y protección a los autores nacionales, así como la formación del editor y las estructuras correspondientes para el desarrollo de un proceso de distribución y difusión de la cultura nacional, atravesando un camino difícil, lleno de obstáculos del orden económico, inexperiencia en el campo, problemas de relación humana, etc. Nos encontramos con que existen casas editoriales que llenaron los requerimientos mínimos para optar sus nombres, pero hicieron falta otros elementos que no les permitieron desarrollarse eficientemente.

Por ejemplo, en el caso de la Editorial Nueva Nicaragua, esta se quejó siempre de no contar con los canales de distribución adecuados, ni se dio la comercialización profesional. La promoción ha sido un trabajo de improvisación por la falta de formación profesional en el ramo de la comercialización, y en el trabajo editorial hubo en cierta manera "hacedores de libros".[7] No fue esto un problema único de esa editorial. Escritores y trabajadores en libros confirman que hizo falta una verdadera distribución. El libro no se expuso al mercado eficientemente, y ha sido esto una de las principales razones por las que algunas instituciones e individuos han fracasado. En lo que se pudo constatar al hacer este trabajo, quizás, entre las editoriales, sea la editorial Vanguardia la que mejor comercializó y distribuyó sus libros de manera directa.

En el año 1984 se dio el bloqueo económico de los Estados Unidos a Nicaragua, y se inició una nueva guerra entre el gobierno y lo que se llamó "Contrarrevolución", lo que provocó una situación económica de emergencia, teniendo que trabajar con listas de prioridades para la subsistencia del país. A partir de entonces dejó de haber importaciones de libros, materia prima para su producción, y otros materiales indispensables para esta área. Esto significó además que el país se vio limitado de la difusión del pensamiento clásico en las artes y letras, y de libros de textos y consulta para el desarrollo académico nacional. Sin embargo, se continuó produciendo obras nacionales, en su mayoría de carácter literario, social y político-testimonial. Esta situación originó problemas comunes al campo de las publicaciones y a quienes estaban involucrados en ello. Se dio una saturación de bibliografía nacional internamente, así como de libros técnicos y literarios que provenían de países socialistas.

Estos últimos libros servían como referencia, sobre todo la literatura técnica, pero no llenaban los requerimientos nacionales en su totalidad. Otro factor negativo fue que se cerraron muchas bibliotecas públicas y escolares durante esta prolongada guerra, debido a que el estado no podía continuar sosteniéndolas económicamente. Las editoriales y distribuidoras perdieron un sector consumidor de libros: el estado, siendo el más grande comprador de estos, dejó de adquirir para esta importante área. En el peor de los casos, se cerró el Ministerio de Cultura, que al inicio de su fundación tuvo una excelente editorial, conocida como Editorial del Ministerio de Cultura; más tarde fue llamada Ocarina, y finalmente, al desaparecer su ministerio, el fondo de esta fue pasada a la Editorial Nueva Nicaragua. Se fundó más tarde el Instituto de Cultura, ya casi al final de esta etapa, pero no se logró constatar hasta donde tuvo un rol en el campo de producción y distribución de libros.

Hay otro factor que fue parte de los problemas de esta etapa, y que se puede considerar tiene dos aspectos. Primero, en esas instituciones que el estado apoyaba, hay quienes sienten que no hubo suficiente amplitud para permitir la publicación de autores que no fueron considerados con la calificación necesaria, o que no estaban políticamente de acuerdo con el gobierno. Segundo, había conciencia entre los sectores involucrados en el quehacer del libro de "la falta de balance en la publicación de libros culturales, creación literaria y libros científicos, pero eso no dependía de las políticas editoriales, sino de la ausencia en el país de la producción científica en las ciencias sociales, ciencias exactas, investigación".[8]

Se finaliza esta etapa, si bien con editoriales establecidas, y con instituciones dedicadas a la distribución y comercialización de libros, sin políticas definidas para realizar esta última tarea, y con una ley de derecho de autor únicamente en proyecto. No obstante, deja un hermoso precedente: Nicaragua se ha dado a conocer a una buena porción del mundo, y ha habido un reconocimiento y fomento de los valores nacionales.

Situación actual

Llegamos a la era que estamos viviendo. Empezamos con los problemas que acabamos de expresar en la etapa anterior, y al parecer sin muchas esperanzas de cambiar pronto el panorama. Se da un cambio de gobierno, y el país sufre también una serie de transformaciones concretamente a nivel político y económico. Esto significa que el país es manejado hacia una nueva tendencia de vida.

Probablemente la principal característica de esta etapa es que se arrastra y recrudece la pésima situación económica del país. Aunque algunas estructuras permanecen iguales, el nivel de vida se deteriora aún más, y en lo que corresponde a la situación de la producción bibliográfica, esta parece deteriorarse considerablemente.

A pesar de que el gobierno ratifica la existencia del Instituto de Cultura, lógicamente con una administración que corresponde a la nueva política gubernamental, este no se ha pronunciado aún en cuanto a publicar alguna obra que les represente, o a dar algún tipo de apoyo al campo editorial-distribuidor existente.

Las editoriales tienen inventarios enormes sin poder ser promovidos porque también haría falta publicar nuevos libros para ofrecer esos fondos, pero hace falta el apoyo económico, y las distribuidoras, aunque también batallan por sostenerse en pie, también adolecen del mismo problema: hace falta financiamiento para mover los fondos e imprimir nuevas obras, y realizar las importaciones de libros necesarios para cubrir en general las necesidades académicas de escuelas, universidades, y las pocas bibliotecas públicas existentes. El único movimiento que hasta ahora ha hecho el gobierno en este aspecto ha sido a través de un convenio con la Agencia para el Desarrollo Internacional, para la edición de varios textos escolares, que los está distribuyendo en las escuelas primarias del país, a precios razonables. Estos libros han sido editados en Colombia.

El pueblo en general no está adquiriendo libros cuando lo primordial es subsistir dentro de la deteriorada economía del país. Si en la mayoría de los elementos básicos del desarrollo de la nación la situación está muy mal, la producción bibliográfica parece deprimida, afectando tanto a los editores, distribuidores como a los autores.

Algunos autores sienten que han llegado hasta el punto de encontrarse con la situación previa a 1979: hay que tener fondo propio o un soporte económico externo y arriesgarse a vender personalmente sus obras, o a quedarse con ellas. Este asunto se agrava al punto de que se podría profundizar una crisis de nivel social y cultural ante la evidencia de que el gobierno ha cortado presupuesto a las universidades, y cancelado subsidios a centros de apoyo social que fueron mantenidos durante el gobierno anterior. Esto le ha creado al gobierno una imagen negativa, como si no considera que es importante el aspecto cultural y que es parte del desarrollo de la nación.

El peor problema en este sentido sería que una buena parte de esas instituciones que ya han hecho un camino, puedan deteriorarse visiblemente si no se encuentran los canales externos adecuados, y el mismo gobierno, si no tiene ahora los recursos necesarios para apoyarles, les permita por su medio canalizar otras actividades o establecer convenios de manera que puedan sobrevivir y mejorar los aspectos que fueron manejados de manera errónea o empíricamente en la etapa que les antecede.

Observaciones

Hemos de concluir con editoriales y distribuidoras con altos inventarios de libros, con la necesidad de publicar obras indispensables para el desarrollo social, académico, científico y cultural del país, pero deprimidas económicamente, y sin mucha esperanza de mejorar en su futuro inmediato. Sin embargo, a pesar de la incertidumbre político-económica del país, hay deseos y entusiasmo por cambiar este panorama.

Independientemente de las claras divergencias políticas que sin lugar a dudas existen en el país, y particularmente a nivel de algunos de los entrevistados para esta ponencia, ha sido notorio que hay puntos donde todos convergen para buscar la solución al problema del desarrollo editorial y una política de publicaciones satisfactoria: (1) hace falta desarrollar profesionalmente el mercado del libro, nacional e internacional; (2) las editoriales y distribuidoras del país claman al unísono por financiamiento interno o externo para publicar aquellas obras clásicas y representativas de la literatura nacional, y aquellos que además requieren los programas académicos en los distintos niveles para el desarrollo de sus programas; (3) el gobierno debería apoyar el desarrollo de editoriales y publicaciones, por lo menos adquiriendo y distribuyendo la bibliografía nacional a través de sus aparatos educativos y culturales; (4) para completar el proceso libro-producción, se debe revisar y ejecutar el proyecto pendiente sobre la política nacional del libro y la protección de los derechos de autor de forma que todo este conjunto sea manejado como una acción integral en la tarea de protección y desarrollo del patrimonio bibliográfico nacional.

NOTAS

1. Fidel Coloma, entrevista, abril 1991, p. 2.
2. *Cuadernos del Taller San Lucas*, no. 5 (agosto 1951), p. 161.
3. *Políticas nacionales del libro: Costa Rica, Guatemala, . . .* (Bogotá: CERLAL, 1982), p. 42.
4. *Que es la nueva Nicaragua*, p. 1.
5. *Que es la Editorial Nueva Nicaragua*, p. 4.
6. Eric Blandon, entrevista, abril 1991, p. 1.
7. Roberto Díaz Castillo, entrevista, mayo 1991.
8. Sergio Ramírez, entrevista, mayo 1991.

REFERENCIAS

Fuentes bibliográficas
Libros
CERLAL. *Políticas nacionales del libro en Costa Rica, Guatemala, Honduras, Nicaragua, Panamá y República Dominicana*. Bogotá: CERLAL, 1982.

Libro y lector: Textos del Seminario Nacional sobre Investigaciones del Comportamiento Lector y Promoción de Hábitos de Lectura. Managua: Editorial La Ocarina, 1987.

I Festival Internacional del Libro: Nicaragua 87. Managua: Editorial La Ocarina, 1987.

Revistas
"50 Años del Movimiento de Vanguardia de Nicaragua". *El Pez y la Serpiente*, 22/23 (invierno 1978-verano 1979), 7-31.

Meneses, Vidaluz. "La cultura en diez años de revolución". *Amanecer*, 61 (junio-julio 1989), 56-58.

Entrevistas
Blandón Guevara, Eric. Escritor; Director de la Editorial Vanguardia. Managua. Abril, 1991.

Coloma, Fidel. Escritor; Director de la Biblioteca Nacional. Managua. Mayo, 1991.

Cuadra, Pablo Antonio. Escritor; Asesor del Instituto de Cultura. Managua. Mayo, 1991.

Díaz Castillo, Roberto. Director de la Editorial Nueva Nicaragua. Managua. Mayo, 1991.

Kliche, Luiz. Director de la Editorial Nicarao. Managua. Mayo, 1991.

Mayorga, Mario. Director de la Editorial Universitaria de la UNAN, León. León. Abril, 1991.

Meneses, Vidaluz. Ex-Vice-Ministro de Cultura; Escritora. Managua. Abril, 1991.

Miranda, Mayra. Ex-Directora de Bibliotecas y Archivos del Ministerio de Cultura; Directora de la Biblioteca del Banco Central. Managua. Abril, 1991.

Pérez-Valle, Eduardo. Escritor; Ex-Director de la Distribuidora Cultural. Managua. Mayo, 1991.

Ramírez Mercado, Sergio. Ex-Presidente de Nicaragua; Presidente del Consejo Editorial de la Nueva Nicaragua. Managua. Mayo, 1991.

Wallace, Melvin. Director del Fondo Editorial del CIRA. Managua. Mayo, 1991.

Liberty and Justice for All: Human Rights and Democratization in Latin America

16. Do Human Rights Exist in Latin American Democracies?

Alexander Wilde

The early 1970s was a period when students were very interested in Latin America, a lively time. What I would like to try to do is present the human rights issues from a somewhat different perspective. In chapter 18 of this work, Lawrence Weschler presents a brilliant exposition about torture, which is arguably the root of the problem of human rights. I work in the world of policy and politics, and torture is thought about differently. Weschler says torture is used to break down the subjectivity of the human being, which is accurate from a moral perspective. In the world of politics, one could say that torture is used because it works, because it achieves the ends of those who hold power. Moral considerations are only part of the world of politics, but those of us working for human rights through policy are continually searching for ways to connect their protection to other interests in the play of power. The success of the international movement for human rights over the last thirty years shows that these efforts can enlarge the real significance of moral concerns in the public realm.

Democracy, the arrival of elected civilian government in Latin America, has changed the nature of human rights problems. It has changed the nature of human rights, and it has changed the nature of work on human rights.

We know that the human rights movement—the idea of the public protection of human rights in Latin America—came into existence under dictatorships. And it had a great deal to do with delegitimating those dictatorships and the methods of repression that they utilized. Human rights also had a lot to do with the international isolation of such regimes. As Weschler put it, the movement succeeded in turning on a light that illuminated the violations previously carried out by dictatorships in the dark. As the light grew, it became something that created real international difficulties for regimes like that of Pinochet in Chile, beyond what they would have faced if they could have kept their practices in the dark. I would stress the genuinely international—or transnational—character of this force. It was not—as too many in Washington complacently assert—just the light of the great American

187

city on the hill shining into the world. Under dictatorships human rights became a language, a public language, for voicing what was otherwise private and dark. As this moral language became public and legitimate—often sponsored and protected by the church—it became a real factor of power delegitimating dictatorships. And it helped to create "space," as Latin Americans put it, for individual and collective rights, the basis for the renewal of public life.

Human rights exist in Latin American "democracies" today. And there are really two ways to understand that: one is the *state* of human rights, the other the *cause* of human rights. First the former. In policy circles, it is commonly asserted that free and fair elections and democratic transitions have really removed the need for any particular concern with human rights per se. Many policymakers, in Latin America as well as the United States, argue that the existence of elected governments negates the underlying rationale of the human rights movement of an earlier time. These energies, it is now held, should now be turned toward improving and deepening democracy.

Clearly, that greatly overstates the change brought by elected governments, even in countries where the situation is relatively good, such as Chile or Uruguay. We can make a couple of generalizations about the state of human rights in Latin America today. One is that where transitions to elected civilian regimes have taken place, it has meant the end of the most egregious systematic violations of human rights. Obviously there's a range here and particularly where the military and their civilian allies hold a great reservoir of veto power, it becomes an enormous gap in cases like Guatemala, or in a less violent way, Paraguay. A state within a state, really. So I would say first that transitions to elected governments have meant limited but real gains. Certainly where there are continuing armed insurgencies in Latin America, Peru, Colombia, Guatemala, El Salvador, there are ongoing violations and abuses of human rights by both sides, and those abuses are rising in the Andes. Real gains in those situations where there are insurgencies will depend on peace. To paraphrase Pope Paul VI, the real name of human rights in these societies is peace.

We can say that almost everywhere in Latin America in this new period of civilian rule (or at least civilian reign), there is greater awareness of endemic problems of human rights. In contrast with the old violations, carried out directly by the dictatorships, there is more consciousness of what we might call sins of omission on the part of the government. Thus, the new problems of human rights trace to governmental failures to remedy widespread institutional problems—for example, in justice systems. Many civilian governments show no ability to control ordinary crime, even while they may tolerate various *operaciones de limpieza social*, and condone the persistent use of force by paramilitary thugs, whether that be in the Urabá or in the Magdalena Medio in Colombia, or in the Amazon in Brazil or in the interior in Paraguay, or in the south of Mexico.

Now the *cause* of human rights. I would point to two tendencies in this new context. I do think that even in Guatemala and certainly in El Salvador, Peru, and Colombia, human rights has become more legitimate as a cause today than it was five or ten years ago. It has come to mean something more in those societies than simply the respectable face that the left tries to put on. It is that kind of universalism that Beatriz Manz (chap. 17) talks about that we all know should be there.

In all these places, human rights groups need to carry on, as Beatriz points out for Guatemala, the classic kind of work that was done under dictatorships, which is the work of *denuncia*, the condemnation of crimes carried out by the agents of the state. But in all of them as well, and I think it's particularly notable in Colombia and El Salvador today, it is very important for the human rights movement also to show some capacity of *propuesta*. This implies the capacity to respond to limited space that exists to work with *fiscales* or the *procuradores* or the ombudsman or whatever to see whether it is possible in fact to enlarge that space. This new work has to be approached cautiously and critically, but things can go forward. Even in El Salvador, they are going forward.

The other tendency in the human rights movement in Latin America today is an increasing concern with civil, economic, and political rights. Mexico is an extraordinary case for this. It is of course undergoing a kind of basic crisis of political legitimacy. It's a country with very serious human rights problems, and yet at the same time there is an extraordinary growth of human rights organizations in civil society. It's happened quite fast and it has spread rapidly. They are diverse. And of course it's happening just at the time of the proposal of the North American Free Trade Agreement which will go forward. The question at this stage is what role will a human rights movement in Mexico, working with labor unions or peasant organizations or other politic forces, such as the Cardenistas, play in seeing that their concerns are part of that agreement. It's a challenge, of course, that exists on this side as well.

On U.S. policy, I would say just one thing. The United States is officially committed today—through the long, tortuous Reagan presidency—to human rights within a support for democracy in Latin

America. Secretary Baker last year said that, "beyond containment is democracy." That's the official policy. Part of the policy, however, which isn't proclaimed quite so loudly, is the drug war. The Andes is now a larger recipient of military aid from the United States than Central America. Colombia, not El Salvador, is now the number one recipient of military aid in the hemisphere! The United States is, in fact, remilitarizing Latin America, reestablishing those relationships that were cut off as a result of human rights pressures in the '70s and '80s. I fear this new "War on Drugs" is putting forces in motion which very much contradict the commitments that are otherwise made to human rights and democracy.

17. Elections without Change: The Human Rights Record of Guatemala

Beatriz Manz

There is an easy equation between elections and democracy. Countries such as Guatemala with a long history of undemocratic regimes, extreme social inequities, and ethnic discrimination illustrate the fallacy of automatically equating elections with democracy. I focus on the election of Vinicio Cerezo Arevalo in December 1985 and examine the meaning of elections in the context of the human rights record during his administration.

An important point of reference in assessing the significance of a civilian administration is to determine the forces that led to elections as well as under what circumstances the elections were held. Unlike failed coups or discredited armies facing a strong democratic movement, in Guatemala a strong, confident, victorious military decided elections should be held. It was the military itself who chose to turn over the administration of the state to a civilian. Several reasons motivated the army in that direction. Trends in Central America toward civilian governments, economic problems, and aid that would be more accessible to an elected civilian administration were one factor. In addition, by 1985 the Army had already set roots in the society, particularly in the rural areas, to such a degree that civilian rule would not undermine military power. Most important, from the Army's perspective, only candidates acceptable to the military were allowed to run. This factor, combined with a culture of fear that had demobilized the population, guaranteed a smooth continuation of military programs and lack of participation in a democratic process. [1]

Vinicio Cerezo Arevalo, a member of the Christian Democratic Party, was elected president in a two-round voting process on December 8, 1985. [2] Some analysts, such as George Fauriol, hailed the election of a civilian, contending that it was more than a symbolic change of clothes: "This is an auspicious moment for both Guatemala and the United States." The election signaled that "a refreshing political climate has taken hold." [3] While the State Department, some academics, and a few members of Congress were willing to place enormous faith in the civilian administration, virtually all human rights monitors soon realized that, unfortunately, little was changing from the previous military administrations.[4] Anyone familiar with Guatemala's history since 1954 would have been skeptical of the character of a civilian administration, particularly given the context under which the elections took place.[5]

In assessing the context of the elections and the role of the military, let me explore the record of human rights prior to the elections. Is that record an aberration or part of a long-term policy? How has the legal system functioned? Have those responsible been brought to justice or are they, in fact, firmly entrenched in power and holding even higher positions of authority? Is there any sign that the military will submit to the authority of an elected president or, more likely, will the President be compelled to continue military policy? Is democracy possible in a society subjected to institutionalized fear? And finally, what would it take to liberate citizens from fear?

I have characterized the period before the elections of 1985 as a period of "mass terror" in which the military carried out a fierce counterinsurgency campaign and, even more effectively, a war against an unarmed population.[6] Despite the fact that human rights organizations such as Americas Watch and Amnesty International[7] have characterized the human rights record of Guatemala as the worst in the hemisphere, the Guatemalan case is among the least known, as it is seldom covered in the United States media. Whereas Chile, Argentina, neighboring El Salvador, and Nicaragua received wide coverage in the international press, Guatemala's human rights atrocities were and continue to be largely hidden from the rest of the world.

It has been estimated that since the 1954 coup more than 150,000 Guatemalans have been victims of abductions and assassinations. An additional 1 million (out of a population of 8 million) have been displaced by the violence, mainly in the rural Indian areas. Of these, a quarter million have become refugees in Mexico and the United States.[8]

The human rights situation in the last three decades can be characterized as follows: the military has either directly controlled or indirectly dominated every national government to the present. Elections such as those that brought to power Julio César Méndez Montenegro in 1966 or Vinicio Cerezo Arevalo in 1986, even if technically without fraud, have not changed the pattern of military domination. The repression against independent organizations has created a culture of fear and terror that undermines the foundations for a true democracy. In the 1980s an additional dimension was introduced: the penetration of the military, directly or through its instruments of control, into even the most remote Indian villages, in effect creating a militarized countryside.

The challenge for a civilian president was to break with the past. In its favor, the civilian administration had a popular mandate, having won with an impressive majority of the popular vote. In addition, the Christian Democratic Party had in its favor an effective organization and base of support both in urban and rural areas. Vinicio Cerezo also had diplomatic support in Europe and the U.S. Congress. In addition, Mr. Cerezo was a seasoned politician. The military had obviously recognized the need to turn over the presidency to a civilian in order to end Guatemala's political isolation in the international community and secure needed economic aid from the European Economic Community and the United States. These factors provided Mr. Cerezo with an opportunity—tenuous, to be sure—to change course and exercise his power not only over the military but also over the traditional intransigent elite.

With all these prospects for change, what happened between 1986 and 1990? Unfortunately, in terms of human rights, events left much to be desired. As one human rights organization stated, "President Cerezo has embarked on a clear strategy of avoiding confrontation with the military, which has been and continues to be the source of the majority of human rights violations in Guatemala."[9] In fact, it has been widely reported that Mr. Cerezo assured the military prior to taking office that he would not repeal the amnesty for past abuses. In terms of new violations, "he has turned responsibility for prosecution of new violations entirely over to the judiciary, not the executive—a dubious proposition in Guatemala, where a weak and at times corrupt court system has little opportunity or will to operate independently of the all-powerful military."[10]

The respected *Inforpress Centroamericana* reported the first massacre during the Cerezo administration: "[it] became known on July 11 [1986], when the daily *La Hora*, reported that Catholic Church pastoral agents from the department of Izabal had sent a letter to the President of the Republic, dated June 30, requesting the investigation of disappearances in Izabal."[11] For me personally, the signs were ominous early on in Cerezo's administration. While coincidentally in Guatemala on a human rights monitoring mission with Aryeh Neier of Americas Watch, I witnessed the execution of a University student just a few blocks from the presidential palace. The absence of an investigation and of any reporting of the incident in the Guatemalan press, and the defensive reaction of Elliott Abrams, U.S. Assistant Secretary of State, to my account of the incident in an op-ed piece in the *New York*

Times all underscored the problems with human rights in Guatemala.[12] Soon headlines referred to the "marked deterioration of human rights" in the country[13] and "political violence out of control."[14] The British Parliamentary Human Rights Group and Americas Watch issued a grim report on Mr. Cerezo's first year in office: "The election of a civilian to the office of the Guatemalan presidency has by no means ended the military's authority. . . . Throughout 1986, violent killings were reported in the Guatemalan press at the rate of over 100 per month and abductions and disappearances have also continued."[15] The violent toll of Mr. Cerezo's second year (1987) was assessed as among the worst since the wave of violence in 1984. In the last month of the year 78 assassinations were reported, totaling 1,021 for the year. November 1987 had the highest number of kidnappings reported.[16] Yet the U.S. State Department "consistently ignores the military's domination of all aspects of rural life and accepts at face value government assurances that the civil patrols are now 'voluntary,' despite considerable evidence to the contrary."[17] Human rights monitors concluded that while "Institutions have been established to protect human rights and to investigate abuses, their impact has been limited by a lack of will and executive support. Indeed, the Christian Democratic government consistently has refused to acknowledge human rights abuses by the military, a position which has all but ruled out serious investigations of such abuses."[18]

The lack of support for institutions on the part of the government has been a repeated complaint: "Unfortunately, the government has demonstrated a consistent lack of support for those institutions—both government and private—created to monitor or investigate past or present abuses."[19] Several human rights monitoring organizations were established within the country, just before Mr. Cerezo was elected and during his administration, such as the Mutual Support Group (GAM), the Runujel Junam Council of Ethnic Communities (CERJ); the Center for the Investigation, Study and Promotion of Human Rights (CIEPRODH); the National Coordination of Widows of Guatemala (CONAVIGUA); the National Council of Displaced of Guatemala (CONDEG) and, in January 1990, a human rights office under the auspices of the Catholic Archdiocese in Guatemala City—the "Miraculous Virgin" Social Service Office of the Archdiocese of Guatemala. What this reflects is that while the State Department and the Guatemalan civilian government could point to these organizations as a sign of improvements regarding human rights, in fact human rights abuses continued with impunity.[20] In 1988 human rights violations, killings, and disappearances were occurring at a rate of about 100 per month.[21] Some critics have asserted that the U.S. government has exerted pressure on the Guatemalan government for political aims in the region rather than to observe the human rights of its own citizens: "A significant factor behind the ongoing aid to the Guatemalan military has been the untoward pressure that the Reagan administration has exerted on the Cerezo government to end its mediating role in the Central American peace process and to place itself squarely in the Administration's anti-Sandinista camp."[22] Lamentably, halfway into President Cerezo's term, Americas Watch issued a report, appropriately titled *Closing the Space*, in which it evaluated the Cerezo administration thus far:

There has been little improvement in Guatemala's human rights record; the military has ceded no authority to civilians in rural areas; and rights violators among the military have not been brought to justice. (In November and January 1988, the GAM accused some two dozen Army officers of responsibility for kidnappings in the past. Almost all listed are active-duty officers who, under the Cerezo government, have received promotions within the officer ranks. None has been charged or tried.)[23]

This appalling state of affairs prompted the Archbishop of Guatemala, Próspero Penados del Barrio, to comment that "The Army hasn't changed at all. . . . The Army is a law unto itself."[24]

While human rights organizations were severely criticizing Guatemala, an even more condemnatory and harmful denunciation came from the Harvard University Law School in testimony before Congress. Professor Philip B. Heymann explained why Harvard's project was being terminated in Guatemala. Harvard Law School had been contracted by USAID to "provide assistance to the appropriate Guatemalan authorities in dealing with two types of violence that seemed to threaten a new democracy: street violence and politically motivated violence."[25] Unfortunately, according to Professor Heymann, "Too many leaders in Guatemala have too much to gain by declaring that Guatemala must be satisfied either with crude and brutal alternatives to a modern criminal justice system or with continuing political violence on a scale that is once again destroying the nation's reputation abroad."[26] He went on to accuse the civilian administration of not wanting to rock the boat: "The claim that nothing can be done about political violence is a way of avoiding direct confrontation with the forces responsible for it."[27] In an earlier testimony before Congress, I had urged that economic and military aid to Guatemala be suspended:

Under current circumstances, any economic or military aid to the government of Guatemala would send a strong statement to the military and the rest of the society: atrocities are acceptable, funding will be provided to the military to reconstruct what they themselves have destroyed. As the army continues to consolidate its power over civilian life, any aid channeled through the government—regardless of the humanitarian purposes of the aid—will simply strengthen military control. [28]

The Harvard project also felt it was a waste of U.S. taxpayers' money to continue to provide funding to Guatemala: "[It] is not a useful expenditure of United States money to provide training or advice to the police, prosecutors, or judges of any country whose political and military leaders are unwilling to support law enforcement efforts against every form of political violence, including that initiated by security forces or political/economic groups to which the government leaders may be sympathetic." [29]

Were there some positive developments during the Cerezo administration? Certainly toward the end of his administration, the region and the world experienced profound changes. Within the country, there was a resurgence of popular organizations, including unions, peasant organizations, and human rights organizations. The price these organizations have paid, however, is high. Victims of killings and disappearances continue to be trade unionists, students (particularly from the University of San Carlos), rural promoters, catechists, human rights monitors. The repression against university students in 1989 over a period of weeks proved the continued targeting of a particular segment of the society. As Harvard's Heymann stated before Congress:

We thus saw our job as helping to build a criminal justice structure that could investigate political violence if they were encouraged to do so by the President and the Minister of Defense. The murder of five and disappearance of another five students from San Carlos University in August and September of 1989 was a particularly dramatic and visible moment in what has been a far larger course of political violence, particularly in rural areas. [30]

Professor Heymann expressed his concern directly to President Cerezo, but to no avail: "I made clear that I believed the military may have been involved in the killing of the students. I said that I saw no sign of a willingness to investigate such crimes seriously . . . [that kind of criminal justice system] was a travesty of justice and hardly a contribution to democracy." [31] Professionals, such as journalists (several press offices were attacked and two weekly newspapers were closed) and independent researchers, have also paid a high price. The most notable case is that of Myrna Mack, a highly regarded Guatemalan anthropologist assassinated on September 11, 1990. [32]

Refugees in Mexico began to press for certain conditions for repatriation as did the internally displaced populations—the

Communities of Population in Resistance (CPR)—for their rights. The case of the Guatemalan refugees and the CPRs is illustrative of the frustrations and lack of progress on the part of the government toward finding solutions to human rights problems. While other countries in Central America, such as Nicaragua and El Salvador, are making strides to bring the political/military conflict to a resolution and address the human tragedy created by forced displacement, the Guatemalan refugees remain the last refugees in the region. In 1992 the United Nations High Commission for Refugees (UNHCR) will cease to provide protection and aid for the Guatemalan refugee camps in Mexico. At that point the Guatemalans will have to decide to remain in Mexico, and become part of that society, or return to Guatemala. This approaching deadline has created anxiety and a new vigor to negotiate the conditions of their return. Their tenacity springs from the strength that comes from years of persecution and collective exodus, even though they have not been able to count on much national or international support. Principal among their concerns are guarantees for their safety. Through their elected representatives—the Permanent Commissions (CCPP), the refugees have articulated a six-point demand: (1) the return must be voluntary, collective, and organized; (2) the land situation and dispute must be resolved; (3) the right to free organization and association must be guaranteed; (4) the right to life, personal and communal integrity must be guaranteed; (5) the right to be accompanied by international and national solidarity organizations must be ensured; (6) the right to freedom of movement must exist.[33]   The CPRs, through their organization, the National Council of Displaced Peoples of Guatemala (CONDEG) formed in September 1989, began to place paid ads in the Guatemalan newspapers describing their conditions and declaring their demands to national and international public opinion.

The Cerezo administration began with expectations that it would curb the excesses of past military regimes, that it would make a break with the past. Unfortunately, as Mr. Cerezo handed the presidency to Jorge Serrano Elías in January 1991, the new President inherits a legacy of the past. During the last year of President Cerezo's term the human rights conditions looked bleak. According to Americas Watch's assessment, "the military remains a law unto itself and human rights violations have risen sharply. Instead of bringing the perpetrators to justice, the Cerezo administration has consistently tolerated and, worse still, apologized for, unspeakable abuses committed by the men the President supposedly commands."[34]   An end-of-the-year report in Guatemala shows that in 1990 there were 1,748 reports of human rights violations: 599 assassinations, 210 disappearances, 140 kidnap-disappearances, and 146 illegal detentions.[35] Among the victims that year were two United States citizens, Michael Devine, who was killed in the Peten, and an Ursuline nun, Diana Ortiz, who was kidnapped and tortured. Another prominent foreigner killed was the Salvadorean Hector Oqueli.

At the time Cerezo left office, no police officer or military officer had been convicted for a human rights violation. However, there is hope that the new government of President Serrano Elías, having inherited the despicable and brutal assassination of Myrna Mack, will bring those responsible to justice. The United States Embassy seems willing to cooperate. Her death has mobilized all sectors of the population in a call to end the impunity that has reigned for so long in that country. What has made Myrna Mack's case possible has been the persistence of her family in bringing the material and intellectual authors of the crime to justice. Should the family, and specifically Helen Mack, sister of the victim, succeed in making the Guatemalan justice system operate or take the case to an international court, it will be the biggest human rights victory won for Guatemala. It would signal the beginning of an end to impunity and a major step to end the culture of fear in that tortured society. If that happens, it will be one further contribution to peace that Myrna Mack made possible for Guatemala.

NOTES

1. For a broad analysis of the elections and Guatemalan society during this period, see Susanne Jonas, *The Battle for Guatemala: Rebels, Death Squads and U.S. Power* (Westview, 1989); James A. Goldston, *Shattered Hope: Guatemalan Workers and the Promise of Democracy* (Westview, 1989); Robert H. Trudeau, "The Guatemalan Election of 1985: Prospects for Democracy," in John Booth and Mitchell A. Seligson, eds. *Elections and Democracy in Central America* (Chapel Hill: University of North Carolina Press, 1989); James Painter, *Guatemala: False Hope, False Freedom* (London: Catholic Institute for International Relations and Latin American Bureau, 1987).

2. In the first round, on November 3, 1985, the Christian Democrats received 38.65 percent of the vote (648,681 votes) against eight contenders. The two leading candidates faced each other in a runoff, and on December 8 Vinicio Cerezo received 1,133,517 votes (68.37 percent). He took office on January 14, 1986.

3. Georges A. Fauriol, Prepared statement, "Development in Guatemala and U.S. Options," Hearings before the Subcommittee on Western Hemisphere Affairs of the Committee on Foreign Affairs, U.S. House of Representatives, Ninety-ninth Congress, February 20, 1985.

4. For an assessment of the military administrations of Lucas García and Ríos Montt, see Carlos Figueroa Ibarra, *El recurso del miedo: Ensayo sobre el estado y el terror en Guatemala* (San Jose, Costa Rica: CSUCA, 1991).

5. The only democratic period in Guatemalan history occurred between 1944 and 1954, during the administrations of Juan José Arevalo and Jacobo Arbenz. A CIA-backed coup overthrew Arbenz and brought about decades of repression. See Piero Gleijeses, *Shattered Hope: The Guatemalan Revolution and the United States, 1944-1954* (Princeton University Press, 1991).

6. Beatriz Manz, *Refugees of a Hidden War: The Aftermath of Counterinsurgency in Guatemala* (Albany: State University of New York Press, 1988) p. 16.

7. Americas Watch, *Creating a Desolation and Calling it Peace* (1983); ibid., *Human Rights in Guatemala: No Neutrals Allowed* (1982); ibid., *Guatemala: A Nation of Prisoners* (1983); Amnesty International, *Guatemala: A Government Program of Political Murder* (1981); ibid., *Massive Extrajudicial Executions in Rural Areas under the Government of General Rios Montt* (1982). Of these, the two most influential are Americas Watch's *A Nation of Prisoners* and Amnesty International's, *A Government Program of Political Murder*.

8. Americas Watch, *Guatemalan Refugees in Mexico, 1980-1984* (New York, NY: Americas Watch, September 1984). See also Beatriz Manz, *Repatriation and Reintegration: An Arduous Process in Guatemala*, Hemispheric Migration Project, Monograph Series, (Washington, D.C.: Georgetown University, 1988). The United States Immigration and Naturalization Service considers most of the Guatemalans entering the United States to be economic migrants. However, one could argue that this population is leaving a country where a coup overthrew a democratically elected president who was carrying out an economic reform program as a cornerstone of his administration. The coup initiated a period of military repression and the absence of democratic participation denying the population a say in the political and economic direction of the country. Therefore, directly or indirectly, people are fleeing political repression. It is also important to note that Guatemala has one of the most unequal distributions of land in the hemisphere. To change the economic conditions requires political participation.

9. Americas Watch, *Closing the Space: Human Rights in Guatemala: May 1987–October 1988* (New York, NY: Americas Watch, November 1988), p. 8.

10. Ibid.

11. *Inforpress Centroamericana*, July 17, 1986.

12. Beatriz Manz, "A Guatemalan Dies and What It Means," *New York Times*, Op-ed, July 14, 1986. See also a series of other articles I wrote related to the civilian administration: "Who Rules Guatemala?" *Boston Globe*, October 22, 1986; "Guatemala: Military's Shadow Clouds Election," *Boston Globe*, Focus Section, December 8, 1985; "Dollars that Forge Guatemalan Chains," *New York Times*, Op-ed, March 18, 1985. A discussion of Elliott Abrams's position can be found in Americas Watch and British Parliamentary Human Rights Group, *Human Rights in Guatemala during Cerezo's First Year* (New York, NY: Americas Watch, February 1987), pp. 86-88.

13. *Inforpress Centroamericana*, November 24, 1988.

14. Ibid., January 21, 1988.

15. Americas Watch and British Parliamentary Human Rights Group, *Human Rights in Guatemala*, p. 7.

16. *Inforpress Centroamericana*, January 21, 1988.

17. Human Rights Watch and Lawyer's Committee for Human Rights, *The Reagan Administration's Record on Human Rights in 1988* (New York, NY: January 1989), p. 66.

18. Ibid., p. 62.

19. Americas Watch, *Closing the Space*, p. 8.

20. For more information on two of these organizations see, Americas Watch, *Guatemala: The Group of Mutual Support* (1985) and Americas Watch, *Persecuting Human Rights Monitors: The CERJ in Guatemala* (May 1989).

21. Ibid., p. 63.

22. Ibid., p. 65.

23. Americas Watch, *Closing the Space*, p. 7.

24. Quoted in ibid., p. 8.

25. Philip Benjamin Heymann, Statement Concerning "Options for United States Policy in Guatemala," before the Subcommittee on Western Hemisphere Affairs of the Committee on Foreign Affairs, U.S. House of Representatives, July 17, 1990.

26. Philip B. Heymann, "Two Views about the System of Criminal Justice in Guatemala," draft, n.d., later published in *Cronica*.

27. Ibid.

28. Beatriz Manz, Prepared statement on "Development in Guatemala and U.S. Options," Hearings before the Subcommittee on Western Hemisphere Affairs of the Committee on Foreign Affairs, U.S. House of Representatives, Ninety-ninth Congress, February 20, 1985.

29. Heymann, "Options for United States Policy in Guatemala," July 17, 1990, p. 15.

30. Ibid., p. 11.

31. Ibid., p. 13.

32. See my opinion piece on Myrna Mack's killing in Beatriz Manz, "In Guatemala No One Is Safe," *New York Times*, Op-ed page, October 29, 1990.

33. Consejo de Instituciones de Desarrollo (COINDE), *Diagnóstico sobre refugiados, retornados y desplazados de Guatemala*, Guatemala, July 1991.

34. Americas Watch Report, *Messengers of Death: Human Rights in Guatemala November 1988–March 1990* (New York, NY: Americas Watch, March 1990).

35. *Inforpress Centroamericana*, February 7, 1991. As an epilogue, the first year of President Jorge Serrano Elias showed how durable and dismal the human rights crisis can be. Like a bad weed, it is hard to get rid of. Near the end of 1991 there were already, according to the human rights office of the Archdiocese, more than a thousand violations reported, or about three per day.

18. A Miracle, A Universe: Settling Accounts with Torturers

Lawrence Weschler

In this paper I talk about torture and about the recovery from torture—not only of individuals but of entire societies, which is the subject, in part, of my book *A Miracle, A Universe*.

One way to start is to think about why torture happens, what it is for in the places where it happens. And to me a useful way of thinking about that was actually provided by Polish Solidarity, by the people there in 1980-81 who spoke of solidarity as an expression of "the subjectivity of the Polish nation," by which they meant its capacity to act as the subject of history rather than the object of history, to be the one who initiates sentences on its own behalf instead of having things done to it. That's a grammatical transformation. It seems to me that that is the transformation inherent in any kind of assertive, progressive, revolutionary moment in history. Conversely, for example, in Poland martial law was taking people who had been acting like subjects and trying to turn them back into objects once again through various techniques, and it seems to me that that is the nature of oppression where it happens. And in certain places in the world what is required in that transformation, or what is used in that transformation, is torture. Torture is a device to take people who have been acting like subjects and turn them back into objects again. To the extent that that's true, it is used by the regime, by the torturer, as a kind of teaching. Elaine Scarry in her book *The Body in Pain*, similarly speaks of torture as a sort of discourse, and to the extent that it is a discourse, a teaching. What is being taught is abject objecthood. And it's being taught both to individuals and to the entire society. The torturers take the people who have been most assertive, or who have been kinds of nodes of subjectivity in their societies—and that, by the way, may be people who aren't even activists, just students or lawyers or people who are somewhat recalcitrant—and the torturer tries to turn them back into objects, through the fear that their example engenders to turn the whole society likewise back into an object.

How is that done? It seems to me, without being too intellectual about it, that torture attacks the victim at two of the most primordial and mysterious aspects of his or her being, his or her human being—which is to say incarnation and solitude. With regard to incarnation, what the torturer is doing is taking people, especially people who have been behaving particularly selflessly, beyond their immediate physical requirements, that is to say, behaving on behalf of others, in effect behaving soulfully, and he teaches them that the soul adheres in a body and that it can in fact be completely undercut through attacks on that body, so that the wide, wide horizon of possibilities can be narrowed completely by attacks specifically on the body, on the physical body, until the body gives up the soul or its soulful behavior. Similarly, torture forces people, and especially people who have been behaving on behalf of others, to recognize the primordial reality of life, which is solitude, and finally solitude before death. That's a kind of realization—you know, that I could die within a few minutes—that people ordinarily are able to sustain at best for a few minutes at a time once in a very long while; they are called existential crises, when they happen to ordinary people. And torture forces it to happen to people for hours, days, weeks on end. Once again, with an ambition or a will to break down the subjectivity, the subjecthood, of the person who is being tortured.

As I say, it's being done, it's being drilled into a particular person, or a particular group of individuals, but in effect, because of the fear, the terror that their example breeds, it's being done to the whole society. For example, it's often the case when you read about torture that torture takes place in downtown areas. In Montevideo, Uruguay, it took place, for example, in this one building right in the middle of downtown, and people would talk about how in the morning you could hear the screams and in the daytime the screams would be drowned out by the traffic and in the evenings you could start hearing the screams again. Well, the screamings have a function within the entire society, and that's to break down the whole society.

In trying to think about how to rehabilitate torture victims, it's not enough, obviously, to just bring them out, to get them out, to liberate them. I remember belonging to various amnesty groups and how you'd work and work and work, the kind of ridiculous work you do when you're got an amnesty prisoner, or one of these adopt-a-prisoners, and you send all the telegrams, you do all the lobbying to governments and so forth, and eventually—lo and behold—years later you get word that the torture victim has been released and you throw a whole wonderful celebration with all the people in your group, and everything seems fine. You might, however, upon occasion have a chance to meet that person years later and you realize very quickly that his having been released from prison was only the *beginning* of a rehabilitative process, that he is, in fact, a broken man long after he's been liberated. In the same way, a torture society, a place where there has been torture, does not become liberated simply because they hold an election, for example, and the military is "thrown out." There is a whole legacy of victimhood that the entire society has to throw off, and that is an extremely complex process. And that is basically what my book *A Miracle, A Universe* was about.

How is that process for both victims and the societies to proceed? It seems to me that the way to understand that is to go back to that moment of torture. When you read Amnesty reports or Human Rights Watch reports over and over again you come upon the same moment in the torture session: the victim is screaming and at some point the torturer says, "Go ahead, scream all you like, nobody can hear you, nobody would dare to hear you, nobody will ever know what's going on in this room." Now that assertion has two functions. On the one hand, it's designed to break the torture victim, to tell him that he is all alone and nobody will ever aid him; but on the other hand, it is also designed to buttress the torturer. What is going on in the room is fundamentally secret. That torture is going on is public, and it's usefully public, but who exactly is doing it and exactly what they are doing has to be a secret. Those people go home, they have children, they live their everyday lives, and it would be disfiguring for the torturer to have what he's doing become known and broadcast about. Which is why one of the main things that militaries in retreat will do as they see democratization coming on for whatever reason, is that they will put an amnesty into effect to prevent what's going on in that room from ever being known. And conversely, that's why the truth telling after a period of torture becomes so important.

The torturers in many cases, particularly in Latin America, still have a tremendous amount of power, often a monopoly of physical power in these countries—in Argentina, in Uruguay and Brazil and Chile—and they will not abide any settling of accounts. And each of these countries, in turn—and, by the way, Guatemala, El Salvador, all these countries coming up, will be faced with the same dilemma—their military has either given itself an amnesty of some sort, or has extracted one through some sort of extortion, and people have to decide whether to try and push it. To the extent that they do not push it, to the extent they accept that amnesty, the torture in effect is going on. I mean, that claim made in that torture room—when the person was screaming and the torturer was saying nobody will ever know what's going on—was not only about the present, it was about the future. And to the extent that the society, the democratizing society, accedes to that, the torture not only for the victims but also for the society as a whole continues in a fundamental way to achieve its purpose.

You talk about what it takes to have a democracy. It's not just elections; it's not even just people having free speech. It's due process. It's equality under the law. And if people, for example, in Uruguay, a small country, where people are meeting their torturers on the street all the time—if there's one group of people who are above the law, you don't have a democracy.

But it's very complicated. In my book, half of which was primarily set in Uruguay, I have a dialectic, and I have a lovely quote from Zbigniew Herbert, the Polish writer, who wrote a poem called "Mr. Cogito and the Need for Precision." "Mr. Cogito" is the poet's alter ego. He wrote it at the end of World War II, when people were saying, "Well, you know, we'll never know how many people died. Let's just forget it, let's go to the future, it's useless to try to make lists." And he said about such needs, about such things, "Accuracy is essential. We must not be off even by a single one. We are, after all, the guardians of our brothers. Ignorance about those who have disappeared undermines the reality of the world." *Undermines the reality of the world.* So that you can have these democracies that have all the trappings of democracy, but if as a kind of willful social gesture an entire polity willfully chooses to ignore what happened to those who have disappeared, been tortured, the democracy itself becomes unreal.

There are, however, very strong arguments the other way. When I quoted that line to Julio Maria Sanguinetti, the president of Uruguay, he quoted me back poem for poem. He said, "Well, as Ernesto Renán said, 'Nations are a plebiscite everyday, and they are built on great rememberings and great forgettings.' If the French were still arguing about the St. Bartholomew's Day Massacre, you know, they'd be killing each other to this day." And there is something to be said for that.

At one point I called Jacobo Timmerman and asked him what he would do with regard to the Uruguayan plebiscite that was coming up, whether or not to overturn the amnesty—this is what half of my book is about, I assume most of you in this group heard of the situation there—should they do it, and if the population as a whole decides to overturn the amnesty, will the military throw a coup, will they go right back to torturing people (they'd done a damned good job of it in the years before that)? I asked Timmerman what they should do and he said, "Well, it's a tough decision. You want to be ethical, but do you mean short-term ethics or long-term ethics? Short-term ethics helps the victim, but long-term ethics, you try to save democracy and maybe for that reason you should just allow the amnesty to stay in effect." In fact, he favored leaving the amnesty in effect. Timmerman of all people! And at one point he said to me, "Well, this reminds me of something that a friend of mine once said in Israel, how he'd been studying with Gershom Scholem, the great cabalistic scholar, going to the lectures, and one day he'd gone up to Scholem and said, 'Professor Scholem, up until today I understood everything that you were saying about Jewish mysticism, all these lectures I've been following completely. But after today's lecture I'm completely confused.' And Scholem said, 'Ah, that means you're beginning to understand.' " When you look really hard at these places, at these cases, at Brazil and Uruguay and so forth, you don't really understand what's going on until you're completely confused. It's a very tough issue.

I don't know how much more time I have, but I'll tell a few more stories. When my book came out, I was invited to be on the Ted Koppel show. Some of you may have seen it, that "Nightline" show. As you may know, part of my book involves this fantastic conspiracy by a group of torture victims in Brazil. After the amnesty, a group of torture victims launched an extremely dangerous, top-secret, nonviolent conspiracy to get even with the torturers. To summarize it very quickly, the Brazilians were technocrats and, in effect, they kept minutes of all their torture sessions, and all these minutes were in the basement of the Supreme Military Court, in the archive. And this group of people kept a secret project going for five years in which they, in effect, smuggled out the entire contents of that archive, Xeroxed them overnight, put them back in the archives, smuggled them down to São Paulo, computerized the records, and eventually came up with lists, and published a book that had lists of torturers, a list of places, a list of people who had been tortured—an incredible documentation. Which was certainly not what the military would have wanted to have happen, since the military denied there was any torture whatsoever taking place, and here it was in their own records! These people had wanted to keep secret, never given their names, and part of my research and reporting involved getting to talk to them anonymously and finding out how they'd done it. At the time the book was coming out in Brazil, a few of them were actually willing to be televised, to go public for the first time, and I called some people I knew at "Nightline" and they went down there; they did an eight-minute report of these people talking about what they'd done—it was really spectacular, exciting footage. There was a break, a commercial break, Koppel came back and had me on with Pepe Zalaquett of Chile; we were the two guests, Zalaquett being the guy who in effect has been heading the Truth and

Reconciliation Commission in Chile. So basically we had the potential of an interesting conversation at that point, and the first question Ted Koppel asked was, "Tell me, Mr. Zalaquett, what bearing does all this have on Romania, on what's going on in Romania today?" I mean American television cannot stay focused on Latin America for one half hour a year! It's incredible; he had to relate it for the American people, to refocus the discussion onto something that Americans could understand, or that he could understand. In any case, we eventually drifted on to a kind of conversation about torture in the abstract What is it about you people—in effect, he was asking Zalaquett—what is it about South America that you people, that you neighbors are able to torture each other? What is this weird thing about the Latin temperament? At that point, I interrupted to say, "Ted, we were paying for this, we were implicated in this up to here." On "Nightline," by the way, there's a kind of video tunnel where you can see him and he you, but you don't know what's going out over the air. As I spoke, he frowned very angrily, cut me short, and I disappeared from the program. That was the last comment I made.

But I think it's important to try to understand that complicity of ours. Because on the one hand, there's a simplistic Leftist view that it was all caused by the United States, that the United States sponsored the coups, and so forth. My book goes into some detail on General Vernon Walter's involvement, or Dan Mitrione's involvement in Uruguay, Walter's in Brazil, in Chile, and so forth, and it's obvious it was U.S. policy to have these military regimes and so forth. I think, though, that strangely it's almost racist for us to imagine the Latin Americans incapable of coming up with a lot of this stuff on their own. As one Leftist in Latin America, a progressive fellow, put it to me, "You know, our monsters were just as good as your monsters; in fact, our monsters taught your monsters a thing or two." And I think that's quite accurate. I mean, look at what Oliver North was doing in the period of the Reagan administration. You may remember, his first six-months' job was to design an emergency plan for the imposition of martial law in the United States, and he did that while hanging out with the Argentines who were training the Contras. So the national lessons of Security Doctrine went back and forth. And it's very simplistic to put it all in one direction.

I think it more useful to quote from a 1948 statement by George F. Kennan, writing about the Far East, in a top-secret memo to ambassadors which was eventually circulated to South American ambassadors and to U.S. ambassadors as well:

We, the United States, have about 50 percent of the world's wealth, but only 6.3 percent of its population. In this situation we cannot fail to be the object of envy and resentment. Our real task in the coming period is to devise a position of disparity without causing detriment to our national security. To do so, we will have to dispense with sentimentality and daydreaming, and our attention will have to be concentrated everywhere on our immediate national objectives. We need not deceive ourselves that we can afford today the luxury of altruism and world benefaction. We should cease to talk about vague and unreal objectives, such as human rights, the raising of living standards, democratization. The day is not far off when we are going to have to deal with straight power concepts. The less we are hampered by idealistic slogans, the better.

This is George F. Kennan, a liberal in the State Department, who within a couple of years was out of the State Department, in part, one suspects, for writing that, for being too liberal. I mean, the fact that he'd even *heard* of the concepts of human rights and democratization of living standards! But it seems to me that in each of the countries we're talking about—especially in El Salvador, Guatemala, Argentina—that statistic of 6 percent/50 percent, is replicated. In Salvador, 3 or 4 percent own 80 percent of the land. It varies. You find the same situation in Guatemala. And I think the way to think about the disparity is that that group, wherever they are, are Americans; that, in effect, you define Americans as people who do their shopping in Miami, who send their children to American schools; that, conversely, there are pockets of the Third World in the United States as in the South Bronx; and that it makes more sense to speak of "America" as distinct from the United States, as this kind of group with dovetailed interests of privilege, of wealth; that those people across the board engage in a National Security Doctrine that is there essentially to secure their wealth; and finally, that together they use torture as one of the methods for destroying the subjectivity of people who are trying to rise up against them.

A few more comments on human rights. The notion of human rights as a real, looming force in world affairs, the demand for human rights, the assertion that human beings have human rights are actually relatively recent, certainly at the level that it's working now. And it's a remarkable phenomenon to watch. In a way it's almost magic . . . . At one level, obviously, human beings don't have any special rights, I mean, it's a *fiction*; people are making it up; it's smoke and mirrors; human beings are, you know, just sacks of flesh on stumps; they don't have any special rights. The extent to which they do is an entirely fictional assertion. I say this as somebody who believes that fiction is the highest aspiration of human consciousness, of civilization, but it starts with people who just started talking, with a small group of people, of activists, some former victims, lawyers, U.N. people, people in Amnesty, people in Human Rights Watch, who just started making the bald, outrageous assertion that you should not torture people, that it is absolutely unacceptable. And, as I say, at first it was just smoke and mirrors. But a strange thing began to happen. As more and more people acted as if that were the case, as if people have rights, as if it's evil to torture them, this light, this ball of light began to hover in the room. It took on a strange kind of reality, and in fact it not only hovered there, shedding light on everything, but it began melting totalitarian regimes. All over the world. It's the most remarkable thing. And it is an exciting development in the progress of human affairs. Period. But it's always embattled, and this business of truth telling, for example, of having human rights recognized, acknowledged, not only for the future but also with regard to the past—it was terribly difficult to achieve and important to watch as it happens.

Finally, let me share with you a fax that I got. Sounds dramatic, but I actually received it just a few days ago. Pinochet was in Brazil and a newspaper in Rio reported his visit to the Bará shopping center in Rio with his wife for a shopping expedition, and I'll read you the translation of one paragraph.

During a visit to the Curly Bookstore in the Bará shopping center, Pinochet went as far as leafing through some books, among them *A Miracle, A Universe: Settling Accounts with Torturers* by the American journalist Lawrence Weschler. [It's been translated, by the way, into Portuguese; it has not been translated into Spanish, unfortunately.] The book deals with political torture in Latin America, especially Uruguay and Brazil. Pinochet looked through the first page, smiled in derision and commented, "It's all a lie. The author is a hypocrite, a liar." ("Todo mentira, este autor es um hipocrita, um mentiroso".)

Anyway, I thought I'd died and gone to heaven when I heard that.

19. Comments

Ariel Dorfman

It's always very difficult to comment on diverse positions that one has heard before. So, I'm going to try to be rather brief in my comments and then perhaps speak about a personal experience which I think might be of some interest to you. I think that we see from the three presentations (chaps. 16, 17, 18) a mixture of hope and despair, as if we had advanced so far, with so much effort, and at the same time as if we were treading water, and were somehow in a cycle, an infernal cycle, in which we find ourselves not only where we were yesterday, but in some sense worse than we were before, because there seems to be no hope for the future. And with fear that if we do not address the issues that brought about these violations of human rights, they're going to be repeated. My basic vision of why these things happen is extremely psycho because I think you only torture somebody, you only make disappear a person, you only execute a person, if that person has inflamed the world with a little spark of rebellion. In other words, it is only because the person *appears* that they are disappearing. If they had engaged only in the acts that have been called "the weapons of the weak," as an anthropologist has said it, they probably would be weakly repressed. It is the savagery of what happened that indicates to us the silhouette of what might have happened. It is the fear of another sort of a future that is behind human rights violations.

What we're seeing in each one of the panelists is this mixture of these lights and this darkness and that we have to look into it very deeply. Now, I've just come out of an experience which is as deep as any I've ever had: I've spent seven months in Chile, last July to January. I had been going back for different reasons during the previous year. In fact, the last time I saw you, Alex [Wilde], was at Allende's funeral. You were one of few people who came invited. What has happened in Chile is very significant and very, very interesting, because in one sense they've gone about as far as they can go, as they used to say in *Oklahoma*, in the musical comedy (to give a bit of levity to this *charla*), but in another sense we are *trabados*; we are stuck in a rut. As you may know, the president designated April of last year a commission to look at the human rights violations during the military dictatorship.

They came up with a report in February of this year, which was given to the President. The President gave it to the country on March 4, as I understand, and it created an extraordinary impact in public opinion in Chile, though not too much elsewhere, to tell you the truth. And here a little parenthesis about my own anecdotes of the Ted Koppel sort of "What does relate to Romania?" When Patricio Aylwin was elected President of Chile in December of 1989, I had managed through my publisher, Viking, to be the guest on "CBS This Morning." It was the only transmission by satellite that was going to be in, from Chile, about the election. And the only reason why they would do it was because I had just brought out a book of stories called *My House Is on Fire*. They called me at 4 o'clock in the morning to say that Sakharov had just died and that therefore they were bumping Chile off the air. My answer to the people who were there was that I certainly had fought very, very hard for Sakharov and for human rights everywhere, certainly including the Soviet Union, but it's interesting that you're more interested in the death of a Russian dissident than in the resurrection of a people.

So there was not very, very much interest in this human rights report, but in Chile it had a major impact. Why? Fundamentally because it was to recognize an official truth, to make public what Ren Weschler said was private. Even if there were no naming of names, it was the fact that this became part of the official history of the country; it was under the Chilean flag and the President went on television and with his voice choking with emotion asked forgiveness, begged forgiveness of the victims in the name of the Chilean state. Then he asked for a series of things that have not come to pass at all: He asked for the army to show some sort of gesture, for instance, to tell the people where the bodies were, the executed bodies, if they had the information, which they do; to show some gesture of repentance, of reconciliation. None of this has come to pass. What *has* come to pass, strangely enough, is that after this was made public, it was as if a great part of Chile has wanted to forget. And I say this with enormous sorrow, and I'm not blaming my compatriots for this, because there is a point at which you really say "enough is enough, it's time to look toward the future." We cannot continue looking at the past. We can't be captured by the past. We have to get rid of the Janus face of looking at the past only. And people are saying, "*Basta*. We can't stand it anymore."

And then there were a series of violent incidents in which different people were murdered, among them Jaime Guzmán. He was a prominent ideologue of the right wing. And lamenting as I do the death of anybody and the death of a person who also contributed to the transition, certainly his death was considered to be balancing the death of all the people during the Pinochet dictatorship, in the sense that the *Mercurio* said we can no longer say, *"los muertos son nuestros"* as the Socialists had said. No *los muertos son de todos*. And it was as if Chile had been transformed all of a sudden. It was as if the report on human rights had been buried.

My vision of this problem is that it is absolutely useless to try to promote human rights in the long run if this is not something that belongs to the whole community. In other words, I hate those phrases saying that, basically, we deserve the governments we've got; but there is some truth in this, as much as I hate to say it. In other words, because friends of mine on the left would say, and as you know, I'm on the left side of the spectrum, they would say to me that the government is doing *this*, Aylwin is not denouncing, he is not bringing them to justice, the government is not *this*, the government is not *that*. My answer, and certainly this is a break with the left and with many other positions, is that the government will do nothing that we do not do first. That doesn't mean that we have to judge these people. Unless we are all prepared, each of us individually, there is no possibility of a profound democratization in those countries. Because we cannot ask a government that represents the people to do more than the people want it to do. It can lead, certainly, and I would hope that the government in Chile would have led a bit more forcefully, though I think that President Aylwin has given a great example in that sense. But unless we realize that these incidents come out of a deep contradiction and history of our own countries, we are not going to get over them.

I would like to finish by saying that we have a great responsibility, the people in this room, not only the academics in this room, but certainly all those who deal with books, because the truth does come out. If those little tiny seeds, and those books are there, people can't say, "I did not know." It's up to you, many of the people in this room, to get some of those books into the libraries, at least into the libraries, at least into the private libraries, at least onto the streets. It's very important to get these things said. I can do that in my literature, I can do that in my writing, I can do that in my plays. I can do that. I can reach people and we can create some sort of language in which we begin to understand that only through the truth, only by telling the whole story, will we be able to look in the face of the people who have done terrible things to us. Unless they recognize—and part of the recognition has to do with the writing of this and the publication, the making public—unless they recognize this there can be no unchaining of the past. The past will haunt us. So, I'm saying we have to bury the past, but we have to give it a good funeral, because if you don't give a corpse a good funeral, it stinks and it comes back as a ghost.

One last thing, to what Beatriz said. The reason why the Guatemalans are so left out is because they're Indians. I just wanted to add that.

Challenge 500: Focus on Membership

20. SALALM Membership, 1956-1990: A Brief Overview

Suzanne Hodgman

In preparing this brief survey of SALALM membership, I was struck by the discrepancies in statistics from one publication to another. Therefore, I want to make clear the source of my figures. I have used the membership lists that are prepared for the annual meetings. I would prefer to have used end-of-year totals, but they do not tell us anything about the additional members who joined after the meetings but before the close of the membership years. Consequently, to have used these year-end totals would have skewed the percentages (see table 1).

In June 1956, twenty-six[1] person met, at the instigation of Marietta Daniels (Shepard), at Chinsegut Hill, Florida, to discuss problems pertaining to the acquisition of library materials from Latin America and the Caribbean area. Although they did not realize it at the time, they were laying the foundation of SALALM.[2] I was not able to determine the position of each of them, but by no means were all librarians. Of these twenty-six attendees, I can definitely identify only seven as "librarians' librarians." At least three were professors of Spanish and/or Latin American studies. One was the representative of Stechert-Hafner, a publisher/bookdealer. One represented the Grace Chemical Company, and may, or may not, have been a librarian. At least five were library directors, and several others were what we know today as "administrative types." Thus we see that a majority of our founding members were academics and/or administrators, and a minority were "working librarians." Contrast that with today's membership. With the exception of directors of special libraries within library systems (e.g., the Benson Latin American Collection at the University of Texas), I cannot think of any library directors who are presently SALALM members, and professors have become an endangered species to be cherished.

From 1956 to 1968, it was not possible to say exactly who was a member of SALALM. Attendance at the annual meetings was by invitation to institutions. Registration fees were paid, but there were no dues. Ninety-four institutions participated in the first seven seminars.[3] The same institutions were often represented year after year by the same person.[4]

In 1968, SALALM incorporated. Incorporation brought many changes, including the establishment, in 1969/70, of a membership committee, whose charge was to promote membership in and wider participation in SALALM. For the first time, we had membership dues. Personal dues were $5 per year ($3 for person from Latin America and the Caribbean). Institutional dues were $10 per year. Lee Williams was the first chairman of the membership committee.

After 1968/69, it is possible to track some of the changes in the composition of SALALM's membership. At the close of the first year, our membership stood at 201. Of the 143 personal members, I can identify eight academics, nine library directors, six bookdealers, and six "administrative types." The remainder were, presumably, librarians filling various positions. But, remember I am drawing on memory. Believe it or not, I don't recall all these people, even though I was one of them.

In the first year of incorporation, SALALM counted in its membership nineteen non-U.S. plus twenty Puerto Rican personal members and fifteen non-U.S. and four Puerto Rican institutional members. In other words, non-U.S. members accounted for 16.9 percent of our total membership, and the Puerto Rican contribution was also very significant—11.9 percent of the membership.

By 1980/81, the first year of my incumbency as executive secretary, South America had 363 members (241 personal and 112 institutional). And by 1989/90, the final year of my tenure, it had grown to 464 members (316 personal and 148 institutional). The geographical distribution of our membership for those four reference years of 1956, 1968/69, 1980/81, and 1989/90 is interesting:

Year	Non-U.S.	Puerto Rico	U.S.	Total
1958	0	0	26	26
1968/69	34 (16.9 percent)	24 (11.9 percent)	143	201
1980/81	97 (27.5 percent)	10 (2.8 percent)	246	353
1989/90	142 (30.6 percent)	10 (2.1 percent)	312	464

Tables 2 and 3 show the geographical distribution of our non-U.S. membership during the decade of the 1980s. Puerto Rico is included with the Caribbean.

It is gratifying to see that the participation of non-U.S. members is increasing, but it was a shock to me to realize how many Puerto Rican members we had in our early days and how few, comparatively, we have today.   (It seems reasonable to suppose that most Puerto Rican members migrated to ACURIL when it was organized, with SALALM's assistance and blessing, in 1969.) The majority of members we did have from Puerto Rico throughout the 1980s were institutional members.

In early 1973, Stechert–Hafner ended its Latin American Cooperative Acquisitions Program (LACAP). (We like to think that SALALM had been so successful that LACAP was no longer needed.) At any rate, by the time of incorporation, several other bookdealers had joined the Stechert–Hafner representative (Dominic Coppola) as SALALM members.   After the discontinuation of LACAP, more bookdealers became active each year. In 1975/76, we had eighteen bookdealer members, representing 6.5 percent of the total (personal and institutional) membership; in 1980/81, thirty-seven bookdealer members, or 10.5 percent of the total membership (see table 4). This segment of the membership has not only continued to grow, but it has also been becoming more influential. The Library/Bookdealer/Publisher subcommittee is the largest committee/subcommittee in SALALM, with thirty-four members in 1990/91. I think we have all been very aware in recent years of the presence of our bookdealer members.

At the same time the number of bookdealers in SALALM was increasing, the number of both academics and library directors was decreasing (see table 5). I can think of only one or two professors active today, and I believe it has been quite a few years since a library director participated actively in SALALM. Our personal membership today consists principally of working librarians—catalogers, selectors, reference librarian—types that were, for the most part, absent from that first meeting at Chinsegut Hill back in 1956. One far-reaching result of this change in the composition of our membership is that, in contrast to yesteryear, nowadays very few SALALM members are in positions to make binding commitments on behalf of their libraries.

Not at all surprisingly, the majority of our institutional members are, and always have been, academic libraries (see table 6). However, special libraries, which include law libraries, library school libraries, and national libraries (as well as the Library of Congress), make up a larger percentage (as high as 25 percent) than I would have expected before making this tabulation. Public libraries have been limited mainly to the New York Public Library and the Los Angeles Public Library (neither of which has had a continuous membership record) and, in recent years, the Miami–Dade Public Library. The other public libraries that appear in the statistics from time to time are, with few if any exceptions, in the Caribbean.

Most bookdealers join SALALM as personal members. Consequently, the percentage of bookdealers in the institutional membership is not large, although in recent years it has been growing. A category of institutional membership which has never been represented to the extent to which I believe it should be is that of the publishers. It is my opinion that companies like G. K. Hall, Bowker, Scarecrow Press, and Greenwood Press, which count on SALALM members as customers for their publications, should contribute to SALALM financially, if in no other way. The same logic applies to jobbers like Faxon and Ebsco.

Statistics seem to bear out what we all thought we knew about SALALM membership: (1) Although the early members were primarily administrators and academics, the present personal membership consists overwhelmingly of "working librarians," with consequences both predictable and unpredictable; (2) the percentage of non–U.S. members has continued to grow (but that of Puerto Ricans has declined); (3) the participation and contributions of the bookdealers have been growing steadily since the early 1970s; (4) academic libraries comprise the majority of SALALM's institutional members, with special libraries accounting for a larger percentage than heretofore believed; and (5) publishers and jobbers are underrepresented in the membership.

NOTES

1. The first incidence of contradiction. Other sources say "thirty" or "about thirty."

2. Those founders who remained active in SALALM until their retirements have been made honorary members. They are: Alice Ball, Nettie Lee Benson, Arthur Gropp, Felix Reichmann (deceased), Marietta Daniels Shepard (deceased), Emma C. Simonson (deceased), A. Curtis Wilgus (deceased), and Irene Zimmerman.

3. Marietta Daniels Shepard, *The Seminars on the Acquisition of Latin American Library Materials* (Washington, DC: Pan American Union, 1962), pp. 77-84.

4. William V. Jackson, "Twenty-third Seminar on the Acquisition of Latin American Library Materials," in *Encyclopedia of Library and Information Science*, vol. 31 (1983), pp. 250-251.

Table 1. SALALM Membership, 1968/69–1989/90

Year	Personal	Institutional	Total
1968/69	143	58	201
1969/70	119	46	165
1970/71	163	91	254
1971/72	178	85	263
1972/73	219	96	315
1973/74	225	83	308
1974/75	255	82	337
1975/76	219	59	278
1976/77	268	109	377
1977/78	260	118	378
1978/79	266	118	384
1979/80	270	121	391
1980/81	241	112	353
1981/82	248	126	374
1982/83	273	122	395
1983/84	274	123	397
1984/85	294	128	422
1985/86	295	134	429
1986/87	313	138	451
1987/88	311	146	457
1988/89	313	145	458
1989/90	316	148	464

Source: Figures taken from the lists prepared for the annual SALALM meetings. Not final figures.

Table 2. Non-U.S. Personal Members, Geographical Distribution, 1980/81–1989/90

Year	Total	Percentage Non-U.S.	Latin America	Percentage	Caribbean[a]	Percentage	Europe	Percentage	Canada	Percentage	Other	Percentage
1980/81	241	25.3	22	9.1	12	5.0	15	6.2	8	3.3	4	1.7
1981/82	248	25.8	25	10.1	11	4.4	19	7.7	7	2.8	2	0.8
1982/83	273	26.4	27	9.9	20	7.3	13	4.8	9	3.3	3	1.1
1983/84	274	23.8	29	10.6	15	5.5	12	4.4	6	2.2	3	1.1
1984/85	294	24.2	31	10.5	17	5.8	12	4.1	7	2.4	4	1.4
1985/86	295	25.8	34	11.5	20	6.8	14	4.7	4	1.4	4	1.4
1986/87	313	26.8	40	12.8	20	6.4	16	5.1	6	1.9	2	0.6
1987/88	311	26.0	43	13.8	18	5.8	14	4.5	5	1.6	1	0.3
1988/89	313	23.7	40	12.8	13	4.2	14	4.5	6	1.9	1	0.3
1989/90	316	28.1	57	18.0	14	4.4	13	4.1	5	1.6	1	0.3

a. Includes Puerto Rico.

Table 3. Non-U.S. Institutional Members, Geographical Distribution, 1980/81–1989/90

Year	Total	Percentage Non-U.S.	Latin America	Percentage	Caribbean[a]	Percentage	Europe	Percentage	Canada	Percentage	Other	Percentage
1980/81	112	41.1	7	6.3	10	8.9	13	11.6	12	10.7	4	3.6
1981/82	126	38.0	10	7.9	9	7.1	15	11.9	10	7.9	4	3.2
1982/83	122	41.8	7	5.7	16	13.1	14	11.5	10	8.2	4	3.3
1983/84	123	39.1	6	4.9	13	10.6	14	11.4	11	8.9	4	3.3
1984/85	128	41.4	10	7.8	12	9.4	14	10.9	12	9.4	5	3.9
1985/86	134	37.4	10	7.5	12	9.0	12	9.0	11	8.2	5	3.7
1986/87	138	41.3	12	8.8	11	8.0	17	12.3	12	8.7	5	3.6
1987/88	146	38.3	14	9.6	10	6.8	16	11.0	12	8.2	4	2.7
1988/89	145	38.0	13	9.0	13	9.0	13	9.0	11	7.6	5	3.4
1989/90	148	41.9	16	10.8	10	6.8	19	12.8	12	8.1	5	3.4

a. Includes Puerto Rico.

Table 4. Personal and Institutional Members,
Bookdealers, 1980/81–1989/90

Year	Number	Percentage of total membership
1980/81	37	10.5
1981/82	39	10.4
1982/83	42	10.6
1983/84	44	11.1
1984/85	57	13.5
1985/86	62	14.5
1986/87	62	13.7
1987/88	57	12.5
1988/89	63	13.8
1989/90	60	12.9

Table 5. Personal and Professorial/Academic
Members, 1980/81–1989/90

Year	Number	Percentage of total membership
1980/81	15	6.2
1981/82	15	6.0
1982/83	18	6.6
1983/84	15	5.5
1984/85	9	3.1
1985/86	10	3.4
1986/87	15	4.8
1987/88	10	3.2
1988/89	8	2.6
1989/90	9	2.8

Table 6. Institutional Members by Type, 1968/69–1989/90

Year	Academic libraries Number	Percentage	Special libraries[a] Number	Percentage	Associations[b] Number	Percentage	Public libraries Number	Percentage	Bookdealers Number	Percentage	Publishers Number	Percentage	Other Number	Percentage	Total
1968/69	34	58.6	10	17.3	3	5.2	4	6.9	2	3.4	3	5.2	2	3.4	58
1969/70	31	67.5	8	17.4	2	4.3	1	2.2	2	4.3	2	4.3	0	0.0	46
1970/71	58	63.7	15	16.5	2	2.2	6	6.6	5	5.5	0	0.0	5	5.5	91
1971/72	49	57.6	14	16.5	4	4.7	4	4.7	5	5.9	1	1.2	8	9.4	85
1972/73	52	54.2	21	21.9	4	4.2	6	6.2	4	4.2	1	1.0	8	8.3	96
1973/74	51	61.5	18	21.7	3	3.6	2	2.4	4	4.8	0	0.0	5	6.0	83
1974/75	51	62.2	14	17.1	3	3.7	4	4.9	1	1.2	0	0.0	9	10.9	82
1975/76	42	71.2	12	20.3	3	5.1	0	0.0	0	0.0	0	0.0	2	3.4	59
1976/77	66	60.6	18	16.5	7	6.4	3	2.7	1	0.9	1	0.9	13	12.0	109
1977/78	73	61.9	28	23.7	6	5.1	2	1.7	2	1.7	0	0.0	7	5.9	118
1978/79	72	61.0	37	31.4	2	1.7	1	0.8	0	0.0	0	0.0	6	5.1	118
1979/80	77	63.7	30	24.8	4	3.3	1	0.8	0	0.0	1	0.8	8	6.6	121
1980/81	68	60.7	28	25.0	4	3.6	2	1.8	1	0.9	1	0.9	8	7.1	112
1981/82	75	59.5	32	25.4	4	3.2	2	1.6	3	2.4	3	2.4	7	5.5	126
1982/83	82	67.3	26	21.3	4	3.3	2	1.6	1	0.8	2	1.6	5	4.1	122
1983/84	79	64.2	28	22.8	4	3.3	1	0.8	3	2.4	3	2.4	5	4.1	123
1984/85	79	61.7	32	25.0	5	3.9	1	0.8	4	3.1	1	0.8	6	4.7	128
1985/86	79	59.0	33	24.6	4	3.0	1	0.7	8	6.0	0	0.0	9	6.7	134
1986/87	81	58.8	34	24.6	4	2.9	2	1.4	7	5.1	0	0.0	10	7.2	138
1987/88	86	59.0	32	21.9	5	3.4	3	2.1	10	6.8	0	0.0	10	6.8	146
1988/89	78	53.8	36	24.8	4	2.7	3	2.1	10	6.9	1	0.7	13	9.0	145
1989/90	82	55.4	34	22.9	4	2.7	4	2.7	14	9.5	1	0.7	9	6.1	148

a. Law libraries, library school libraries, business libraries, as well as the Library of Congress and national libraries.
b. Library associations, such as the American Library Association.
c. Entities not readily identified or which do not fit into another category (e.g., area studies programs, state archives).

21. SALALM and the Public Library

Luis Herrera

This paper will address the topic of how SALALM has or has not served the interests of the public library community. In order to provide a backdrop for my comments, I would like to begin by offering some perceptions of SALALM's identity within the library community. These fall into three specific areas:

1. That SALALM is academic and scholarly in orientation and mission. In other words, the primary purpose is perceived as one of bibliography and research. From a practical viewpoint, this mission is too narrow and specialized. Public librarianship deals with a more mundane, but relevant, array of contemporary, social, and day-to-day concerns. Indeed, the information and collection-development issues typically focus on the general public and the practical, real life arena.

2. That SALALM is known in limited circles of librarianship. That is to say, recognition is strong in academic libraries but there is only limited awareness among public librarians involved in Latin Americana. For example, members of REFORMA are much more likely to have an awareness and understanding of SALALM than the general public library establishment.

3. That there is a lack of understanding by public librarians of SALALM's role in librarianship. For example, in the manual *Developing Library Collections for California's Emerging Majority*, a publication produced as part of a statewide workshop on library service, SALALM is listed as a resource organization that "deals with all types and levels of materials and disseminates bibliographic information about all types of Latin American and Caribbean publications." However, this purpose statement is not widely known among public librarians.

Thus, the ultimate question is whether SALALM needs to reexamine its mission and broaden its focus to include a role for the public library or simply market its current mission more effectively.

Forging Partnerships for the Twenty-First Century

This section sets forth two broad areas of recommendations. The first set calls for the development of stronger ties with other library associations, specifically those with emphasis on public libraries.

First and foremost is the development of a close working partnership with REFORMA, the National Association to Promote Library Services to the Spanish-speaking. This organization, which celebrated its twentieth anniversary in 1991, is committed to the improvement of the full spectrum of library and information services to the approximately 19 million Spanish-speaking and Hispanic people of the United States. REFORMA and SALALM share a common mission in promoting the development of library collections to include Spanish-language and Hispanic-oriented materials, and the establishment of a national and international information and support network among individuals who share these goals. REFORMA is further committed to the recruitment of more bilingual and bicultural library professionals. SALALM could become a significant ally in addressing the acute shortage of bilingual/bicultural librarians. Indeed, the number of Hispanic librarians currently represents less than 2 percent of all librarians, and the effort to recruit and train librarians to serve our diverse and growing communities is extremely critical.

Specific examples of this partnership could include the expansion of mentor programs, international exchange progams, internships, and the joint development of recruitment projects.

The second area of recommendations is that SALALM should explore a closer link with the Public Library Association, a 6,500-member division of the American Library Association, which seeks to advance the development and effectiveness of public library service and public libraries. PLA exists to provide a diverse program of communication, publication, advocacy, continuing education, and programming at national conferences. One of their priorities is improved access to library resources, which supports the primary mission of SALALM.

PLA's Committee on Multilingual Materials and Library Services serves to collect and disseminate information on existing multilingual public library collections, to develop these collections, to develop guidelines, and to investigate the viability of cooperative acquisitions

programs. Once again, these goals fall within the scope and realm of
SALALM's purpose.

It is my recommendation that SALALM join forces with these
PLA entities to present and publish position papers that focus on issues
of concern to Latin American librarianship. Moreover, this partnership
can serve as an effective public relations vehicle for the association. To
this end, ALA and PLA journals should provide a supportive venue for
the publication of articles that address specific topics of Latin American
collection development and public libraries.

Two other groups merit special attention: the Ethnic Materials
and Information Exchange Roundtable (EMIERT) of ALA and the
Reference and Adult Services Division's (RASD) Committee on Service
to the Spanish-speaking. Both of these bodies are committed to similar
goals, focusing on service to the Spanish-speaking and ethnic minorities.

These partnerships with REFORMA, the Public Library Association, and other entities of the American Library Association can
strengthen SALALM's posture and future role in Latin American
librarianship. Programs could include financial incentives and support
to students interested in Latin American studies, recruitment on a
broader scope, and heightened awareness of the importance of
collections, services, and programs for and about the Spanish-speaking.

Sharing the Wealth: SALALM'S
Collection Development Expertise

Public Libraries are lagging behind in the development of strong
collections to serve Latino communities in the United States. Yet, this
population continues to grow at a phenomenal pace. I would welcome
SALALM's proactive involvement and participation in providing the
tools to assess how well (or poorly) our libraries are doing in
developing these types of collections. All too often, public libraries do
not have the in-house expertise to evaluate or determine the focus or
type of materials that should be part of their purview.

This effort could begin with a listing of core materials recommended for acquisition by any medium-to-large public library collection.
Along with the type of materials recommended, the sources and
vendors for these titles could be identified. This shared expertise could
take the form of committee recommendations or a listing of resource
librarians in the region who could assist on a formal or informal basis.
Public librarians would value SALALM's involvement in a practical and
significant effort to identify gaps in our collections, especially as they
affect service to Latino and Hispanic populations.

SALALM could also undertake research and scholarly projects aimed at addressing specific concerns to the library field, for example, the use patterns of libraries serving Hispanic communities. Furthermore, SALALM could utilize new technologies such as electronic newsletters, the Internet, and other databases to provide a network of resources and expertise to public libraries.

Conclusion

SALALM is at a crossroads. Its strength and vitality in the next century will come by forging coalitions and partnerships with associations sharing similar goals and objectives. It is my belief that the association needs to focus on four areas. First, it must reexamine its scope and broaden its mission to encompass a changing and complex environment. Librarianship is at a critical juncture, and SALALM must relate to the issues affecting the profession. Second, SALALM should develop strong cooperative ties with REFORMA, PLA, and other associations in order to advance the cause of Latin American bibliography and librarianship. Closely connected to this concept is the third goal, which calls for sharing SALALM's expertise with the library community-at-large. And fourth is SALALM's need to market its strengths. Its contributions to librarianship are significant and should be promoted. I commend SALALM for its leadership role and for its foresight in examining the challenges that lie ahead. I hope that public libraries can be a part of its future agenda.

22. Algunas reflexiones sobre lo que SALALM podría ofrecer a los bibliotecarios nicaragüenses

Conny Méndez Rojas

Es necesario iniciar esta presentación haciendo la consideración de que para la mayoría de los bibliotecarios nicaragüenses la sigla SALALM es totalmente desconocida. Esto significa que no se conoce del todo qué es y qué hace esta organización. Teniendo la tarea de expresar aquí qué podría hacer SALALM como organización profesional bibliotecaria, es meritorio señalar lo que, como trabajadora de este campo, he tenido la oportunidad de haber aprendido respecto a esta organización. A pesar de que no hay nada escrito respecto a lo que a continuación se menciona y que me baso únicamente en mi propia memoria, estoy segura que más de alguna persona podrá recordar haber sido parte de ello.

En junio de 1983, un grupo de bibliotecarios de SALALM que participarían en un congreso en Costa Rica, se detuvieron por más o menos entre 4 a 7 días en Nicaragua. Lo que en ese entonces se llamaba en Nicaragua Dirección de Bibliotecas y Archivos, perteneciente al hace ya algunos años desaparecido Ministerio de Cultura, preparó una agenda para que estos bibliotecarios hicieran un recorrido por las principales bibliotecas (incluyendo Biblioteca Nacional, bibliotecas universitarias, bibliotecas públicas, etc.) y librerías del país. Estos miembros de SALALM participaron con mucho interés, y fueron y vinieron por las principales ciudades, cumpliendo así con la apretada agenda que les fue preparada. Aprovechando la visita, estos bibliotecarios adquirieron mucha de la producción bibliográfica nacional disponible en ese momento.

De acuerdo a lo expresado por los ex-funcionarios del desaparecido Ministerio de Cultura, quienes también participaron en el congreso que se realizó en Costa Rica, ahí se les expuso a los miembros de SALALM cuál era la situación bibliotecaria nicaragüense, pero aparte de eso, nunca se logró concretar ningún tipo de comunicación, mucho menos algún tipo de acuerdo.

Año y medio después, a inicios de 1985, un bibliotecario miembro de SALALM, Dan Hazen, quien estuvo integrando el grupo que visitó Nicaragua en 1983, vino a apoyar a la Escuela de Bibliotecología de la

Universidad Centroamericana por un período de dos semanas. Impartió charlas a los estudiantes sobre selección y adquisición, y participó en otros trabajos dentro del curriculum de la Escuela, con el personal de ésta. Este apoyo estuvo patrocinado por uno de los programas de Fulbright. Es hasta aquí lo poco que se conoce de SALALM.

La oportunidad de participar en este panel es meritoria para enfocar algunos aspectos que competen a los bibliotecarios nicaragüenses y si revisamos los objetivos de SALALM, y concretamos en lo que se ha sido plasmado en la ponencia "La producción bibliográfica nicaragüense" durante este seminario, quizás SALALM tiene mucho que ofrecer a Nicaragua.

Sin embargo, hace falta referirse, aunque de manera general, a la situación de las bibliotecas y bibliotecarios en Nicaragua. En cuanto a las bibliotecas universitarias, es importante hacer notar la situación en que se encuentran: Afectadas económicamente como casi todo en el país, las bibliotecas universitarias prácticamente carecen de presupuesto mínimo para las adquisiciones de libros y materiales para procesamiento. Durante los últimos siete años por lo menos, las bibliotecas han sobrevivido únicamente en sus servicios básicos, tanto a nivel de personal como a nivel del servicio a los usuarios. Las universidades mantienen los salarios y proporcionan algunos materiales para funcionamiento, a través de un modesto presupuesto que les asigna el estado. El ingreso de libros se ha dado gracias a la solidaridad de algunas instituciones externas, y de materiales que proporcionaba el gobierno hasta 1990. Gran parte de estos materiales venían como convenios de solidaridad, pero en la mayoría de los casos eran materiales que no llenaban los requerimientos de los programas académicos.

Para el procesamiento de los materiales se da un caso similar. Las universidades han recibido donaciones de tarjetas, ficheros, marbetes, etc. que han llegado de bibliotecas norteamericanas, instituciones privadas, convenios, etc. y con esto se ha logrado subsistir.

El aspecto de la capacitación ha sido un caso particular. En la Universidad Centroamericana de Managua existe la carrera de Bibliotecología, donde cada año salen entre 10 y 20 licenciados. En los últimos años se pudo observar que un buen porcentaje de estos graduados (por lo menos un 55%, y es algo que se ha dado en casi todas las carreras) salían de Nicaragua tan pronto terminaban sus estudios. En la mayoría de los casos salían por la presión económica que se ha ido acentuando en los últimos años. Los bibliotecarios que han permanecido en el país han tenido muy pocas oportunidades para

actualizarse y capacitarse en campos especializados de la Bibliotecología. Se han dado algunos casos de bibliotecarios que han logrado
sacar cursos de especialización en México, Cuba, Brasil, etc., y quizás
cinco o seis bibliotecarios que han logrado obtener un grado de
maestría en Venezuela, Puerto Rico y los Estados Unidos.

Actualmente, quizás la situación es más grave en cuanto a que se
unen la falta de recursos para capacitar personal con el alto grado de
desempleo a nivel de bibliotecas que dependen directamente del estado.
Es este el caso de las bibliotecas públicas y escolares (en 1989 fueron
cerradas la mayoría de las bibliotecas escolares por falta de presupuesto), donde las pocas que existen sobreviven gracias al esfuerzo
personal que hacen sus bibliotecarios, y una buena parte de ellos son
personal que carece de técnicas bibliotecarias para realizar su trabajo.

En las bibliotecas universitarias, por lo menos el último año, sus
administraciones han logrado mantener el personal, aunque con un
servicio mínimo a los usuarios. La situación en relación a las condiciones de los bibliotecarios no va a cambiar fácilmente si se toma en
cuenta que los salarios dependen de un aporte estatal. Sin embargo,
las administraciones de las universidades hacen grandes esfuerzos para
establecer convenios y cooperación con instituciones afines en el
exterior del país con el objeto de mejorar y actualizar sus acervos
bibliográficos.

Después de revisar cuál es la situación de Nicaragua en cuanto a
sus servicios bibliotecarios, es posible señalar algunas consideraciones
sobre qué podría SALALM ofrecer a los bibliotecarios nicaragüenses.
En principio, hace falta que se desarrolle un programa publicitario
dando a conocer a los bibliotecarios nacionales qué es esta organización
y cuáles son sus objetivos. Esta tarea de difusión de los principios de
SALALM debe incluir un programa de integración de los bibliotecarios
nicaragüenses, haciendo las consideraciones del factor económico
posible de estos que les pueda facilitar la asociación correspondiente.

El segundo aspecto que se podría considerar es si a través de
SALALM, las bibliotecas universitarias, la Biblioteca Nacional, y otras
bibliotecas e instituciones homólogas en los Estados Unidos podrían
crearse los canales para establecer un intercambio de bibliografía
nicaragüense con materiales en español que se editan en los Estados
Unidos y que son de interés para Nicaragua. Esto obviamente traería
un beneficio inmediato para los servicios a los usuarios de las
bibliotecas nicaragüenses, y de la misma manera las bibliotecas
norteamericanas que tienen interés en las colecciones latinoamericanas
tendrían la opción de captar este tipo de bibliografía a través de este
recurso.

Otro asunto donde SALALM podría colaborar con los bibliotecarios nicaragüenses es en relación a la posibilidad de concretar con
esta organización un intercambio de bibliotecarios que facilite la
capacitación del personal de las bibliotecas nicaragüenses, dentro y
fuera de Nicaragua. Sobre todo a nivel de las bibliotecas universitarias,
sería de mucho provecho para sus bibliotecarios si algunos pudieran
conocer de cerca la experiencia de bibliotecas norteamericanas en el
aspecto de la automatización, por ejemplo. También, en el aspecto de
desarrollo de las publicaciones, cómo se maneja la selección y adquisición de materiales bibliográficos en las bibliotecas universitarias y qué
tipos de políticas desarrollan para la realización de estas actividades,
etc., así como en otras áreas de la bibliotecología que son importantes
para la efectividad de su funcionamiento.

A nivel de la producción bibliográfica nicaragüense, tema que ha
sido cubierto en la ponencia "La situación de la producción bibliográfica nicaragüense", a presentarse también en este seminario, han
habido solicitudes concretas en cuanto a la colaboración que SALALM
puede dar a Nicaragua. Considerando que esta es una organización, en
la que uno de los principales objetivos es el desarrollo de colecciones
latinoamericanas de bibliotecas, para las editoriales y distribuidoras de
libros nicaragüenses, SALALM es la mejor fuente en los Estados
Unidos para la distribución de los recursos bibliográficos con que se
cuenta en el país. Quizás esto se justifica de mejor manera cuando se
ha tenido la oportunidad de escuchar a un director de una editorial
nicaragüense expresando que: "Una forma de favorecer la industria del
libro sería de establecer comunicaciones con las editoriales de cada país
a fin de adquirir sus fondos bibliográficos. Por ejemplo, sería una
iniciativa de que las editoriales pudieran venderles a las bibliotecas
norteamericanas a precios muy favorables el stock de títulos nuestros a
fin de que el libro nicaragüense estímulo de parte de las bibliotecas,
porque se estarían adquiriendo para una población mucho mayor y
estaría distribuido en otros países. Eso ayudaría a las editoriales que
tienen sus libros estancados".*

Finalmente, quizás hay algo más en lo que SALALM podría tener
una gran contribución con Nicaragua: Las posibilidades de ser un
enlace más para apoyar y facilitar proyectos de desarrollo técnico de las
bibliotecas de Nicaragua. Esto podría concretarse en la sugerencia de
instituciones que puedan proveer fondos para ejecución de programas
específicos de los que en el momento oportuno se darían los detalles
necesarios.

NOTE

*Eric Bladón, Director de la Editorial Vanguardia, entrevista, Managua, Nicaragua, abril 1991.

The Conspectus Ten Years On: Achievements and Future Prospects

23. The Latin American Conspectus: Panacea or Pig in a Poke?

Dan C. Hazen

Introduction

The development of a national conspectus is a project of potential significance approaching that of the development of the National Union Catalog of past generations. Through this effort, scholars and librarians everywhere will have a better concept of the location of major research collections. By understanding existing patterns of strength, and by distributing responsibility on the basis of collaborative self-interest, the research libraries of the nation may develop even stronger research collections with less undesirable redundancy and unnecessary expenditure. [1]

The Latin American Update or Conspectus, as devised in 1984–85, sought to incorporate Latin American library collections within the Conspectus approach to collection evaluation. In so doing, it also addressed some perceived drawbacks of then-existing Conspectus components. Other flaws in the Conspectus approach have since become more apparent, as have the practical difficulties of completing and using this instrument. Yet the Conspectus has during the same span been embraced as the basis for the North American [and beyond . . .] Collections Inventory Project (NCIP). It remains an implicit centerpiece for library cooperation.

My rather curmudgeonly remarks will first consider the Conspectus independent of its Latin American manifestation. [2] In turning to the Latin American Update, which was designed in order to both strengthen the Conspectus and extend it to our field, I emphasize particularly the instrument's relation to cooperation. I close by speculating on the role of collection evaluation in our emerging age of information access. What are the possibilities, and the limits, of the Conspectus approach?

The RLG Conspectus and NCIP: Evaluation Tool or Collections Panacea?

In 1979, the American Library Association published a task force report on collection development that included a lengthy section entitled "Guidelines for the Evaluation of the Effectiveness of Library

Collections." Collection evaluation, while a somewhat intractable enterprise, was perceived as both important for individual libraries and increasingly necessary in an age of resource sharing and cooperative collection development. Yet the "guidelines," in recapitulating existing evaluation approaches and listing the advantages and drawbacks of each, were ultimately conservative. The state of the evaluation art was reflected in the document's rather tentative conclusion: "In any evaluation of a library collection, a combination of these procedures may be used, the one complementing or verifying the other. Some tend to be quantitative, some qualitative, both together possibly producing a reasonable, reliable result. . . ."[3]

Collection development officers from the Research Libraries Group, with Stanford's (now Penn's) Paul Mosher leading the charge, subsequently developed the "Conspectus" methodology in order to establish a common framework for collection evaluation. The Conspectus approach entails standardized instruments with normalized categories and codes that are applied to describe both existing holdings and current and prospective collecting. The instruments themselves were generally devised by teams of subject specialists. RLG's Collection Management and Development Committee oversaw the gradual extension of Conspectus components to cover most library collections.

The Conspectus approach was further refined through a small number of "verification studies," and the promise of more. "Verification studies" are intended to calibrate and reconcile the values attributed to specific Conspectus lines by individual bibliographers at different institutions. Specially constructed, "standard" bibliographies are created for each category under consideration, and holdings levels then confirmed by each participant. A collection claiming a high Conspectus ranking but owning only a small share of items from the test bibliography would be expected to lower its rating. This kind of "reality check" promises the objective, comparable, practical information that could underpin programs of cooperative collection development and resource sharing.

The Conspectus methodology, by appearing to provide "standard approaches to determining and reporting collection strengths and weaknesses [to] provide essential information for making collection decisions on acquisitions responsibilities," stimulated the Association of Research Libraries to initiate the North American Collections Inventory Project (NCIP).[4] As more libraries signed onto the effort, the expected values of the results became ever greater. The Conspectus boasted technical support through a state-of-the-art online file and institutional backing from both ARL and RLG. Although many claims for the Conspectus were somewhat qualified, the casual impression was that effective cooperation was at last within our grasp. Similar hopes have influenced the Conspectus's adoption in other parts of the world.

The Conspectus and Cooperation: An Appearance of Order
The Instrument

The order, comparability, comprehensiveness, and usability of Conspectus data—and of the Conspectus approach itself—may be more apparent than real.[5] The first Conspectus sections were, for the most part, devised as subject specialists developed ad hoc categorizations of their disciplines. These instruments covered their fields well, but many bore little relation to the systems by which libraries organize their holdings. In a sense, the Conspectus architects were inventing new systems to organize knowledge, on top of the library classification schemes (and HEGIS terms, specialized thesauri, and the like) already in existence. Later Conspectus efforts, among them the Latin American Update, sought rather to align each category with a measurable component of library collections—in our case through rigorous utilization of the Library of Congress classification. As we will see, this response generated its own problems.

The Conspectus is completed as bibliographers assign a series of codes to describe both existing and prospective collections. Numerical ratings from 0 through 5, for instance, identify topics that range between "out of scope" (level 0) and those represented by "comprehensive" (level 5) collections. The scores assigned by bibliographers are inevitably subjective. A "verification study" for French language and literature thus revealed that five collections rating themselves as "Research Level" held between 31 and 62 percent of the items on a test bibliography.[6]

The Conspectus response to scoring subjectivity has taken two directions. "Verification studies" of the sort that revealed the French literature discrepancies are so time consuming that very few have been conducted. A somewhat similar "reality check" is prospective in application. "Benchmarks," or "supplementary guidelines," are brief statements of the levels of holdings from specific bibliographies and reference sources that might justify particular Conspectus scores. Most "benchmarks" are a priori creations: they in effect substitute a single subjective scale for the many individual standards applied as bibliographers work independently. Subjectivity is thus boosted to a higher level of abstraction.[7]

Problems are again apparent in the Conspectus coding scheme. The 0-5 rating scale at first glance suggests a simple continuum between "out of scope" and "comprehensive." The intermediate values include "Basic Information Level" (2)—a category essentially representing a reference collection. Yet a reference collection pursues different objectives and is therefore qualitatively different from a collection designed for "Instructional Support" (3). And the "Instructional Support Level" is, once again, qualitatively distinct from either the "Research Level" (4) or the "Comprehensive Level" (5). Library collections fall into a matrix that incorporates function as well as size. The Conspectus coding system unsuccessfully attempts to reduce this matrix to a single-dimension scale.[8]

I have so far suggested that Conspectus rhetoric fostered unrealistic expectations and that the approach itself—though superficially plausible—was flawed in both concept and methodology. A perhaps more compelling criterion for evaluating the Conspectus, however, centers on its more tangible results. What has the Conspectus allowed us to do, and what have we done with it? The record appears mixed.

The Instrument's Uses

The literature describing the Conspectus is impressibly consistent in reporting local advantages. Improved understandings of local collections, more tightly defined collection development policies, data to aid in allocating materials budgets within libraries and library budgets within institutions—these and similar benefits are repeatedly asserted. They may well justify the institutional decision to complete all of the Conspectus.

The multi-institutional benefits are less obvious. One aspect involves the panorama of collections information—the "map" of strengths and weaknesses—that the Conspectus can provide. In some mainstream disciplines, the number of potentially significant collections may indeed both warrant and require highly structured evaluation and information instruments. Less populated fields, however, might manage with less formal tools. The information value of the Conspectus, in other words, may not be uniform across all fields: it is best seen in the broader context of what librarians and scholars are able to know through personal contacts, printed sources, and other vehicles.

The actual track record of Conspectus-based cooperation affords another dimension for assessment.[9] Cooperative uses can be divided between those that focus on existing library holdings (RECON, preservation) and those addressing prospective needs (cooperative collection development, cooperative cataloging). Grant applications for retrospective conversion or preservation typically mention Conspectus scores to demonstrate the target collection's importance. Actual grants for RECON and preservation generally reflect the same collection strengths.

The Conspectus is not the only factor at play. Our prevailing operational ideology for preservation projects focuses on single items. The eventual result of intensive, dispersed preservation microfilming will be a collectively comprehensive collection of preservation masters. Further down the road, these scattered resources may be digitized and made available through some universal document delivery system. Strong local collections often provide the logic for allocating preservation funds, but filming operations focus on single items for which microfilm does not exist. Conspectus data, while sometimes germane to the fund-finding process, are thus irrelevant to both filming operations and the dispersed array of preservation masters that result.

The Conspectus has provided an occasional organizing focus for cooperative RECON. A series of music RECON projects, for instance, have employed LC classification segments/Conspectus categories to order the workflow among participating institutions. On the one hand, the initial effort at each participating library focused on areas rated high on the Conspectus, with follow-up in segments already addressed somewhere else. Cooperative projects for Latin American RECON, on the other hand, have employed much broader country categories, with the large countries sometimes divide between the humanities and the social sciences. Other preservation and RECON projects, including the NEH "Comprehensive" [microfilming] grants to Berkeley and Yale for Western European humanities material, have likewise carried only indirect connections to the Conspectus.

At yet another level, grants follow funding requests. Money is ordinarily available to funding agencies during a limited term. If a strong collecting library fails to apply for want of a filming lab or because it isn't ready for RECON, the funds will certainly be spent somewhere else. Practicality and expediency weigh heavily in grant and project decisions: the Conspectus can only guide the funding process to the extent that applications represent strong collections.

Both preservation and RECON focus on existing library holdings. The Conspectus is more successful in mapping these holdings than in characterizing current activity or future intent. Yet cooperative collection development is an area in which these more volative data are essential. The designation PCR (primary collecting responsibility) affords perhaps the closest link between the Conspectus and cooperative collection development. A library accepting a PCR promises to maintain that collection at its reported "current collecting intensity." The 300 PCRs current as of 1986 (out of more than 7,000 Conspectus lines overall) for the most part represented "narrow subject areas outside the academic mainstream."[10]   I am aware of no analysis of the practical impact of PCR assignments, though such inquiry might clarify how institutions interpret and support these commitments, as well as how PCRs have affected our collective research capability.

Current Collecting Cooperation

Most cooperative collection development involves levels of collecting not associated with Conspectus divisions: individual titles in the first instance, but also some categories of materials like statistical serials, ministerial *memorias*, or local newspapers.   Conspectus categories only occasionally match the operational categories that structure most cooperative endeavors, and these occasional matches are often only coincidental. The reasons lie within the general Conspectus approach.

The Conspectus has been built around the LC classification system in order to ensure an immediate connection with the library collections that it evaluates.   For existing collections ordered by LC, the Conspectus categories can indeed facilitate analysis.   But these categories carry far less meaning for such prospective activities as selection and acquisitions.

Selection is an enterprise structured by dealer capabilities, institutional needs, available resources, each discipline's research agenda, and bibliographic tools.   None of these elements follows Conspectus categories or reflects the Conspectus approach. Both title-by-title selection and gathering plans thus respond to a logic, and to subject categories, distinct from those of the Conspectus.   The Conspectus can only exceptionally be adapted to the selection process— yet selection is the key to cooperative collection development.

The Conspectus suffers from similar drawbacks for resource sharing. Its advocates claim that reference librarians, bibliographers, interlibrary loan staff, and scholars themselves will consult the Conspectus in order to identify strong collections. Once again, the fundamental issue is whether and how Conspectus categories correspond to real-life questions and needs. Compilations like Lee Ash's *Special Collections* may well be more useful in addressing these inquiries, especially for areas outside the academic mainstream. Finally, of course, most library quests center on specific items. Here the Conspectus is simply irrelevant.

With the Conspectus as fairly active background, other approaches to cooperative collection building have moved to the fore even within RLG. As early as 1984, RLG staff identified a choice "between continuing with the development of the Conspectus and the assignment of primary collecting responsibilities, or developing 'our opportunities for meaningful and statistically significant cooperation in mainline fields.'"[11] The latter approach was explored with a CONOCO-funded study on the potential for cooperation in German literature and Geology. This study, which revealed bibliographers' perhaps surprising willingness to rely on shared resources and interlibrary loan, was based on surveys using specific sample titles. A more recent RLG effort to identify core journals in a field, and then ensure their availability somewhere within the consortium, likewise reflects an approach based on the very specific.

This section has explored some of the weaknesses in the Conspectus approach, considered the uses to which the Conspectus has been put, and surveyed current directions in library cooperation. The Conspectus carries fairly clear local utility, though its broader benefits seem to entail communication and consciousness-raising as much as any rationalization of collecting efforts. The Conspectus may have a role in communicating collection information where resources are very widely distributed. Of the few direct Conspectus applications in support of cooperation, those focusing on existing collections—RECON and preservation—have been most prominent. On the other hand, the mobilization of collection development and cooperative energies enabled by the Conspectus may itself have had a major impact on subsequent endeavors. Its primary value may lie within this area of galvanizing interest and support.

The Latin American Update: A (Typically?) Unruly Example

Our own example of Conspectus promise, pitfalls, and performance is the so-called Latin American Update. This Conspectus component, developed in 1984-85, particularly addressed two presumed defects in the structure then prevailing. In the first place, the Latin American Conspectus sought to rigorously employ categories intelligible in terms of library collections. This was accomplished by reviewing the entire Library of Congress classification system and noting every value corresponding to Latin America. The preliminary result was a list of more than 6,000 categories, ranging from topics like "Brazilian Literature since 1960" to such arguably more marginal themes as "Protection of Animals—Paraguay."[12]

The Update next validated its categories in terms of their demonstrated significance to Latin American library collections. This was accomplished through shelflist counts at four institutions with substantial bodies of Latin Americanist material in the Library of Congress classification system: Berkeley, Stanford, the Library of Congress, and the Benson Collection at Texas. The numerical tallies (none of which represented the corresponding institution's full holdings) enabled a working group to eliminate most categories falling beneath a certain threshhold, with special exceptions for a few rapidly expanding classification segments like that for Nicaraguan history since 1979. A few categories exceeding the minimum level of holdings at one or more test institutions were also dropped. The result was an instrument of about 800 "objectively" validated categories.

The Research Libraries Group accepted and massaged this Latin American Update within its existing Conspectus structure. (For instance, RLG had previously decided to omit the entire "A" classification from the Conspectus: the Latin American "A"s thus disappeared. Some categories from the Latin American Update likewise did not fully correspond to preexisting Conspectus categories.) In 1989 RLG announced that it "has folded the Latin American Conspectus into the appropriate subject divisions, and therefore no longer inputs this data."[13] It is not altogether clear how this change has affected either specific Conspectus categories or the overall Latin Americanist coverage now available.

The Latin American Update was devised to minimize subjectivity in the selection of Conspectus categories. Other drawbacks to the Conspectus approach were not addressed. Thus, for example, the Latin American Update ignored the issues surrounding the 0-5 Conspectus coding levels. Perhaps more interesting to us, the Latin American Update exacerbated some difficulties in its effort to resolve others. The Update's organizing principle is the LC classification system. Yet many of our most important Latin American collections are not even minimally understandable in Library of Congress terms. Old and often idiosyncratic classifications persist in many collections now employing LC. Accession-number variants are increasingly employed for both current arrearages and materials not destined for full processing. Abbreviated, general classification numbers are used for some "minimal level cataloging." Hanging the Latin American Conspectus on the LC classification scheme has compromised our ability to evaluate a major share of our collective holdings.

Verification studies for the Latin American Conspectus, while occasionally considered, have not been pursued. SALALM-based groups have proposed "benchmarks" [aside from the shelflist tallies upon which the original instrument was based] for Latin American literature, though these have not to my knowledge received formal sanction.[14] At least part of the reason may reflect the fairly even split of North America's largest Latin American collections between institutions using OCLC and those belonging to RLG. The Research Libraries Group has also consistently opposed a Latin American Program Committee, apparently from misgivings over a possible proliferation of "special interest" groups. And SALALM, an organization of individuals rather than libraries, can do little more than encourage cooperation.

The Latin American Update, finally, is a long and complicated instrument—reflecting the size and complexity of our field. Conscientious responses require significant time and energy. This kind of commitment comes most readily when the payoffs are clear. Yet the Latin American Conspectus has, to my knowledge, informed no cooperative programs—for collection development or for anything else. RECON and preservation grant proposals include obligatory passing references to Conspectus values, but the practical uses have been scant.

Latin American Collections and the Bases for Cooperation

The Conspectus approach seeks to subdivide library collections, both retrospective and prospective, into discrete components that can be evaluated and scored at a host of institutions. Completing the entire Conspectus at a single institution can provide crucial local information. Completing a single Conspectus section at different institutions carries separate possibilities. Examining the scores enables us to compare many collections and collecting emphases. At least for Latin American studies, however, the number of significant North American collections is probably smaller than 25. With so small a universe, separate descriptions of individual collections and their strengths may as effectively meet our needs.

This approach would merely expand on what we now know. We are already more likely to recall Tulane, Bancroft, and Texas's Taracena Flores Collection for scholars requesting Guatemalan materials than to parse through the Conspectus. If a user seeks a specific title, we will turn to OCLC, RLIN, and the *National Union Catalog*—not the Conspectus. The Conspectus is simply not something that we use with either rigor or consistency. Local collection guides—not just limited to the print materials emphasized in the Conspectus, and perhaps ideally distributed on floppy disks with keyword searching software—might provide a better basis for improved common knowledge.

Nevertheless, several steps might improve the Conspectus as a tool for collection evaluations and comparisons. An exploration of conversion ratios between Dewey and LC might enhance its applicability to collections classified by Dewey. "Benchmark" and "verification" bibliographies could produce more reliable scores. The possible relationship between collection quantity or strength, as determined by shelflist counts, and collection quality, as represented by the combination of Conspectus values and results from verification studies, could also be examined. Arguments abound on this issue: in theory, large collections may be laced with junk, so that size means nothing. In practice, large collections are those most likely to have been built by professional subject specialists, with consequently enhanced quality. Only further investigation can establish whether correlations exist—but the possibility that shelflist counts do reasonably reflect collection strength might significantly simplify evaluations.[15]

It is by no means clear that these or similar efforts to improve the Conspectus are worth the effort. It is fairly apparent that the Conspectus has not provided a base for Latin Americanist cooperation. Our endeavors have focused on different approaches for analyzing library resources and drawn upon a broad array of individual and institutional underpinnings. Some cooperative projects—addressing prospective needs as well as existing collections, and including RECON, preservation, and the "Modified Farmington Plan" for collection development—have been based on country-level divisions of responsibility, sometimes further informed by a "humanities"/"social sciences" split. Other efforts have been structured in terms of narrow and very discrete categories. LAMP for the most part focuses on individual titles, though its "memorias" project addresses a category of materials. The Intensive Cuban Collecting Group also emphasizes individual titles.

On another level, committed individuals have provided the impetus for our most effective cooperative efforts. These inspirations have rarely coincided with the language, approach, or logic of the Conspectus. The Intensive Cuban Collecting Group, for instance, has reacted to perceived needs for rather specialized research materials in an analysis although independent of the Conspectus. The Latin American Microform Project has followed its membership's initiative in identifying and preserving research materials. Multi-institutional proposals for RECON and preservation, while employing any available Conspectus data to buttress their appeals, again reflect needs and an operational logic removed from the Conspectus.

While the Conspectus/NCIP framework might provide a focus for successful cooperation, there appears to be neither individual nor institutional interest in applying it. The level and locus of the Conspectus approach seem inevitably to limit its application in cooperative collection development. The prospects might differ in other parts of the world, where systems of scholarship and research resources are more centrally controlled.

Collections and Collection Evaluation in the Age of Information Access

Discussions concerning library collections must consider what these collections are becoming as well as what they have been. From this perspective, the Conspectus may soon be obsolete. At varying rates among disciplines—and with Latin American studies well toward the rear—the library world's former organizing principle of "collections" is giving way before the concept of "information access." "Access" subsumes several divergent strands. Electronic information entails data that do not readily respond to our current concepts of "ownership." As such resources become more important, the Conspectus's emphasis on library holdings will become ever less useful.

Changing relationships of economics and technology are also affecting library practices concerning printed materials. Most libraries will as a matter of policy *not* microfilm a deteriorated local copy of a title already filmed somewhere else. Preservation funds are ordinarily not applied to purchasing such existing film, either. The practical effect is to erode local collections, even as the aggregate corpus of preserved materials continues to grow. The economistic logic of filming efficiencies, buttressed by an eventual prospect of ubiquitous digital reformatting, appears to render the Conspectus—and local library collections—both inadequate and irrelevant. Visions of electronic information entropy and/or utopia are not necessarily compelling vis-à-vis our immediate concerns. They nonetheless form part of the context within which the Conspectus must be evaluated.

Even for the print collections that continue to support Latin Americanist scholarship, online bibliographic databases can address ever more needs for aggregated as well as title-specific information. MARC tags and indicators, in conjunction with improved searching software, could enable a researcher to—for instance—search OCLC or RLIN for materials defined by country and date of publication, classification number, subject heading, or other features; and to generate comparative holdings tallies. As RECON progresses, such tallies would become ever more reliable. This kind of online search might, for instance, enable a scholar to identify the strongest collections of Venezuelan fiction published during the Pérez Jiménez years. Could such searches eventually replace the Conspectus's more abstract, static, and subjective data?

As we assess the Conspectus, we must more fully articulate our strategy for cooperation. On the one hand, the Conspectus/NCIP, RLG/ARL structure does not appear to have immediately benefited the Latin Americanist community. Ad hoc consortia, LAMP, and SALALM itself have been far more successful. On the other hand, the Conspectus may have moved us to think and work together in a way that we neither could nor would have before. Is the Conspectus therefore a necessary step on the road to cooperation—even though it may ultimately be superseded and shunned? Or does its local value alone warrant its pursuit, regardless of cooperative usages?

NOTES

1. Nancy E. Gwinn and Paul H. Mosher, "Coordinating Collection Development: The RLG Conspectus," *College and Research Libraries* 44, 2 (March 1983), 139.

2. My observations are based on my experiences in helping design the Latin American Conspectus (in an outgrowth of a collection evaluation project at Stanford University in 1983/84), completing the instrument (at Berkeley), running Conspectus workshops and explaining Conspectus theory to groups both here and in Latin America, and working on a number of specific cooperative endeavors.

3. American Library Association, Collection Development Committee, *Guidelines for Collection Development* (Chicago: ALA, 1979), p. 19.

4. "Collection Description and Assessment in ARL Libraries," ARL *SPEC Kit* 87 (Sept. 1982), cover page.

5. David Henige, "Epistemological Dead End and Ergonomic Diaster? The North American Collections Inventory Project," *Journal of Academic Librarianship* 13, 14 (Sept. 1987), 209-213.

6. See Jeffry Larson, "The RLG French Literature Collection Assessment Project," *Collection Management* 6, 1/2 (Spring/Summer 1984), 97-114. Henige (pp. 211-212) pointedly restates the results. Also see Thomas A. Lucas, "Verifying the Conspectus: Problems and Progress," *College and Research Libraries News* 51, 3 (March 1990), 199-201.

7. Updating Conspectus values as collection emphases gradually shift is another dilemma with both theoretical and practical aspects. The initial Conspectus sections are now almost ten years old. How does one determine whether changed collecting intensity over a decade translates into a corresponding change in "existing collection strength" as well as "current collecting intensity"? Among other considerations, the rate at which scholarship evolves in different fields would suggest that different Conspectus sections will have different half-lives. On a practical level, despite the technically straightforward operations entailed in updating online Conspectus values, how many libraries have actually revised their reports?

8. Some of these points are made in Ross Atkinson, "The Language of the Levels: Reflections on the Communication of Collection Development Policy," *College and Research Libraries* 47, 2 (March 1986), 140-149.

9. Authorities within both RLG and ARL have urged that the Conspectus be regarded as a tool rather than an end in itself. See, e.g., Scott Bennett, "Commentary on

the Stephens and Haley Papers," in Wilson Luquire, ed., *Coordinating Cooperative Collection Development: A National Perspective* (New York, NY: The Haworth Press, 1986), 199-201; or Millicent D. Abell, "The Conspectus: Issues and Questions," in *NCIP: Means to an End: Minutes of the 109th Meeting (October 22-23, 1986, Washington, DC)* (Washington, DC: Association of Research Libraries, 1987), 26-30.

10. See Stephen Hanger, "Collection Development in the British Library: The Role of the RLG Conspectus," *Journal of Librarianship* 19, 2 (April 1987), 94.

11. Jim Coleman, *Report on the Conoco Project in German Literature and Geology* (Research Libraries Group, April 7, 1987), p. 18.

12. The listing work at Stanford was independently corroborated by Laura O. Loring's—now Shedenhelm's—1983 MLS thesis at UCLA, entitled "Latin America: A Conspectus Extracted from the Library of Congress Classification Scheme."

13. *Association of Research Libraries Newsletter* 144 (March 8, 1989), 18.

14. See "Latin American Conspectus: Benchmarks for Literature, 3/87 Draft."

15. See William E. McGrath and Nancy B. Nuzzo, "'Existing Collection Strength' and Shelflist Count Correlations in RLG's *Conspectus for Music*," *College and Research Libraries* (March 1991), 194-203. This article correlates shelflist counts with Conspectus values. It does not report whether all holdings at the test institutions are represented in LC shelflists, and thereby omits a potentially decisive piece of the argument.

24. Collection Evaluation Techniques: A British Pilot Study

Patricia Noble

This paper is principally a report of the first stages of an exercise in collection evaluation techniques which is being carried out by a group of members of ACOLAM, the United Kingdom Advisory Committee on Latin American Materials. In order to explain how and why the project came into being, I begin by giving some idea of the place of Latin American area studies within the general context of British research libraries.

It is important first of all to recognise that, even with the cuts being experienced now by U.S. libraries, there are still considerable disparities of scale between British and North American concepts of what constitutes a major collection in this field. For obvious geo-political reasons, Latin American studies as a field never ranked as highly in British universities as it does on this side of the Atlantic, and even our biggest and longest established research collections are, correspondingly, much smaller than their North American counterparts. For example, in a paper presented at SALALM XXXIII in 1988,[1] Carl Deal offered some criteria for major status; amongst them was an annual expenditure of $100,000 and a minimum collection size of 150,000 to 200,000 volumes. No British library has Latin American holdings of that magnitude. It seems reasonable to predict that only two of them, the British Library itself and the Bodleian, with their large collections of older material, are likely to be able to reach even the lower edge of Carl Deal's target size before the end of this decade, and then, I think it is safe to say, only if non-Latin American imprints are included in the total. As for the funding minimum he specified, few, if any, British libraries have ever benefited from that level of expenditure for Latin American material, and certainly not for Latin American imprints alone. In fact, the relatively high level of current acquisitions that was reported by the British Library and the Bodleian to the British Union Catalogue of Latin Americana almost certainly had a good deal to do with their ability to claim free copies of British and North American imprints under copyright deposit.

The 19 years between 1968 and 1987, during which the British Union Catalogue of Latin Americana (BUCLA) was compiled, saw the greatest general expansion of British research libraries of this century. This period included the 10 years of the Parry grants, funds earmarked for Latin American studies by the University Grants Committee in a scheme similar to Title VI funds in the United States but on a much smaller scale. Only 5 institutions[2] received Parry funds, but 37 libraries contributed to BUCLA, not all of them, unfortunately, for the whole period. During those 19 years, however, only 4 reported an average annual accession rate in excess of 1,500 items; 3 reported between 1,000 and 1,500, and 10 between 500 and 1,000. The figures for the remaining 20 libraries range between 70 items per year over 7 years, to 970 a year over 17 years. To sum up, over the full period of 19 years a total of 368,284 locations for 202,776 titles was reported by the 37 contributing libraries altogether.

These statistics are the record of an era of maximum expansion, and what now seems, in retrospect, to have been amazing generosity on the part of the keepers of the national pursestrings. It may be imagined, therefore, what level of funding is now generally available for Latin American acquisitions today, when British higher education, which suffered savage cuts in the early 1980s, is being faced with further demands for at best rationalization, at worst retrenchment. It is important to understand, moreover, that in many libraries, budgets assigned to Latin American studies must also cover the provision of English-language undergraduate texts; some libraries, in fact, particularly those in which budget formulae based on student numbers are applied, cannot even provide a full range of the publications of major British and North American academic publishers, let alone of material published in Latin America itself.

One must conclude, therefore, that it is unlikely that many British libraries will feel able in practice to assume primary collecting responsibility (which implies of course long- or at least medium-term commitment of funds) for even the most strictly limited and defined topic within the field of Latin American studies. Nevertheless, there is at the same time considerable pressure to rationalise research and library resources generally, and as a result different forms and methods of cooperation are being actively considered in many institutions and groupings, at both local and national levels.

As a contribution to this debate, a working group of 12 members of ACOLAM[3] came together, last year, to examine various methods of collection evaluation and in particular to attempt to identify some way of producing a benchmark for Latin American materials which could be applied in any exercise of collection assessment, and which might also be effective in identifying particular strengths and concentrations of specialist or hard-to-obtain material.

The group began by considering four possible approaches: Conspectus worksheets, shelf-measurement, evaluation by subject specialists, and the creation of benchmark bibliographies. It soon became apparent that there were serious obstacles to using the first three methods. The essentially interdisciplinary nature of Latin American area studies was itself a problem, which was further complicated by the great diversity of methods of bibliographical control and stock management favoured by British libraries.

Bibliographical record formats, for instance, still vary widely, despite the almost universal adoption of computerization over the last decade. Before automation, many libraries prepared their own entries in-house, often to fairly basic standards; and even after automation some still continue to do so, rather than using the full records obtainable from one of the bibliographical cooperatives. Even in those libraries which do use full AACR2 records for new stock, MARC retro-conversion of traditional card or guardbook catalogues is not likely to be completed for some time yet; meanwhile, older material tends to be added to the online catalogue only if it is circulated, and then with not much more than author, title, and callmark.

Systems of stock arrangement also vary widely. Some libraries still use in-house classification schemes (Garside at University College, London, is one example) which, whatever their intrinsic merits, do nothing to facilitate comparison of holdings. Even where LC or Dewey schemes have been applied, they have sometimes been modified over the years quite radically, and to idiosyncratic local guidelines.

These factors, which suggested that the use of Conspectus worksheets, whether based on Library of Congress or Dewey, would be far from easy, also militated against linear shelf-measurement. Since very few libraries shelve Latin American material separately, measurement of relatively small sections of various mutually incompatible classification schemes did not seem likely to produce any realistic indication of either quality or currency (or even reliable figures for quantity).

The third option, evaluation by a subject specialist, was also rejected (although it has been used in other British exercises of this kind). It was felt that the recruitment of willing, expert independent observers (faculty, for instance) would not be easy, and that assessment of a collection for much of which the assessor was personally responsible might offer too many conscious or subconscious temptations, whilst mutual inspection of each other's holdings might not achieve the necessary objectivity either, and would be equally difficult to organize effectively.

It was finally agreed, therefore, to begin by experimenting with the creation of a statistically sampled checklist of titles in one topic, preferably an interdisciplinary one. Obviously, the topic would have to be one which was the subject of a reasonably up-to-date bibliography; we also felt it should be one of some current research interest, so that the final result might produce information of some practical benefit to library users.

Achieving the necessary combination of up-to-date bibliographical source, interdisciplinary status, and research significance proved more difficult than we had expected. Eventually, we settled on the topic of "The military in politics," which was the subject of a bibliography compiled by Herbert E. Gooch, *The Military and Politics in Latin America*.[4] However, this was published as long ago as 1979, so it was decided to supplement it with items derived from appropriate index headings in vols. 45, 47, and 49 of the *Handbook of Latin American Studies*. To simplify the process of compilation as well as of checking, we decided to confine the checklist to monograph items. The sampling was carried out according to the guidelines in B. H. Hall's *Collection Assessment Manual for College and University Libraries*.[5] The samples, which were produced separately from each source, gave a grand total of 328 references; this size of sample is valid, according to Hall, for a population of 2,200, which is much greater than the total number of monograph citations in the two sources we used.

Each library then checked the list. In several libraries it was necessary, as I have described, to check against both a card catalogue for earlier holdings and an online catalogue for more recent material. This accounts for the variations reported by different libraries in the length of time taken to complete this operation: from as little as two to as much as eight hours.

The validity of translations or other editions as full matches was not specified in the covering document; as a result, some libraries noted variant editions and translations separately, whilst others did not record them at all, or recorded them as full matches. Since it was not always clear what each checker had decided to do, hits were registered in the final tables as full matches unless otherwise described, and two overall totals were given for those libraries which had drawn a distinction.

As the checklists were received back the results were entered on a master list. From this information three tabulations were produced.

Table 1 analyses the results in terms of total hits and language balance; table 2 analyses them in terms of date of imprint, to give some indication of currency; and table 3 records patterns of availability and duplication according to language of text. Two libraries with very specialised collections reported only two hits in all, and their returns have therefore been used only for table 3, but not for tables 1 or 2, where they would have distorted the averages downward. Since the main object of the project was to establish the validity of the particular method being tested, institutions have been identified in the tables only by letter, and are entered in order of magnitude of the total number of hits. The main points that emerged from the survey can be summarised as follows:

Of 328 items, locations were reported for 270 items (83 percent).

No locations at all were reported, however, for 57 items (17 percent); of these over four-fifths were foreign-language texts, or pre-1980 imprints, or both.

London locations were reported for 74 percent of all items; of 27 items *not* held in London, 15 were at Oxford, Cambridge, or Essex, all within about an hour or two of London, so that it may be said that 79 percent of all the items on the list were available somewhere within what is sometimes referred to as the Golden Triangle of South-East England.

As far as currency is concerned, there were found to be locations for 91 percent of the post-1980 imprints, but only 79 percent of the pre-1980 imprints. Given the cuts of the last few years, the reverse might have been expected, but presumably the figure reflects the fact that most of these institutions have only been collecting Latin American material intensively since 1970, whereas 40 percent of the titles in the checklist were over 20 years old.

The highest hit rate for pre-1980 imprints for any individual library was only 52 percent, and for post-1980 only 66 percent. As the overall hit rate for each library declines down table 2, the proportion of post-1980 hits within each total declines also, from 37 percent at the top to 17 percent at the bottom. This may reflect the concentration of Latin American studies into centres with a longer tradition of Hispanic studies in general, which has taken place as levels of funding have fallen.

As far as language balance is concerned, there was found to be at least one location for 92 percent of the English-language material, but for only 75 percent of the foreign-language material. Whereas foreign-language material represented

55 percent of the total checklist, no single library reported a proportion of more than 48 percent of foreign-language items within its total hits; the average level in fact was only 32 percent, and the smaller the total of hits, the smaller the proportion which was of foreign-language material. In other words, it appears there is a distinct bias, even in the largest research collections, towards English-language, and against foreign-language publications, a finding which may be thought to have serious implications for the availability of primary material and hence for future research needs.

The results of this survey can be considered from two viewpoints: as an exercise in a measurement technique on the one hand, and for the quality and quantity of the information which it produced, on the other.

As an exercise, it proved rather more labour-intensive than we had anticipated. The compilation of the checklist in itself took about 80 hours of work (shared between two people), and was complicated by the decision to supplement the original sources with citations from the *Handbook*. It seems reasonable to assume that the selection of a source for citations will always be difficult if the aim is to evaluate collections longitudinally, rather than to produce a snapshot of the situation at one point in time.

Evaluation of coverage over a defined, relatively short period (in which case annual bibliographies, drawn from the *Handbook*, could be used) would obviously be much simpler.

Over all the libraries concerned, the checking occupied about 50 staff hours, and the tabulation took about another 20 hours. In any repeat exercise it will be essential to employ a spreadsheet, which would have speeded up considerably this part of the project, as well as allowing for more refined statistics to be calculated.

The list itself proved relatively easy to check, apart from one or two misspellings or misdescriptions which were, however, easily picked up by the checkers. A major omission, already referred to, was the failure to define a full match exactly, and this may well have produced some distortions in the final figures.

The results themselves were valuable, but not surprising, since they told us little that in general terms we could not have predicted from personal knowledge; however the high overall hit rate was gratifying. The general preponderance of English-language material was depressing but not surprising, given the shortage of funds and the need in many libraries to give priority to undergraduate provision. The principal value of these figures, in fact, is that they go some way toward quantifying what could only previously have been described (however accurately) in impressionistic and subjective terms. The method must, of course, be tested again in other subject fields, and we are currently planning to try a literary topic next. We are reasonably optimistic, however, that it may prove to be a statistically valid method of producing a benchmark for use in a Conspectus exercise or similar comparative survey, provided a satisfactory citation source can be agreed on.

The amount of staff time needed is, however, quite significant, particularly for smaller institutions, and it may be that libraries that are unable to provide a comprehensive collection of undergraduate teaching materials in English are unlikely also to be able to commit significant funds to any project of cooperative collection development in what is after all a relatively specialized field. Nevertheless, exercises of this kind can still provide a valuable service in identifying and recording existing collection strengths, even in those libraries which no longer find themselves in a position to be able to fill any retrospective gaps in holdings or to maintain currency.

NOTES

1. Carl Deal, "Latin American Collections: Criteria for Major Status," in Paula Ann Covington, ed., *Latin American Frontiers, Borders and Hinterlands: Research Needs and Resources*. Papers of SALALM XXXIII, Berkeley, California, June 5–10, 1988 (Albuquerque, NM: SALALM, 1990), pp. 163-168.

2. Parry funds were awarded to the following centres for a period of ten years, beginning in 1965: Cambridge, Glasgow, Liverpool, London, and Oxford. The University of Essex (although not a Parry centre) received substantial support from the Nuffield Foundation between 1967 and 1972.

3. The institutions that took part were: The Bodleian Library; the British Library; the British Library of Political and Economic Science; Cambridge University Library; Essex University Library; Glasgow University Library; the Institute of Education, University of London; the Institute of Historical Research, University of London; Liverpool University Library; London University Library; Portsmouth Polytechnic Library; University College London Library.

4. Herbert E. Gooch, *The Military and Politics in Latin America* (Los Angeles: Latin American Studies Center, California State University, 1979).

5. Blaine H. Hall, *Collection Assessment Manual for College and University Libraries* (Phoenix, AZ: Oryx Press, 1985).

Table 1. Titles Held by British Research Libraries

Library	Includes variant editions but excludes translations (maximum 328)		Includes variant editions and translations[a]		English-language titles held and as percentage of all English-language on list (maximum 146)		Foreign-language titles held and as percentage of all foreign-language on list (maximum 182)		English titles held and as percentage of all titles held (44 percent of total)	
	Number	Percentage	Number	Percentage	Number	Percentage	Number	Percentage	Number	Percentage
A	185	56	186	57	109	75	76	42	109	59
B	167	51	170	52	97	66	70	38	97	58
C	155	47			97	66	58	32	97	62
D	152	46	157	48	79	54	73	40	79	52
E	148	45			99	67	49	27	99	67
F	124	38	126	38	89	61	35	19	89	72
G	112	34			86	59	26	14	86	77
H	108	33			83	57	25	14	83	77
J	99	30	100	30	78	53	21	11	78	79
K	65	20	66	20	55	38	10	5	55	85
Average	131	40			87	59	44	24	87	68
Average excluding libraries J and K	144	44			92	63	52	28	92	58

a. Not all libraries reported translations.

Table 2. Titles Held by British Research Libraries

Library	Holdings of pre-1980 imprints (maximum 328)		Holdings of post-1980 imprints (maximum 105)		Holdings of post-1980 imprints as percentage of all items held (32 percent of total list)
	Number	Percentage	Number	Percentage	Percentage
A	116	52	69	66	37
B	112	50	55	52	33
C	101	45	54	51	35
D	99	44	53	50	35
E	116	51	32	30	22
F	90	40	34	32	27
G	83	37	29	28	26
H	85	38	23	22	21
J	77	34	22	21	22
K	54	24	11	10	17
Average	93	42	38	36	27
Average excluding libraries J and K	100	45	44	41	25

Table 3. Patterns of Availability and Duplication by Language of Text

Language of text	Number of locations recorded											
	0	1	2	3	4	5	6	7	8	9	10	11
English	11	8	10	6	9	11	8	18	23	26	14	2
Foreign (including French, German, etc.	46	31	33	16	23	13	12	7	1	—	—	—
Total	57	39	43	22	32	24	20	25	24	26	14	2

25. European Approaches to the Conspectus

Ann Wade

Introduction

Although the Conspectus has been around for longer than ten years, this panel commemorates a rather personal milestone: nearly a decade of my own interest in it. I first heard of it at SALALM XXVII, in March 1982, in a paper by Deborah Jakubs on "Sharing Collection Responsibility and the Problem of Database Compatibility." I was immediately fascinated by the potential of the Conspectus, and have since charted its development in North America, the United Kingdom, and then farther afield, initially with a passive interest, but with active involvement since 1989, when I was given the opportunity to spend half of my time furthering its development in the British Isles and continental Europe as National Conspectus Officer in the British Library. I soon became aware of the widespread, but by no means universal, unease that the Conspectus could not deliver all that it had appeared to promise. I hope that the papers in this panel will help to identify what, if anything, has gone wrong, and where the future lies for the Conspectus. Will it be relevant in any way to "Latin American Studies in[to] the Twenty-first Century"? In an attempt to answer this question, I assembled speakers to cover a broad spectrum of topics: from the Latin American Conspectus in the United States, through an experimental evaluation of Latin American collections in the United Kingdom, the approach to the general Conspectus adopted by European research libraries, to the place of Conspectus in the broad field of collection management. A survey of the Conspectus in Australia by John Horacek was summarized at the panel, and is to be published as "Conspectus and Australian collections (with some comments on DNC)," in G. E. Gorman, ed., *Australian Studies: Collection Development and Acquisitions for Librarians* (London: Mansell, 1992).

European Approaches to the Conspectus

In Europe, the first library to carry out a Conspectus evaluation was the British Library. When the Library was established in 1973 it was not created from scratch as a single entity but was formed from several existing national collections. There was need for some rationalization and coordination among the major elements and for a clear public statement of the Library's collecting profile. An article that fully describes how the survey was carried out also explains the background:

In 1983 . . . a divisional [then Reference Division] Collection Development Group was created. . . . Its brief was to assist management in "deciding the priorities of current and future acquisitions in an era of recession." The group was asked to consider how the division's collecting activities might best be co-ordinated with those of other parts of the British Library, and those of the British Library as a whole with the collecting of other libraries—"leading to a national acquisitions plan on a sector-by-sector basis."[1]

The Conspectus was adopted as the method of documenting the findings of the Group, and the survey was carried out in 1985. The results were made available internationally on Conspectus On-line, a special database of the Research Libraries Group (RLG), and were also published in summary form. The resulting volume, *Conspectus in the British Library*,[2] included a statement of the priority assigned by the Library to broad subjects in its collecting policies, and a listing of the categories and formats of material the Library does not collect.

The data have since been used in a variety of ways. For example, the original survey revealed potential areas of overlap and duplication between the science/technology and humanities/social sciences collections. Using the Conspectus framework, a statement of collecting boundaries was drawn up, and a manual was produced for the guidance of staff. In planning the future development of the collections, the Conspectus has been used to identify subjects that the library does not aim to collect to a high level, with a view to establishing whether the level could be reduced further in order to free up resources for maintaining the strong collections. It is also used to answer queries from staff and readers about the strength of the collections in certain subjects.

The Conspectus was next adopted by the consortium of Scottish libraries: the National Library of Scotland together with the eight Scottish university libraries and the public libraries of Edinburgh and Glasgow carried out Conspectuses in 1987. The consortium is now using the data to identify those subjects for which member libraries claim to have a level 3, 4, or 5 collection. Those libraries are then invited to accept responsibility for maintaining their collections at that level in whichever subjects they choose, and to confirm their original assessment of the level of those collections for which they accept responsibility. When volunteering for a Cooperative Collecting Responsibility (CCR), a library does not incur additional purchasing commitments, but there is a commitment to inform the group if the level of collecting cannot be maintained. When as many subjects as possible have been covered, the group will review the overall picture, to see if several libraries have taken the same level of responsibility for the same subject (in which case one or more may wish to relinquish responsibility), and if some subjects are not covered at all (in this case the group may ask a member to volunteer to take on that subject, or may choose to rely on the holdings of a library outside the group). The benefit of the CCR scheme is that members can channel their scarce resources into those subjects that are of core priority to them with a degree of confidence that subjects of lower priority will be covered by other members of the group.

The Conspectus is being used in other ways in Scotland. The German Studies Scottish Library Group is using it as a basis for compiling a guide to resources. The Fine Art libraries group (UCABLIS) is using Conspectus methodology to describe current collecting and is also assigning CCRs. The Scottish Working Group on Official Publications has published a directory of official publications in Scotland containing the results of the Conspectus survey of government documents expressed as descriptive text rather than codes. (The Conspectus experience in Scotland is described further by Matheson[3]).

So far, the Conspectus has not been adopted in the United Kingdom as widely as was hoped. Nevertheless, it is spreading. A Conspectus survey has been done at the National Library of Wales, and the National Art Library is doing one at present. A couple of major university libraries are doing feasibility studies, and the Library and Information Co-operation Council (LINC) will be assessing the potential value of the Conspectus to its work.

The British Library maintains the National Conspectus Office as a source of information and advice to other libraries planning Conspectus surveys, and as the home of the database which it created to provide ready access to U.K. information nationally. The Library has under-taken to enter other libraries' data into the system and to provide them with a copy of the resulting database.

The focus for European Conspectus activity is the Conspectus Working Group of the Ligue des Bibliothèques Européennes de Recherche (LIBER). LIBER was set up in 1971 to "establish close collaboration between the research libraries of Europe. . . . Its intention is to bring together professional knowledge and experience of European librarians and thereby help in finding practical ways of improving the quality of the services which their libraries provide."[4]   Within that context the Conspectus Working Group was set up in 1987 with the following terms of reference:

-to promote the use of the Conspectus for resource sharing in the fields of collection development, retrospective conversion, and conservation and preservation

-to map and assess this use

-to consider the need for translations of existing Conspectus materials

-to consider the need for European, national, regional, and local adoptions of the schedules and look to their respective compatibility

-to advise the Executive Committee on the developments of European infrastructural elements (e.g., relating to networking, Conspectus databases, etc.)

-to gather and promote information among European research libraries concerning use and development of the Conspectus.

The Group has the task of creating the necessary framework for Conspectus surveys to be carried out and is consequently addressing the practical problems of assessing collections, recording the information, and making it accessible in a European context.   The aim is to create a network of Conspectus databases among national libraries, compiled to a common standard.

So far the Chair has been from a Scottish library (currently the National Library) and the Secretary has come from the British Library, an arrangement that reflects the greater experience with the Conspectus in Britain.   Currently there are one or two members, acting as a national focus, from each of the following: Austria, Catalonia, France, Germany, Italy, Netherlands, Portugal, Spain, Sweden, and Switzerland. There is scope for involving other countries, particularly in Eastern Europe.

The Group is still in the process of establishing the infrastructure for a European Conspectus, and a major task has been to adapt the worksheets for use in Europe.   The Divisions that were identified as needing a significant amount of work were: History; Linguistics, Languages and Literatures; Law; Philosophy and Religion; and Political Science.   This has generally involved expansion of the existing lines, often giving a country up to a dozen lines when it may previously have only had one.   The worksheets now need to be translated, at least into French (it may only be necessary to translate the Europeanized versions, as the rest may be available from the National Library of Canada), German, Italian, Spanish, and Portuguese.   The language codes have had to be adjusted to cater to a broader linguistic base and to remove the English-language orientation. The codes and the definition of the levels will also need to be translated. A user manual is needed, and training will have to be arranged for national coordinators and then for individual library staff. The supplemental guidelines may need to be expanded to include more European references, and the problem of developing a suitable verification technique will need to be addressed. The Group is also considering the issues involved in automation of Conspectus data, such as the standards to be used for data capture and exchange, where the data are to be held, and how they are to be accessed. In all this work the Group has not entirely gone its own way. Close consultation has been maintained with RLG, and the principles of international compatibility have been respected.

From the following examples it is clear that the appeal of the Conspectus to research libraries varies markedly from country to country, and that most are still in the early stages of refining their plans to implement the Conspectus. In France a group of libraries designated "specialized acquisitions centres" has been considering the Conspectus as an approach to a distributed national acquisitions policy. The Bibliothèque Nationale has unfortunately had to suspend its Conspectus activities while resources are directed toward the occupation of the Bibliothèque de France. In Portugal the national bibliographical database PORBASE is the focal point of a network of libraries and provides the cooperative framework for rationalization of technical and bibliographical resources. The Conspectus will fit into that framework, and the eventual national Conspectus database will complement the bibliographical database. Portugal has a national conspectus officer at the Biblioteca Nacional. In the Netherlands a national conspectus officer has also been appointed and a Conspectus of the Koninklijke Bibliotheek and thirteen university libraries is underway, looking at Current Collecting Intensity in the first phase. A national classification scheme for research libraries has recently been adopted, and there are plans for automated links to be made between the libraries' own classification schemes and Conspectus numbers via the national scheme. Conspectus numbers can thus be associated with individual titles. In Austria the major libraries already have clear statements of their individual priorities, so there are no plans to use the Conspectus to provide a national overview, but it is seen more as an internal housekeeping tool, as an aid to surveying existing collections in greater depth. In Sweden the Kungl. Biblioteket and the university libraries of Stockholm and Uppsala have used a Conspectus-based technique to construct detailed acquisitions plans. A group of Swedish research libraries has evaluated the Conspectus in the areas of Agriculture, Medicine, Psychology, Education, and International Economics and has concluded that it is useful, but has not progressed further as yet. In Germany the Deutsche Bibliothek is interested in the Conspectus as a basic classification scheme for the national and international exchange of information. At present various classification schemes are used, and the Conspectus would provide a top layer, through a concordance. Its use in national bibliographical records is being assessed. (There is also interest in this in Scotland, Wales, and the Netherlands.) The Conspectus is also being considered in Germany as a means of indexing a directory of rare books collections. (There is interest elsewhere in the idea of associating the Conspectus with the more detailed, descriptive surveys of collections, rare or otherwise.) It is not intended to be used for cooperation in acquisitions at a national level, as the German Special Subject Fields Programme has been in place for many years.

Progress by the Group as a whole has not been rapid, but there are difficulties intrinsic to any international working group which tend to make progress rather slow. First, there is communication: many languages are represented within the Group, but the Group has adopted English as its working language. The command of English by the members is impressive, and their willingness to use it is much appreciated, but at times communication is not as rapid as it would be in a monolingual group. Moreover, each country has its own framework for libraries, with different priorities and interests, and the members consequently come from a variety of backgrounds and start with different assumptions. Mutual understanding is fundamental, so positions need to be clarified frequently, and this necessarily slows the pace of the discussions. Second, there is the cost of travel within Europe. Member libraries fund attendance of their delegates at meetings, which take place two or three times a year. Most libraries are suffering severe financial problems, and travel budgets are often the first to be cut. It is extremely unusual to have every member country represented at a meeting, and this also reduces the momentum of the programme. The Group is seeking alternative sources of funds, but has not yet secured them.

The major challenge to the Group is to convert not just the working materials but the whole Conspectus technique into an international tool. European Conspectors will need to adopt an international perspective when coding collections and base their assessments on a knowledge of the universe of available publications—a truly international universe. In all its work the group needs open channels of communication to RLG and ARL. European work must be compatible with and informed by what happens in the United States.

The future vision offered by the European Conspectus is exciting. It will provide an overview of the collections of important European libraries and will thus facilitate access by scholars to the great wealth of material held in the continent. It will enable a coordinated approach to collection building and preservation, and ultimately to resource sharing. At a practical level, there is still a long way to go, but a good start has been made.

NOTES

1. Stephen Hanger, "Collection Development in the British Library: The Role of the RLG Conspectus," *Journal of Librarianship* 19:2 (April 1987), 89-107.

2. Ann Matheson, "The Conspectus Experience," *Journal of Librarianship* 22:3 (July 1990), 171-182.

3. Brian G. F. Holt and Stephen Hanger, *Conspectus in the British Library: A Summary of Current Collecting Intensity Data as Recorded on RLG Conspectus Worksheets with Completed Worksheets on Microfiche* (London: The British Library, 1986).

4. LIBER statutes, as amended in draft in 1991.

Latin American Studies, Information Resources, and Library Collections: Whither and How?

26. Latin American Studies, Information Resources, and Library Collections: The Contexts of Crisis

Dan C. Hazen

The following sections react to today's imperiled information base for Latin American studies and for area studies scholarship in general. Each section pursues a separate tack, but all respond to a crisis that has roots in at least three distinct contexts. These contexts or systems respectively encompass higher education in North America, scholarly communication, and Latin America itself. Understanding these separate, though overlapping frameworks will help clarify both needs and possibilities as we look toward the future.

The Academic Marketplace

Latin American studies is an academic endeavor embedded in a general system of higher education and intellectual activity. This larger structure defines relative and absolute levels of funding, and also helps channel prestige and other intangible resources.

Higher education in the United States grew tremendously after World War II. Economic prosperity, North American hegemony (whether imagined or real), baby boom demographics, and an apparent sensitivity to the relationship between knowledge, productivity, and innovation all supported growth. Sputnik and the Cold War injected a less benign educational imperative. Results included a quantitative explosion in higher education, substantial diversification of academic programs and approaches, and widespread public and foundation support.

Today's picture is quite different. Tax revolt, an aging population, and perceptions of universities as just another self-serving bureaucracy have sapped support for higher education. "Comprehensive" academic programs are beyond the financial reach of all but a few institutions. Successful colleges and universities must increasingly operate as businesses as well as academies: professional schools and programs in science and technology afford the greatest potential returns in an ever more economistic academic marketplace.

Area and Latin American studies have faced varying and somewhat contradictory pressures over the past generation. America's postwar/Cold War role encouraged area studies expertise through the late 1950s and the 1960s. Fidel Castro propelled Latin American studies to the vanguard of this expansionary surge. Fields related to science and technology have subsequently moved to the fore. The once-central disciplines of the social sciences and humanities have for the most part been left to squabble over the bones of more (though occasionally less) culturally inclusive "core curricula."

Underlying trends may nonetheless bode well for area and Latin American studies within higher education. The diversifying demographics of American society should have a positive effect. As North American colleges and universities increasingly function as service institutions for the world, foreign student populations will likewise both demand and produce more "international" academic programs. For the same reasons, North American universities will continue to showcase the academic superstars of the entire world. Finally, the business and commercial strategies underlying much of Pacific Rim studies, among other emerging international interests, may reinforce support for area studies and for Latin Americanist research.

In sum: Latin American studies falls within a larger structure of formal and informal academic endeavor. Academic funding, interest, and program development follow many impulses, only some of which are purely scholarly. Today's academic marketplace fully reflects the commercialization of higher education. The probable result will be continuing ebbs and flows in the fortunes of area studies in general, and of Latin American studies in particular.

Scholarly Communication

A second context for our deliberations carries the code name "scholarly communication." This system entails the process—which varies among disciplines—through which academic inquiries are framed, pursued, reported, and shared. A series of economic and technological changes are transforming this process. The changes affect all fields of study, albeit with substantial variations.

Traditional scholarly communication entailed a rather straightforward sequence from the production of knowledge, through dissemination, to consumption. Researchers, most commonly associated with universities or independent institutions, pursued "new" knowledge. Research results were packaged as articles and books that were produced by a relatively small number of specialist publishers. The resulting print products were disseminated both directly and through an established network of booksellers and distributors. Academic libraries were among the principal consumers: their well-defined stocks of research publications in turn fueled new cycles of research and publication.

The traditional system of scholarly communication was never as neat as this caricature might suggest. International fields like Latin American studies were particularly anomalous in both addressing and reflecting areas with very different cultural understandings of research and publication. Nonetheless, much of scholarly communication reflected a fairly well-ordered structure encompassing researchers as knowledge producers, publishers as knowledge disseminators, book-sellers as marketing intermediaries, and libraries as knowledge holders and consumers on behalf of both student and researcher clienteles. Libraries, though at the end of the information food chain, filled a necessary, accepted, and fairly predictable role.

Commercialization, exploding research output, and new electronic technologies have complicated this model. As scholarship and higher education have focused on instrumental disciplines embodying technological or commercial possibility, profits have increasingly propelled the "knowledge industry." Ever-larger cadres of researchers and scholars, vying for recognition within traditional structures that above all reward publications, have fueled scholarly publishing. The "serials crisis" is but one very painful result.

Another dimension of change is embodied in electronic tech-nologies, which can substantially reduce the need for intermediaries in the process of scholarly communication. Research findings more and more travel directly between their researcher-producers and researcher-consumers. The traditional model by which libraries acquire and own published research results has become correspondingly fuzzy. Direct access to electronic information, as well as mediated access through libraries, is increasingly central to both scholarship and librarianship. And the library's archival role is less and less certain.

Even within libraries, models of appropriate activities and priorities have shifted over time. Building area studies collections—collections that represented the last frontier of traditional print resources—remained a major focus through the 1960s. Subsequent budget shocks forcibly curtailed most libraries' acquisitions appetites. Technological innovation, including both in-house automation and the provision of electronic information and formats, has subsequently absorbed increasing energy and attention. Area studies collections, which had comprised the library vanguard, are perceived as relics of an outdated library philosophy emphasizing ownership over access, and of disciplines somewhere between quaint and archaic in their dependence on print formats.

New information technologies, spiraling costs, and the intensifying user demands associated with new directions in scholarship have engendered new approaches in scholarly communication. Our tools are not yet adequate to the need. Resource sharing and cooperative access remain legal thickets in light of copyright restrictions and uncertain interpretations of "fair use." Appropriate understandings of libraries' archival responsibilities are both uncertain for electronic information and under challenge for traditional materials. Latin American library collections have been innovators in addressing the special challenges of our field, as both the Farmington Plan and LACAP (among many other initiatives) suggest. But our current acquisitions model, characterized by duplicative blanket orders channeled through a far-flung dealer network, may require rethinking.

Scholarly communication in general, as well as for area and Latin American studies, is becoming ever more complex. The evolving process is straining all aspects of the traditional system. For research libraries, reduced buying power and diminished coverage are among the most immediately dramatic results. Our efforts to anticipate, react to, and utilize these changes will become increasingly crucial as we attempt to maintain the information base necessary for our scholars.

Latin America

A final context for our discussions, obvious even though often only implicit, is Latin America itself. Sustaining Latin Americanist research and providing the resources to support it force us to examine the general contexts of the academic community and of scholarly communication. But this scholarship fundamentally draws from, reflects, and contributes to the region itself.

At the most elementary level, awareness of the Latin American context demands our recognition of Latin American reality. Major issues and trends of the moment include democratization, debt, and privatization; the larger dilemma of a "developing region's" role in a world system of emerging regional spheres and intensifying Northern Hemisphere hegemony; and the region's incessant and almost ubiquitous challenges of poverty and violence.

Even as we recognize and reflect Latin America, we must avoid romanticization. Latin America is not ours to remake in our image, nor ours to freeze in archaic patterns of research or information. As librarians, this means that our efforts to document contemporary Latin American life and culture must incorporate not only electronic datafiles from central banks and government agencies but also self-published poetry from the continent's hinterlands. We must acquire the scholarly monographs of universities and research institutes as well as representative subsets of gray literature. We must recognize ephemeral serials, and also the sound recordings, comic books, and video resources so crucial in a semiliterate land.

Other regional trends may both allow and require more active responses. Recent phenomena, again within our librarians' purview, include rising book prices accompanied by declining publishing output. The emergence of multinational nongovernmental organizations as principal locuses for research and publication carries major implications for local and national research agendas and for the viability of many Latin American universities as sources of alternate social and political visions. On another level, the region generally lacks resources with which to control and preserve local cultural and intellectual patrimonies.

The issues that may compromise Latin America's viability—or, in a narrower sphere, the viability of its systems of scholarly communication—are by no means ours alone to address. But we must recognize Latin America itself as one of the central contexts for our efforts, and contribute to as well as draw from Latin America in our role as information specialists.

The three systems or contexts here outlined—of academic inquiry, of scholarly communication, of Latin America itself—inevitably shape both the momentary challenges and the enduring dilemmas with which we must grapple. Especially now, all three systems seem in crisis. Our analyses and proposals must reflect the full range of both problems and possibilities.

27. Resource Sharing: The Only Reasonable Whither

George J. Soete

The collections programs in most academic research libraries are in crisis. The crisis has been building since the mid-1980s. In the University of California, for example, though state-budgeted library materials budgets have increased 23 percent since 1985-86, the cost of library materials has increased by an estimated 54 percent. What this means is that if a library had a $3 million book budget in 1985-86, its effective 90-91 budget has dropped to less than $2.1 million. While this picture differs somewhat among academic research libraries—and even among the University of California libraries—it is, in general, the situation that we all share. And for all of us, the situation is not likely to improve soon; it will probably get a great deal worse before we reach the end of the 1990s.

We are in crisis. It's important to stress this fact in a conference panel setting, which is usually given over to contemplation of conceptual matters and analyses of issues. I am not talking about concepts or issues; I am talking about a steeply declining ability to pay our bills and support our researchers. We must continue to analyze the causes and debate the issues that face us, but we must also act. Libraries *have*, of course, been acting to cope with the crisis in a number of ways. Thousands of subscriptions to research journals and other serials have been canceled. Monographic buying, particularly of foreign imprints and retrospective materials, has been cut back drastically. External funding efforts have been intensified. We routinely try to supplement our budgets by transfers of operating funds and by shameless begging from our parent institutions.

One strategy that we have not exploited very much at all is resource sharing, specifically a resource sharing program that we've been developing at the University of California. Librarians have been

Author's note: Some of the material in this paper has been excerpted from George Soete and Karin Wittenborg, "Applying a Strategic Planning Process to Resource Sharing: The Changing Face of Collaborative Collection Development among the University of California Libraries," in Jennifer Cargill and Diane Graves, eds., *Advances in Resource Sharing*, vol. II (Westport, CT: Meckler Publishing, 1991), pp. 51-59.

272

been developing at the University of California. Librarians have been writing and talking about resource sharing for decades. There are still few well-established, significant programs underway. And few of those, it seems to me, are equipped to deal with the present crisis in any significant way.

There appear to be good reasons for the underutilization of resource sharing. Many institutions find the obstacles to resource sharing too difficult and the incentives too few. Participating institutions often serve different constituencies and experience conflict between local culture and priorities and those of the consortium. Sometimes, resource sharing simply seems to promise more losses than gains. On the bright side, much progress has been made in recent years on a technical level in tearing down some of the barriers to collaboration. Databases now provide reasonable bibliographic access to the holdings of other institutions. Facsimile transmission and other improved delivery systems facilitate physical access. Use of electronic mail systems has made communication among subject specialists in different libraries easy and relatively inexpensive. Technically, we are in pretty good shape. What we haven't done very much is to sit down and hammer out the kinds of agreements and commitments that will enable us to acquire, cut back, cancel, preserve, and manage collections in ways that are mutually beneficial, especially to our users.

Though the UC Libraries are in many ways uniquely situated to share resources, the development of cooperative programs has been steady but slow. Some may be familiar with our Shared Purchase Program, instituted in 1977. Recently, however, a new program is underway which has already resulted in more proactive, formal, and pervasive collaboration. A key component of this program expansion has been the implementation of several collaborative collection development pilot projects. In these projects, our goal was to make resource sharing a normal—even attractive—strategy for developing and managing all but core collections. We developed three pilot projects, two of which are particularly interesting, I think, to area studies librarians.

Science Translation Journals. This project was chosen because it dealt with a body of low use, expensive material. The goal was to ensure that at least one copy of each science and engineering translation journal essential to UC programs was retained somewhere in the UC system or at Stanford. Project designers identified three categories of importance: the most important titles were designated as local campus responsibilities; titles of medium importance were picked up on Shared Collections funds; titles of low importance were canceled or referred to the Center for Research Libraries as purchase proposals. Campus libraries accepted holding responsibility for journals in high and medium importance categories for a five-year period.

Pacific Rim Trade Journals. This project aims at supporting new programs in the University within the framework of a no-growth budget. Active programs in Pacific Rim Studies developed on several UC campuses during the 1980s. Trade journals provide important information about economic developments in the region, yet, because of budgetary problems, the UC libraries had subscribed to very few titles. Three libraries (Berkeley, Los Angeles, and San Diego) accepted formal responsibility by geographic area; subscriptions to some ninety trade journals were instituted and paid for with Shared Purchase funds.

East Asian Newspaper Backfiles. A growing academic interest in the Pacific Rim meant that existing programs were expanding and that new East Asian programs were introduced on several campuses. Newspaper backfiles were identified as important research material which was prohibitively expensive to acquire in multiple copies and could easily be shared. Participating campuses have assumed voluntary commitments to acquire backfiles with local funds; Shared Purchase funds are used for additional titles to strengthen our collections systemwide. As a by-product of this project, the East Asian librarians have expanded their collaborative efforts to several other areas of their collections, using Conspectus levels as a tool for indicating commitment levels.

We've learned a great deal during the pilots:

Agreements do not have to involve all libraries in the UC system. We found a wide range of relevance, need, and readiness among the libraries with respect to the individual programs. Only one—the Science Translations Project—involved all UC campuses and Stanford. Moreover, an unwilling or reluctant participant tended to slow down— even stop—the planning process.

Those responsible for selecting materials on the front lines are best able to plan and implement collaborative projects. The most effective planning groups were composed of a small number of selectors and a member of the UC Collection Development Committee as a resource person and guide.

The most effective agreements are positive and enabling, not negative and forbidding. In thinking about resource-sharing, there can be a tendency to focus on what might be lost rather than what will be gained. We found that focusing on positive commitments was the most useful approach; by ensuring the maintenance of selected subscriptions or a level of buying in a subject area, the formal agreement enables participants to make appropriate local collection management decisions, which may include cancellation or other kinds of cutbacks, but does not force such decisions on anyone.

Motivation and incentives are key elements in gaining acceptance of formal resource sharing. Resource sharing typically involves giving up something in return for something else. It is also hard work to plan and implement a formal resource sharing agreement. Though the Collection Development Committee began with the rather idealistic view that resource sharing was obviously good and necessary for the UC Libraries, participants quite reasonably wanted to know what they and their libraries were going to get out of the projects. Incentives included funding from the Shared Purchase Program; savings from cancellations; and improved and better rationalized systemwide collections. At a less tangible level, participants reported that they valued the sense of team accomplishment and the opportunity to work with colleagues on other campuses.

Written guidelines, especially an outline of the components of an effective written agreement, were helpful to the planning groups. Our guidelines suggested that each agreement include a clear statement of overall commitments (such as levels of collecting responsibility and language coverage, etc., expressed as much as possible in NCIP terms); a minimum time commitment (e.g., five years); the minimum notification required if an institution was unable to continue its agreement; special commitments, such as timely processing and record inclusion in MELVYL, the UC online catalog; a brief plan for monitoring the agreement; and the endorsement and signatures of authorized administrators of the participating libraries.

An accommodation to the copyright laws had to be developed early in the process. Inevitably, the question of copyright arises in any discussion of resource sharing. From the beginning, the UC libraries participating in these projects were careful to observe copyright laws, with the local campuses taking responsibility for paying special copyright-related charges.

With the pilot projects successfully implemented, the libraries have, we believe, taken a decisive step toward mainstreaming collaborative collection development. A dozen more projects are being worked on in areas such as government documents; contemporary English-language belles lettres published outside the United States and England; Eastern Europe; music; California newspapers. The Guidelines have been revised to reflect what we have learned in the pilots. A training program has been developed for selectors.

In summary, it strikes me that, as an overarching strategy in coping with this crisis, the UC libraries are very deliberately moving from acquisition as the focus of our collections programs to access. We are shifting from a conceptual framework in which individual libraries focus all their attention on developing local collections to one in which we view all UC collections as a single resource with specialized, often distinctive, strengths on the campuses. Though this shift is being driven by the budgetary crisis, I think we are coming to recognize that it simply makes good sense to share resources, to avoid unnecessary duplication, and to enrich the total library research resources available within the UC libraries. This is a new way of thinking and behaving for many of us, especially for some of our users, who are not as aware of the collections crisis as we are. So far, so good.

Why do I say that resource sharing is "the only reasonable whither"? Well, to get your attention, for one thing. Yet, I also believe that no other strategy within our reach holds so much promise for dealing with the present crisis. Consider the alternatives. There is really little that we can do very soon about exchange rates, about the publish-or-perish syndrome, about allegedly greedy publishers. Electronic publishing holds some promise, but its capacity to help us in our hour of need is, I think, far in the future. We can continue to cancel journals and cut back in other areas, but these strategies are becoming exhausted. By process of elimination, I come up with resource sharing.

Though we are working in some new project areas in the UC system, the next big move for us, I think, will be outside the "family." Stanford is already a participant in some of our projects, and recently, at UC San Diego, we are developing agreements with San Diego State in the areas of Latin American Studies and Women's Studies. It is my view that formal resource sharing can take place among unrelated regional libraries and even among libraries in different countries. It will take initiative. It will take hard work. It will take trust. It will be slow. But it is possible.

28. Scholarship, Research Libraries, and Foreign Publishing in the 1990s

Jeffrey Gardner

Introduction

In December 1989, staff of the Association of Research Libraries issued an exploratory paper titled *Research Libraries in a Global Context* to the Association's Board of Directors and Committee on Collection Development. The paper described the pressures placed on American research library collections programs by increased global publishing output, the internationalization of research and research publishing, and the interdependence of nations and their economies. In that context, it outlined a situation that combines increased foreign publishing activity with decreased ability of North American research libraries to acquire foreign materials. In October 1990, the Board of Directors of the Association of Research Libraries reaffirmed the Association's historic commitment to the provision of access to foreign materials by issuing the following statement:

Research libraries have been forced to reduce their commitment to foreign acquisitions at a time when international research materials are becoming increasingly important to research and economic development. Increases in global publishing output, the internationalization of research, and increased interdependence of national economies have intensified the need for foreign materials even as individual libraries are becoming less able to fulfill that need.

The Association of Research Libraries places paramount priority on the formulation of cooperative strategies for developing and providing access to foreign materials located both in North America and abroad. The Association urges the development of improved understanding of needs for foreign materials by research libraries and scholars, leading to the creation of cooperative structures and systems designed to ensure improved future access to international research materials.

The situation addressed by the ARL board reduces American research libraries' ability to support their users' research, posing a serious threat to the long-term educational, political, and economic interests of the United States. This proposal builds on the resulting discussion of that earlier paper and presents a strategic response to the challenges that it identified and described. These discussions have expanded to include representatives of major foreign and international studies associations, foreign area library associations and committees, the Library of Congress, and scholarly groups including the American Academy of Arts and Sciences.

These meetings and discussions have led to this proposal, which assumes that one component of an effective response to foreign acquisition needs[1] will be additional financial support for access to foreign research materials, whether from the federal government, the business community, research libraries' parent institutions, foundations, or some mix of all sectors. It is also assumed that, to be viable, any approach to the problem must be beneficial to a broad range of scholars and researchers. As part of the development of that support, ARL has joined efforts with the Council of National Resource Center Directors, the American Association of Universities, the American Council of Education, and other higher education and library associations to ensure continued authorization of Section 607 of Title VI of the Higher Education Act. Efforts have focused on securing substantial funding for that section, that is, specifically for foreign research materials. At the same time, an additional strategy of developing broader, more formal cooperation in the acquisition of foreign materials by research libraries is required, and the proposed project is viewed as an essential initial step.

The project described in this proposal is aimed at creating a better understanding of the current dynamics affecting access to foreign materials and developing a commitment to a coherent strategy for raising and allocating funds that will be required to provide access to foreign materials in the future—through both acquisitions and improved cooperative access programs. A major intent of the project is to develop consensus on what strategic actions ARL, its member libraries, and its colleagues in the scholarly and research community need to take. During the development of this proposal, ARL has worked with the following groups in identifying the issues and securing broad support: the Council of National Resource Center Directors (which includes representatives of major area studies associations), the American Academy of Arts and Sciences, the American Council of Learned Societies, the Library of Congress, the Center for Research Libraries, the Archives–Libraries Committee of the African Studies Association, the Western European Specialists Section (WESS) of the Association of College and Research Libraries, the Seminar on the Acquisition of Latin American Library Materials (SALALM), the Committee on Bibliography and Documentation of the American Association for the Advancement of Slavic Studies (AAASS), the

Committee on Research Materials on Southeast Asia (CORMOSEA), the Committee on East Asian Libraries, the Committee on South Asian Libraries and Documentation (CONSALD), and the Middle East Library Association (MELA).

There is broad agreement among these groups that library resources in support of foreign and international studies in the United States need major improvement. There is also a clear consensus that the ongoing development of foreign and international studies will benefit directly from closer cooperation between the research library and area studies communities. The discussions leading up to the development of this proposal have already contributed to increased cooperation, with movement toward initiating a national council of foreign area library associations and committees that would mirror the Council of National Resource Center Directors. Under the leadership of ARL, this proposed council is currently viewed as an opportunity to institutionalize greater cooperation between research libraries and scholars, and to further the needs of all foreign studies scholars through an organization able to view the issues from a broad, international perspective.

Background

Entering the 1990s, American research libraries face unprecedented challenges to their historic mission of collecting, preserving, and disseminating research materials from around the world. Operating in a dramatically changing political, social, and economic international landscape, research libraries must continue to fulfill that mission with severely limited financial resources. Nowhere, perhaps, is the challenge more obvious than in the area of providing access to research materials published in other countries. Several developments highlight the challenge:

The importance and frequency of research and scholarship in the humanities and the social sciences focused on foreign cultures are increasing as national boundaries become less significant in the cultural, commercial, and technological arenas. Foreign monographs in the humanities, arts, and social sciences are proliferating, and the cost of acquiring them has risen dramatically.

At the same time, the internationalization of scientific and technical research has led to increased importance of foreign publications—especially serials—from Western Europe and Asia. This trend will continue through the 1990s. In January 1991, the ARL Board of Directors appointed a Task Force on a National Program for Scientific and Technical Information whose work will complement the efforts described in this proposal.

While North American book production is increasing, it represents a decreasing proportion of the world's book production, whereas the proportion coming from Asia and selected European countries (especially Germany) is increasing dramatically. Latin American and African publishing output is also reported as increasing, although somewhat less dramatically. The *1989 UNESCO Statistical Yearbook* reports that the world's book production rose from 572,000 to 835,000 between 1975 and 1987. During the same period, the percentage of the world's output from North America as reported by UNESCO dropped from 16.2 percent to 12.7 percent.

Publishing in Eastern Europe is experiencing major changes during this decade, changes likely to include increased output and already resulting in higher costs to research libraries as subscription invoices replace historic exchange agreements. A dramatic example exists in Germany, where publications formally available from East Germany increased in cost 47 percent on July 1, 1990, when East and West Germany's currencies were integrated. In addition, Otto Harrassowitz, the major German bookseller serving U.S. research libraries, reported in January 1991 that the publishing industry in East Germany is in considerable turmoil, raising serious acquisitions problems, beyond mere price increases.

The rising costs of foreign materials are severely exacerbated by a weakened U.S. dollar. Representatives of the Council of National Resource Center Directors (covering all geographic areas) estimate that the combination of the decline of the dollar on international currency markets and sharply rising costs of foreign materials has resulted in a 40 to 50 percent decrease in acquisitions of foreign materials since the Plaza Accord (which depreciated the U.S. dollar against other major currencies) in 1985. Since that accord the Japanese yen and the German mark have appreciated against the dollar at a 50 to 60 percent rate, effectively halving the purchasing power of the dollar against those currencies. Somewhat lesser levels of appreciation have occurred for the French franc, Spanish peseta, and British pound. More recently, the Korean won and Taiwan dollar have risen rapidly against the

U.S. dollar. While there has been considerably less change in the value of the dollar against the currencies of socialist countries, other changes in their economic systems are creating similar pressures.

The increased availability of information in digitized format is leading to shifts in research libraries' acquisitions patterns, reducing the portion of library budgets available for conventionally published materials. However, current and predicted increases in availability of digitized information from Third World countries are minimal.

The costs of providing access to foreign materials are exacerbated by the high costs of providing bibliographic control (i.e., cataloging) and of preserving the materials. While national bibliographies in machine-readable form are available from most developed countries, it is less frequently true for Third World countries, requiring major investments by research libraries in both language and discipline expertise. In addition, the poor paper quality of much foreign material requires significant additional investment. Both of these issues require careful consideration of existing and potential cooperative mechanisms and procedures to ensure both timely and ongoing access to material.

While developments in information technology make it possible for American research libraries to gain access to some types of information from some parts of the world via networks, the need for development and maintenance of U.S. research collections remains for many, if not most, disciplines.

Research libraries in the United States have traditionally developed collections intended to serve the needs of current and future scholars. These collections have represented an enormous investment in the future. However, during the past fifteen to twenty years, available resources have been inadequate to maintain that investment, and the rate of acquisition of foreign materials has decreased at the same time that foreign material has increased in quantity and importance. For example, from 1985 to 1989, the average number of monographs acquired by ARL members decreased by 19 percent—and member libraries indicate that an inordinate proportion of that decrease has occurred in the acquisition of foreign materials. While the impact is most immediately noticeable at those individual research libraries with very large, comprehensive collections, to the degree that those collections in the aggregate represent a national resource the problem affects current and future scholars in virtually all academic institutions.

There are several additional forces at work that mandate stronger, coordinated efforts toward ensuring continued access to foreign materials. Government and business leaders publicly recognize the need for increased investment in the country's capacity to compete and participate in the global economy. Educational leaders are, once again, actively promoting the development of stronger foreign language programs in colleges and universities, and there is increased scholarly interest in all aspects of foreign cultures—including social, political, and economic systems, scientific and technological developments, and popular culture.

Research libraries in the United States face a difficult challenge in addressing the foreign materials needs of the country's scholars. There are, however, precedents for a successful cooperative effort. For many years libraries cooperated in the collection and maintenance of foreign materials through the Farmington Plan. It assigned to individual libraries the responsibility for collecting and cataloging material from specific countries and/or areas, with the intent of building a distributed national collection of foreign materials ensuring coverage of all major areas. Begun in 1947 under the leadership of the Association of Research Libraries, the Farmington Plan counted on the participation of more than sixty research libraries for more than twenty years. The Plan's demise in the early seventies has been attributed to several factors, including the lack of a mechanism to monitor the degree of implementation, budgetary constraints of the early seventies that led many libraries to turn inward in their collection development efforts, and real or perceived deficiencies in the services of bookdealers designated for the different parts of the plan. At the same time, there was some thinking that libraries' new approval plans for foreign materials were—at least into the early eighties—reducing the need for the Plan. This thinking now appears to have been shortsighted, and new approaches to maintaining national collections of foreign materials will need to consider the lessons of the Farmington Plan.

Currently there are several cooperative efforts in the area of foreign materials that form a base upon which the research library community can build. Perhaps foremost among these are the cooperative acquisitions programs of the Library of Congress. The Library's overseas offices cover 59 countries and involve 73 participating American research libraries. While this program continues to be an essential component of national foreign acquisitions efforts, L.C.'s statistics indicate that for many areas the proportion of published material acquired has declined since 1980.

The Center for Research Libraries (CRL) makes a major contribution in the area of foreign acquisitions by collecting low-demand, yet important, foreign research materials. The Center's foreign collections complement and supplement the strong, broader based collections at other major research libraries. The Center provides lending services to libraries throughout the world and is a national, cooperative program whose members include 85 ARL libraries. The Center also manages cooperative regional microform acquisitions programs that are funded by participating libraries. These cover Africa, Latin America, Southeast Asia, South Asia, and the Middle East. Finally, a foreign newspaper project that was developed in the early 1950s was administered as a separate project by CRL until 1982, when it was absorbed into the Center's core collection program. It continues as a cooperative preservation microfilming project of more than 250 foreign newspaper titles.

The cooperative efforts described above provide both an illustration of the ability of the research library community to address foreign materials needs and a base on which to build future efforts. They are, however, inadequate in the current and likely future higher education and research library environments. Continued reductions in the overall availability of foreign materials in conjunction with the increased national need for studying, understanding, and participating in the international community demand a stronger, more cohesive national response.

Project Goals

The context described above exerts intense pressures on research libraries. While there appear to be several possible long-term approaches to the challenge, an essential initial step is to develop a greater understanding of the problem. Six major areas require investigation, and existing data are either inadequate or inadequately compiled to support a comprehensive understanding of the situation or the development of a rational, cohesive strategy for addressing the challenge of providing access to foreign materials into the twenty-first century. Project goals include the following:

To develop an accurate understanding of current and future trends in international publishing. While very gross data on countries' publishing output exist, specific information is needed in the following areas: estimates of current and future publishing output, by country or area, relevant for disciplines in the sciences, humanities, and social sciences; price forecasts for monographs and serials, by country and broad discipline, taking into account currency fluctuations; the assessment of the impact of information technology developments on research library delivery systems; identification and analysis of the technical challenges facing research libraries in acquiring material from both industrialized and developing countries; and a greater understanding of developments in international publishing such as the shift of Eastern European publishing to a private sector system.

To define more explicitly current and emerging needs for foreign materials. This includes: The determination of scholars' current and emerging needs *and priorities* for foreign materials in various disciplines and languages; the compilation and analysis of measures or indicators of demand for foreign imprint materials in research libraries, including use by scholars from outside the collection-holding institution, through both interlibrary loan and visiting scholar programs; an analysis of the impact of reduced foreign acquisitions on area studies programs and the preparation of future area scholars; and an analysis of scholars' approaches to fulfilling their foreign materials requirements.

To describe and analyze research libraries' historic and current collecting patterns for foreign material. Needs within this topic include: the quantitative analysis of research libraries' historic and current acquisitions of foreign materials; an assessment of current strategies for dealing with reduced purchasing power as well as identification of optional approaches available to the research library community; the identification of those research libraries with historic strengths in specific foreign materials collections; and the review of current and potential cooperative roles of individual libraries and organizations, including especially the Library of Congress and the Center for Research Libraries, but also various university and research library consortia and associations.

To develop decision-making structures and processes for managing the cooperative development of foreign materials collections. Concerns to be addressed in this area include: whether cooperative acquisitions is best organized purely around geographic divisions, or a mixed approach of geography and discipline; the degree to which enhancements of current exchange programs between U.S. and foreign institutions can improve access to foreign acquisitions; the need to define how any newly available funds might best be allocated among institutions or programs; the degree to which libraries will retain autonomy in their use of any funds which might be made available as a result of this project; the determination of appropriate cooperative approaches to support the processing and preservation of foreign materials; and the need for a process and structure to manage a national foreign acquisitions program and to adapt the program to changing circumstances.

To identify foreign materials collection priorities. It is a given that research libraries will not be able to acquire all that might be desired by the nation's scholars. It is also clear that the fundamental question of relative emphasis on core collections versus specialized collections needs to be addressed. Criteria as well as procedures for applying the criteria need to be designed and implemented. The role of scholars—particularly those in area studies programs—will be critical in this effort.

To develop a broad consensus among scholars and research librarians for a long-term funding strategy. While efforts in this area have begun with the development by representatives of the higher education community of recommended new language for the re-authorization effort for Title VI of the Higher Education Act, additional efforts are required. Strategies are likely to include the development of additional federal support, but will inevitably require the research library community to assess possible new approaches to cooperation—both for the acquisitions of materials and for providing access to materials to scholars throughout the country.

Methodological Overview

Analysis of Scholarly Need

Clearly, scholars and their organizations will play a role in advising the research library community on both the problem and its solution. The issues will vary widely among both geographic areas and disciplines, and identifying and involving appropriate scholars or their representative societies in appropriate ways will be essential. Several approaches are intended, including: the development of a joint working group, representing the American Academy of Arts and Sciences, the Council of National Resource Center Directors, and the Association of Research Libraries to develop approaches for determining scholars' priority needs for foreign collections; and the design of data-gathering techniques and instruments to interview and/or survey faculty in research institutions.

Contacts with the scholarly community will define the significance of the problem from scholars' perspectives, increase scholars' understanding of the challenge facing research libraries, and build stronger cooperative working relationships among research librarians, scholars, and their respective professional associations.

Analysis of International Publishing Output

Developing a thorough understanding of trends in international publishing presents a difficult challenge. While gross data on book production are collected and published by UNESCO, those data have serious limitations.

It is necessary to develop better information, including: quantitative and price/cost data for various geographic areas, information on current and potential availability of machine-readable national bibliographic information (including the potential role of national libraries), and information related to vendors and the delivery of materials from the various geographic areas. A mix of approaches will be used, including written contact with foreign publishers' associations and vendors, surveys and interviews of acquisitions specialists (librarians and scholars), and, if needed, visits to specific areas by area specialists.

Analysis of Research Libraries' Acquisition and Delivery of Foreign Imprint Collections

Identifying and analyzing historic and current collecting trends for foreign materials in research libraries are perhaps less problematic. Selected ARL member libraries will provide budget and acquisitions data from acquisitions systems related to country of origin; and analysis of data from the Conspectus On-line can identify both historic and current collecting strengths for at least a portion of the research library community. Existing data from library area studies associations and committees will also be identified and compiled. Among the issues to be explored is that of the relationship of needed core collections at the nation's 100-plus Title VI National Resource Centers to the need for broader, national research collections.

Analysis of Existing Approaches to the Provision of Bibliographic and Physical Access to Foreign Materials

Developing current and future cooperative arrangements among libraries is an important component of the project. The issues include: timely processing and preservation of materials; delivery mechanisms for full text as well as bibliographic information to scholars throughout North America; and the need to further understanding broadly among librarians and scholars that the physical location of foreign language collections need not limit their utility geographically.

A further need is to form and develop the administrative and political alliances required to develop and maintain a cohesive national program. This will require the development of funding strategies and the design of governance structures and procedures within an inevitably political environment.

Project Design

The proposed project consists of four phases. The first includes the design of a project advisory structure and the further development of project cooperation among ARL, National Resource Centers, the American Academy of Arts and Sciences, foreign area library associations and committees, key research libraries (e.g., Library of Congress, Center for Research Libraries), other scholarly groups, and appropriate government agencies. Much of this effort will focus on the formation of a Working Group on scholars' needs for foreign materials. Phase II includes the design and implementation of one to three pilot test analyses of: trends and developments in international publishing and the acquisition of foreign materials, the state of foreign imprint collections in American research libraries, and the relative need for foreign imprint materials from selected areas and in selected disciplines. The third phase is designed to refine the pilot test methodologies, to extend the analyses to remaining geographic areas, and to develop procedures for the ongoing monitoring of the state of access to foreign materials in the United States. The fourth phase is intended to institutionalize cooperative acquisitions programs through the development of appropriate cooperative structures and procedures.

Phase I. Project Organization, Formation of the Working Group on Meeting Scholarly Needs for Foreign Materials, Design of Data Collection Efforts, and Development of Scholars' Interest and Participation in the Project. Phase I is estimated to last four to six months. Major activities in Phase I include:

During the initial phase of the project a Project Advisory Committee, consisting of ARL member library directors, area collection development specialists, representatives of major scholarly associations, and national libraries will be appointed. The committee will have responsibility for advising project staff, responding to findings, monitoring progress, providing liaison between the project and their respective constituent communities, and formulating the broad strategies needed to address the foreign acquisitions challenge over the long term.

ARL, the American Academy of Arts and Sciences, and the Council of National Resource Center Directors will form a jointly sponsored Working Group on Access to Foreign Materials that will bring together scholars and research librarians to design strategies and methodologies to identify and address priority national needs in this area. Participants will include foreign area library specialists, area center directors representing the major area studies programs in the

United States, and selected scholars, drawn from the American Academy of Arts and Sciences, with particular interest in disciplines requiring access to foreign materials. During a design session, the Working Group will assist project staff in designing and carrying out the major data-gathering effort aimed at increasing understanding of scholars' current and emerging needs for access to foreign material. Major goals for the Working Group will include:

> To define the scholars' groups that need to contribute to our understanding of national needs
>
> To recommend information-gathering approaches and methodologies for determining research priorities
>
> To identify approaches to improving research library-scholar cooperation
>
> To identify approaches for determining relative priorities among geographic areas and disciplines
>
> To begin the exploration of long-term strategic options available to the research library and scholarly communities.

An additional task for the Working Group will be to develop the means to focus national attention on the issue. Considerations will include: the impact of reduced investment in the information infrastructure on the future economic and technical status of the United States, and the potential interest in and role of the private and governmental sectors in addressing the need for stronger foreign research information resources, and governance issues related to the possible ongoing operation of a distributed national research collection.

Based on the Working Group's advice, project staff will identify necessary information, determine data-gathering strategies, and design data-gathering instruments for the analyses to be carried out during Phase II of the project.

Project staff will continue efforts to identify areas of unmet needs through discussions with key interest groups, including the following groups committed to cooperating in the project: the Council of National Resource Center Directors, the American Academy of Arts and Sciences, the area studies library groups listed in the Appendix, and other area studies groups (also listed in the Appendix).

Project staff will make site visits to selected ARL libraries with historically strong foreign acquisitions programs to explore the issues related to foreign acquisitions in depth with collection development staff, faculty, and administrators. These visits will also focus on the development of strategies to collect additional needed data during Phase II.

Phase II. Pilot Test Analytical Studies on International Publishing, State of Foreign Imprint Collections in American Libraries, Current and Emerging Needs for Foreign Imprint Material, and Assessment of Current and Emerging Document Delivery Systems. Phase II is estimated to last four to six months.

The second phase of the proposed project consists primarily of pilot analytical studies intended to assist in designing methodologies that can be used for assessing adequacy of geographic coverage. For test purposes, one to three geographic areas will be selected. While the final selection of pilot areas will be influenced by the Advisory Committee and the Working Group, coverage within each geographic area will include a range of disciplines representing the humanities, social sciences, and sciences. Criteria for selecting test areas will include: representation of both industrialized and developing areas, research libraries available and willing to cooperate in data-gathering efforts, relative interest of area scholars, and relative urgency in relation to national interests. Potential areas include the following, or subsets of the same: African studies, European studies (including Eastern Europe and Slavic studies), Asian studies (including East, South, Southeast, and Central, and Inner Asian Studies), Middle Eastern studies, Latin American studies, and Slavic studies. Data-gathering and analytical methodologies developed and tested during the project will be revised based on the pilot test(s) experience and then made available for the additional analyses during Phase III, as well as ongoing monitoring after this project. Methodologies to be considered for testing include the following:

> A survey of ARL libraries to identify existing data describing recent trends in allocations to and/or acquisition of foreign imprint material. Specific efforts will be made to identify specific disciplines suffering neglect;
>
> Site visits for in-depth interviews of bibliographers at selected research libraries with historic collection strengths in the areas being studied. These collections will be identified via surveys of libraries, input from area scholars, and review of Conspectus Online data.
>
> Project staff will develop tools to be used by participating libraries in carrying out analyses of specific collections. This will include use of the Conspectus approach to collection description and assessment, and the analysis of data from acquisitions records, online catalogs, and interlibrary loan

transaction records. One to three studies will be completed, each representing an area of urgent interest, and each carried out at a library with an historic collection of strength in that area.

A survey of major vendors representing publishers from the selected countries and/or areas will be designed and carried out. The survey will be aimed at collecting data on purchasing patterns of the American research library community in relation to research publishing output.

A survey of national libraries and publishers' associations will be carried out to determine trends in publishing output, in terms of quantity, format, and price. In addition, the issue of national libraries' role in providing worldwide access to countries' machine-readable bibliographic data will be explored.

Consideration will be given to visits to selected countries of the test areas by bibliographers, scholars, or project staff. These would include meetings and discussions with staff from national libraries and other major foreign research libraries, vendors, major publishers, and representatives of foreign scholarly groups. Visits are most likely to be necessary for developing areas lacking strong central bibliographic systems and strong vendor support.

All results of these efforts will be documented and made available through formal ARL publications.

Phase III. Phase III of the project will be directed toward the consolidation and dissemination of the research carried out during Phases I and II, refinement of the methodologies based on the test experience, extension of the methodologies to remaining areas requiring study, and the development of procedures for the ongoing monitoring of the state of access to foreign materials in America. Phase III is estimated to last from six to ten months. Major activities in this phase include the following:

The preparation of a detailed report of findings from the pilot tests, as well as summary reports for wide distribution.

The revision and production for distribution of data-gathering methodologies tested during Phase II. These will include surveys, interview guides, approaches to analysis of library statistics, guidelines for needed information from foreign publishing associations, and national libraries. The intent will be to provide a package of materials that area specialists can utilize in assessing trends and needs for their areas.

The coordination of data-gathering and analysis projects for the areas not covered in the Phase II tests. Those foreign area library associations and committees listed in the Appendix are committed to participating in this project, and it is expected that the analysis will be carried out by those groups, with ARL staff assistance.

The development of an ongoing program for monitoring the state of access to foreign materials in North American research libraries, through the publication of annual reviews for each of the areas of the world. It is expected that the collection and publication of data will be centralized at ARL and rely on foreign area library specialists and their associations to provide the needed information.

Phase IV. Phase IV of the project is intended to develop a national consensus on an overall strategy for addressing the challenge of providing library support for foreign and international studies by mobilizing the involved constituencies to act collaboratively. Strategies are likely to include institutionalizing cooperative acquisitions programs for foreign materials through the development of appropriate cooperative structures and procedures, and developing needed funding. While the process of building consensus on needed actions will have been proceeding throughout the project, Phase IV is estimated to last from three to six months. Activities would include:

A strategy session on access to foreign materials, bringing together scholars and research librarians to develop broad strategies for addressing national needs. Participants will include ARL member library directors representing those collection-based libraries with historic commitments to foreign acquisitions, representatives of those scholarly associations and societies with particular interest in disciplines requiring access to foreign materials, and foundation and government officials. The session will be designed to develop an overall strategy for mounting a U.S. response to the challenge of maintaining access to important foreign materials collections. Major strategic issues to be resolved will include: funding of foreign materials collections, long-term cooperative strategies that are workable for both research libraries and the scholarly community, appropriate utilization of emerging information technologies such as national and international networks, and effective cooperation in the provision of bibliographic control and preservation of foreign materials in North American libraries.

Formation of effective administrative structures and procedures for ensuring the effective collaboration of institutions involved in addressing the issue as well as continuing to ensure access to collections of foreign materials by scholars. This effort has begun with the movement toward the formation of a council of foreign area library associations and committees, initiated in February 1991.

NOTE

1. In this proposal, "foreign acquisitions" refers to material published in countries other than the United States and Canada, in English and other languages.

APPENDIX
Area Studies Library Associations and Committees, 1991

African Studies Association. Archives–Libraries Committee. Chair: Peter Malanchuk, University of Florida.

Committee on East Asian Libraries (CEAL). Chair: Thomas Lee, Indiana University.

Committee on South Asian Libraries and Documentation (CONSALD). Chair: Merry Burlingham, University of Texas.

Committee on Research Materials on Southeast Asia (CORMOSEA). Chair: John Badgley, Cornell University.

American Association for the Advancement of Slavic Studies. Bibliography and Documentation Committee. Chair: Hugh Olmstead, Harvard University.

American Library Association. Association of College and Research Libraries. Western European Specialists Section (WESS). Chair: Eva Sartori, University of Nebraska.

Seminar for the Acquisition of Latin American Library Materials (SALALM). President: Deborah Jakubs, Duke University.

Middle East Librarians Association (MELA). President: Fawzi Khoury, University of Washington.

PROJECT STAFF

Jeffrey J. Gardner, Director
Office of Research and Development
Association of Research Libraries

Jutta Reed-Scott
Senior Program Officer for Collection Services
Association of Research Libraries

Brigid Welch, Information Officer
Association of Research Libraries

Project consultants will be provided by the foreign area library associations and committees listed in a Appendix, as needed.

The American Academy of Arts and Sciences—Midwest Center is co-sponsoring the working group of Phase I. Center staff would be Dr. Marian Rice of the Midwest Center of the American Academy of Arts and Sciences.

29. The Progress of Alliance: Confronting the Crisis in Resources for Foreign Area Studies in the United States

Gilbert W. Merkx

The history of foreign area studies in the United States and of the library collections that support area teaching and research is one of boom and bust. Throughout most of American history the study of non-European peoples was the preserve of esoteric communities such as orientalists, antiquarians, philologists, and ethnographers. Broader foreign area studies movements developed in the United States during both World War I and World War II, only to collapse with the advent of peace. For example, some Latin Americanists may remember that the first academic journal in their field, the *Hispanic American Historical Review*, was founded in 1918 toward the end of World War I and featured a foreword by President Woodrow Wilson. This noble experiment ceased publication in 1921 and had to be reestablished some years later. During World War II a crash program was likewise set up to develop foreign area expertise for the war effort. After the war federal investment in foreign area studies was abandoned, leading to what Cline described as "the cataclysmic, catastrophic tumble from 1942-1945 heights" as foreign area courses and programs disappeared from university campuses.[1]

The current institutional edifice of foreign area studies in the United States is also a product of national mobilization for defense. By the early 1950s the Cold War had already resulted in major confrontations such as the civil war in Greece, the Berlin Blockade, and the Korean War. In 1957 the successful launching of Sputnik added a new and far more threatening dimension to the Soviet challenge. Soviet leadership in ballistic missile technology directly menaced the continental United States and gave new impetus to Soviet advances in the Third World.

The Eisenhower Administration responded to the Soviet challenge in more than military terms by proposing the National Defense Education Act (NDEA), which provided federal subsidies for the training of scientists and engineers, and, under its sixth title, of foreign language and area specialists. The original NDEA Title VI legislation envisioned a 50-50 partnership in which the costs of foreign area centers would be equally divided between the universities and the federal government (a munificent arrangement in comparison with the current 20-1 ratio of university to federal support for Title VI centers.)[2] Federal support for foreign area studies was augmented by sizable investments from the philanthropic community, led by foundations such as Ford, Rockefeller, Mellon, Carnegie, and Tinker. The Ford Foundation alone contributed about $27 million annually between 1960 and 1967 for advanced training and research in international affairs and foreign area studies, more than federal appropriations for Title VI in the same period.

Latin America was not considered a foreign area worthy of federal funding under the original NDEA legislation passed in 1958. This oversight soon proved embarrassing. On January 1, 1959, Fidel Castro and his 26th of July Movement marched into Havana. United States security interests in the Western Hemisphere could no longer be taken for granted. The NDEA was amended the same year to permit the funding of foreign area programs focusing on Latin America.[3] The Cuban missile crisis of 1962, which nearly precipitated nuclear war, symbolized both the technological and the foreign area challenges that were the raison d'être of the NDEA.

The establishment of foreign area programs was a costly venture for universities even with federal and foundation subsidies. Yet universities responded to NDEA Title VI with enthusiasm. This reflected a consensus between academia and government on national needs in the field of international education, forged by World War II and reinforced during the early stages of the Cold War. Many, if not all, foreign area scholars, university administrators, and foundation executives had served in State Department, intelligence, or military positions during World War II or the Korean War. The boundaries between government and academic institutions were permeable and amicable. The relatively small size of the community of foreign area specialists inside and outside government meant that people knew one another. Perhaps most important of all, they shared a similar perspective on the U.S role in world affairs. The alliance between academia and government for foreign area training and research was a natural outgrowth of these affinities.

The Title VI experiment proved highly successful. Within a decade the United States had established a network of centers covering most foreign areas, generating unprecedented quantities of research, and producing substantial numbers of new foreign language and area specialists. Ancillary institutions such as foreign area studies associations and research journals quickly multiplied. As Lambert has noted, this system of university-based foreign area centers was unique in the world both for its diversity (many centers were found on many campuses) and for its integration with the academic disciplines (foreign area programs represented the intersection of specialists housed in different disciplines who shared a country or area interest). Foreign area expertise in most other countries, in contrast, tended to be concentrated in a small number of nonacademic governmental institutes that were entirely area-defined and nondisciplinary.[4]

At the same time, the overall size and diversity of the American system tended to conceal the fact that the individual campus-based centers were likely to be thinly staffed and poorly funded in comparison with the disciplinary departments, which housed the tenure-track program faculty. This, combined with the high mobility of individual faculty members, created considerable program fragility. Given the right combination of administrative neglect and budget-cutting, well-regarded foreign area programs could disappear with surprising rapidity. Therefore the presence of federal subsidies through NDEA Title VI, and its successor, Title VI of the Higher Education Act (HEA), remained extremely important despite representing a shrinking proportion of center funding. The prestige and the funding conveyed by Title VI designation continued to be rewarded by university administrations.[5]

Following the promising early start of Title VI came the Vietnam War, which by the late 1960s led to funding freezes and then to declines. Moreover, the Vietnam War itself produced a significant deterioration in the relationship between government and academia. Academic dissent from U.S. foreign policy in Southwest Asia began to grow during the Johnson Administration and reached high levels during the Nixon Administration. The events of Watergate did little to increase academic confidence in government. Resentment by government officials of criticisms from academia, including from some of the very foreign area specialists trained under Title VI, grew as well. The gradual retirement of the World War II generation of leaders further contributed to the growing gulf between academic and government cultures.

The Carter Administration made some effort to improve relations with the academic community. Carter appointed a Presidential Commission on Foreign Language and International Studies (known as the Perkins Commission), which in 1979 issued a strong call for increasing federal support of international education to more than three times existing levels.[6] Among its recommendations were the establishment of undergraduate and regional foreign area centers as complements to the Title VI national resource centers and the provision of annual federal grants of $50,000 to each of the national resources centers for library costs. However, the timing of the Perkins Commission report was not propitious. Double-digit inflation and high interest rates were leading to reductions, not increases, in federal expenditures.

A more successful initiative by the Carter Administration was to repeal NDEA and incorporate its Title VI functions in a new Higher Education Act (HEA). This step ratified the separation of university-based foreign area studies from the national defense needs that had been the original justification for federal funding. While pleasing many campus-based area specialists, the change of name made Title VI a more vulnerable target for those in the next administration, who were to argue that federal subsidies were no longer in the national interest. The Higher Education Act was also accompanied by the controversial establishment of the Department of Education (ED) as a cabinet-level institution, despite strong objections from the Republican minority in the Congress.

Within months after the establishment of the Department of Education, President Carter lost the 1980 elections to Ronald Reagan. The Department of Education and Title VI were among the targets singled out by the incoming Republican administration. Reagan's Office of Management and the Budget (OMB) recommended elimination of all Title VI appropriations and continued to do so for all of the first seven Reagan budgets, even after the White House had conceded defeat on its goal of eliminating the Department of Education. University-government relations were not enhanced by faculty criticisms of the Reagan Administration's increased emphasis on defense expenditures and its aggressively interventionist stance in Third World zones of conflict, nor by Administration insinuations that foreign area specialists were unpatriotic partisans of the countries they studied.

Thus the early years of the Reagan Administration represent the nadir of the partnership between academia and government in foreign area studies. Owing to the high inflation of the late 1970s and early 1980s and essentially level funding in current dollars, Title VI appropriations in real terms were at their lowest level since the inception of the program, falling to well below half their 1967 high point. The Administration was formally opposed to the program. Higher education in turn was suffering from the consequences of inflation, the growth of university enrollments had taken a sharp downturn for demographic reasons, and foundation support for international education had evaporated.

Nonetheless the partnership between government and academia survived. Support for Title VI came from three directions. A few well-placed government officials recognized the value of Title VI research and training and were moved to intervene on its behalf. Perhaps the most famous example is the letter of 11 March 1983 sent by Secretary of Defense Caspar Weinberger to Secretary of Education Ted Bell, with a copy to OMB Director David Stockman, requesting reconsideration of the zero-funding of Title VI. Weinberger noted, "My concern is shared by other officials within the Department of Defense, and members of the academic community on whom we depend for both a solid research base in area studies, as well as for production of foreign language specialists." The Deputy Director of Central Intelligence, Rear Admiral Bobby Inman, was another outspoken defender of Title VI programs.

A second source of support came from the directors of Title VI-funded area centers, who were galvanized by the realization that the survival of Title VI programs could no longer be taken for granted. The second-generation center directors of the 1980s lacked the Washington contacts and political knowledge of the founding generation. They were forced, however, to increased activism by the disastrous implications of a total cut-off of federal support for their programs. After the failure of their efforts to reverse the Reagan Administration zero-funding of Title VI in the early 1980s, the center directors focused on the Congress.[7] These early attempts at congressional relations were for the most part uncoordinated individual initiatives, but were not without effect. Congress proved more responsive to the universities than the Administration had been, and Title VI funding survived, albeit at the relatively low levels of the Carter period.

The third source of support came from individuals outside of government and academia that were affiliated with institutions involved directly or indirectly with international education, such as the major foundations, higher education associations, and professional organizations. Some of these persons had served on the Perkins Commission. Others were involved with the successful effort to obtaining funding for Soviet Studies that led to the passage of the Soviet–Eastern European Research and Training Act of 1983 (Title VIII of the Department of State Authorization Act). From this sector came two important studies calling attention to inadequacies in the U.S. international studies, the 1981 NCFLIS *Report of the Task Force on National Manpower Targets*

for Advanced Research on Foreign Areas [8] and Richard Lambert's 1984
Beyond Growth: The Next Stage in Language and Area Studies. [9]

The growing sense of shared concern about the chronic under-
funding of international education in general, and the threat to Title VI
in particular, coalesced in an initiative that began with a dinner at the
Smithsonian Institution in late 1984 "to discuss what might be done to
stabilize long-term federal support for international studies and foreign
language training." [10] Several foundations funded, under the aegis of
the Association of American Universities (AAU), a study that resulted
in Richard Lambert's 1986 monograph *Points of Leverage: An Agenda
for a National Foundation for International Studies,* [11] accompanied by
the recommendation of an AAU advisory committee chaired by
Kenneth Prewitt of the Rockefeller Foundation. [12] The Prewitt
committee offered draft legislation for the establishment of a National
Foundation for Foreign Languages and International Studies. The
intent of the proposal was to centralize federal support for international
education in a single entity, as opposed to the existing 196 international
studies and exchange programs in 35 departments of the federal government. It was thought that this would allow supporters of international
education to focus their advocacy on a single, high-profile institution
that would be analogous to the National Science Foundation or the
National Endowment for the Humanities.

The AAU legislative proposal was intended to serve as a rallying
point for the various international education constituencies. It had the
opposite effect. The proposal was viewed with suspicion as being the
product of the elite institutions associated with the AAU. It was widely
misinterpreted as constituting a threat to existing programs. The
process by which the proposal was developed was criticized for having
too narrow a base and not including a sufficiently broad spectrum of
international education interests. Perhaps the most positive thing that
can be said of the reaction was that its vigor reflected the growth of
concern about the future of the U.S. international education effort.

In a constructive response to these criticisms, the AAU obtained
additional foundation support to broaden the dialogue about international education needs, establishing in 1987 a two-year planning effort
known as CAFLIS, the Coalition for the Advancement of Foreign
Languages and International Studies. An open invitation to participate
was sent to virtually every type of group that might be interested.
Ultimately some 150 organizations participated in one or more stages of
CAFLIS discussion, including most higher education associations, area
studies associations, language groups, organizations engaging in foreign

exchanges, peak organizations in the social sciences, and professional associations.

Despite, or perhaps because of, the inclusive nature of the process, CAFLIS ultimately ended in failure. The various constituencies represented in the CAFLIS process had different agendas and found difficulty coming to an overall agreement. A fundamental cleavage existed between those groups that emphasized the need for increased investment to meet the original Title VI goals of advanced training and research in foreign language and area studies (a focused and less costly agenda), and those who were advocating federal subsidies for language training in primary and secondary schools, for internationalization of undergraduate education, or for adding international dimensions to professional training in fields such as business, medicine, and engineering (a diffuse and more costly agenda). Even after the recommendations of the three CAFLIS working groups were watered down and widened to satisfy groups dissatisfied with the original Title VI agenda, some of these groups refused to ratify the final recommendations, which appeared in late 1989. [13] The result was a proposal for a new federal foundation that would not incorporate existing federal programs but merely add to them, an agenda that failed to generate the enthusiasm required for enactment.

The disappointing outcomes of both the AAU legislative proposal and the CAFLIS process led some of the participants to refocus their attention on Title VI, as the remaining target of opportunity, and something of an endangered species, since the Higher Education Act was to expire in 1990. The AAU, NASULGC (the National Association of State Universities and Land Grant Colleges), and the other higher education presidential associations began to organize a series of meetings on Title VI reauthorization that culminated in the appointment of an Interassociation Task Force on HEA–Title VI Reauthorization staffed by Miriam Kazanjian. The Title VI center directors proceeded to organize themselves in a new Council of Title VI National Resource Center Directors (CNRC). The foreign area studies associations organized a coordinating group of executive directors and presidents known as CASA (Council of Area Studies Associations).

A parallel concern was arising from the community of foreign area bibliographers, facing a growing crisis in acquisitions of foreign materials owing to the declining value of the dollar on international currency markets and a sharp absolute rise in serials prices. In 1990 the president of the Seminar on the Acquisition of Latin American Library Materials, Deborah Jakubs, and the director of the Hispanic Division of the Library of Congress, Cole Blasier, asked the Executive

Council of the Latin American Studies Association (LASA) to appoint a task force to address this problem and to make contact with other foreign area studies associations about library problems.

This more or less spontaneous resurgence of concern led to the emergence of a strategy that was to build support for Title VI programs in particular, and international education in general, by building upon the core campus constituencies of language and area programs (faculty, centers, libraries, and language programs), to their professional associations (e.g., LASA, SALALM, and AATSP), and finally to their peak national organizations (e.g., CASA, CNRC, ARL, AAU, ACLS). At the invitation of the center directors a meeting of all these groups took place at the Library of Congress on February 4, 1991, for the purpose of agreeing on a common agenda with respect to Title VI reauthorization and to achieve an informal working arrangement among the various organizations represented, which is hereafter referred to as "the coalition."

The existence of the coalition proved useful when in May 1991 the Interassociation Task Force submitted its recommendations on HEA Title VI reauthorization.[14] The coalition offered a common front on reauthorization issues, in contrast with the divisions of the past. Consultations with congressional staff were facilitated by the ability of members of the coalition to discuss their differences and agree on common strategies. When the final law reauthorizing HEA was approved by the Congress in 1992, Title VI incorporated, virtually intact, almost all of the recommendations of the Interassociation Task Force and of the coalition. Among the provisions approved was an expansion of Section 607 authorizing federal grants for the acquisition of foreign area periodicals to include *other research materials*, with a first-year authorization level of $8.5 million.

The coalition also was able to obtain increased appropriations for Title VI. Funding for Title VI programs has increased by more than 50 percent in real dollars since the low point of the early 1980s, returning awards for centers to about two-thirds of their 1967 high point. Section 607 was funded for the first time in fiscal year 1991 at the $500,000 level, with funding for fiscal year 1992 rising to $990,000.

Thus positive incremental change in federal support for international education has begun to come about. This improvement, however modest, is highly fortuitous given the worsening funding situation in higher education and the particularly grim picture for research library acquisitions. The lesson to be learned is that the campus alliance that underlies each and every foreign area studies program can be reproduced on the national level to make the case for federal support. Indeed, if those most familiar with foreign language and area studies are not there to make that case, who will take their place? There are potential allies in government agencies, in the Congress, in the Administration, and in nongovernmental organizations. The challenge for the core organizations of the international education community, such as SALALM, is to continue to work with such allies toward more ambitious goals.

NOTES

1. Howard F. Cline, "The Latin American Studies Association: A Summary Survey with an Appendix," *Latin American Research Review* 2, 1 (1966), 57-79.

2. Lorraine M. McDonnell et al., *Federal Support for International Studies: The Role of NDEA Title VI* (Santa Monica, CA: The Rand Corporation, 1981), p. 38.

3. The sociologist Joseph Kahl described to me receiving a telephone call in 1959 from the Ford Foundation offering to fund an area studies program for Latin America at Washington University in St. Louis. Two years earlier Kahl had submitted such a proposal to the Ford Foundation only to have it turned down. The rejected proposal had been found in the files by foundation officials looking for programs to support.

4. Richard D. Lambert, "Blurring the Disciplinary Boundaries: Area Studies in the United States," *American Behavioral Scientist* 33, 6 (July/August 1990), 712-732.

5. Gilbert W. Merkx, "Title VI Accomplishments, Problems, and New Directions, *LASA Forum* 21, 2 (Summer 1990), 1, 18-23.

6. *Strength Through Wisdom: A Critique of U.S. Capability*, A Report to the President from the President's Commission on Foreign Language and International Studies, U.S. Department of Health, Education, and Welfare (U.S. Government Printing Office, November 1979), 156 pp.

7. For example, I met with Vice President Bush's chief of staff, Boyden Gray, in 1981 to submit several proposals concerning Title VI funding and administration, which were then transmitted to the Vice President in writing, eliciting from him a pleasantly noncommittal response.

8. "Report of the Task Force on National Manpower Targets for Advanced Research on Foreign Areas" (National Council on Foreign Languages and International Studies, 605 Third Avenue, New York, NY 10158, 1981), mimeograph, 320 pp.

9. Richard D. Lambert et al., *Beyond Growth: The Next Stage in Language and Area Studies* (Washington, DC: Association of American Universities, 1984), 436 pp.

10. Kenneth Prewitt, "Preface," in Richard D. Lambert, *Points of Leverage: An Agenda for a National Foundation for International Studies* (New York, NY: Social Science Research Council, 1986), p. v.

11. Ibid.

12. "To Strengthen the Nation's Investment in Foreign Languages and International Studies: A Legislative Proposal to Create a National Foundation for Foreign Languages and International Studies," Association of American Universities, Washington, D.C., October 1, 1986, 26 pp.

13. "The Federal Government: Leader and Partner." Report on the Recommendations and Findings of the Coalition for the Advancement of Foreign Languages and International Studies: Working Group on Federal Support for International Competence," December 1989 (One Dupont Circle NW, Suite 710, Washington, DC 20036), 10 pp.

14. "Recommendations on the Reauthorization of the Higher Education Act of 1965, As Amended for Title VI, International Education Programs and Fulbright-Hays (102(b)(6))" (Washington, DC, May 1991), 30 pp.

Analyzing Latin American Library Materials Price Indexes

30. Latin American Book Prices: The Trends of Two Decades

David Block

Maybe it's the time of the year—you know, one budget cycle winding down, while another looms ahead. Or maybe it's just a fund manager's pathological concern with making a compelling argument. but whatever the reason, I have lately found myself obsessing on questions such as: What are Latin American library materials likely to cost next year, and what areas of the budget are most in need of triage? All the papers in this volume offer ease to this bibliographer's lament by describing projects designed to chart trends in Latin American library expenditures. My contribution examines the longest lived of these, the annual inventory of books and costs received by major libraries in the United States. Amid a welter of charts and graphs, I offer you a history of this project, now in its twentieth year, describe its current state, critique its strengths and weaknesses, and suggest ways of making it a more useful instrument.

History

Regular studies of library materials costs long predate the advent of the automated systems that currently crunch our numbers, and anything else that gets in their way. The price index, as applied to library materials, resulted from a report compiled for the U.S. Office of Education in 1961.[1] Later in the same decade, the American Library Association recognized the increasing need for authoritative statistics on the costs of books and serials by establishing a Library Materials Price Index Committee. Since its inception, this body has sponsored the production of a series of compilations that measure trends in materials costs and index them against a base year. These instruments, published in the *Bowker Annual of Library and Book Trade Information*, rechristened *Library and Book Trade Almanac* in 1989, currently measure, among other things, the prices of trade and academic books in the United States and Canada, daily newspapers in the United States, library microfilm, nonprint media, and British and German academic books.

Latin Americana made its appearance early in the Library
Materials Price Index enterprise when William H. Kurth and David
Zubatsky compiled statistics for Mexican imprints extracted from the
entries in *Boletín bibliográfico mexicano*. Kurth and Zubatsky produced
their tables from 1965 (when the 487 volumes surveyed cost an average
of $2.74) to 1970 (when 766 volumes averaged $3.51). A more
comprehensive approach to Latin American book prices came out of
the SALALM XIX meeting which, in the wake of LACAP's demise in
1973, established a Subcommittee on Cost Statistics, chaired by Robert
Sullivan of the Library of Congress. In 1976 this group began
to publish reports which established the contours for subsequent
compilations (see table 1).

From the beginning of its labors, the subcommittee recognized a
set of constraints. It confined its attention to receipts from U.S.
libraries and to those data traditionally collected by Latin American
library specialists: that is, monographs received on blanket orders rather
than serials or series or firm orders; and country, rather than subject,
counts. It also established a rather modest intent, to establish "a cost
index to assist libraries that do not maintain their own payment or
average cost statistics in preparing budget estimates or justifications."[2]
Even though the subcommittee has withered away, libraries continue to
collect data and Sullivan's successors—Peter de la Garza oversaw the
compilation from 1980 to 1985, I have done so since—have dutifully
ground out the statistics in annual fashion.

Description and Critique

The fruit of our labors is shown in table 2, which displays total
receipts and total costs by country of publication. Let me stress that
this is an inventory project, not a true index; it measures submissions
made by the library contributors, regardless of source. Let me stress
also, that it is an aggregate. No attempt is made to separate monographs from series, to screen out duplicates, or to measure what each
library may be paying for a particular title or titles. In this aggregated
form, our compendium is limited in its utility for further analysis. For
instance, it cannot be used to measure the increase or decline of Latin
American book production, since imprints from a number of years may
arrive at a contributing library during any given reporting period. And
more importantly, the vagaries of statistics gathering, a change in
counting practices, or a change in the mix of reporting libraries can
distort annual volume counts.

But cost statistics have always driven the inventory, and for the present, it represents the best barometer I know for trends in the prices of Latin American books.

Consider the linear representation in figure 1 of mean costs derived from the survey since 1977. Its major topographic features are a series of plateaus: 1978–1979, 1981–1983, 1985–1987, each higher than the last. The only real "spike" in the gradual ascent was 1980–1981, when the mean cost increased by 33 percent. If there can be such a thing as an "average" Latin American book, its price rose 90 percent in the 14 years represented in the graph, an average of some 6.5 percent a year. On the whole, we have not done badly in a world market where double-digit increases have become the norm. But before we begin to congratulate ourselves, notice the tail of this figure and its trajectory. Since 1987, mean costs have risen steadily, if unspectacularly, some 20 percent in three years. I wonder what the booksellers make of this? Will current rends continue for the foreseeable future, or will we establish a new plateau? I also wonder what the audience thinks are the critical factors in explaining price changes in the national book markets of Latin America and the Caribbean.

It is dangerous to presume how information is used, of course. But may I suggest that the originators of the project had it right. The annual inventory furnishes an authoritative and widely circulated compendium of country-based price trends for books, still the most important channel of information exchange in the region. It offers a context for locally gathered data and a reliable stand-alone source for budget planning.

Of course, none of us buys the average Latin American book. The trend line smooths 26 separate trajectories. Figure 2 is a representation of computer graphics run amok, with mean costs from seven countries dipping and soaring like kites in a Santa Ana windstorm.

A more intelligible representation is found in figure 3, which graphs mean costs from Argentina, Brazil, and Mexico. It illustrates the same point, that national trends are anything but smooth and that a heavy commitment to any country within the region will likely deflect a budget in the short term.

Again, I would ask the reader to help me understand this chart. It shows three rather different trends, one steady-state, one marginally lower, one substantially higher. I would add in passing that although the full year's data are not yet in, 1991 will give a different look to these lines. Argentine books received by Cornell to April 1991

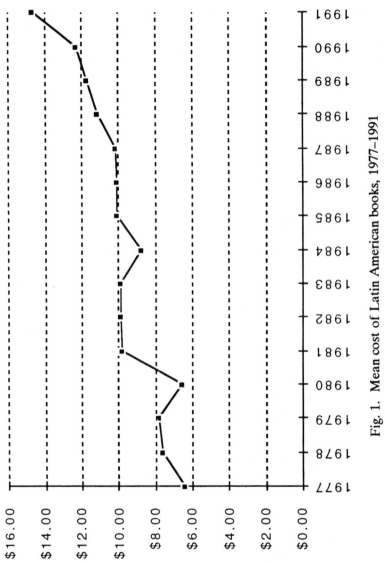

Fig. 1. Mean cost of Latin American books, 1977–1991

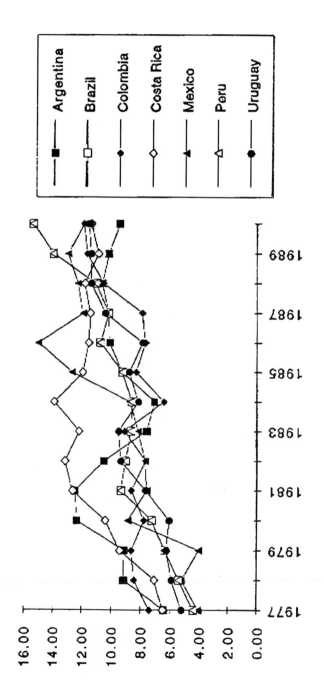

Fig. 2. Mean cost of books for seven Latin American countries

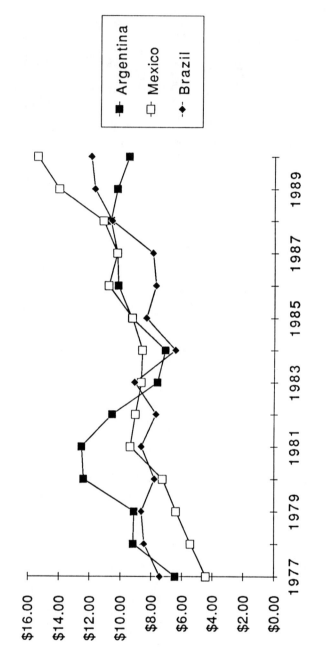

Fig. 3. Mean cost of books for three Latin American countries

averaged $12.94 per volume and Brazilian books would be off the chart, averaging $17.02 each.

Where Do We Go From Here?

Let us consider the product as it now stands. The title of table 2 varies with the number of reporting libraries: last year nine libraries reported their accessions, this year we are down to six. While volume counts of even this reduced number of participants is extensive, the absence of past contributors—often attributable to a change in personnel or in data collection policies—could have a statistically significant impact on the counts. See also the note, "Some figures include binding costs." Past compilations have included postage as well. Again, we are captives of the kinds of information the contributing libraries choose to report.

Compare these compilations with the others done by members of the Library Materials Price Index Committee. Both the British and German compilers base their work on data supplied from sources in the book trade. The British index was originally based on the *British National Bibliography* and now relies on information furnished by the Oxford bookseller, B. H. Blackwell. The German index has a similar experience, with Otto Harrassowitz supplanting *Buch und buchhandlen in zahlen*. These data represent selections made by commercial firms on behalf of library approval plan customers and allow the presentation of nonduplicative, comprehensive, subject-based indexes, recognized for their accuracy.

The state of bibliographic control in Latin America does not allow us to rely on such tools as national bibliographies for our cost compilations. However, the option of booksellers' participation remains a possibility. Over the years a few vendors have approached me about the possibility of including their statistics in the inventory. To date I have been inhibited by the piecemeal nature of the requests. The advantage of the project as it currently stands is its extension: the entire region is represented. However, recent developments in this organization and in technology have given me the opportunity to rethink my position.

The vendors' group has shown what can only be described as a refreshing enthusiasm for additional involvement. Perhaps the inventory would be something they could consider as a project. Surely most of the vendors keep statistics on their selections and costs that could be translated into the kinds of data currently reported by libraries.

Table 1. Latin American Books: Average Costs for
Fiscal Years 1973, 1974, 1975, and 1976

Country	1973	1974	1975	1976
Argentina	$5.84[a]	$4.70[a]	$6.48[a]	$5.85[a]
Bolivia	5.14[a]	4.78[a]	5.87[a]	6.79[a]
Brazil	5.85	5.88	7.09	6.52
Chile	4.79[a]	4.50[a]	6.60[a]	6.44[a]
Colombia	4.04[a]	3.91[a]	5.23[a]	5.35[a]
Costa Rica	—	2.73	4.31	7.95
Cuba	—	—	—	3.03
Dominican Republic	—	5.40	5.73	5.41
Ecuador	5.48	2.99	5.24	4.17
Guatemala	6.31	4.76	6.24	6.23
Guyana	3.07	2.82	1.92	4.40
Haiti	6.33	2.80	4.68	4.53
Honduras	5.65	4.65	6.10	5.61
Jamaica	7.11	5.38	4.43	5.23
Mexico	4.28[a]	4.59[a]	4.05[a]	4.64
Nicaragua	6.92	—	—	6.91
Panama	4.13	—	3.84	3.99
Paraguay	5.59	4.19[a]	5.01[a]	5.86[a]
Peru	5.40[a]	4.72[a]	5.13[a]	6.40[a]
Puerto Rico	5.71	5.73	6.01	5.45
El Salvador	4.96	4.41	3.50	4.51
Trinidad	—	2.74	4.06	4.38
Uruguay	5.54	5.00	5.28[a]	4.58
Venezuela	7.19	5.44	5.54	6.56

a. Some binding costs included.

Compiled by Robert C. Sullivan, Seminar on the Acquisition of Latin American Library Materials (SALALM), Subcommittee on Cost Statistics, from reports on the number and cost of current monographs purchased by the libraries of Cornell Univ., Univ. of Florida, Univ. of Illinois, Library of Congress, Univ. of Minnesota, New York Public Library, Univ. of Texas, and Univ. of Wisconsin. A full explanation of the methodology employed is contained in SALALM XXI Working Paper No. A-4, dated May 1976.

Table 2. Number of Copies and Average Cost of Latin American Books Purchased by Six Selected U.S. Libraries in FYs 1989 and 1990

Country	Number of books		Average cost[a]		Percent increase/ decrease in cost over 1989
	FY 1989	FY 1990	FY 1989	FY 1990	
Argentina	8,805	7,114	$10.19	$9.45	−7.26
Bolivia	1,612	1,638	10.14	9.22	-9.11
Brazil	7,197	6,927	11.63	11.87	2.06
Chile	2,279	1,612	13.67	15.22	11.28
Colombia	3,500	2,727	10.88	11.35	4.31
Costa Rica	1,495	1,203	12.99	11.87	−8.64
Cuba	301	363	14.17	13.58	−4.17
Dominican Republic	452	221	19.19	19.04	−0.77
Ecuador	2,559	1,652	8.15	8.85	8.66
El Salvador	302	229	11.23	10.76	−4.15
Guatemala	328	208	13.55	14.21	4.83
Guyana	22	5	5.96	8.80	47.59
Haiti	127	36	17.98	16.58	−7.74
Honduras	268	266	10.89	12.99	19.30
Jamaica	154	62	10.80	18.32	69.71
Mexico	7,646	7,523	13.98	15.35	9.77
Nicaragua	236	420	11.99	11.50	−4.11
Panama	261	226	12.05	12.23	1.44
Paraguay	867	536	12.19	14.18	16.32
Peru	3,846	2,503	11.39	11.49	0.95
Puerto Rico	313	72	15.99	23.54	47.24
Surinam	23	11	20.45	28.18	37.81
Trinidad	76	67	16.26	17.70	8.88
Uruguay	2,427	2,173	12.79	13.84	8.20
Venezuela	2,634	2,088	9.10	13.69	50.38
Other Caribbean	2,132	994	13.11	11.80	−10.01
Total	49,862	40,876	11.71	12.27	4.80

a. Some figures include binding costs.

Compiled by David Block, Seminar on the Acquisition of Latin American Library Materials (SALALM), Acquisition Committee, from reports on the number and cost of current monographs purchased by the libraries of Cornell University, University of Wisconsin, University of Illinois, University of Arizona, Library of Congress, and University of Texas.

I have also begun to consider using Latin American databases as a source for the inventory. *Latbook*, because of its Pan–Latin American scope, certainly offers the potential for extracting volumes and price information for the region as a whole, and its coding would allow subject descriptions as well. Its computational capabilities bear investigation. (See chapters 41 and 42 for more information about *Latbook*.)

My colleagues on this panel will introduce you to two new statistics gathering projects. But as I yield the dais, I wonder if the time has not come to change the way we have compiled Latin American monograph costs for the past two decades.

NOTES

1. Frank L. Schick and William H. Kurth, *The Cost of Library Materials: Price Trends of Publications*, OE-15029A, October 1961 (Washington, D.C.: Office of Education, 1961).

2. Robert Sullivan, "Latin American Book Pries Fiscal Years 1973 through 1975," in *Twenty Years of Latin American Librarianship, Final Report and Working Papers of the Twenty-first Seminar on the Acquisition of Latin American Library Materials* (Austin, TX: SALALM, 1976), p. 80.

31. A Survey of Latin American Collections

Carl Deal

This second and revised survey of Latin American collections provides a description and profile of quantified data about the respondents' collections and their patterns of staffing and expenditures from 1986 to 1991. It builds upon similar information collected a year earlier and presented at the SALALM conference in Rio de Janeiro in 1990. Where it has been possible, similar information for institutions which did not take part in this second survey, but which participated in the first, is included in the tables and collections profile. This has provided a wider profile especially for the Group II and Group III libraries. Each library in the United States and Puerto Rico with a SALALM personal membership was sent a survey form. A total of 23 responses to this survey and 9 from the first survey are the basis for the combined information in the text and tables that follow.

Methodology

Information is reported for three library groupings, by size. Group I includes those with 190,000 or more volumes. Group II is for libraries with 100,000 to 189,000 volumes, and Group III includes libraries with fewer than 100,000 volumes. For comparative purposes, the Library of Congress and the Columbus Memorial Library appear separately in the tables and the Latin American Collections Profile.

Allocations

Library materials allocations in all subject categories for the fifteen Group I libraries identified in table 1 ranged from a low of $1,314,873 to a high of $6,761,400. The median of allocations for this group was $4,262.204.

For eight Group II libraries, allocations ranged from $2,195,000 to $7,025,686, with a median of $3,916,668. A low of $712,000 and a high of $4,252,721 resulted in a median of $2,213,843 for four Group III libraries.

Expenditure Totals

Latin American expenditures for eight of the fifteen Group I libraries in 1986 were $901,694. By 1990 expenditures had risen to $1,060,925, an increase of only 17.7 percent. Calculated on the increase in costs measured against current Latin American monographs purchased on blanket orders at Illinois, unit costs of Latin American materials increased by 43 percent, from $8.51 in FY1986 to $12.31 in FY1990. The difference between the lower percentage of increase in expenditures and the costs of materials demonstrates that there has been a severe national decline in Latin American collections. The total 1990 Latin American expenditures equaled 2.9 percent of the total allocations in all subject areas reported for these seven libraries.

Five Group II libraries reported allocations in all fields at $9,392,407. The $277,066 allocated for Latin America was 3 percent of those allocations. In Group III, six libraries expended $186,421 in FY1986 and raised expenditures in 1990 to $317,764, an increase of 70 percent. Latin American expenditures in FY1990 equaled 3 percent of these total allocations.

Expenditures on Blanket Orders and Other Funds

Every Group I library maintained a separate Latin American blanket order. These ranged from $14,296 to $77,700 for the six libraries. The Library of Congress expended $138,000 on Latin American blanket orders in 1990. Three Group II libraries reported blanket orders of $17,920, $44,3218, and $17,920. Seven Group III libraries had blanket orders, but only one was specific in reporting $15,000.

Six from Group I included materials received on United States approval plans in their total Latin American expenditures, but only four were able to cite specific amounts, which ranged from $1,782 to $4,714. Two from Group II reported $7,800 and $5,500, and two from Group III reported $500 and $193 in this category.

Similarly for fourteen Group I libraries reporting materials on Latin America arriving on other foreign approval plans, only three specifically reported amounts at $600, $2,695, and $7,091. One Group II member reported $1,500, and two in Group III acknowledged that $1,500 and $1,600 were expended for this purpose.

Title VI funding for nine libraries supporting National Resource Centers ranged from approximately $1,000 for four libraries and $3,000 and $11,782 for the other two. Seven libraries reported materials received from other subject funds, but only three gave specific figures of

$600, $14,414, and $38,000.   No library was assessed charges for bibliographic utilities, preservation, or database searches.

Serials

Cancellations for Latin American serial collections have varied in severity from one collection to another since 1986. In Group I, one institution reported approximately $2,000, one $4,300, one $3,500, and four libraries less than $1,000 for the period of 1986 to 1991. In the second group, one member canceled 40 titles at $2,600 and another reported 8 at $700. One from Group III reported $400 in cancellations. The Library of Congress canceled an estimated 250 titles in 1990. One may assume that there has been less money for new serials during the same period owing to the overall decline in purchases and rising costs of materials already noted.

The number of current serial titles annually purchased averaged 929 for twelve libraries in the first group, and the median was 685. Expenditures for serials ranged from $5,250 to $45,000 in ten institutions, where they averaged $24,780, with a median expenditure of $26,738. In the ten libraries where they could be compared, serials equaled 21.7 percent of Latin American materials costs. Costs per title in seven libraries averaged $30.32 per title. In Group II three libraries used 25 percent of their allocations for serials. Four from the last group utilized 12.4 percent of their allocations for serials. Costs per title could not be measured for the second group, although seven libraries from the third reported an average cost of $36.80.

Gifts and Exchanges

Gift and exchange titles received by eight Group I libraries ranged from a total of 232 to 3,878 in 1990. Texas received the largest number, and the median was set at 891. One library from the second group reported receiving 8,451 titles, and five from Group III averaged 499 titles.

Size of Collections

Total volume counts in fourteen Group I libraries ranged from 192,000 at the University of Puerto Rico to 596,000 at Texas. The average was 301,574 and the median was 275,000 volumes. Uncataloged backlogs ranged from 330 to 98,540 volumes at Southern California, where a major collection recently acquired is being processed. Uncataloged Latin American backlogs at eleven libraries represented 4.9 percent of their collections.

In Group II the size of Latin American collections ranged from 90,000 to 170,000 volumes. The low for the third group was 25,000, and the largest collection contained 80,000 volumes. Backlogs for six Group II members equaled 3 percent of their collections, and four in the final group reported backlogs that represented 15.3 percent of their Latin American holdings.

The ratio of serial volumes to monographs received in 1990 was 16.7 percent as reported by nine of the first group's collections. Four in Group II reported a 21 percent ratio, and the third group did not respond. Control of microform holdings in all three groups is not very accurate and is complicated by several libraries' maintaining statistics by rolls and some by exposures.

The total number of volumes received annually varied from 2,518 to 20,934 volumes in eleven of the largest libraries. Nine reported 83.3 percent of the volumes (a serial title equaling 1 volume) were monographs. This total varied from 6,000 to 6,800 volumes in four Group II libraries, where 79 percent of the volumes received were monographs. Group III libraries did not report in this category.

Of special interest for this survey is the method each library reported for arriving at a volume count for their Latin American collections. Cornell and Wisconsin have utilized a strict shelflist count, whereas eight others have set a base figure to which they annually make additions. Illinois, North Carolina, and University of California, Los Angeles utilized other methods. In Group II, one library employed a shelflist count, two used a set base, and one reported for other methods. One Group III member used a shelflist count and a second employed a set base.

Staffing Patterns

Twelve libraries in Group I showed an average of 2.6 Full Time Equivalent (FTE) in professional staff were involved in FY1990 in managing the collections, an increase over the FY1986 average of 2.4 FTE. The average of Latin American support staff and graduate students in eleven libraries decreased from 3.2 FTE to 2.7 FTE during the same period.

In the second group of six libraries, the number of professional staff grew slightly from 1986 to 1990 to 2 FTE. In the same period, the average of 2.43 FTE support staff and graduate students also increased slightly. Group III libraries experienced some growth in professional staff to 2 FTE in 1990, with support staff increasing to 2.43 FTE by 1990.

It has proven difficult, particularly with the impact of automation on acquisition and processing practices, to determine the time of staff in other departments allocated for acquiring, processing, and accessing Latin American materials. Texas reported 6.95 FTE professional staff and 11.65 FTE other support staff and graduate students, but it is a separate and major library unit with heavier public service requirements than most other collections.

A better comparison of staffing patterns is derived from the combined total of professional and support staff which in 1990, after excluding Texas, averaged 7.9 FTE and had a median of 8.4 FTE for the other twelve libraries. The combined total of professional and support staff for six Group II libraries averaged 6.1 FTE. For the final group the average was 3.2 FTE.

Division of library activities in nine Group I libraries showed that, on the average, 29 percent is provided for collection development, 29 percent for technical services, 31 percent for cataloging, and 11 percent for other processes. Nine Group II respondents compared rather closely with percentages of 37.4, 28.1, 25.2, and 9.3 in the same order of categories. Group III libraries reported a different range in percentages of 39, 6, 31, and 27, respectively, for these activities.

Cooperation

Fifteen Group I, six Group II, and three Group III libraries are members of the Center for Research Libraries (CRL) as of 1991, and all from the first, and two from each of the other two groups are members of the Latin American Microforms Project (LAMP). Activities through CRL, especially through LAMP, offer the strongest evidence of formal cooperative agreements. Only six libraries reported the existence of other formal agreements.

Perhaps the model for formal cooperation to which libraries might aspire is the heavily coordinated collection development and resource sharing agreements between the University of North Carolina and Duke University. Conditions for cooperation between these two institutions are ideal, since their libraries are fifteen minutes apart, since both collections are managed by Latin American subject specialists, and since the curricula of the two teaching programs are integrated through the Duke–University of North Carolina Program in Latin American studies. Students from each campus can take courses for credit at the other. Informal cooperation for all three groups is not very prominent, and only seven libraries reported in this category. These results point toward a need for greater cooperation among our Latin American collections in the future.

Conclusions

A number of conclusions can be drawn from the results of the study. Importantly, the average expenditures from 1986 to 1990 for the major collections in Group I libraries rose 17.7 percent, wherein average costs of monographs reflected an increase of 43 percent. This measures a significant and alarming decline in acquisitions experienced by the nation's largest Latin American research collections in the past four years.

Expenditures for all groups showed that 3 percent of the total library materials allocations were spent on Latin American materials. With 4.9 percent of the collections of the large Group I libraries reported to be uncataloged, the problem of cataloging backlogs seems to be in decline. This probably can be attributed to the major retrospective conversion projects that have been funded by the United States Department of Education through its Title II C program, by foundations, and through locally funded conversion efforts.

Serial expenditures for the large Group I libraries represented 21.7 percent of the total spent for monographs and serials, and the average cost of a serial title for this group was $30. For these libraries, a ratio of 16.7 percent of serial volumes to monograph volumes received was reported. Serials cancellations were not as serious as the decline in the rate of acquisition for monographs. The most serious cancellation took place in the Library of Congress, where 250 titles were reported canceled in 1990.

Finally, staffing patterns can be measured best by the total of librarians and support staff. For Group I libraries, excluding figures for the very high number of staff for the University of Texas, staff averaged 7.9 percent. In Group II libraries the average was 6.1 percent, and for Group III libraries it was 3.2 percent. These conclusions are supported in the tables below.

Table 1. Volumes and Expenditures for the Library of Congress,
the Columbus Memorial Library, and Group I Libraries

		Expenditures	
Library	Volumes	1986	1990
Library of Congress	2,000,000		$334,492
Columbus Memorial	750,000	$ 58,223	$ 39,202 [c]
GROUP I LIBRARIES			
Cornell	269,000		$109,260
Duke	230,900		$ 47,727
Florida	267,000		$111,125
Illinois	343,300	$109,240	$119,482
New Mexico	317,000	$152,300	$166,067
North Carolina	200,000		$ 59,880
Pittsburgh	281,000	$112,171 [b]	$112,171
Princeton			
Puerto Rico	191,800	$ 38,204	$ 19,250
Southern California	192,000	$ 56,000	$125,577 [d]
Stanford	234,000	$108,000	$138,000
Texas	596,000	$175,032	$237,500
University of California, Los Angeles	300,000	$125,000	$135,000
Wisconsin	425,000 [a]	$ 81,747	$133,455
Yale	378,000		

a. Wisconsin includes Ibero-American Studies for Latin America, Spain, and Portugal.

b. FY1986 allocations.

c. FY1989 expenditures.

d. FY1990 allocation.

NOTE: Figures for the Columbus Memorial and Southern California libraries are from the first survey taken in 1990. Princeton's collection is in excess of 190,000, even though specific numbers were not given for the survey. Although Princeton's financial information cannot be reported, it is included for other information used in the Profile of Latin American Collections (table 3).

Table 2. Volumes and Expenditures for Group II
and Group III Libraries

Library	Volumes	Expenditures 1986	Expenditures 1990
GROUP II LIBRARIES			
Arizona	110,000	$37,134	$ 63,412
Arizona State	105,000 [a]		$ 85,083
California San Diego	170,000	$51,000	$129,600
Massachusetts	100,000	$72,378	$ 82,432 [b]
Miami	125,000		$ 38,845
Minnesota	100,000	$38,375	
San Diego State	90,000		
Vanderbilt	155,000		$ 96,697 [c]
GROUP III LIBRARIES			
Brigham Young	80,000	$35,000	$ 30,000 [b]
London	35,000	$32,230	$ 39,645
New York University	56,000	$43,771	$ 83,086 [b]
Notre Dame	44,438		$114,236
Ohio State	65,000 [d]	$44,200	$ 40,100 [b]
Pennsylvania State	25,000	$ 7,970	$ 10,697 [e]
Rutgers	31,514	$23,250 [f]	$ 23,250 [c]

    a. 90,000 to 120,000 volumes were reported on the survey.

    b. FY1989 expenditures.

    c. FY1990 allocation.

    d. 60,000 to 70,000 volumes were reported on the survey.

    e. FY1988 expenditures.

    f. FY1986 allocation.

NOTE: Only London and Notre Dame in Group III completed this second survey. Figures for all other Group III libraries are from the first survey completed in 1990. Minnesota includes Latin America, Spain, and Portugal.

Table 3. Profile of Latin American Collections

Category	Average			OAS	LC
	Group I	Group II	Group III		
Expenditures FY1990	$132,615 (8)	$ 52,961 (6)	$31,000 (6)	$39,202 FY1989	$ 334,492
Number current serials	929 (12)	379 (5)	238 (7)		1,300 [a]
Current serial expenditures	$ 27,276 (7)		$10,055 (4)	$28,654 FY1989	$ 160,000 [b]
Percentage of expenditures for serials	21.7 (10)			73	47.8
Gift, exchange titles received	1,350 (8)		499 (5)	5,200 FY1989	3,680 [a]
Total volumes FY1991	301,574 (14)	119,375 (8)	48,136 (7)	750,000 FY1990	2,000,000
Uncataloged backlog FY1991	15,414 (11)	6,075 (4)	8,250 (4)	14,000 FY1990	33,900 [c]
Volumes received from all sources	6,340 (9)				108,000
Percentage of monograph volumes received	83.3 (9)				
FTE Latin American professionals	2.6 (12)	2 (6)	.95 (7)		

Table 3 (cont.)

Category	Average			OAS	LC
	Group I	Group II	Group III		
FTE Latin American support staff and graduate students	2.7 (11)	2.43 (7)	.5 (3)		
FTE Latin American and other staff	7.9 (12)	6.10 (6)	3.2 (7)		70[d]
Percentage of time devoted to:					
Collection development	29 (9)	37.4 (6)	36 (2)		29
Technical services	29 (9)	28.1 (6)	6 (2)		24
Cataloging	31 (9)	25.2 (6)	31 (2)		43
Other	11 (9)	9.3 (6)	27 (2)		4

a. Figures for Washington only.
b. Includes newspaper microfilming.
c. Includes all Spanish and Portuguese titles.
d. Total for LC and its overseas operations.

NOTE: All information reported is for FY 1990 except where it is indicated otherwise. Numbers enclosed in parentheses are for the number of libraries reported in that category.

32. Stretching the Budget: Developing Latin American and Caribbean Serial Collections for University Libraries

Nelly S. González

Importance of Serials

Serial publications, particularly those from Latin America and the Caribbean, are an important medium for rapid communication, since they are one of the better thermometers of the daily function of societies. Serials published in these areas are also a popular method to disseminate the cultural life of these countries and reflect their intellectual production. In Latin America serials are generally less expensive and more accessible than books, which is a significant factor for these economically depressed regions. Despite difficulties in staying abreast of serial acquisitions and needs, domestic and foreign serial publications are heavily relied upon by academic libraries to support the research functions of their institutions.

Serials are also important because they provide an excellent forum for the introduction of fresh ideas. In this way, the medium helps to promote discussion, research, and development of conclusions for these new ideas until they become more refined products that may later be published in book form.

Another facet of the importance of serials for library collections is the diverse nature of the topics that may be discussed in this type of publication. As a result, there is a dichotomy between serials that are general in scope and those that are more specialized. A serial with a general treatment of knowledge, for example the *Latin American Research Review*, would be necessary in a library with limited resources that serves a general curriculum. Serials that are general in scope address a wide range of current topics from disciplines in the social sciences as well as the humanities, providing a source for broad research interest. A serial with a specific subject focus, such as *Historia Mexicana*, concentrates on a more specialized audience, which makes it appropriate for collections of academic institutions with specialized curricular programs.

Finally, currency is the strongest feature of serials, since their contents are ready for public access as soon as the journals are checked in.[1] This last feature is a primary justification for the prominent place given to serials in academic library collections.

Factors Influencing Serial Collection Decisions

The important role that serials have in collection development influences the factors that must be considered when making serial collection decisions. Some of the main points to consider are: (a) size of the library; (b) curriculum served; (c) amount of budget; and (d) nature of the collection.

The size of the library is often parallel to the size of the academic institution it serves. A large university supports a substantial body of research which in turn requires a large library collection. In most academic institutions, these two components, research needs and size of library collection, are interdependent. Research could be severely hampered unless it is supported by an adequate library collection, and vice versa.

A preestablished collection development program determines the serial subscriptions according to these requirements. This means that the curriculum of each institution is closely followed by the library's collection development policy in order to fully support the institution's objectives.

A well-planned and carefully administered budget is a principal consideration for maintaining an orderly acquisitions program. The serials subscription plan must conform to the amount allocated for their purchase. Furthermore, it should be closely monitored owing to the volatile nature of trends in serials pricing. Marifran Bustion clearly states the situation facing libraries with regard to serials in an article in *The Serials Librarian*:

Stagnant materials budgets and increasing serials prices are forcing libraries to monitor expenditures closely and to review collection development practices regarding serials. Most libraries, especially the longtime large university libraries considered at one time the best in the country, are suffering from state budget cuts and increased serials prices. For the last five years most of the large libraries have been doing an intensive serials review process, where academic faculty had to rate serial publications and come out with a list of titles to be canceled. Furthermore, some large academic libraries that formerly carried duplicate subscriptions for the convenience of their clientele, had to cancel them, thus this is a luxury that only will be remembered as "how it used to be, in the good old days, when money was not a problem."[2]

Bowker's serials staff refer to 1990 as "the Year of the Horse . . . serials prices rode roughshod over many a library budget."[3] In effect, the serials librarian is a juggler in the library circus, where s/he must be monitoring the ups and downs of prices, inflation, cessations, sudden deaths, mergers, splits, name changes, subscription expenditures, irregular receipts, and so on, and be prepared to order, cancel, and claim subscriptions to successfully manage the serials budget.

Building and Maintaining the Collection

An article in *Collection Building* makes an interesting observation regarding the development of serial collections. The authors state that librarians may tend to prefer to subscribe to journals that are covered in abstracting or indexing services but that the faculty's preference is to have journals that, although often not indexed, provide the opportunity to browse and expand their information sources. This is especially true with foreign journals. [4] Both of these factors influence the composition of each library's serial collection. It is no different for a collection of serials from and about Latin America and the Caribbean.

Building and maintaining a good Latin American serials collection requires knowledge of appropriate information sources and continuous checking on the status of the titles. Over the years, my experience has indicated that the most important sources to consult for bibliographic information are the following established bibliographies:

1. *Hispanic American Periodicals Index (HAPI)*
2. *Handbook of Latin American Studies (HLAS)*
3. *Indexed Journals: A Guide to Latin American Serials* [Provides some journals not listed in *HAPI*]
4. *MLA Directory of Periodicals*

The first three are the most authoritative, important, and unique bibliographic tools in Latin American studies. The *MLA Directory of Periodicals* is the premier periodical listing of journals in literature and related areas of study, and since those subjects constitute one of the major components of Latin American collections, it is included in the list of recommended sources for bibliographic information.

Subscription verification is another critical step during the selection process. Excellent sources to consult include:

1. Faxon's *Librarian's Guide to Serials*
2. Ulrich's *International Periodicals Directory*

Faxon is an international serials subscription agency and publisher of the *Librarian's Guide to Serials*, which contains an alphabetical listing of more than 200,000 serials along with ordering information (price, ISSN, frequency, etc.). Types of serials covered include periodicals, annuals, continuations, Government Printing Office (GPO) publications, monographic series, newspapers, proceedings, transactions, yearbooks, and CD-ROM titles. It does not provide the address of publishers, but it has a title number assigned by Faxon to each particular title, which facilitates the identification of the publication. No country codes are provided—only an 'N' when the publication is a non-U.S. periodical. Nevertheless, it has a variety of Latin American and Caribbean journals for which Faxon provides subscription service.

Faxon also offers the DataLinx service, which has an electronic mail component to speed orders and the claiming process. The convenience of this system is that each library may be connected to DataLinx and have instant online communication.

Ulrich's *International Periodicals Directory* is another very good source for information on the acquisition of serials, listing more than 116,000 serials currently published throughout the world. There are approximately 7,000 journals included that are from Latin America and the Caribbean. Access to periodicals is by subject and by title. Each entry has a country code, publisher's name and address, ISSN, frequency, circulation data, and price of publication. An added feature is that it provides a list of ceased serial titles along with a list of refereed journals. With the circulation information, the selector is able to find out which serials have the highest circulation in a specific field.[5] It is important to note that Ulrich's is also available on CD-ROM.

Most academic libraries have a separate serials unit for maintaining an organized serial acquisitions program. This separation permits the division of fund allocation, acquisition system, and processing.[6] There are also several different approaches to accounting processes in libraries. Some libraries may manage their funds within their acquisition units. Others have a more centralized approach to payments control, involving a central business office which controls disbursement of all funds. Payments could be by direct subscription to the publisher, by blanket order through a jobber servicing all the serials of the library, or by payment upon receipt of titles.

Budget control is the most important operation in serials collection development. The diversity of publication sequences requires the division of the type of serials being ordered into separate funds: serials that are published daily, weekly/bimonthly, yearly, and irregularly. Monographic series should be treated as a separate category because they appear so irregularly. This separation of funds permits a more precise account of the monies spent on serials. One must remember that most serials are long-term commitments. It is therefore important to have a clear idea of the funds involved to cover subscriptions.

Once the budget is allocated for serials, how can the serials selector deal with a shrinking budget, price escalation, and increased publication volume of serials? All these problems meet on common ground, which is inadequate funding. As a consequence, it is becoming increasingly difficult to maintain a balanced budget. With this situation, a well-defined serials collection development policy is an absolute necessity.   Subject specialists and collection development officers oversee the serials allocation for the collection within the respective disciplines of their institutions. This means that detailed consideration must be made by each department with regard to its primary interests. Other aspects to review are the interdisciplinary nature of certain serials, the institutional support for instruction and research, student enrollment, size of faculty body, historical precedent, growth rate of collections, and subscription prices.

Finally, every policy should fulfill the needs of the university's curriculum. For an institution supporting an undergraduate program in Latin American studies, a good basis for selection would be the acquisition of all or part of the titles indexed in the *Hispanic American Periodicals Index (HAPI)*. The *HAPI* serials make a useful core list for selection of serials that focus on Latin American studies. These serials generally cover the humanities and social sciences curricula. Deciding which journals to purchase also depends on the size of the institution: the larger the institution and the stronger the programs, the more inclusive and extensive the serials subscription list needs to be. In sum, balancing the serials budget becomes a real challenge for the serials librarian, where planning and evaluation enter into the decision-making process for serials acquisition.

Close supervision of serial collection procedures is necessary to ensure a successful serials department. The unit in charge of receiving (serial check-in) is predominantly clerical in nature, and is well served by paraprofessionals and clerks.   Nevertheless, the serials librarian should oversee the processing of serials to make certain that efficiency is maintained. Speed and competency would improve if the clerical staff processing the serials had some knowledge of foreign languages. This avoids problems that arise for several reasons, such as confusion of titles (e.g., *Análisis político*, published in Mexico, vs. *Análisis político*, published in Colombia).   Often titles are checked in on the wrong classification number (i.e., printing errors), which results in snagged materials—impeding the normal flow of serials and their rapid availability.   These problems demonstrate the importance of the supervision of the check-in process by a knowledgeable librarian or paraprofessional. Another source of confusion is addresses. Many times a serial publication is claimed from the wrong vendor, wasting precious time, or maybe even being disregarded and not answered at all. By the time the problem is caught, that specific issue could be out of print, or otherwise unattainable. Therefore, it is crucial for the collection to have an advanced serials control system, which is beneficial for the user as well as for the serials department.[7] The value of serials relies to a great extent on the continuity and completeness of the collection. For example, it is frustrating to try to find a bibliographic entry on a specific serial when the issue is not included in the holdings of the library.

Maintaining the collection also requires a policy for the conservation of serials. An important and expensive part of this effort is binding. Also necessary is the provision of an adequate number of conveniently located copiers with reasonable copying prices. This cuts down on the possibilities for mutilation and losses, which make a serial worthless for the next user.

Claiming serials is a time-consuming task, yet it is extremely necessary. Large collections need a knowledgeable support staff to keep the collection current and complete. Serials departments that have been automated may have an added feature of "action date," when the computer generates claim records. These are sent to publishers, jobbers, dealers, and the like. Other systems do not have this capability, so the claiming is done manually. Usually it is accomplished by filling out a form, which the serials claim staff sends at the request of the claiming library. The claiming system requires constant follow-ups to work satisfactorily. The main reason for this is that large serial subscription vendors only accept claims for items published within the year. If a certain title was not claimed between those dates, a dealer such as Faxon will not honor the request. Thus, the library has to attempt to buy from the publisher at greater cost the issues that were not received. In this way there is an economic loss, and sometimes it is not possible to fill the missing issues because the publication is unavailable. This is a problem for serials in general but much more so with Latin American and Caribbean serials, since they are generally published in small quantities and become out of print almost immediately after publication.

Automated serials check-in systems do a lot to alleviate persistent problems with serials maintenance. But the problem still exists with serials that were not received and later became unattainable. EBSCO is better than Faxon in this respect because they collect a pool of back issues of serials to be used to fill gaps in their clients' holdings. However, this pool is a representative number of particular serials and not inclusive for all of the titles they serve. Furthermore, Latin American serials are unlikely to be collected for this pool since they are difficult to obtain.

As we have seen, serials collection development is a complex operation. Latin American and Caribbean serials in particular pose many difficulties because all of the problems that have already been discussed occur regularly with these serials. With this in mind, a domestic jobber, although experienced with servicing U.S. publications, is not recommended for supplying Latin American and Caribbean serials. In some cases the use of foreign jobbers is a more successful operation. For one thing, it is easier to initiate claims to these dealers since they know the publishers and thus can almost always obtain the issues claimed.

To decide upon the appropriate jobber, each institution must consider the unique constraints and possibilities of its operation. A large institution with a large serials collection might benefit by ordering from local book dealers in each country or region. A smaller collection might obtain better results by dealing with a domestic jobber who services all of its serials subscriptions. Finally, processing costs must be considered. This is often the deciding factor on choice of vendors.

Alternative Methods for Serial Collection Development

Libraries and librarians have in the past been involved in developing alternative methods of acquisitions. Perhaps these activities began as a natural process of communications in life, where one cooperates with another, exchanging something for something else. In some libraries the gifts and exchange activity has gradually developed until it has become a very important part of the operation. Many library collections can credit active gifts and exchange programs for a substantial portion of their holdings.

In today's climate of budgetary restraint, escalating serial subscription prices, and increased production, gifts and exchange should receive more serious consideration than in the past. This activity could be pursued by contacting government agencies, academic institutions, and research centers, or through any other creative method. It usually involves extensive letter writing, making known the service that your institution provides and the problems faced by the institution owing to budget cuts. Very often the response is positive, and sometimes even overwhelming.

Most large academic institutions have a well-established gifts and exchange department staffed by a gifts and exchange librarian and some support staff. Directories of institutions interested in exchanging materials exist and are circulated among institutions. Furthermore, one could contact the librarians of academic institutions to share information. The key to the success of this endeavor is to make certain that each participating institution benefits from it.

The most important facet of a gifts and exchange operation is an ongoing commitment to communication for acknowledgment of publications received, comments, encouragement, and so on. It is advantageous for this correspondence to be done in the language of the country in question, because the reaction to the request is generally more positive when written in the native language.

Another way to cope with budget restraints is the development of national cooperative programs. The first extensive effort to establish a national plan for collecting foreign area materials was the Farmington Plan, developed by the Association of Research Libraries in 1948, shortly after the end of World War II. This program was very successful and greatly influenced the development of research collections in academic institutions. In 1960, the first Latin American Cooperative Acquisitions Project (LACAP) was established. The Farmington Plan and the LACAP projects prospered owing to the economic affluence of the period. It was during this time that the excellent collections of Latinamericana of today began, and the idea of cooperation evolved. There is an excellent study on "The Implementation of a National Plan for Latin American Library Collections in the United States," presented by Carl W. Deal of the University of Illinois and William E. Carter of the Library of Congress to the 27th Seminar on the Acquisition of Latin American Library Materials (SALALM) conference in 1982 which discusses in more detail the history and implementation of these national plans for cooperation.

At SALALM in 1982 it was noted that "The steeply rising costs of area studies library collections calls for more inter-library cooperation."[8] This cooperation continues to be necessary if librarians are to cope with today's serials problems. Several cooperative programs have recently developed. Some libraries have committed to extensively collecting materials from and about a specific country or region while maintaining the collection activity in general and in accordance with each institution's economic situation. This effort is paying off, since the libraries in the United States are still the strongest depositories of publications from and about Latin America and the Caribbean.

One alternative for serial collection development is private fundraising conducted by organizations such as the Library Friends. The Library Friends organization serves as an increasingly important source of support for varied library activities. This support is generously given by volunteers who spend many hours assisting with library activities from technical services to preservation. Furthermore, they are involved in fund-raising campaigns for specific programs or acquisition of materials that they consider important for the library to have. For example, the University of Illinois Library Friends group has a constituency of "nearly 3,000 members dedicated to ensuring the Library's place among the world's greatest research libraries . . . and since 1972, they have contributed more than $1,250,000 in annual funds." [9] By working through the Library Friends or library development offices to prepare lists of titles suitable for acquisition, librarians may enlist support for funding of materials which otherwise would not be available.

Conclusion

Serial publications play a vital role in the holdings of university libraries. This is especially true for libraries with Latin American and Caribbean collections, since serial publications within these regions function as an increasingly important medium for the rapid communication of information, thoughts, and ideas.

The process of collection development for these publications is complex and varied, beginning with the selection of serials and continuing through ordering, receiving, control, payment, and binding, up to the final stage, availability for patron use. An important factor to be considered in this process is that serials are a more rapid means of communication than most other scholarly materials; hence, there is an inherent urgency to their acquisition and availability.

Because of the difficulties surrounding serial acquisitions, it is necessary for libraries to come up with alternative methods for developing their collection of serials from and about Latin American and the Caribbean. In particular, it is necessary to monitor and expand gift and exchange relationships with other institutions or through government agencies. Cooperative acquisition programs with similar libraries within our country can provide better access to a wide range of materials. We might better solve the needs of each particular institution and the larger scholarly community by working in closer cooperation with other libraries and organizations. By applying the methods discussed in this paper, one might truly be able to stretch the serials budget.

NOTES

1. Peggy Keeran and Gunter Angermayr, "The Impact of UnCover on the Use of Current Periodicals at the University of Denver's Penrose Library," *The Serials Librarian* 20, 1 (1991), 70.

2. Marifran Bustion et al., "Methods of Serials Funding: Formula or Tradition?" *The Serials Librarian* 20, 1 (1991), 75-89.

3. *Ulrich's News* 4, 1 (January 1991), 1.

4. Lois Olsrud and Anne Moore, "Serials Review in the Humanities: A Three-Year Project," *Collection Building* 10, 3-4 (1990), 7.

5. F. Jacso, "Coverage and Accessibility in *Ulrich's Plus* and EBSCO-CD," *The Serials Librarian* 10, 1 (1991), 31.

6. Karen Schmidt, "The Acquisitions Process in Research Libraries: A Survey of ARL Libraries' Acquisitions Departments," *Library Acquisitions: Practice and Theory* 11 (1987), 6.

7. Betsy Kruger, "Serials Management at the University of Illinois at Urbana-Champaign Library," *The Serials Librarian* 19, 1-2 (1990), 27.

8. Carl W. Deal and William E. Carter, "The Implementation of a National Plan for Latin American Library Collections in the United States," in Pamela Howard, ed., *Public Policy Issues and Latin American Library Resources*, Papers of SALALM XXVII, Washington, DC, March 2-5, 1982 (Madison, WI: SALALM, 1984), p. 153.

9. *The Library Is Looking for . . .* (Urbana: University of Illinois Library Development Office, 1990), p. 2.

33. Latin American Periodical Prices Revisited

Scott Van Jacob

During the June 1990 SALALM conference in Rio de Janeiro, I presented an analysis of Faxon's survey of periodical subscription prices annually published in *The Serials Librarian* for the Latin American countries of Argentina, Brazil, and Chile. My findings indicated that the table, "Price Comparison by Country of Origin," included in the survey, was not an accurate index of Latin American periodicals prices. With this information, as well as useful observations from a number of my colleagues and the SALALM Serials Subcommittee, I have spent the past year developing an index for Latin American periodicals which examines the prices from five Latin American countries. In this paper I summarize last year's findings, outline the criteria established for this index, and report the findings of the index thus far.

Faxon Subscription Analysis, 1990

Last year I examined the periodical price index information published annually in *The Serials Librarian*. This index charts periodical subscription prices and is probably the index most utilized by librarians for tracking and forecasting periodical prices. Of special interest to me was the table "Price Comparison by Country of Origin," which listed the average cost per periodical title by country of publication. Since only those countries with 25 active titles (titles to which Faxon clients currently subscribe) carried in the Faxon database were listed, only nine Latin American countries were represented: Argentina, Brazil, Chile, Colombia, Costa Rica, Jamaica, Mexico, Peru, and Venezuela. Although 25 titles may be too few to represent accurately a country's actual periodical costs, it is a starting place to begin investigating the cost behavior of these periodicals.

The Faxon table, "Price Comparison by Country of Origin," in table 1 for Argentina, Brazil, and Chile, illustrates subscription price variations for the first six years of its use. I selected these three countries for examination because they have some of the largest and most active publishing industries in Latin America.

Table 1. Faxon Average Price, 1985-1990
"Price Comparison by Country of Origin"

	1985	1986	1987	1988	1989	1990
Argentina	72.35	78.49	81.75	103.43	107.14	107.48
Brazil	96.64	97.41	107.34	113.37	116.11	121.34
Chile	65.71	68.13	66.98	85.18	97.32	100.85

NOTE: Faxon provides an average price and a weighted price. The weighted price takes into account the number of libraries subscribing to the journal through Faxon. The price used in this graph is the average price.

SOURCE: This table was first published in "Periodical Prices 1985-1987 Update," *Serials Librarian* 13, 1 (Sept. 1987), 49-57.

Two observations can be made from table 1, even though only six years of data may not adequately represent a trend. First, subscription prices for these three countries together have increased over this period by 40 percent. During the same period and from the same Faxon table, the combined periodical prices of the United Kingdom, United States, and West Germany increased by 67 percent. It is no wonder that our profession's attention is focused on North American and Western European periodical prices. Second, the average price per title seems quite high. For example, the 1990 average price for all three countries was over $100, with Brazil leading the way at $121.34 per title. One would expect titles from developing countries to be much less expensive than what the Faxon table indicates. One possible reason for these high prices may be that Faxon's mix of titles for these countries includes a disproportionate number of traditionally expensive titles such as law journals, science and technology journals, and daily foreign newspapers. Of course, it is also possible that the cost of these types of journals in Latin America may not reflect the high cost of the same journals in the United States and Europe. Both of these points are examined below.

An analysis of the mix of Faxon titles by content can be found in table 2. To ensure that only periodical prices were examined, monographic series, reordered titles, and "bill laters" were omitted. The remaining titles were placed into six general subject areas (social science, humanities, science and technology, general, law, and newspapers) according to the Library of Congress classification found on their MARC record. When the record could not be located on OCLC or RLIN, it was not included.

Table 2. Faxon Periodical Titles by Subject Analysis

	Argentina		Brazil		Chile	
	Number of titles	Average price	Number of titles	Average price	Number of titles	Average price
Social Science	26	$63	24	$42	11	$74
Humanities	14	$37	7	$19	5	$38
Science/ Technology	24	$46	50	$60	18	$41
General	4	$165	3	$60	3	$211
Law	5	$142	1	$102	4	$60
Newspapers	5	$360	1	$1,290	1	$1,480

As might be expected, the majority of the titles fall into the first three categories, social sciences, humanities, and science and technology. Within this grouping, science and technology titles make up 51 percent of the total. In fact, Brazil's 50 science titles make up 58 percent of all Brazilian titles listed. While in the United States and Europe science and technology journals tend to cost more than humanities or social science journals, table 2 demonstrates that this is not the case for Argentina and Chile. In both cases, the social science journals are more expensive than the science and technology journals. These data demonstrate that science journals are not responsible for the average cost given by Faxon. It is apparent that general, law, and newspaper titles are largely responsible for the high average price of the Faxon results even though they make up only a small portion of the Faxon database. This is the case among all three countries. Of the general, law, and newspaper titles, the cost of newspaper subscriptions inflates the average price per serial considerably. For example, the cost of the Brazilian newspaper *Jornal do Brazil* was $1,650 in 1990. While this is only one year of data, it illustrates the phenomenon.

These results highlight the need for a periodical price index that can adequately measure Latin American subscription prices. Faxon should be commended for tracking the subscription information for the developing world, but their catalog of titles is influenced significantly by newspaper and law subscriptions. What follows is the first attempt at measuring Latin American periodical prices.

A Latin American Periodical Price Index

The objective of the Latin American Periodical Price Index (LAPPI) is to provide an accurate picture of each Latin American country's periodical subscription prices on an annual basis, thereby allowing for comparison of price variations over a period of years. An accurate depiction of Latin American periodical prices must include a representative sampling of titles from each country. The procedures to achieve this are described below.

Method

To ensure that the sample is consistent and reliable, the *American National Standard for Library and Information Sciences and Related Publishing Practices—Library Materials—Criteria for Price Indexes* (ANSI Z39.20-1983) will be utilized as a guideline for creating the index. The following criteria have been established to provide a consistent and reliable sample based on the ANSI guidelines.

1.   All periodicals included in the sample must fall within the following definition of the above ANSI standard: "A continuous series under the same title published at regular or irregular intervals, over an indefinite period, individual issues in the series being numbered consecutively or each issue being dated."

2.   The currency of choice here is the U.S. dollar. All subscripton prices will be given in this currency.

3.   When there is both an airmail price and surface price listed for the same title, only the surface mail price will be included in the index.

4.   The subject categories of social sciences, humanities, science and technology, general, law, and newspapers will be utilized to provide a fuller analysis of each country's subscription prices. Titles will be categorized by their LC classification number, given in the MARC record. If no LC class number is listed, subject headings will be used for this purpose.

5.   When both microfilm and paper prices are available for the same periodical, only the paper subscription price will be included in the sample.

6.   In order to maintain a consistent number of titles for price indexing purposes, a ceased title will be replaced with a like title.

7.   The index figure shall be calculated using the equation:

$$\text{Index figure} \quad = \quad \frac{\text{Average price x 100}}{\text{Average price in the base year}}$$

The Faxon Company has graciously agreed to provide their list of titles for all the countries of Latin America as part of the index's sample. In an effort to improve the accuracy of the sample, the number of titles will be increased by including the Library of Congress (LC) list of Latin American periodical subscriptions. Using the six subject categories employed in table 2, the subject content of the Faxon and LC 1990 subscription prices for Argentina, Brazil, and Chile is analyzed in table 3. (When both Faxon and LC have the same title with different prices, both prices have been included.) It is apparent that the LC titles are oriented toward the social sciences and the humanities. For example, LC subscribes to 63 Brazilian social science titles, while Faxon carries only 24. The reason for this difference is that

Table 3. LC–Faxon Subject Comparison

	Argentina		Brazil		Chile	
	LC	Faxon	LC	Faxon	LC	Faxon
Social Science	62	26	62	34	8	23
Humanities	25	25	31	14	5	5
Science/ Technology	11	24	30	58	2	18
General	9	4	20	14	7	4
Law	11	6	24	1	4	2
Newspapers	8	5	3	3	4	1
Total	136	90	170	124	30	53

the LC collection is determined by a collection development policy, whereas the Faxon catalog of titles is determined by client demand. Thus Faxon has little concern for the types of periodicals they carry as long as their clients subscribe. Conversely, LC attempts to represent a country's social, cultural, and political milieu through its periodical literature. Together these two groups of periodicals provide a large and balanced set of titles that will provide a representative sample of the actual prices of Latin American periodicals.

Preliminary Results

Table 4 shows the initial results of the index of the 1990 subscriptions for the combined Faxon and LC titles as well as the average periodical prices for Argentina, Brazil, Chile, Paraguay, and Uruguay.

Weighted Prices

In order to ensure that the titles reflect the holdings of Latin American collections, table 4 contains both an average subscription price and a weighted subscription price by subject category for each country. This weighted price is reported by multiplying the number of libraries holding a title by the title's subscription price. These totals are then added together and divided by the total number of holding libraries within that category. Consequently, titles held by more libraries influence the weighted price more than those held by fewer libraries. The libraries were identified by reviewing the holdings record attached to the OCLC bibliographic record for each title. Libraries with notable Latin American holdings were selected for this list (see Appendix) Many of these collections were logical choices, such as the Benson collection at the University of Texas at Austin, the Library of Congress, and the University of California, Berkeley. Others that have much smaller but still significant holdings were also included.

Although the data reflect only one year, or a "snapshot" of subscription prices, they show some significant trends. First, in all five countries the daily newspaper is by far the most expensive of the six subject areas. The small number of newspapers included in the sample are mostly the dailies from major cities of Latin America, for example, *El Mercurio* from Santiago de Chile. If newspapers from the smaller cities were included in this sample, the cost may be much lower. Since most libraries are only ordering the major Latin American newspapers, the price for newspapers given here is probably an accurate reflection of what libraries are spending on Latin American newspapers.

Table 4. Average and Weighted Price by Country

Subject	Titles	Average price	Holding libraries	Weighted price
		Argentina		
Social Science	94	$ 57.66	539	$ 58.54
Humanities	41	43.70	251	48.64
Sciences	35	42.57	145	41.63
General	15	99.70	57	117.50
Law	17	195.90	44	209.30
Newspapers	12	378.90	36	364.00
Total	201	88.35	1072	73.53
		Brazil		
Social Science	96	$ 26.40	521	$ 27.79
Humanities	38	22.62	207	29.33
Sciences	74	53.58	256	48.38
General	27	48.60	220	67.60
Law	25	111.70	48	96.30
Newspapers	4	768.00	21	714.00
Total	264	51.42	1273	52.97
		Chile		
Social Science	31	$ 68.90	336	$ 44.30
Humanities	10	32.55	73	22.90
Sciences	20	44.29	74	47.37
General	8	137.70	64	190.40
Law	4	62.60	9	50.59
Newspapers	4	300.50	4	300.50
Total	77	$76.60	561	63.08
		Paraguay		
Social Science	14	$30.80	59	$ 29.26
Humanities	2	10.00	3	10.00
Sciences	–	—	–	—
General	3	25.00	13	22.69
Law	5	32.15	9	29.30
Newspapers	1	440.00	2	261.00
Total	25	21.51	86	
		Uruguay		
Social Science	15	$ 30.78	94	$ 24.97
Humanities	5	17.00	23	10.70
Sciences	1	25.00	1	25.00
General	9	54.90	35	59.54
Law	12	92.20	18	68.60
Newspapers	6	865.00	6	865.00
Total	48	153.30	177	

Law journal prices are not surprising. Since the law degree is one
of the most common graduate degrees given in Latin America and since
law is unique to every country, there is a real need and market for
scholarly law journals.[1]

The "general" category includes all areas not appropriate to any of
the five other areas. Examples are education, bibliography, and library
science periodicals. These periodicals are not very expensive. The high
average price for this category is generated by the cost of news
magazines such as Venezuela's *Resumen* or Brazil's *Veja*.

As noted in table 2, the most surprising finding is the cost of social
science journals compared with science journals. With the exception of
Brazil and Uruguay (which has no science journals), social science
journals are substantially more expensive than the science journals.
The most expensive social science journals tend to be in economics,
banking, and legislation. One possible explanation of the low cost of
science periodicals is that they are more organs of information for
associations such as newsletters than research publications as we
generally know science journals from the United States or Western
Europe. It is likely that Latin American scientists publish in U.S. and
European journals. One example of evidence supporting this view is a
bibliometric survey of Mexican health science research (Licea de
Arenas and Cronin, 1989) that found more than 70 percent of the
articles in their sample were published in foreign journals. Further study of the difference in cost between Latin American science and social
science journals is needed to truly understand these initial findings.

The results of the index show that weighted prices have no
significant relation to the average price. This indicates that the cost
that libraries with strong Latin American collections actually pay is
different from the average price of Latin American periodicals. It is
interesting to note that the weighted price of science journals is greater
in three of the five countries, a striking contrast from the average price
tables.

Conclusion

The annual publication of the Latin American Periodical Price
Index will begin a systematic survey of Latin American periodical
prices. Charting these periodical prices over time will give us a better
understanding of their publishing industry, particularly in the academic
sector. This information will be of use in securing funding for Latin
American materials. Certainly, the more we know about our expenditures the more persuasive we can be in maintaining and increasing

funding. Such knowledge will help to build collections that serve present and future scholars,

APPENDIX
Selected Libraries

Arizona State University
Cornell University
Duke University
Florida State University
Florida International University
Georgetown University
Harvard University
Indiana University
Kansas University
Library of Congress
Louisiana State University
New York Public Library
Ohio State University
Purdue University
Princeton University
San Diego State University
Southern Illinois University
Tulane University
University of Arizona

University of California, Berkeley
University of California, Los Angeles
University of California, San Diego
University of California, Santa Cruz
University of Florida
University of Georgia
University of Illinois at Champaign-Urbana
University of Massachussetts
University of Miami
University of Minnesota
University of New Mexico
University of North Carolina at Chapel Hill
University of Notre Dame
University of Pittsburgh
University of Southern California
University of Texas at Austin
University of Utah
University of Virginia
University of Wisconsin at Madison
Yale

NOTE

1. For more information on the number of students enrolled in law school, see "Higher Education: Distribution of Students by Sex and Field of Study," *Statistical Abstract of Latin America*, Vol. 28 (Los Angeles, CA: UCLA Latin American Center Publications, 1990), table 912, .

BIBLIOGRAPHY

American National Standard for Library and Information Sciences and Related Publishing Practices—Library Materials—Criteria for Price Indexes. New York, NY: American National Standards Institute, 1983.

Licea de Arenas, Judith, and Blaise Cronin. "The Contribution of Higher Education Institutions to the Development of the Mexican Health Sciences Base." *Journal of Information Science*, 15 (1989), 333-338.

Lenzini, Rebecca T. "Periodical Prices 1985-1987 Update." *Serials Librarian* 13, 1 (Sept. 1987), 49-57.

Wilkie, James W., et al., eds. *Statistical Abstract of Latin America*, Vol. 28. Los Angeles: UCLA Latin American Center Publications, 1990.

Librarianship and Library
Collections in Brazil

34. Computer Training in Brazilian Library Schools

Iratí Antonio and Claudia Negrão Balby

The objective of this research is to investigate the practices followed by Brazilian library schools in training librarians for computer use in undergraduate, extension, specialization, and graduate programs. Preliminary results present information on matters such as courses and syllabi, the academic profile of instructors, and the computer resources (hardware and software) available. The research outlines a historical profile of computer training in Brazil, presenting data collected through questionnaires and through a survey of the literature. It also approaches themes such as the job market, the professional profile of librarians, and new technology, that together with critical analyses form a picture of the present conditions of the area. The conclusion suggests possible further avenues of study and follow-up on these matters.

Objectives and Methodology

The project, "The state of computer training in Brazilian library schools," investigates the current situation of that subfield of library education in Brazil at undergraduate, extension, specialization, and graduate levels.

The project is composed of field research in several phases. The present and first stage reports on data collected through a questionnaire sent to public and private library schools in Brazil. Thirteen questions covered the following major points for the academic year 1990: titles, contents, and number of hours of the courses; academic profile of faculty involved; hardware and software available for student use; research projects and programs; and relevant literature published by faculty involved.

A bibliography was also compiled, listing books and articles published by Brazilian authors. It provided a frame of reference for the paper and helped to identify researchers working on the topic.

Authors' Note: We wish to thank Dr. Dinah Aguiar Población and Dr. Neusa Dias de Macedo for their collaboration in this paper, as well as the Conselho Regional de Biblioteconomia—8a. Região, and Mr. Fabio Negrão Balby, computer programmer.

A historical profile of the subfield in Brazil was also outlined. Related themes, such as professional skills and the job market, were discussed as well.

Computer Science and Library Science

The history of library education in Brazil can be divided into four phases. The first covered the period from 1879 to 1929 and was led by the Biblioteca Nacional under French influence. The second, which spanned 1929 to 1962, was marked by the influence of a course offered in São Paulo by professionals who had received their training in the United States.

A third phase, which began in 1962, brought a greater degree of uniformity to the programs. This was due to the official acknowledgement of the profession by the Brazilian Ministry of Labor, which also established a minimum mandatory national curriculum for undergraduate programs. The trend toward the use of new technology in information processing can be seen in one of the courses in that curriculum, which was called Reprodução de Documentos.

A fourth phase began in 1970 and was marked by the proliferation of undergraduate programs and by the emergence of graduate study. Brazilian libraries started to use computer resources at this time. The literature of the decade shows an increasing concern with the training of personnel to plan and operate library computer systems. Reviewing that fourth phase, Suzana Pinheiro Machado Mueller states that

desenvolvimentos na educação superior no Brasil, aliados ao desenvolvimento tecnológico, especialmente o referente à área de comunicações, e às mudanças sociais e econômicas do País, tiveram . . . muita influência nos programas de formação profissional para Biblioteconomia, pois provocaram a expansão dos cursos de pós-graduação stricto sensu e lato sensu e empurraram os cursos de graduação para um processo de auto-avaliação de seus programas. [1]

The emerging graduate programs played an important role. According to Gomes, many courses that were first offered—Mecanização, for instance—were later extended to undergraduate programs. [2] Among the courses offered by the Master's Degree Program in Information Science of the IBBD (Instituto Brasileiro de Bibliografia e Documentação), which started in 1970, one could find Processamento de Dados na Documentação as a mandatory course, and Programação as an optional one. [3]

Briquet, however, criticized the mere addition of information on recent technologies to undergraduate courses without changes in their global structure. [4] Along the same line, the final resolutions of the 6°

Congresso Brasileiro de Biblioteconomia e Documentação, held in Belo Horizonte in 1971, include a special recommendation that the ABEBD (Associação Brasileira de Escolas de Biblioteconomia e Documentação) press for changes in the minimum curriculum to include the course Introdução aos Computadores. This measure would, it was believed, bring a degree of uniformity to teaching. The same author states that

as escolas que não oferecem cursos com a denominação específica de Mecanização e Automação, Introdução ao Processamento de Dados, ou Informática incluem no conteúdo dos cursos de Documentação os estudos sobre a aplicação de equipamento convencional e computadores na mecanização de serviços de bibliotecas e na recuperação de informações. [5]

However, the depth in which the subject was approached varied from school to school.

In the late 'seventies one could identify within the schools a growing dissatisfaction with syllabi swollen by the absorption of new subjects in a haphazard way. A group of schools prepared a document for the CFE (Conselho Federal de Educação) in which some courses in the library curriculum were criticized for placing emphasis on some traditional aspects of library work and not on others, ". . . particularmente os surgidos face aos progressos tecnológicos."[6]

A new minimum curriculum for undergraduate programs was approved in 1982, and implemented from 1985 through the definition and application of full curricula by each library school. The curriculum grouped courses in three categories: (a) those that aimed at providing a general foundation for the understanding of culture and society; (b) those that served as tools to improve the quality of professional work (Foreign Languages, Applied Linguistics, Logic, etc.); and (c) those specifically related to library work (e.g., Cataloging, Classification).

According to Mueller,[7] courses in the 1982 curriculum were quite similar to those established twenty years before. No course title makes specific mention of computer applications in libraries. The author views the development of new technology as a factor to motivate change but believes that dissimilarities between Brazilian library schools will lead to unequal developments at the local level.

In her evaluation of graduate programs, Mueller finds that

outra tendência notada entre os cursos de mestrado é a introdução do computador como meio normal de trabalho. Quase todas as escolas possuem pelo menos um microcomputador e fazem uso regular das instalações disponíveis nas suas universidades. O que se percebe é o desejo de aumentar as experiências nessa área, tanto para ensino quanto para trabalho, mas ainda se ressentem da falta de pessoal qualificado. [8]

Professional Profiles and the Job Market

The current stage of human development, which has been called "the information age," is characterized by the extensive use of media such as the telephone, television, and computers. Those media have enormous influence on society and are marked by the power to dissolve the constraints of time and space in human communication.

Information is now seen as a commodity, and given that perspective, information services acquire a privileged status. They are regarded as basic elements of the economic system, and therefore must undergo frequent changes to meet market needs. Thus a demand develops for information professionals who can understand and effect change in increasingly complex services.

In Brazil, however, there are no extensive, up-to-date studies on the characteristics now required of the information professional. This is attributable on one side to the great diversity in existing roles and needs and on the other to the lack of concrete data about the information market that could serve as a basis for definitions.

Calls for change in views of this new library professional are somewhat vague and self-referential. Greater clarity is found in statements concerning the need to transform library programs to meet market requirements and to provide specific training in the use of new technology through formal and continuing education.[9] According to Tarapanoff: "A necessidade do profissional da informação de se adaptar a mudanças (sociais, tecnológicas, e outras), para não sofrer progressiva marginalização, tem sido a preocupação de muitos autores."[10]

Computer Training for Librarians: The Situation in Brazil

The questionnaire was mailed to the country's 33 library schools, and responses came from 13 institutions, representing 39.3 percent of the total:

Universidade de Brasília (UNB)

Faculdades Integradas Teresa D'Avila (FATEA/SA; Santo André, SP)

Universidade do Rio Grande (URG; Rio Grande, RS)

Universidade Federal de Minas Gerais (UFMG; Belo Horizonte)

Universidade Federal de Pernambuco (UFPE; Recife)

Escola de Biblioteconomia e Documentação de São Carlos (EBDSC; São Carlos, SP)

Universidade Federal do Paraná (UFPR; Curitiba)

Universidade Federal de Goiás (UFGO; Goiânia)

Universidade Federal da Bahia (UFBA; Salvador)
Faculdades Teresa Martin (FATEMA; São Paulo, SP)
Pontifícia Universidade Católica de Campinas (PUCCAMP; Campinas, SP)
Universidade Estadual Paulista (UNESP; Marília, SP)
Universidade de São Paulo (USP).

Nine of the surveyed institutions (69.2)* are government funded at state or federal levels, and 4 (30.7) are privately funded. Seven (53.8) are located in the Southeast region, and 2 (15.4) each in the Center-West, Northeast, and South. These figures present a very close correspondence to the geographical distribution of the total number of library schools in Brazil: of the total 33 schools, 17 (51.5) are located in the Southeast, 7 (21.2) in the Northeast, 5 (15.2) in the South, 2 (6.1) in the North, and 2 (6.1) in the Center-West. The same correspondence applies to the main source of financial resources: 23 are funded by the government (69.7) and 10 (30.3) are privately funded. The sample may thus be considered valid according to geographical and funding criteria.

Computers in the Library Curriculum

The 13 schools surveyed reported that a total of 39 courses on computers were offered to librarians in 1990. Twenty-eight of them (71.8) were offered at the undergraduate level; 5 (12.8) at specialization level; 2 (5.1) at extension level, and 4 (10.3) at the graduate level (the last three categories all refer to Master's degree programs).

This paper does not intend to make a qualitative analysis of the variation in course titles and syllabi. From a quantitative perspective, table 1 presents the number of hours of mandatory undergraduate courses offered in 1990 by surveyed institutions.

Comparison of course titles to course syllabi made it possible to classify courses in two groups, as follows: (*a*) specific courses, dealing directly and specifically with computers, their hardware and software, and their application to library and information services; (*b*) general courses, which, as broader courses on Technical Services or Library Administration, deal indirectly with computer use.

Most course titles correspond to their contents (e.g., Automação de Bibliotecas, Introdução à Informática); however, there are cases in which an extensive and detailed course on computer applications in libraries is disguised under a generic course title—Administração de Bibliotecas or Disseminação da Informação, for example. Regardless of the titles, those courses were classified as "specific" in this paper.

---

*All figures in parentheses are percentages.

Table 1. Number of Hours of Mandatory Undergraduate Courses

Institution[a]	Number of hours of courses	Number of hours of program	Percentage of each course[b]	Percentage of total[c]	Type of course
FATEA/SA	72	3,510	2.05		
	72	3,510	2.05	4.1	Specific
URG	30	2,970	1.0	1.0	Specific
UFPE	75	2,770	2.7	2.7	Specific
UFMG	60	2,790	2.1		
	60	2,790	2.1	4.2	Specific
EBDSC	60	3,120	1.9		
	30	3,120	0.9	2.8	Specific
UFPR	60	2,970	2.0	2.0	Specific
UFGO	60	2,970	2.0	2.0	Generic
UFBA	75	3,375	2.2		Specific
	75	3,375	2.2	4.4	Generic
FATEMA	144	3,456	4.1		Generic
	72	3,456	2.0	6.1	Specific
USP	90	2,940	3.0		
	60	2,940	2.0		
	60	2,940	2.0		
	60	2,940	2.0	9.0	Generic
UNESP	90	2,940	3.0		
	60	2,940	2.0	5.0	Specific

a. See pp. 350-351 for full name of institution.

b. Percentage of each computer course in relation to total number of hours of library program.

c. Sum of computer course percentages in relation to total number of hours of library program.

Note: UNB and PUCAMP, which have not declared the total number of hours of the library program, were not represented in this table.

Most courses are compulsory, but very few are prerequisites for others.

The majority of computer-related courses were introduced in the institutions surveyed in the 1980s. The oldest reference is Introdução ao Processamento de Dados, taught since 1971 at PUCCAMP. It should be noted that UFMG offers a total of 11 courses at all levels, the first one dating from 1972, most starting with the implementation of the new curriculum, and 4 beginning in 1990. This information is based on data provided by the schools in answer to the questionnaire, but it should be noted that Cavalcanti indicates that Mecanização e Automação de Bibliotecas (Documentação II) was offered at UNB beginning in 1969;[11] it is also known that other schools introduced similar courses in the 1970s.

Qualification of Faculty

Of the 32 specific courses, which represent 82.1 percent of all courses, 13 (40.6) are taught by instructors qualified in Library Science; 12 (37.5) by instructors holding degrees in Library and Computer Science, and 7 (21.9) by instructors qualified in Computer Science.

The 7 general courses account for 17.9 percent of all courses. Four of them (57.1) are taught by instructors who have degrees in Library Science; 2 (28.6) by instructors qualified in Computer Science, and 1 (14.3) is taught by instructors qualified in both areas.

Regarding the total number of courses offered, 17 (43.6) are taught by instructors qualified in Library Science; 13 (33.3) by instructors qualified in Library and Computer Science, and 9 (23.1) by instructors qualified in Computer Science.

Considering that computer training for librarians combines two different areas, faculty should aim for qualification in both. The schools surveyed either have instructors who are doubly qualified or form teams of people who complement each other in qualification. However, only 33.3 percent of the courses belong in this category, not ideal for library education.

Table 2 presents the qualifications of faculty as related to course types—generic or specific.

Available Hardware

The Brazilian computer market was dominated by 8-bit machines compatible with the Apple II-IIe standard until 1984. The 16-bit IBM-PC compatibles became available the following year, and their relative decrease in price over time helped them become the computer standard for the country. By 1988, 85 of every 100 computers in Brazil

Table 2. Course Type vs. Qualification of Faculty

	Specific Courses					Generic Courses			
School	Qualification in library	Qualification in computers	Qualification in both	Total	School	Qualification in library	Qualification in computers	Qualification in both	Total
UNB	0	0	1	1	UNB	0	0	0	0
FATEA	4	0	0	4	FATEA	0	0	0	0
URG	0	1	1	2	URG	0	0	0	0
UFPE	0	0	2	2	UFPE	0	0	0	0
UFMG	5	1	5	11	UFMG	0	0	0	0
EBDSC	1	0	2	3	EBDSC	0	0	0	0
UFPR	1	0	0	1	UFPR	0	0	0	0
UFGO	0	0	0	0	UFGO	1	0	0	1
UFBA	1	1	0	2	UFBA	1	0	0	1
FATEMA	0	0	1	1	FATEMA	0	0	1	1
USP	0	0	0	0	USP	2	2	0	4
PUCCAMP	1	2	0	3	PUCCAMP	0	0	0	0
UNESP	0	2	0	2	UNESP	0	0	0	0
Total	13	7	12	32	Total	4	2	1	7

were compatible with the IBM-PC-XT; in 1989, 250,000 such machines were reported to exist in the country. At present IBM-PC-AT compatibles based on the 80286 chip are becoming more common, but those based on the 80386 and 80486 chips are still rare.

Only 3 institutions were found to have 8-bit equipment (5 machines, of which 4 are Apple compatible). Use is shared with administrative staff in 2 cases (UNB and UFBA) and with courses not offered by the Library Department in 2 cases (UFBA and PUCCAMP). Table 3 shows the availability of such equipment in the surveyed institutions.

The relative scarcity of 8-bit equipment probably indicates that the majority of the schools were only able to acquire computer equipment after 16-bit machines were introduced.

Eleven schools have 16-bit equipment (53 machines, of which 51 are IBM-PC-XT compatible). Use is shared with courses not offered by the Library Department in 7 cases and with administrative staff in 4 cases, as represented in table 4.

Table 5 presents information on peripherals used with 16-bit equipment, as well as other lines of equipment.

Available Software

Articles on software in the surveyed literature often describe (and rarely discuss) experiences at the institutional level, and sometimes concentrate on describing specific programs. Attempts to answer the question "What software should be taught?" have yet to produce a comprehensive list of relevant programs or program categories.

In her reflection on computer training for librarians, Paranhos[12] divides the syllabi of courses in that subfield into two sections: one theoretical and one experimental. She believes that in the first section the basic notions of data processing and data processing equipment should be taught, with an emphasis on word processing. The second section should be dedicated to practical demonstrations of library applications of computers. In both there is a need for adequate attention to hardware and software.

Microcomputers were not as widely disseminated at the time she wrote her article as they are now. Despite the differences in scale of production between Brazil and other computer-producing countries, and the negative effects of the Lei de Política Nacional de Informática—the associated effect of which caused locally produced computers to cost up to ten times as much as similar models in the United States—it is no longer possible for library schools to disregard the need to own at least one microcomputer for student use. As this

Table 3. Availability of 8-Bit Equipment

Institution	Quantity	Quantity of printers	Quantity of 5¼" disk drives	Quantity of modems	Quantity of CPM cards	Quantity of memory cards	Capacity of each memory card	Quantity of 80-column video cards
UNB	3	1	6	1	2	2	64	2
UFBA	1	1	2	1	0	0	0	0
PUCCAMP	1	0	0	0	0	0	0	0
Total	5	2	8	2	2	2	–	2

Table 4. Availability of 16-Bit Equipment and Form of Its Use

Institution	Quantity	IBM-PC-XT compatibles	IBM-PC-XT compatibles	Used solely by computer courses	Used jointly with		
					Other library department courses	Other department's courses	Adminis-tration
UNB	4	yes			yes	yes	yes
FATEA/SA	1	yes					yes
URG	2ᵃ	yes			yes		
	14ᵇ		yes			yes	
UFPE	1	yes			yes		
UFMG	7	yes			yes	yes	yes
EBDSC	1	yes			yes	yes	
UFBA	1	yes			yes	yes	yes
FATEMA	3	yes				yes	
USP	5	yes			yes	yes	
PUCCAMP	10ᵇ	yes		no	yes	yes	
	1ᵃ	yes		c	c	c	c
UNESP	2ᵇ	yes	yes		yes	yes	
	1ᵃ				yes	yes	
Total	53						

a. Equipment owned by the Library Science Department.
b. Equipment owned by the University's Computer Laboratory.
c. Form of use was not indicated.

Note: UFPR and UFGO were not included because they do not have any equipment.

Table 5. Peripherals Used with 16-Bit Equipment and Other Lines of Equipment

Institution	Dot matrix printers	3½" disk drives	5¼" disk drives	Hard disk drives	Capacity each hard drive	Modems	Mice	CD-ROM reader	Other peripherals	Other lines of equipment
UNB	2	0	8	0	0	0	0	0		2 terminals for the mainframe computer UNISYS A-9
FATEA/SA	1	0	1	1	30	0	0	0		
URG	1	0	4	2	30	1	0	0		Terminals for the mainframe IBM 4381 (on-line access to databases)
	3	0	28	3	40	0	0	0		Terminals for the mainframe IBM 4381 (on-line access to databases)
UFPE	1	0	2	0	0	0	0	0		
UFMG	not indicated	0	not indicated	5	15[a]	0	0	1	1 data show	IBM terminal and Digirede 8000 super-micro
EBDSC	1	0	2	0	0	0	0	0		
UFBA	0	0	2	1	30	[b]	0	0		

Table 5 (cont.)

Institution	Dot matrix printers	3½" disk drives	5¼" disk drives	Hard disk drives	Capacity each hard drive	Modems	Mice	CD-ROM reader	Other peripherals	Other lines of equipment
FATEMA	0	0	3	3	30	0	0	0		
USP	5	0	5	5	20	0	0	0		
PUCCAMP	5	10	0	0	0	0	0	0		
UNESP	1	0	4	0	0	0	0	0		
	1	0	1	1	20	1	1	0		
Total										

a. Besides the indicated 15 Mb hard disk drive, there are one with 20 Mb and three with 40 Mb each.
b. Quantity was not specified.

survey shows, most schools have chosen (or only managed to buy) the same equipment as the majority of the country's computer users: 16-bit IBM-PC-XT compatibles. But the question of what software to teach still remains unanswered.

It is impossible to know precisely what the job market needs owing to the lack of definition in Brazilian library schools concerning the type of professional needed. However, many courses have already been developed, and it is time to reflect upon experience. Besides word processing software, which professionals in any area need to understand, it is no longer possible to educate librarians who do not know at least: (a) one operating system compatible with available hardware; (b) one utility program for floppy and hard disk management; (c) one utility program for diagnosis and elimination of computer viruses; (d) one database management program for cataloging and retrieval of information about the collection and the users; (e) one spreadsheet for administrative applications; (f) one desktop publishing software at basic level to assist in editing library publications.

Ideally, instructors should also strive to have students experiment with: (a) computer-assisted construction of thesauri, through the use of advanced functions of word processing software or of specific programs; (b) access to online and/or optical disk databases, which requires additional equipment. Additionally, librarians who dedicate themselves to research might need to learn how to operate statistics programs.

Given the growing availability of software in the market, it seems advisable to stop teaching pure programming languages at the undergraduate level, in favor of teaching the programming languages available in some database and word processing software. Table 6 presents the types of software taught by the surveyed institutions.

No studies are available that cover the whole of the country's software market. It is common to hear that if one adds the percentage shares that each company claims to have, totals always reach over 100 percent. From what little information is available, it can be said that library schools reproduce the overall market situation in two software categories: database management and spreadsheets.

DBase III leads in the first category, as it does in the general Brazilian market. However, it is closely followed by UNESCO's Micro-CDS/Isis, which has gained increased penetration in the library market due to its free distribution by IBICT, the Instituto Brasileiro de Informação em Ciência e Tecnologia (interested institutions only have to pay postage fees). Lotus 1-2-3 is the leading spreadsheet, as it is in the general market.

Table 6. Types of Software Taught

Database management		Spreadsheets		Word processors		On-line retrieval		Desktop publishing	
DBase	7	Lotus 1-2-3	4	MS-Word	7	Biblio	1	News	1
Micro-Isis	5	Quattro	1	Wordstar	6	MSIBMPC	1		
Procite	2	Visicalc	1	Redator	2	MSPCTRAN	1		
Stairs	2					SIURG	1		
REFBIB	1					STM	1		
SRI	1								
Other	1								

Operating systems		Others	Programming languages		Utility programs	
MS-DOS	2	Matriz-Catalogação	Basic	1	PCTools	2
PC-DOS	1	Microstat	Cobol	1	CopyII PC	1
Sisne Plus1	1	PC-Produção Científica	DBase	1	SCAN67	1
		SPSS	Fortran	1		
		Tecer	Pascal	1		
			Other	1		

Note: The numbers in each column present the number of institutions that teach each program.

It is common knowledge among computer specialists that the use of disk management utilities warrants the safe storage of data on hard or floppy disks, allowing for more speed and ease of use in file organization, and extending the life of disk drives. It is also widely accepted that programs for diagnosing and eliminating computer viruses prevent logical damage to files (which can imply partial or total loss of stored information) and physical damage to equipment, repair can be extremely costly. It is thus a matter of concern that only 2 schools teach disk management utilities, and only 1 teaches virus diagnosis utilities.

It should also be noted that only 4 institutions teach on-line access to databases, and 2 of those programs are taught by the same school. The only institution to have an optical disk reader did not indicate which databases are used.

Preliminary Conclusions

The analysis of data shows that library schools in Brazil follow two different trends in computer training.

The first, and major trend (9 out of 13 schools or 69.2 percent), bases training on specific courses, where computers figure as the main element. Courses are not interrelated (i.e., they rarely are prerequisites for others despite often being mandatory). Contents comprise a definition of data processing, some basic notions on its history and development, computers and their functioning, software and programming languages.

The second and minor trend (3 of 13 schools or 23.1 percent) bases training on generic courses, opting for the presentation of computers as one of the existing resources for doing library and information work. Contents focus on the study of library techniques (cataloging, subject analysis, and so on) and make use of computers as a work tool. One school (7.7 percent) balances the two trends and offers the same number of generic and specific courses.

In reality, the two trends reflect old quandaries of Brazilian library education: technical training *vs.* critical education; conservativeness *vs.* adaptability to change; ideals and mystification *vs.* real necessities; an integrated curriculum *vs.* a curriculum divided into tight compartments that do not relate to each other in either theory or practice. The question remains the same: how to structure a computer course for librarians?

Most institutions surveyed seem to have opted for concentrating and individualizing teaching in the area. Some universities offer introductory courses on computers taught at Engineering or

Mathematics schools by instructors qualified in those fields. Others have preferred to integrate such courses into their curricula and have attracted engineers and systems analysts to be responsible for instruction. Most of the other courses on library applications of computers are taught by instructors who only hold a library degree.

For McCarthy, "a preocupação primordial deveria ser para a implantação de um ensino eficaz na área da automação de bibliotecas," and he defines two different teaching fields according to professional activities: automated cataloging and retrieval of information from databases.[13] He believes that the two fields are large and diverse enough to justify their being taught as "duas disciplinas distintas."[14]

Fujino proposes that "a profissão e consequentemente o profissional seja definido a partir das necessidades e potencialidades do mercado, adequando a sua formação a estas necessidades e potencialidades."[15] Differing from McCarthy, she believes that

o curso de biblioteconomia deveria assentar-se sobre duas linhas básicas: -- a primeira que lhe possibilitaria uma visão macro de seu universo, através do conteúdo das disciplinas básicas da área de planejamento/organização/administração; -- a segunda que lhe possibilitaria um domínio sobre o seu objeto de trabalho "a informação," através do conteúdo das disciplinas básicas da área de análise documentária.[16]

Computer training becomes thus a "complementação de conteúdos" of the basic courses.[17]

For Barsotti, "ao bibliotecário não interessa a Informática pura e conceitual," but "sua aplicação na área. Em outras palavras: a Informática deve ser um meio para o bibliotecário e não um fim."[18] Along that line, integration of the various courses of the library program can be attained by having training in the use of computers as a common element among them. "Isto se justifica pelo simples fato de que todas as disciplinas básicas do curso devem incorporar doses de Informática que podem chegar inclusive a modificar o perfil de muitas delas."[19]

That line of thought can also be observed in Robredo: when describing the experience of the Universidade de Brasília, he states that automated systems are used as "instrumentos de apoio para o ensino de diversas disciplinas."[20]

Some authors propose the possibility of qualitative change in professional education with the inclusion of computer training in library programs. However, training in the use of new technology cannot bring structural change on its own—nor can it transform the social role or the image of librarians.

According to Miranda, "Mas o ensino, em geral, ainda é conservador e não assumiu plenamente o desafio colocado pela revolução tecnológica, iniciada pela indústria da informação de nossos dias, em escala internacional."[21] This statement can be extended in two ways: first by analyzing the contents of the courses regarding scope, approach, bibliography, and so forth; second by analyzing the form of the programs regarding curricular structure, connections between courses, educational resources, and teaching methods.

If the adoption of new technology by society changes the relationships between people, institutions and work, it can act as an element to transform teaching and training relationships. However, experiences of the schools from the inception of the new 1985 minimum national curriculum have not yet been sufficiently examined and analyzed. It is thus impossible to evaluate performance and results at this point. It is hoped that the questions that were raised and the data that were presented here will make it possible for the subject to be studied in more depth.

Final Considerations

The transformations in the economic, social, and technological systems require changes in professional activities and profiles. The need for changes in library education and professional performance is unquestionable, and change is the only way for the profession to progress. After a long period of debate, librarians in Brazil have finally reached a consensus regarding the need to integrate the area into productive and social systems. What remains to be done is to propose and to discuss policies of professional action and education—and it cannot be done without an understanding of scientific and technological development, Brazilian geopolitics, economic conditions, the job market, and the needs of the scientific and professional communities.

In keeping with the political and historical view, it is possible to study library education in its multiple dimensions, beginning with its structure, facets, and problems. The understanding of the development of computer training for librarians in Brazil is the main contribution of these first analyses. From the organization and analysis of data it was possible to outline the theme and to indicate its fundamental problems. The results point to an effective approach to the subject and its debate, establishing a basis for future comparative studies. This core of information presents complex interdisciplinary relationships that address the points below:

Professional Skills and the Job Market

Although professional skills and the job market are both subjects that are identified frequently in the literature as parameters to teaching, there are no extensive or timely studies on the state and on the professional demands of the information and computer markets. The same is true of the professional skills currently required of librarians. Many authors subordinate education to market needs, and curriculum changes have been made in conformity with that view. However, there is no evidence that either institutions or researchers have approached these themes scientifically. [22] Considerations of the job market, professional skills, and their transformation are only made through inference. The need is clear to know both the market and its professionals broadly and deeply. Because of their wide applications to library science as a whole, those subjects could form an independent project to address: What kind of information professionals does the job market need in Brazil today? and What are the skills required of the modern librarian?

Professional Education

What kind of professionals are presently being educated in the country? Are they qualified to meet the requirements of society? These questions are closely linked to those raised above on the job market. The intention here is to evaluate the degree of professional capacity of the librarian as well as the adequacy of education in relation to the market.

The data in this report show that Brazilian library schools have opted to provide students with a basic knowledge of computer science and library automation through specialized courses. At the undergraduate level, the contents of such courses are generally homogeneous both in breadth and in depth; educational methods remain traditional, with few possibilities for training in real work conditions. Therefore, it is correct to state that the librarian holding an undergraduate degree in Brazil nowadays has notions on computer science and its applications in information services—notions of the same level of other courses, such as cataloging and reference service. This professional still is a "general librarian" (one with no specialization in any particular subject) and is also a technician (one who is instructed on library techniques).

No evaluation of courses at the graduate and specialization levels was possible, since there was no access to their syllabi. Further considerations on the curriculum and its contents will be approached in a future phase of this study.

Qualification of Faculty

To identify faculty qualified both in computer science and library science has become an essential problem for library schools. The efficient development of those programs depends on faculty profiles, their qualification, and potential for teaching. Library schools have found different solutions for this problem: from the recruitment of instructors from the computer science area to the training of their library science faculty in that field. Common projects occur that bring together both kinds of instructors, but the majority of faculty carry out their activities independently as much from professional cooperation as from the program itself. It is supposed that on one side an excessively technical orientation to computers predominates, and on the other a restricted view of library work prevails. These conditions lead to compartmentalized teaching and learning. In rare cases, the computer instructor holds a double qualification that gives learning a broader as well as more detailed view of the subject.

Some authors have discussed faculty preparation and stressed the need for an equilibrium of both areas. The quality of faculty is a major determinant in the educational process; however, it has not received enough attention from schools. There is no effective orientation to the development and implementation of the curriculum in the classroom; there are no official statements on faculty skills (in relation either to field of specialization or ability to teach); there are no consensual and objective forms for evaluating faculty performance; there are no satisfactory conditions for the academic career (salary, promotion, resources). It is a serious problem, which is also linked to the questions raised above. Some aspects have also been regarded at times as matters for political action (career, for instance). This study intends to promote an active debate that involves the discussion of faculty skills in the context of the establishment of a policy for library education.

Educational Policy

The development of an educational policy is the most important project for library science in Brazil. It means establishing basic guidelines on professional education that can be used as parameters by Brazilian library programs at different levels—an outline of general statements that support fundamental needs and allow for diversified actions according to regional requirements.

A policy on computer training for librarians should be subordinate to a broader policy on library education. As such, it should be established from an accurate knowledge of the job market and of the information needs of users and should be in accord with the overall scientific, technological, and educational policies of the country. It should propose specific policies and suggest contents and programs. It should outline the main skills required of faculty. Finally, it should serve as a tool for designing academic activities, and at the same time provide a basis for political action.

Basic directives should guarantee minimal resources for adequate operation of the programs (faculty, administrative staff, equipment, facilities); they should require regular evaluation of programs, as well as promoting continuing education and research in the area (from market conditions to the development of software).

The Project: Proposals for Continuity

The job market, professional skills and education, faculty preparation, educational policy: these are the main topics that emerge from this report on computer training in Brazilian library schools. Research on this matter should have continuity, depending, however, on the availability of institutional and financial support. A description of some local experiences will be of interest, particularly those of the Universidade de Brasília and the Universidade Federal de Minas Gerais.

The next phase should include: (a) the active involvement of more schools; (b) checking of some inconsistencies in answers; (c) a detailed study and comparison of course syllabi; and (d) preparation of criteria for the evaluation of programs.

The present and future results should become the basis for discussion of courses by library educators, for dissemination of experiences, for evaluation of diverse institutional realities, and also for the establishment of educational and research policies.

NOTES

1. Suzana Pinheiro Machado, Mueller, "O ensino de biblioteconomia no Brasil," *Ciência da Informação* 14, 1 (January/June 1985), 8.

2. Hagar Espanha Gomes, "Experiência do IBBD em programas de pós-graduação," *Revista da Escola de Biblioteconomia da UFMG* 3, 1 (March 1974), as quoted in ibid.

3. Antonio Agenor Briquet de Lemos, "Estado atual do ensino da biblioteconomia no Brasil e a questão da ciência da informação," *Revista de Biblioteconomia de Brasília* 1, 1 (January/June 1973), 55.

4. Ibid., p. 56.

5. Ibid., p. 54.

6. *Proposta de currículo mínimo de biblioteconomia* (Brasília: MEC/Secretaria de Ensino Superior, 1981). Documento produzido pelo Grupo de Trabalho reunido no período de 24 a 28 de novembro de 1980, as quoted in Suzana Pinheiro Machado

Mueller, "Avaliação do estado da arte da formação em biblioteconomia e ciência da informação," *Ciência da Informação* 17, 1 (January/June 1988), 76.

7. Mueller, 1988, p. 74.

8. Ibid., p. 79.

9. Irati Antonio, "Do bibliotecário ao agente da informação: seu perfil diante de novas tecnologias," *Revista Brasileira de Biblioteconomia e Documentação* 24, 1/2 (January/June 1991), xx.

10. Kira Tarapanoff, Silvia H. L. Santiago, and Dauí A. Corrêa, "Características e tendências do profissional da informação," *Revista Brasileira de Biblioteconomia e Documentação* 21, 3/4 (July/December 1988), 75-76.

11. Cordélia Robalinho Cavalcanti, "Ensino de informática na formação de bibliotecários," *Revista de Biblioteconomia de Brasília* 13, 1 (January/June 1985), 137.

12. W. M. M. Paranhos, "Reflexões sobre o ensino de informática para bibliotecários," *Revista de Biblioteconomia de Brasília* 13, 2 (July/December 1985), 182.

13. Cavan Michael McCarthy, "Direções no ensino de automação em bibliotecas: a definição de estratégias para uma época de mudança," *Cadernos de Biblioteconomia* 10 (1988), 119-120.

14. Ibid., p. 121.

15. Asa Fujino, "O ensino de informática no curso de biblioteconomia: algumas considerações," *Palavra-Chave* 6 (May 1987), 3.

16. Ibid.

17. Ibid., p. 4.

18. Roberto Barsotti, "A informática no ensino de biblioteconomia: depoimento de um ex-professor da ECA/USP e FATEA," *Revista Brasileira de Biblioteconomia e Documentação* 22, 1/2 (January/June 1989), 116.

19. Ibid., p. 117.

20. Jaime Robredo, "Uma experiência de aplicação do computador no ensino de biblioteconomia e ciência da informação," *Revista Brasileira de Biblioteconomia e Documentação* 16, 3/4 (July/December 1983), 9-10.

21. Antonio Miranda et al., "Informática, sistema de informação e ensino de biblioteconomia no Brasil: o caso da Universidade de Brasília," *Revista da Escola de Biblioteconomia da UFMG* 15, 1 (March 1986), 89.

22. Jaime Robredo, "Tendências observadas no mercado de trabalho dos bibliotecários e técnicos da informação, nas bibliotecas especializadas do Distrito Federal, e qualificações requeridas," *Revista de Biblioteconomia de Brasília* 12, 2 (1984), 123-147, a survey on the job market for special librarians.

35. A Regional Database for the Brazilian Northeast

Cavan M. McCarthy

Local publishing is a major channel for preserving and spreading regional culture. Data on book production in the state of Pernambuco, Brazil were obtained by a team of ten library school students who visited organizations of all types in Recife which publish books and took details of any item issued in the five years from 1980 to 1984. Over 1,300 books and pamphlets were recorded from more than fifty sources. The information was registered in a database on a PC-XT compatible microcomputer, using PRO-CITE software and a format specifically developed for local publications. Data for 1981 were revised and indexed, permitting detailed statistical analysis.

Introduction

The book continues to be one of the most effective means of transmitting knowledge and culture. This is especially true in Northeast Brazil, which has a rich literary tradition. All types of publication are issued there, from the traditional poetry pamphlets known as "literatura de cordel" (10), short stories, poetry, and historical texts, to the reports and planning documents necessary for regional development. The visitor to any reasonably sized bookshop will observe a variety of books and pamphlets from local publishers, authors, and institutions; many deal with subjects of wide interest. Any sizable city will have several institutions for research, planning, or development which produce research documents in significant quantities. Despite this, there is a strong tendency in Brazil to treat books as a product of Rio de Janeiro and São Paulo. Laurence Hallewell began a chapter of his *Books in Brazil* with a comment from Moreira Campesinos: "Publishing a book in the provinces is dropping a stone down a well" (3). All states and regions of Brazil traditionally publish books, but this activity is scattered over a huge geographic area, and materials are rarely available outside the state where they were published (8). No research into local

---

Editor's Note: The numbers in parentheses refer to the numbered entries in the Bibliography.

369

publishing is being done, nor is there encouragement for regional authors and publishers, despite a general feeling at grassroots level that these activities deserve support (2, 4, 7).

The Department of Librarianship of the Federal University of Pernambuco, Recife, considered that a systematic survey of local publications would be a valuable project, encouraging teachers and students to support local cultural activities. There is currently much interest in setting up databases in Brazil, because microcomputers are beginning to have a significant impact on the activities of library professionals; this project would provide relevant experience. Database software also permits the rapid analysis of the elements recorded. The survey had the additional objective of recording "fringe" or "gray" literature, documents which are not normally preserved in larger libraries or registered in general bibliographies. It appeared that such materials were being published in significant quantities, but they had never been systematically studied.

Fieldwork

I coordinated this project with the assistance of other professors, students, and graduate assistants, during 1986-1989. Preliminary stages included conducting a literature search and compiling a preliminary list of local publishers. A form was designed so that researchers could describe local publications quickly and systematically, and detailed instructions for participants were drawn up. Ten student librarians, working in pairs, were selected and trained for the fieldwork, which lasted a month, in 1986. By going directly to the source of local materials, it was considered the students would be able to register the largest possible number of publications. All institutions in Recife and nearby cities which publish books or pamphlets were visited, and all items issued in the years 1980–1984 were recorded. This period was chosen because publications should still be available in their organizations of origin; a five-year period would reveal a significant quantity of material; a future survey could complete a decade. "Book" was defined as widely as possible: monographic publications of eight pages or more, including popular poetry pamphlets (frequently of eight pages), reports from research or planning institutions, items produced by mimeo or photocopy, published by any organization or person. Principal exclusions were newspapers, magazines, commercial lists and catalogs, teaching texts, "handouts" or similar compilations for students, and items printed for internal use. The participants were generally welcomed by the organizations they visited. The most serious problem at this stage was that many institutions did not permanently file copies of their publications, or they kept bibliographic materials in disorganized or insecure conditions. During the fieldwork the team registered no fewer than 1,332 books and pamphlets published in Pernambuco state in 1980–1984, almost twice what had been expected. After a rapid statistical analysis preliminary results were publicized locally (1).

Setting up the Database

In 1987 the file was revised and some additional items registered. A Brazilian PC-XT compatible microcomputer was installed in the Department, and a review copy of PRO-CITE, a software package developed in Ann Arbor for bibliographic databases, was received. This system includes preset formats for a wide variety of bibliographic materials and also permits the user to set up formats for special purposes. After testing the package, a special format was designed for regional publishing, combining an entry in AACR/ISBD style with additional data about local publishing. This offered good compatibility with MARC formats and also permitted the registration of the state of birth and residence of authors of local books, number of copies, production method, and so on. (See Appendix for sample entries.) On one hand the keyboarding was easy, because in PRO-CITE any field will accept any quantity of any character, as long as there is sufficient space in memory. On the other hand, data entry was slowed considerably by the inclusion of accents and cedillas. Portuguese uses these in abundance, and it was necessary to enter a three-digit code to register each one. The letter was printed correctly, but a different form appeared on the screen of the microcomputer. One of the principal objectives of the project was to support and encourage local publishing; it was thus important that the final product should be well produced. Therefore the database used accents and cedillas, even though this caused significant difficulties in entering and checking the data. This type of problem is very common in microcomputing in Brazil.

In 1988 the remaining data were keyed in and some additional items were also included, from the interior of the state, via mail. A careful examination of the file, unfortunately, turned up some unexpected problems. It had been generally believed that the bibliographic descriptions were complete and accurate, because the data collection had been carefully organized. In fact, major problems began to emerge. Library school students had frequently been unable to specify the subject of the books, leaving the project coordinator to decide how to index titles such as *Reflecting on Methodology* or *The Desert and the Numbers*. Semilegible student handwriting caused constant problems. Students had been trained simply to transcribe information, but data were only partly transcribed, and some into a form that a library school student considered correct. Transcription itself could cause problems; it is difficult to distinguish between one text with two authors, title, and subtitle and two texts published in the same volume. It was possible to confuse the state-level Education Secretariat with its municipal equivalent. The basic approach of the project, visiting publishers and copying data on paper forms, on the one hand enabled the team to register a large amount of material in a relatively short time. On the other hand, it made it difficult to verify data at a later stage.

Problems owing to a lack of confidence in the information collected exist in surveys of all types, but are especially acute in databases. In "classic" studies in the social sciences, the final results appear in condensed, tabular form. Even if all the data were published, this would be done anonymously and it would be difficult to identify errors of transcription, keyboarding, and so on. But in database projects, all the information is published and informed readers will rapidly identify errors. Certain errors, such as spelling the name of a local author incorrectly or describing a poetry book as a novel, can provoke criticism from the very people whose work is being publicized. The methodology used, having students fill out paper forms while visiting publishers, did not generate error-free results.

A further problem arose because the detailed examination showed that the results were in fact not representative of local publishing, especially in terms of peripheral and minor documents. The term "gray documentation" is used for this peripheral material; one of the principal objectives of the project was to register items of this type. It became clear that certain organizations had offered a wide range of materials, whereas others did not appear in the database. Certain university departments contributed many documents, whereas others, known for their publishing, had not collaborated. This phenomenon was called the "Barrier of the Secretary." Participants in surveys of this type normally meet with a clerk or a secretary. If this contact states that the department or government office does not produce anything relevant, the researcher will go on to the next address. The chosen methodology was also unable to register publishing done directly by the author. In the specific case of 1980-1984, this had little impact, because most items issued directly by the author are poetry books, and there was an extremely active poetry publisher in Pernambuco at that time. Some items were not registered because their publishers had not kept file copies. An absolutely complete survey would probably expand the database by 20 percent to a third.

The opposite problem arose with teaching texts, "handouts," or compilations produced for student use. These are very common in Brazil, and the original intention was to omit such documents. But one course that prepares students for university entry published texts presented just like books from a commercial publisher; they even had an imprint which was different from the name of the course. In other institutions the student texts were easily identified, but one local university occasionally published a text of general interest in the same series as its teaching texts. Theses were also excluded from the survey. At least one department of the Federal University normally mimeographed multiple copies of defended theses.

The original intention was to set up a database that would hold all entries for the five-year period in a single sequence. Unfortunately, the project coincided with a period of decreased funding for Brazilian universities, and equipment with adequate memory was not installed. It was therefore not possible either to create or index a single sequence of all the entries. It was decided that it would be best to revise, check, and exhaustively index one year of the file. The data for 1981, 282 items, were thoroughly indexed on a variety of fields, generating a printout with a total of 316 pages which serves as a practical example of the value of PRO-CITE (7). The indexing was also analyzed to obtain a statistical analysis of the topics covered by books published in Pernambuco.

Even limiting the checking to one year, the process of revising the file was lengthy. PRO-CITE is an extremely safe system; operating in an environment where power cuts are common, no data were lost throughout the entire project, because the software saves the content of each entry before going on to the next. But this same security feature means that making minor changes in a large number of entries is a tiresome process. It is essential to plan database activities carefully so that data can be keyboarded correctly and easily first time around, avoiding later modifications. This, however, is not always possible in real life; in this project the data were collected before the computer and the software arrived.

The inclusion of accented letters continued to cause problems. A small number of entries with accents in the name of the author or at the beginning of the title filed out of order in the printout. Brazilian compound surnames, for example, "Medeiros Filho, João," also caused problems. The solution was to create a special field to hold the data in appropriate form (omitting accents or suffixes such as "Filho") and to use this field to organize the file in alphabetical order. This had to be done for 16 entries or 5.67 percent of the file. It was only possible to get a listing in perfect alphabetical order on the sixth printout. Similar problems arose with index terms; here a different solution was adopted: all accents and cedillas were taken out. Index terms were printed in capitals when printouts in index term order were made, and this was visually acceptable.

Statistical Analysis of Book Production in Pernambuco

The database now contains a total of 1,382 monographs (publication dates are specified in table 1). The state of Pernambuco published an average of 276 books and pamphlets per year in 1980–1984, or more than one item each working day. This is a significant figure for a medium-sized state in the Northeast region; the author considers it probable that other states in the region would show similar statistics. It was clearly confirmed that regional publishing is an important feature of local culture.

Table 1. Books and Pamphlets Published in Pernambuco
and Registered in the Database, by Year of Publication

Year	Items registered
1980	232
1981	282
1982	301
1983	246
1984	227
Not dated, but known to have been published between 1980 and 1984	94
Total	1,382

The publications of a single year, 1981, were checked, indexed, and analyzed in depth. The text that follows is based on the analysis, by PRO-CITE software, of the 282 books registered for this year.

Place of birth was registered for 60 items. Thirty-seven (66.66 percent) were written by authors born in Pernambuco. The authors of nine other titles came from Paraíba, Alagoas, and Ceará, states that share long borders with Pernambuco. Three other states from the Northeast appeared here with one author each, and therefore a total of 49 items (81.66 percent) were by writers born in the region. Ten authors were from other states and one from overseas. These results show that regional publishing is an important channel for the communication of local culture. The survey included similar data on the state of residence of authors. Here the concentration was even greater: it was rare for a nonresident to publish a book in Pernambuco. Of the total of 52 items for which this information was registered, 47 (90.38 percent) of the authors were residents of Pernambuco state. Combining this with the well-known tendency of local publishers not to distribute their books to other states, the conclusion is that local publishing is basically limited to residents of the same state.

Recife, the state capital, naturally dominated the book production of the state, appearing as the place of publication of 253 items. Twenty-five agricultural research documents were published in Petrolina, while Caruaru, a traditional center for *cordel* literature, contributed eight items.   Co-editions were not common; only one example was registered in this year, between publishers in São Paulo and Pernambuco.

A publisher was registered for 275 items (97.5 percent). Major publishers are shown in table 2.

Table 2. Publishers Responsible for Three Items or More, 1981

Publisher	Number of items
Pirata (poetry and short stories)	43
Universidade Federal de Pernambuco	39
CNBB (pastoral documents)	28
Liber (course for university entry)	25
FIDEM (urban planning)	23
Secretaria de Educação	18
CPATSA (agricultural research)	15
SUDENE (regional development)	10
EMATER-PE (agricultural extension)	8
IPA (agricultural research)	7
CONDEPE (state-level planning)	6
Fundação de Cultura Cidade do Recife (local culture)	6
Massangana (regional culture)	6
Casa das Crianças (cordel)	5
Conselho Municipal de Cultura	4
FIDEPE (state-level planning)	4
Guararapes (regional culture)	3

The most obvious feature of this table is the variety in publishers it demonstrates: government agencies, agricultural research and extension institutes, cultural and religious organizations, a university, and publishers of textbooks and poetry. The smallest publisher listed, Guararapes, represents the last attempt to set up a commercial publisher in Recife and was cited by Laurence Hallewell (3). This publisher no longer exists, nor does the publisher that heads the list, Pirata. The same fate overtook the CNBB, the organization that represents Roman Catholic bishops. The Pernambuco branch used to publish numerous pastoral documents, mimeographed texts to take the church's teachings to the masses. When progressive Archbishop Helder Câmara was replaced by a conservative successor, this activity ceased abruptly. Publishing was concentrated in relatively few organizations; the four major sources of books and pamphlets were responsible for almost half the publications. The complete results showed that 16 organizations published one item each in this year.

The method of production was registered for 263 items. Offset was the commonest printing method used, for 147 items (55.89 percent). This shows that relatively modern equipment is available in Recife. Traditional printing from metal type was second, with 50 books. The latest method of reproduction was almost catching up with metal type: 35 items were photocopied and 31 mimeographed. Each publisher or organization normally used one method only. The printing of 64 items had been contracted out, while 173 items came from internal printshops. (The database included a significant number of documents produced internally by mimeograph, photocopy, or offset.) The printshop was recorded for 55 of the items printed externally. There was even more concentration here than among publishers: two printers were responsible for more than half of these publications. Only 4 books printed outside Pernambuco were identified.

The publications on the survey were generally brief. Nearly half (135) consisted of 8 to 50 pages, with 15 or 16 pages the commonest size (cited 14 times). Only 17 items had more than 300 pages. The largest book, with 749 pages, was a compendium of economic analysis compiled by the state bank (see Appendix). The number of copies published was registered for 49 items, and these figures were also low. The commonest print run was 1,000 copies (cited 17 times), with 14 items (almost half those for which the number of copies was specified) in runs of less than 1,000 copies. The largest print run recorded was 5,000 copies, for a popular poetry pamphlet issued by Catholic bishops to inform cane cutters of their rights (see Appendix).

All the documents in the file for 1981 were carefully indexed, using two or three terms for each document. The most frequently used index terms offer a fascinating insight into the subjects of books published in Pernambuco (see table 3).

Table 3. Index Terms Applied to Two Items or More in
Books and Pamphlets Published in Pernambuco in 1981

Subject	Number of items[a]
Poetry	35
Agriculture	25
Textbooks	24
Pernambuco	20
Religion	20
Planning	20
Northeast	19
Education	18
Pastoral documents	18
History	15
Agronomy	13
Economy	12
Nuclear Energy	12
Cordel (popular poetry pamphlets)	9
Agricultural extension	9
Statistics	8
Water resources	8
Childrens literature	7
Irrigation	6

[a]Five items: Biology, Folklore, Health, Municipality, Short stories, Technology.

Four items: "Crônica" (brief prose text), Drought, Geography, Law, Legislation, Portuguese language, Recife, Rural worker, Sociology.

Three items: Agricultural research, Alcohol, Art, Chemistry, Corn, Earth, Ecology, Energy, English language, Exportation, Grapes, Mathematics, Medicine, Milk, Pests (Agriculture), Philosophy, Physics, River, Taxation, Water.

Two items: Agrarian reform, Bandits, Beach, Beans, Biography, Cattle, Coastal areas, Commerce, Drainage, Easter, Fisheries, Folklore dancing, Geology, Handicrafts, Historical archive, Income distribution, Industry, Insect, Literature, Literary criticism, Olinda, Maracatu (folkloric dance), Novel, Physical education, Research, Small and medium-sized industries, Soil conservation, Sorgum, Sugar cane, Tax on the circulation of merchandise, Tourism.

Local publishing is usually the only chance regional authors ever have to bring their work to the attention of the reading public. All large bookshops in the Northeast display numerous books of poetry, short stories, and fiction by local writers. In this survey poetry heads the list of subjects, with 35 titles. Other literary forms, such as cordel, short stories, and criticism are also included, to make a total of 54 index terms. Another common feature of regional publishing is that authors generally avoid novels.

The second subject term, by frequency of use, was agriculture (25 titles). This category is expanded to 77 when all the related terms are included, for example, agronomy, agricultural extension, rural worker, soil, grapes. Thus organizations responsible for agricultural research and extension are major producers of reports and documents.

Teaching texts represent the next most common type of publication. Pernambuco is one of the few states outside the Rio-São Paulo conurbations to have a commercial textbook publisher. Another medium-sized publisher is closely linked to a private course for university entrance. Most documents indexed by terms such as biology, mathematics, or physics are textbooks. It should also be noted that the total quantity of textbooks will be even greater because a high proportion of the 94 items published in this period, but without a specific publication date, were textbooks.

The term "Pernambuco" occupies fourth place in the list (20 items). The entire list shows a strong tendency toward local affairs, with 19 documents on the Northeast. Water resources, a major problem in the region, has 8 documents; other terms include irrigation, drought, and water. The more traditional features of the area are not neglected: folklore is the subject of 5 documents; handicrafts, banditry, folkloric dances, and tourism are also to be found. No fewer than 15 books were published on historical subjects. Catholicism is deeply rooted in the region, so it is no surprise to see 20 items dealing with religion, plus almost the same number of texts indexed as pastoral documents.

Searching for documentation about the more modern aspects of the Northeast, one finds planning (20 items), statistics, sociology, and ecology. Administrative aspects are evident in terms such as "legislation" and "taxation." Nuclear energy occupies a position of relative importance in the list; the Federal University of Pernambuco has an active Department of Nuclear Energy responsible for numerous publications.

Certain other elements registered in the database can be briefly mentioned. Most of the file, 172 items (60.99 percent), was made up of works written by individuals. This includes poetry, short stories, and research reports, documents typically cataloged by personal author. Corporate authors were responsible for 21 books or pamphlets, and 3 conference proceedings were registered. It was common to publish in series. Ninety such documents (31.92 percent of the file) were found, most technical reports. Nineteen works were issued as new editions; one local publication had even reached its eleventh edition (see Appendix). It was a surprise to find that Pernambuco issues occasional works in foreign languages, books for either language courses or the export trade; two items were recorded in this year. Nine books carried International Standard Book Numbers (ISBN).

Information about the method of distribution was collected for 208 books. In 84 cases the books were mainly given away. In 20 cases half were donated, half sold. For 104 items the publisher claimed that the majority of the copies had been sold. At first sight this would indicate that editors work along commercial lines, but the 104 books sold included 41 poetry books, items that traditionally sell slowly, if at all, and 20 pastoral documents mimeographed by the Catholic Church for sale to the masses at nominal prices. An additional 25 items were produced by a publisher linked to a specific university entrance course, student texts sold to a captive market. In fact commercial publishing is not a viable activity in Northeast Brazil.

Conclusions

Local publishing is a vital channel for the transmission of culture and knowledge in Brazil. A book or a pamphlet is issued every single working day in the state of Pernambuco, and this publishing is undertaken by a variety of organizations, representing all sectors of society. There is considerable concentration in this area: a few publishers and printers are responsible for the majority of the items issued. Both modern and traditional printing methods are used. In general the publications are brief and their print runs short, but there are some notable exceptions to this rule.

The indexing of the documents revealed that the subjects of local publications are relevant to the needs of the region. The agricultural foundations of the economy are solidly supported by an extensive publishing program that gives special attention to water resources and local crops. Traditional areas, such as literature, regional studies, history, and religion, are also supported. More modern activities linked to regional planning and administration, also generate documents, while one isolated area on the cutting edge of technological development is visible among local interests. The range of subjects faithfully reflects a society undergoing rapid change.

This study of local publishing was a major project, which lasted more than four years and reached important conclusions in an area devoid of systematic studies. A medium-sized database was created and analyzed. As it was a pioneering activity, this paper includes considerable discussion of the practical aspects of the project. It is essential to bear in mind that the setting up of a database is a complex operation that must be carefully planned. All elements should be thoroughly tested before quantities of data are collected. Thus the data collection instrument can coincide exactly with the format, which will generate output to fully support the objectives of the project. It is best to avoid the tedious process of making minor modifications after keyboarding. Unfortunately, under actual working conditions it is not always possible to follow these theoretical principles.

A small file is sufficient to show how a database works and to demonstrate indexing or information retrieval to library science students. Library school teaching does not require the manipulation of major databases. The creation of even a medium-sized database requires a major effort, not just to collect the data but also to keyboard and check it. Appropriate equipment is essential, including at least a microcomputer with ample hard disk storage, preferably supported by other micros for data entry, word processing of progress reports, and training. Graduate assistants need to be familiar with both library science and the use of microcomputers. The complexity of their training makes it advisable that they remain with the project for a significant period. It is, however, difficult to meet these conditions in the context of a Brazilian university during a recession.

The software currently available for databases does not work well with files that include a large number of accented letters, but Portuguese uses numerous accents. This is a major problem for all Brazilians involved with databases and word processing. Brazilian users of MICROISIS are advised not to use accents or cedillas. But if the final text omits these elements, Brazilian readers will consider the final product to be second-rate, and of low quality. In this project it became clear that accents and cedillas should only be used (1) if they can be keyboarded as on a typewriter; (2) if they appear correctly on both the screen and the printout; and (3) if accented and nonaccented letters are treated identically when put into alphabetical order. The combination of software, microcomputer, and printer to be used for a database should be tested in relation to these three points. Should it test negatively on two or three, it is better to omit accents. Accents can be considered if only one point causes problems. Even so, the decision should not be automatic: if the microcomputer does not sort the entries correctly into alphabetical order, and the project requires frequent printouts in alpha order, it would be best to omit accents.

One of the most important objectives of the project was to record specialized documents, pamphlet materials, "gray literature," and other publications not usually registered in bibliographies or preserved in libraries. In this the project succeeded: it was clearly shown that a large quantity of this material was being issued in the state of Pernambuco. Paradoxically, as the number of items registered increased, the database became less interesting for the general user, and it became more difficult to find the books and pamphlets in libraries. The bibliography was more complete, but it would be much more expensive to print and distribute. It was important that the information be as accurate as possible, but it was difficult to check the data, because the bibliographic information was noted by students during visits to organizations that publish books. This procedure permitted the participants to collect a considerable quantity of data in a short time. But when a bibliographic description was garbled or appeared to be incorrect it was not feasible to go back to verify the information. In a database project it is necessary to publish all the results; this situation is totally different from that of a typical project in the social sciences, where only an analysis of the data is published.

An alternative approach would be to abandon the attempt to register the totality of books and pamphlets, and to concentrate on items of general interest, available in larger libraries. The quantity of information would be reduced and the checking would be simplified. The final product would be easier to reproduce and more useful for the general public. This would be a bibliography, rather than a research project, but could have a greater impact while sparing the compilers some of the more tedious work. The mass of information collected about books in Pernambuco in 1980–1984 could form a basis for this new approach.

APPENDIX
Sample of the Database

This appendix contains a sample of entries from the database that show the variety of materials registered. All items specifically mentioned above were included, such as the pamphlet with the largest print run, the book with the largest number of pages, etc. The first part of each entry is similar to a catalog entry, for books with a personal author.

The second part commences with record numbers; the prefix (e.g., PE81-0297) is permanent, while the suffix (/275) is generated by the software and permits the rapid identification of individual items. This number can be changed if necessary. The entry ends with additional information relevant to local publishing; accents and cedillas were omitted.

Albuquerque, João Antônio Silva de.
    Comportamento da figueira (Ficus carica L.) : cultivar roxo de valinhos no Vale do São Francisco / João Antônio Silva de Albuquerque; Teresinha Costa Silveira de Albuquerque. -- Petrolina : CPATSA, 1981.
    19p. 22cm. (Boletim de pesquisa, 7).

    Número de registro: PE81-0279/275.
    Reprodução: offset. Distribuição: maioria gratuita. Registros bibliográficos: ISSN: 0100-8951. Nomes adicionais: Albuquerque, Teresinha Costa Silveira de. Indexação: Figueira/Agronomia.

Albuquerque, Nancy Lins.
    Ciclo do combustível nuclear : enriquecimento do urânio / Nancy Lins Albuquerque. -- Recife : UFPE, CT, Energia Nuclear, 1981.
    46f. il. 30cm. (Monografia, 15).

    Número de registro: PE81-0233/38.
    Folha de rosto: UFPE/Centro de Tecnologia/Departamento de Energia Nuclear. Reprodução: tradicional. Número de exemplares: 50. Distribuição: maioria gratuita. Indexação: Energia nuclear.

Alves, Antônio.
    História B2 / Antônio Alves. -- Recife : Liber, 1981.
    514p. il. 21cm.

    Número de registro: PE81-0221/50.
    Reprodução: offset. Distribuição: maioria vendida. Indexação: Historia/Texto didatico.

Análise setorial : indicadores econômico-financeiros, análises contábeis, 1980. -- Recife : BANDEPE, 1981.
    749p. il., gráf. 22cm.

Número de registro: PE81-0003/266.
Folha de rosto: Banco do Estado de Pernambuco: BANDEPE/ Governo do Estado de Pernambuco. Tipografia: Liceu, Recife. Reprodução: offset. Distribuição: maioria gratuita. Ordenação: Analise setorial indicadores economico financeiros analises contabeis. Indexação: Economia/Estatistica.

Andrade, Manuel Correia de.
Nordeste : a reforma agrária ainda é necessária? / Manuel Correia de Andrade. -- Recife : Guararapes, 1981.
119p. 21cm. (Cadernos Guararapes, 2).

Número de registro: PE81-0111/159.
Reprodução: offset. Indexação: Reforma agraria/Agricultura.

Areas prioritárias para implantação de programas habitacionais de interesse social. -- Recife : FIDEM, 1981.
55f. 30cm.

Número de registro: PE81-0007/262.
Folha de rosto: FIDEM. Ordenação: Areas prioritarias para implantacao de programas habitacionais de interesse social. Indexação: Habitacao popular/Moradia/Planejamento urbano.

Barros, Homero do Rêgo.
O atentado ao Santo Papa e sua repercussão / Homero do Rêgo Barros. -- Recife : 1981.
8p. 16cm.

Número de registro: PE81-0010/259.
Tipografia: Casa das Crianças, Olinda. Número de exemplares: 1000. Distribuição: maioria vendida. Naturalidade do autor: PE. Residência do autor: PE. Nomes adicionais: João Paulo II (Papa). Indexação: Cordel.

Brazilian handicraft from Pernambuco for export. -- Recife : Secretaria de Indústria, Comércio e Minas, 1981.
30p. il. col. 21cm.

Número de registro: PE81-0016/253.
Folha de rosto: Secretaria de Indústria, Comércio e Minas. Língua: inglesa. Tipografia: CEPE, Recife. Reprodução: offset. Distribuição: maioria gratuita. Indexação: Artesanato/Exportacao.

Carta aos trabalhadores da cana. -- Recife : CNBB, 1981.
15p. 21cm.

Número de registro: PE81-0021/248.
Folha de rosto: Centro de Defesa dos Direitos Humanos/Serviço de Documentação Popular/Pastoral da Juventude. Reprodução: tradicional. Número de exemplares: 5000. Distribuição: maioria vendida. Indexação: Trabalhador rural/Cana de acucar/Cordel.

Coelho, Duarte de Albuquerque.
Memórias diárias da Guerra do Brasil : 1630-1638 / Duarte de Albuquerque Coelho. -- 2a. ed. -- Recife : Fundação de Cultura Cidade do Recife, 1981.
395p. il. 23cm. (Coleção Recife, 12).

Número de registro: PE81-0103/167.
Tipografia: CEPE, Recife. Reprodução: tradicional. Distribuição: maioria vendida. Registros bibliográficos: ISBN: 85-7044-002-2. Indexação: Historia/Pernambuco/Holandeses em Pernambuco.

Como Padre Cícero queria combater a seca. -- Recife : CNBB, 1981.
20p. 21cm.

Número de registro: PE81-0032/237.
Folha de rosto: Serviço de Documentação e Informação Popular. Reprodução: mimeógrafo. Número de exemplares: 1000. Distribuição: maioria vendida. Nomes adicionais: Batista, Cícero Romão (Padre). Indexação: Extensao rural/Seca/Agricultura.

Mello, José Antônio Gonsalves de.
Um mascate e o Recife : a vida de Antônio Fernandes de Matos no período de 1671-1701 / José Antônio Gonsalves de Mello. -- 11a. ed. -- Recife : Fundação de Cultura Cidade do Recife, 1981.
140p. il. 23cm. (Coleção Recife, 9).

Número de registro: PE81-0193/78.
Tipografia: CEPE, Recife. Reprodução: tradicional. Distribuição: maioria vendida. Naturalidade do autor: PE. Indexação: Biografia/Historia/Pernambuco/Recife/.

BIBLIOGRAPHY

PRO-CITE software includes formats and rules for the presentation of all types of bibliographic materials. This bibliography was generated on PRO-CITE using the ANSI standards for bibliographic citations.

1. CARRERO, Raimundo. "Professor inglês faz levantamento de livros publicados em Pernambuco." *Diário de Pernambuco;* Recife; 04 de abril de 1987: B-1.

2. "EDITORES e autores debatem mercado regional de livros." *Nordeste Econômico;* Recife, nov. 1985; 16(11): 30.

3. HALLEWELL, Laurence. *Books in Brazil: A History of the Publishing Trade.* Metuchen, N.J.: Scarecrow Press; 1982; 485p.

4. JORGE NETO, Nagib. "Literatura aqui é heroísmo: e só." *Reclamo;* Recife, out. 1985; 1(1): 42-43.

5. "LIVRO: mercado em expansão." *Revista de Comunicação;* Rio de Janeiro, 1985; 1(3): 14-6.

6. "O LIVRO em Pernambuco: bibliografia preliminar dos livros publicados no Estado de Pernambuco no quinquênio 1980-1984." Recife; 1991; 329p. Computer printout.

7. "O LIVRO em Pernambuco: dimensionamento, controle bibliográfico e perspectivas: projeto de pesquisa...anexo 2 ao relatório da terceira fase: exemplos de indexação pelo PRO-CITE num arqivo de livros publicados no Estado de Pernambuco no ano de 1981. Recife, 1989." 316p. Research report for CNPq. Computer printout.

8. LUCAS, Fábio. *Crepúsculo dos símbolos: reflexões sobre o livro no Brasil.* Campinas, S.P.: Pontes; 1989; 124p. (Coleção Literatura-crítica).

9. McCARTHY, Cavan Michael. "PRO-CITE: um software para gerenciamento de bases de dados bibliográficos." Ci. Inf., *Brasília,* 18(2): 191-198, jul./dez. 1989.

10. McCARTHY, Cavan Michael. "Recent Political Events in Brazil as Reflected in Popular Poetry Pamphlets (literatura de cordel)." Charlottesville, VA: SALALM; 1989; 25p. Paper presented to the Thirty Fourth Seminar on the Acquisition of Latin American Library Materials, Charlottesville, Virginia, May 27 - June 1, 1989.

11. MESQUITA, Vianney. *Sobre livros: aspectos da editoração académica.* Fortaleza: UFC; 1984; 148p.

12. *PRO-CITE: User Manual.* Ann Arbor, MI: Personal Bibliographic Software; 1986?; (400p.) 1 vol. loose leaf.

13. "PROJETO de pesquisa: o livro em Pernambuco: dimensionamento, controle bibliográfico e perspectivas; relatório das atividades no ano de 1986." Recife; 1987; 49p. Research report for CNPq.

14. "PROJETO de pesquisa: o livro em Pernambuco: dimensionamento, controle bibliográfico e perspectivas; segunda fase: montagem de uma base de dados de livros pernambucanos em microcomputador nacional." Recife; 1988; 48p. Research report for CNPq.

15. "RELATÓRIO de projeto de pesquisa: o livro em Pernambuco: dimensionamento, controle bibliográfico e perspectivas; terceira fase: utilização e indexação de uma base de dados de livros pernambucanos." Recife; 1989; 47p. Research report for CNPq. p.36-44: anexo 1: "Campos utilizados no formato bibliográfico."

16. ROBREDO, Jaime. *Manual de editoração.* Brasília: Associação dos Bibliotecários do Distrito Federal; 1981; 158p.

17. "SECRETÁRIO da Cultura defende a implantação de indústria editorial." *Diário de Pernambuco,* Recife; 24 abr. 1986: A-11.

18. SMITH JR., Datus C. *The Economics of Book Publishing in Developing Countries.* Paris: UNESCO; 1977; 44p. (Reports and Papers on Mass Comunication; v. 79).

36. School Libraries in Brazil Facing the Twenty-First Century: New Formats

Paulo Tarcísio Mayrink

... se aqui a vida já é um artigo de luxo,
imagine então o que são os livros. — Lygia
Fagundes Telles, *Revista LEIAI*, April 1990

Brazilian school libraries suffer from a lack of librarians, the prevalance of outdated collections, and an inferior environment. Microcomputers are beginning to be used and educational technology is making possible the use of new formats. The accelerated development of new technology will permit school libraries in Brazil to have sophisticated formats and information services by the twenty-first century.

Introduction

Education in Brazil is supported by the government, with private participation at both the elementary and the university levels. The constitution guarantees education to people at all levels, but the state system of education has been so precarious that private initiative must frequently take over. Despite its shortcomings, the state education system, including federal, state, and city support, is larger than the private one.

Almost every state primary and secondary school has a library, although the staffing, collections, and physical facilities leave a lot to be desired.

In 1986 there were 161,858 primary schools throughout Brazil, with 18,564,481 students and 18,517 libraries. This averages to 1 library for every 1,002 students and a total of 143,331 schools without a library.[1]

Most of the schools have full-time professional and paraprofessional librarians appointed as senior teachers. In the remaining schools, release time from the classroom is granted for the teacher responsible for the library, at principal's discretion. Many schools do, however, allocate part of their auxiliary staff time to library work.

Some states in Brazil have established School Library Service Systems in order to encourage the sharing of resources and the networking of school libraries in the state or region. Such networks have centralized head offices and have two main goals: (1) to ensure that books and other resources are available to students and teachers, in support of the school curriculum; and (2) to provide information, culture, and entertainment to the community.

The School Library Collection and the New Formats

Brazilian school library collections, at present, are acceptable in size, and are composed basically of literature, educational materials, and reference books. More recently, educational videos have been added to the collections, and they are the only modern format that has reached the school libraries till now. They are, however, not yet available for loan. These collections need to be updated, and new technologies require a dynamic acquisitions program for new formats. In order to take the best advantage of this situation, school libraries in Brazil need first of all that the school librarian be properly trained to understand the new resources and to make them available to the users.

School libraries in Brazil do not yet have current serials in their collections, with the exception of some five or six titles on teaching skills. They generally lack local and regional newspapers, nor do they have a well-organized collection of clippings and pamphlets, very basic material that should not be excluded from such libraries.

Multimedia Materials

New and accelerated technological developments have brought radical changes in the availability of different types of media, as well as new demands for different types of resources. The school library must acquire such materials to be able to supply users with new information. Brazilian school libraries have no collections of phonograph records, video cassette tapes, microforms, or other kinds of media that are today very commonplace, such as slides or filmstrips. The revolution in new formats requires school libraries to jump from very traditional materials to the newest ones, therefore leapfrogging the intermediate formats that will soon be obsolete.

Some educators resist the use of media in schools, limiting their adoptions to reading programs, because of the country's high illiteracy rate. [2]

Educational Technology

Educational technology arrived in Brazil in the early 1970s, first conceived as teleducation and later extended to the activities related to wider educational innovations. Educational videotapes are available in many schools of some of the more developed states of the country, both in public and in private schools.

The next step will be the adoption of interactive educational videos, which permits individual participation in dissemination of information, called hypertexts, a complete database about a certain subject. In these databases, the orientation to teaching is through an autodidatic model at three levels simultaneously: picture, text, and audio.

Microcomputers are already used widely by private schools, many of which adopted the language LOGO, taken as a teaching methodology and educational philosophy. In these schools computers are viewed as a basic tool for the educational process.[3] Microcomputers have been used for teaching, especially through educational games that facilitate the construction, understanding, and enhancement of concepts. They are also used for tests, as text editors, or simply as calculator or typewriter to construct number tables, databases, and statistics packages, or for simulating phenomena and processes (chemical or physical reactions study, flight, or direction simulation, games, and the like).

Some research experiences related to the field of "author system" began to appear in Brazil by the 1980s. These included the CAIMI/SISCAI System, developed at the Federal University of Rio Grande do Sul, and the SAB (Brazilian Author System), presented as a Master's thesis at the Catholic University of Rio de Janeiro. In both of these educational software packages a multidisciplinary staff was involved, as a means of allowing more democratic access to the computer technology.[4]

Although the educational software used in Brazilian primary and secondary schools is at present more a question of potential than of reality, it will be quickly introduced as it develops and becomes readily available and understood.

By the twenty-first century, the evolution of information formats will necessarily reach Brazil and the school libraries will certainly have access to sophisticated devices such as those stimulated by voice and tactile reflex. These may also include other bibliographic and audiovisual formats that will be recorded by laser on paper.

NOTES

1. Walda A. Antunes, "A biblioteca na escola," in "Simpósio sobre biblioteca e desenvolvimento cultural," 3, presented at Bienal Internacional do Livro, 9, São Paulo, Brazil, August 25-27, 1986 (São Paulo, SP: Câmara Brasileira do Livro, 1986), 11 pp. (Unpublished).

2. Rizza de A. Porto, "Recursos materiais para a biblioteca escolar," in *Papers of Seminário Nacional sobre Bibliotecas Escolares*, 1, Brasília, Brazil, 5-8 October, 1982 (Brasília: Instituto Nacional do Livro/Centro Regional para el Fomento del Libro en America Latina y el Caribe, 1982), pp. 150-169.

3. Sílvia Branco V. Bustamante, "LOGO: uma proposta pedagógica?" *Tecnologia Educacional* 16, 75/76 (March/June 1987), 43-46.

4. Wilson Faria, "Utilização de computadores no ensino básico," *Tecnologia Educacional* 16, 75/76 (March/June 1987), 27-31; Claudio D'Ipolito, "Desenvolvimento de software educacional: arte exclusiva de informatas ou ao alcance do educador?" *Tecnologia Educacional* 16, 77 (July/August 1987), 40-43.

The ABCs of Preservation Microform Masters: Access and Bibliographic Control

37. Microform Cataloging: Current Issues and a Selected Bibliography

Crystal Graham

A machine-readable database of bibliographic records for preservation microforms is the cornerstone of any large-scale cooperative preservation program. One of the obstacles to creating such a system has been the lack of agreement on bibliographic standards. In fact, microform cataloging is one of the areas of greatest controversy in international cataloging circles. This article provides an overview of the problems and issues associated with microform cataloging.

Before machine-readable cataloging, a library that microfilmed an item in its collection often just noted that fact in its shelflist. The 1949 *A.L.A. Cataloging Rules* and the first edition of the *Anglo-American Cataloging Rules* included a provision for such items, which were called "issues," saying that "if variations between issues are so great that the publications cannot be treated as copies but the title and text of the works are the same, they are cataloged as different issues."[1] These issues were noted on catalog cards by means of a "dash entry."

Often the existence of preservation microfilms was unknown outside of the organization responsible for the filming. The Library of Congress (LC) considered the recording of microfilm replacements to be merely "a housekeeping issue."[2] Gradually the preservation community convinced LC and other libraries that it is imperative to communicate the existence of preservation masters. Users need to know where they can consult microfilmed materials, and preservation librarians need to know what has already been filmed so they do not duplicate those efforts. Clearly, the most expeditious method for making cataloging records for preservation microforms readily available is to include them in the databases of bibliographic utilities where they are accessible to all libraries.

Just as libraries were beginning to understand the importance of sharing records for microforms, the second edition of AACR (AACR2) was published. This new edition of the cataloging code took a different philosophy from the earlier ones. The cardinal principle of the new rules was to describe the physical piece in hand. Rule 0.24 laid down the rule: "The starting point for description is the physical form of the

393

item in hand, not the original or any previous form in which the work has been published."[3]   Chapter 11 of AACR2 prescribes that the catalog entry should first describe the microreproduction, with details of the original relegated to a note.

This new approach caused quite a furor in the library community. Opponents of the AACR2 approach accused the rule writers of "an obsession with principle to the exclusion of common sense."[4] Let me give you an example: A patron comes to the library with this citation for an article:

Seymour, Charles. "University Contributions to Foreign Policy," in *The Pacific Era*. Honolulu: University of Hawaii Press, 1948.

In response to her search in the online catalog, she retrieves the record shown in figure 1. The brief record gives the publisher and date of the

TITLE	The Pacific era [microform] / edited by William Wyatt Davenport ; foreword by Gregg M. Sinclair.
PUBLISHED	La Jolla : University of California, San Diego, 1969.
DESCRIPTION	1 reel ; 35 mm.

Fig. 1. Brief OPAC display of "pure" AACR2 record for microfilm

reproduction. Will she recognize that this is the desired publication? If the patron selects the option to view the full bibliographic record and reads through all the notes (since AACR2 prescribed that the note about the original must be the *last* note), she will find that this is the item she seeks (see fig. 2).

TITLE	The Pacific era [microform] / edited by William Wyatt Davenport ; foreword by Gregg M. Sinclair
PUBLISHED	La Jolla : University of California, San Diego, 1969.
DESCRIPTION	1 reel ; 35 mm.
SERIES	Pacific microforms ; no. 6
NOTE	"A collection of speeches and other discourse in conjunction with the fortieth anniversary of the founding of the University of Hawaii."
NOTE	Originally published: Honolulu : University of Hawaii Press, 1948.
SUBJECT	University of Hawaii (Honolulu)
SUBJECT	Pacific Area.
AUTHOR	Davenport, William Wyatt.
AUTHOR	University of Hawaii (Honolulu)
SERIES	Pacific microform series ; no. 6.

Fig. 2. Full OPAC display of "pure" AACR2 record for microfilm

In response to pressure from the library community, the Library of Congress issued a rule interpretation which instructs catalogers to emphasize the bibliographic data relating to the original item, giving data relating to the reproduction in a secondary position (see fig. 3). This Library of Congress rule interpretation was adopted as network policy by RLIN and OCLC and thus has become the de facto American national standard. Other countries, such as Canada and Australia, implemented AACR2 as published.

TITLE	The Pacific era [microform] / edited by William Wyatt Davenport ; foreword by Gregg M. Sinclair
PUBLISHED	Honolulu : University of Hawaii Press, 1948.
DESCRIPTION	xii, 274 p. ; 23 cm.
NOTE	"A collection of speeches and other discourse in conjunction with the fortieth anniversary of the founding of the University of Hawaii."
NOTE	Microfilm. La Jolla : University of California, San Diego, 1969.
SUBJECT	University of Hawaii (Honolulu)
SUBJECT	Pacific Area.
AUTHOR	Davenport, William Wyatt.
AUTHOR	University of Hawaii (Honolulu)
SERIES	Pacific microform series ; no. 6.

Fig. 3. Full OPAC display of microform cataloged
according to LC rule interpretation of AACR2

Since AACR2 assumes that a new physical format for an item meant a new bibliographic description, it mandates separate records for the same item in hard copy and microform. Likewise, the USMARC Format for Bibliographic Data does not provide a means to "dash" issue information onto a bibliographic record. The only way to convey preservation information such as the publisher and physical characteristics is to create a new record for each microfilm.

Problems of Separate Records

The mandate to create separate records every time an item is acquired or re-formatted in microform has caused several problems for libraries, including user confusion, cataloging bottlenecks, and spiraling costs.

Let's look at a simple example of the confusion caused by creating essentially duplicate records for every version. You are looking for an article published in 1987 in *Information Technology and Libraries*. You search the OPAC and retrieve three citations, as shown in figure 4.

You searched for title: Information technology and libraries

3 titles found; Titles 1-3 are:

1) Information technology and libraries
2) Information technology and libraries [microform]
3) Information technology and libraries [microform]

Please type the NUMBER of the item you wish to see.

Fig. 4. OPAC menu screen for multiple versions.

You select the first item listed and discover that it lists current issues only (see fig. 5).

TITLE	Information technology and libraries.
PUBLISHED	Chicago, IL : Library and Information Technology Association, c1982-
DESCRIPTION	v. : ill. ; 24 cm.

LOC: Current Periodicals Room
CALL: Z678.9.A1I53
HOLD: Current issues

Fig. 5. Brief OPAC display of hard copy record

If you happen to remember that there were other selections, you look at the next item shown on the summary screen. The second selection says microform, but upon calling up the record, you see the holdings are for 1982-1984 only (see fig. 6).

TITLE	Information technology and libraries [microform]
PUBLISHED	Chicago, IL : Library and Information Technology Association, c1982-
DESCRIPTION	v. : ill. ; 24 cm.

LOC: Microform Reading Room
CALL: Film 555
HOLD: 1 (1982)-3 (1984)

Fig. 6. Brief OPAC display for microfilm record

If you are truly persistent, you may notice that there was still another listing on the summary screen. At last you find the record for the item you are seeking (see fig. 7).

TITLE	Information technology and libraries [microform]
PUBLISHED	Chicago, IL : Library and Information Technology Association, c1982-
DESCRIPTION	v. : ill. ; 24 cm.

LOC: Microform Reading Room
CALL: X8065
HOLD: 4 (1985)-

Fig. 7. Brief OPAC display for microfiche record

If you are curious as to why there were three postings, you can call up the full records (see figs. 8, 9, and 10). The library has partial runs in microfilm, microfiche, and paper.

TITLE	Information technology and libraries.
PUBLISHED	Chicago, IL : Library and Information Technology Association, c1982-
DESCRIPTION	v. : ill. ; 24 cm.
NOTE	Vol. 1, no. 1 (Mar. 1982)-
NOTE	Title from cover.
NOTE	Official publication of the Library and Information Technology Association.
NOTE	Continues: Journal of library automation.
SUBJECT	Information science—Periodicals.
SUBJECT	Libraries—Automation—Periodicals.
SUBJECT	Information storage and retrieval systems—Periodicals.
AUTHOR	Library and Information Technology Association (U.S.)

Fig. 8. Full OPAC display for hard copy record

How many patrons are able to navigate through these "duplicate" records? Once a user has located a record for the work desired, he or she often stops searching. If the user subsequently discovers that the version represented on the first record is unavailable, a new search of the catalog may not be made. When examining a serials holdings record appended to the first version's record and failing to see the issues s/he seeks, the user may conclude that the issue is not available at all, rather than resuming the search of the catalog for another version record and examining its concomitant holdings record.

TITLE	Information technology and libraries [microform]
PUBLISHED	Chicago, IL : Library and Information Technology Association, c1982-
DESCRIPTION	v. : ill. ; 24 cm.
NOTE	Vol. 1, no. 1 (Mar. 1982)-
NOTE	Title from cover.
NOTE	Official publication of the Library and Information Technology Association.
NOTE	Continues: Journal of library automation.
NOTE	Microfilm. Ann Arbor, Mich.: University Microfilms. reels ; 35 mm.
SUBJECT	Information science—Periodicals.
SUBJECT	Libraries—Automation—Periodicals.
SUBJECT	Information storage and retrieval systems—Periodicals.
AUTHOR	Library and Information Technology Association (U.S.)

Fig. 9. Full OPAC display for microfilm record

TITLE	Information technology and libraries [microform]
PUBLISHED	Chicago, IL : Library and Information Technology Association, c1982-
DESCRIPTION	v. : ill. ; 24 cm.
NOTE	Vol. 1, no. 1 (Mar. 1982)-
NOTE	Title from cover.
NOTE	Official publication of the Library and Information Technology Association.
NOTE	Continues: Journal of library automation.
NOTE	Microfiche. Ann Arbor, Mich.: University Microfilms. microfiche ; 11 x 15 cm.
SUBJECT	Information science—Periodicals.
SUBJECT	Libraries—Automation—Periodicals.
SUBJECT	Information storage and retrieval systems—Periodicals.
AUTHOR	Library and Information Technology Association (U.S.)

Fig. 10. Full OPAC display for microfiche record

"Duplicate" records are apt to be overlooked when they are adjacent in the catalog. When the records have been created under different catalog codes, often causing the choice or form of entry to differ, it is even more likely that a second record will be missed.[5] AACR2 redefined the source of information for bibliographic description, changed the choice of access points, and modified the rules for formulation of headings. While the LCRI rescinded the application of Chapter 11 to microform reproductions, the other provisions of AACR2 remained in place.

When AACR2 was first published, both RLIN and OCLC required their users to input all new cataloging according to AACR2 (as interpreted by LC). The consequence of this policy was the requirement that catalogers create records for the microforms according to the new code, even when records for the original publications were available. This policy proved especially onerous in the case of serials, because AACR2 bases description on the first available issue in contrast to AACR1, which specified the most recent issue. (Compare the records shown in figs. 11 and 12. The choice of entry, as well as most of the description, differs simply because the records were created under different editions of AACR).

AUTHOR	Seminar on the Acquisition of Latin American Library Materials.
TITLE	SALALM Newsletter.
PUBLISHED	Austin, Tex., etc., SALALM Secretariat, University of Texas.
DESCRIPTION	v. 28cm.
DESCRIPTION	1- 1973-
SUBJECT	Acquisition of Latin American publications—Periodicals.
SUBJECT	Seminar on the Acquisition of Latin American Library Materials—Periodicals.
OTHER TITLE	Seminar on the Acquisition of Latin American Library Materials. Newsletter.

Fig. 11. AACR1 record for the original publication

TITLE	SALALM Newsletter [microform]
PUBLISHED	Amherst, Mass. : SALALM Secretariat, University of Massachusetts Library.
DESCRIPTION	v. ; 28cm.
DESCRIPTION	Began with: Vol. 1 (1973).
DESCRIPTION	Description based on: Vol. 3, no. 1 (May 1975).
NOTE	Microfilm. Vol. 3, no. 1 (May 1975)-v. 15, no. 2 (Dec. 1987). Los Angeles: Filmed for the University of California, San Diego by UCLA Photographic Services, 1990. 3 reels ; 35 mm.
SUBJECT	Acquisition of Latin American publications—Periodicals.
SUBJECT	Seminar on the Acquisition of Latin American Library Materials—Periodicals.
AUTHOR	Seminar on the Acquisition of Latin American Library Materials.
OTHER TITLE	Newsletter.

Fig. 12. Microform cataloged according to LCRI of AACR2

All of this recataloging costs a lot of money. While that was a significant consideration when libraries were simply acquiring commercial microforms, it became a major issue when monies were garnered for preservation programs. Imagine the frustration of preservationists who secured funds for preservation filming when they discovered that a large amount of the money they planned to spend on filming was going instead to what was essentially *recataloging*.

The Research Libraries Group, which has assumed a leadership role in the area of preservation, realized that the requirement to create cataloging records according to current cataloging standards was wasting preservation monies. Therefore, they modified the input standards of their bibliographic utility, RLIN, allowing catalogers to copy records for original publications without upgrading to AACR2.

ARL *Guidelines*

The Association of Research Libraries decided that a national standard was needed for the bibliographic records for preservation microform masters. In September 1990, ARL issued *Guidelines for Bibliographic Records for Preservation Microform Masters*.[6] The ARL *Guidelines*, as they are known, call for the application of "retrospective conversion standards" to the creation of records for microform masters. Whenever a record exists for the original publication, that record can be "cloned" to form the basis of the microform record. In other words, a record is created for the microform either by inputting the data as they appear on catalog cards for the original or by using a "copy" command ("cre*" in RLIN and "new" in OCLC) to create a new record just like the record for the original with the addition of a microform note, preservation information, and a general material designation (GMD). A basic set of data elements must be included, but the description is not changed to conform to AACR2. The choice of access points is not changed, but the headings are checked against the Library of Congress name authority file. If a heading has been established in AACR2 form, that new heading is used in the microform record. (Fig. 13 illustrates a record created according to the ARL *Guidelines*.)

The National Endowment for the Humanities, the major funding agency for preservation microfilming, now requires libraries to adhere to the ARL *Guidelines* as part of its funding criteria. OCLC has agreed to endorse and distribute the ARL *Guidelines* rather than require libraries to create new records according to AACR2 as interpreted by LC for all microform reproductions.

AUTHOR	Seminar on the Acquisition of Latin American Library Materials.
TITLE	SALALM newsletter [microform]
PUBLISHED	Austin, Tex., etc., SALALM Secretariat, University of Texas.
DESCRIPTION	v. 28cm.
DESCRIPTION	1- 1973-
NOTE	Microfilm. Vol. 3, no. 1 (May 1975)-v. 15, no. 2 (Dec. 1987). Los Angeles: Filmed for the University of California, San Diego by UCLA Photographic Services, 1990. 3 reels ; 35 mm.
SUBJECT	Acquisition of Latin American publications—Periodicals.
SUBJECT	Seminar on the Acquisition of Latin American Library Materials—Periodicals.
OTHER TITLE	Seminar on the Acquisition of Latin American Library Materials. Newsletter.

Fig. 13. Microform cataloged according to ARL *Guidelines*

United States Newspaper Program

The United States Newspaper Program (USNP) is a major national program funded largely by the National Endowment for the Humanities, to identify, preserve, and catalog all newspapers ever published in the United States. Catalogers are responsible for determining the publication history of each paper—a formidable assignment, given the generic titles and frequent title changes of many papers—and also for recording the specific issues held by each institution.

The decision was made by the USNP managers to make a single bibliographic record for each newspaper title, with local data records giving holdings information attached to the bibliographic record. This single record approach overcomes many of the problems discussed: it is much easier for users to consult a single record than to flip back and forth among a host of records. It is cheaper than creating, storing, and maintaining duplicate records. It is a lot less work for catalogers. Unfortunately, the local data records do not contain detailed preservation information. The U.S. Newspaper Project is geographically organized, with each state filming its own papers, so there is no danger of duplicate filming efforts. But for libraries preserving newspapers from other parts of the world, duplicate filming can be avoided only by the creation of a comprehensive database of records for microform masters, giving their condition and location. The lack of consistency in the creation of bibliographic records for newspapers complicates resource sharing, preservation efforts, and international exchange of bibliographic data.

The Multiple Versions Problem

The Library of Congress recognized the growing incompatibility of bibliographic records for microforms. Within the CONSER database of serials records, Canadian records follow AACR2 as published, most U.S. records conform to the Library of Congress rule interpretation of Chapter 11, records created under the ARL *Guidelines* follow a "retrospective conversion standard," and the USNP records use a "master record" convention. In 1984, LC decided that a comprehensive study of the problem should be undertaken, with a scope much wider than microform cataloging. The term "multiple versions" or "mulver" was coined to encompass all publications that are identical in content but different in physical format, such as sound recordings on cassette and disk, motion pictures in dubbed and subtitled versions, and video-cassettes in Beta and VHS format. A number of studies were carried out to try to resolve what came to be called the "multiple versions" dilemma, but no universally acceptable idea has been suggested.

At the suggestion of the CONSER Policy Committee, a national forum was held in December 1989 to discuss the issue of multiple versions. The goal of the Multiple Versions Forum was to identify a technique for communicating bibliographic data about versions, that is, items with equivalent artistic and intellectual content but differences in physical format.

The technique recommended by the MULVER Forum is the two-tier hierarchical technique—a fancy name for implementation of the USMARC Format for Holdings Data. The model is hierarchical, with a full independent bibliographic record for one version at the top of the hierarchy and dependent partial records at the second level, each linked to the bibliographic record. In the case of microreproductions, the full bibliographic record describes the original publication and each holdings record describes a reproduction. The details of this plan were referred to various groups, including the ALA Committee on Cataloging: Description and Access. A Task Force on Multiple Versions was formed to make recommendations on handling multiple versions. That group agreed that the technique should be limited to reproductions, at least during initial implementation. The Task Force also proposed a rule revision which would enable catalogers to apply the multiple versions technique. In the proposal, the cardinal principle of AACR2 is reworded to eliminate the directive to use the piece in hand as the starting point for description. An optional rule is suggested which sanctions the use of a multilevel description for reproductions.[7]

Progress on implementing the Multiple Versions solution has run aground because of differences of opinion on the implementation phase. While decisions about the USMARC format fall to the Library of Congress and ALA's Committee on Machine-Readable Bibliographic Information (MARBI), CC:DA has opinions on that aspect as well. The *USMARC Format for Holdings Data* was originally designed to accommodate a limited amount of bibliographic data about reproductions. The format includes an 843 field for reproduction notes (similar to the 533 in the bibliographic format) and an 007 field for coded physical description of microforms. The limitations of the current structure pose a number of problems for implementation of the "multiple versions technique." Additional data elements beyond those allowed in the 843 will no doubt be needed, such as edition statements, series tracings, and notes that relate to the reproduction only. In fact, the CC:DA Task Force has identified the need in the subordinate record for virtually every field in the bibliographic format. Some members of the CC:DA Task Force are uncomfortable with the idea of putting bibliographic data in the Holdings Format and prefer to adopt a three-tier approach, with bibliographic, version, and holdings data in linked but separate tiers.

International Cooperation

The Commission on Preservation and Access (CPA) International Project is taking the lead to foster cooperation among U.S. and foreign libraries to enable worldwide communication of bibliographic records for preservation masters. CPA sponsored a meeting in Zurich, Switzerland, on May 13-16, 1990, to begin work on an international register of microform masters. The intent of the CPA meeting was to "find the common ground" among American, Canadian, and European practices and to ensure that records will be compatible, both bibliographically and technically.[8] Representatives from designated preservation centers, such as the National Library of Venezuela, also attended the meeting.

The biggest problem for bibliographic compatibility is the "AACR2" issue discussed earlier: should the record emphasize the microform or the original? The Canadians, who presently use the "pure" AACR2 approach, hope that universal adoption of the "multiple versions" solution will eliminate the need for such incompatibility. In the meantime, they have graciously agreed to follow the ARL *Guidelines* for preservation masters so that their records will conform to the

American and European practice of emphasizing the original publication.[9] To ensure technical compatibility, libraries are encouraged to use a machine-readable format which can be translated to UNIMARC.

Conclusion

International agreement on microform cataloging policies is essential to the effort to make bibliographic records for microform masters available worldwide. During the last decade progress has been made. The U.S. decision to emphasize the original publication in bibliographic description has provided the opportunity to streamline cataloging without impairing access. The provision for "cloning" existing records set forth in the ARL *Guidelines* and endorsed by the bibliographic utilities has expedited processing of preservation microforms. The USNP "master record" approach has demonstrated the feasibility of using a single bibliographic record to collocate all versions of a library's holdings. The technique identified by the Multiple Versions Forum has the potential for enhancing access, facilitating cataloging, and rationalizing the treatment of materials in different formats. The International Project of the Commission on Preservation and Access should be commended for its efforts to develop internationally compatible cataloging and communication standards.

The need for an international standard encompassing the attributes of these developments is paramount. Given the fragility of many Latin American publications, it is incumbent upon us as Latin Americanists to encourage the development of new and better standards for describing and communicating records for preservation microforms.

NOTES

1. *A.L.A. Cataloging Rules for Author and Title Entries*, 2d ed. (Chicago, IL: American Library Association, 1949), p. 43, rule 4:1; *Anglo-American Cataloging Rules. North American Text* (Chicago, IL: American Library Association, 1974), pp. 100-101, chap. 6, rule 152B.

2. Richard Boss, *Cataloging Titles in Microform Sets: Report of a Study Conducted in 1980 for the Association of Research Libraries by Information Systems Consultants, Inc.* (Washington, DC: Association of Research Libraries, 1983), p. 29.

3. *Anglo-American Cataloguing Rules*, 2d ed., rev. (Ottawa and Chicago: Canadian Library Association, American Library Association, 1988), p. 8, rule 0.24.

4. Louis Charles Willard, "Microforms and AACR2, Chapter 11: Is the Cardinal Principle a Peter Principle?" *Microform Review* 10, 2 (Spring 1981), 75.

5. Additional examples of the problems caused by the creation of independent records can be found in Crystal Graham, "Rethinking National Policy for Cataloging Microform Reproductions," *Cataloging and Classification Quarterly* 6, 4 (Summer 1986), 69-83.

6. *Guidelines for Bibliographic Records for Preservation Microform Masters* (Washington, DC: Association of Research Libraries, 1990). The 1990 guidelines cover both books and serials, superseding the guidelines for books issued in 1989.

7. "Multilevel Description Applied to Reproductions," a memorandum from John Attig to Verna Urbanski, October 13, 1990.

8. Hans Rütimann, Program Officer, Commission on Preservation and Access, telephone conversation with author, March 7, 1991.

9. Margaret Stewart, National Library of Canada, telephone conversation with author, November 30, 1990.

BIBLIOGRAPHY

Association of Research Libraries. *Guidelines for Bibliographic Records for Preservation Microform Masters.* Prepared by Crystal Graham. Washington, DC: ARL, 1990.

Guidelines for cataloging microform masters of books and serials. Calls for "cloning" records for original publications, using a "retrospective conversion standard" rather than recataloging to AACR2. Also includes listings of minimum data elements required in all records.

Boss, Richard. *Cataloging Titles in Microform Sets: Report of a Study Conducted in 1980 for the Association of Research Libraries by Information Systems Consultants, Inc.* (Washington, DC: Association of Research Libraries, 1983).

Study of the problems, history, and prospects for cataloging titles in microform sets. Excellent background for ARL Microform Project. Detailed summary of the AACR2, Chapter 11 controversy.

Clareson, Thomas F. F. "Education, Communication, and Cooperation: OCLC's Preservation Program." *OCLC Micro* 6, 6 (December 1990).

Describes OCLC's preservation program, including efforts to create a comprehensive listing of bibliographic records for preservation masters, through a combination of purchase, exchange, and online input. OCLC libraries may input minimal "decision-to-film" records or they may catalog "prospectively," i.e., they may create a record for the microform in advance of filming.

González Garcia, Pedro. "Historical Documentation and Digital Conversion of Images at the Proyecto de Información of the Archivo General de Indias, Seville." *Microform Review* 18, 4 (Fall 1989), 217-221.

An ambitious project to digitize selected documents of the Archivo General de Indias in Seville, Spain, including the development of an automated information retrieval system that will allow users to search and retrieve cited items as well as the ability to consult the digitized documents on a high-resolution monitor. (This article is not about microforms, but it is essential reading for anyone concerned with preservation of historical documents pertaining to Latin America.)

Graham, Crystal. "Definition and Scope of Multiple Versions." *Cataloging and Classification Quarterly* 11, 1 (1990), 5-32.

Background paper prepared for the Multiple Versions Forum describes the multiple versions problem, cataloging conventions, and criteria for evaluating possible solutions.

_____. "Rethinking National Policy for Cataloging Microform Reproductions." *Cataloging and Classification Quarterly* 6, 4 (Summer 1986), 69-83.

Offers examples of the confusion and expense encountered when cataloging serials on microform according to the Library of Congress rule interpretation of AACR2, Chapter 11. Proposes that a master record concept be applied to cataloging microform reproductions.

Gwinn, Nancy E., ed. *Preservation Microfilming: A Guide for Librarians and Archivists.* Chicago, IL: American Library Association, 1987.

Excellent manual includes a chapter on "Preservation Microfilming and Bibliographic Control." After emphasizing the importance of cataloging microform masters, it provides an overview of cataloging options. Also included is a discussion of the often-neglected area of cataloging archives and manuscripts in microform.

Hazen, Dan. *The Production and Bibliographic Control of Latin American Preservation Microforms in the United States.* Washington, DC: Commission on Preservation and Access, forthcoming.

Summarizes the current state of Latin Americanist microfilming activity in the United States and, to lesser degree, in other world areas. After briefly reviewing the historical context of microfilm production and its bibliographic control, the report points out subject and format areas in which filming has been particularly extensive. Makes recommendations for future filming projects and concomitant bibliographic control.

Hirons, Jean. "Report on Serial Microform Cataloging Activities." *Library of Congress Information Bulletin* 49, 7 (March 16, 1990), 124-125.

Describes LC's current projects to provide bibliographic control of microform serials. The Library of Congress owns a large number of serial titles on microform which for many years were not represented in the catalog. The Serial Record Division is now cataloging microfilms produced through LC's Preservation Microfilming Project and also creating records for items selected for filming. In addition, records for serials in commercially published sets are authenticated and made available from the USMARC tape subscription service.

Jones, James F. "Online Catalog Access to the Titles in Major Microform Sets." *Advances in Library Automation and Networking* 3 (1989), 123-144.

Provides an overview of the historical problems of bibliographic control of large commercially produced microform sets, highlighting the development of OCLC's set-processing capability as the unforeseen and triumphant solution. Also included is a very readable description of remaining technical difficulties, such as insufficient index blocks in local online systems for hundreds of identical series tracings. The most serious problem relates to call numbers. While OCLC can customize records to include a local call number, the number does not reveal the position number of a specific title within the set. Although the examples are specific to OCLC and NOTIS, many of the concerns are generalizable to other online systems.

Kruger, Betsy. "Automating Preservation Information in RLIN." *Library Resources and Technical Services* 32, 2 (April 1988), 16-126.

Examines the Research Library Group's use of its automated bibliographic database, RLIN, to support preservation activities. Briefly reviews efforts to share preservation information in the online environment. Describes enhancements to RLIN which facilitate access to information about preservation master microforms as well as decisions to film.

McClung, Patricia A. "Costs Associated with Preservation Microfilming: Results of the Research Libraries Group Study." *Library Resources and Technical Services* 30, 4 (Oct./Dec. 1986), 363-374.

Results of a study of costs associated with preservation microfilming. Includes figures on the cost of cataloging and mentions the Research Libraries Group's policy allowing for retrospective conversion standards to be applied to cataloging of microform masters.

Mikita, Elizabeth G. "Monographs in Microform: Issues in Cataloging and Bibliographic Control." *Library Resources and Technical Services* 25, 4 (Oct./Dec. 1981), 352-361.

Award-winning article recaps the major issues of microform cataloging: changing cataloging rules, deterrents to cataloging, and the importance of integrating microform records with other records in the library catalog. Includes an excellent discussion of the "facsimile theory" (the AACR1 approach) and the "edition theory" (the AACR2 approach).

Multiple Versions Forum Report: Report from a Meeting Held Dec. 6-8, 1989, Airlie, Virginia. Washington, DC: Network Development and MARC Standards Office, Library of Congress, 1990.

Report of an invitational conference sponsored by the Library of Congress and funded by the Council of Library Resources. The participants evaluated various approaches for communicating data about materials identical in intellectual/artistic content but differing in physical format or characteristics. The group recommended use of the *USMARC Format for Holdings Data* for microforms and serials, with possible extension of that technique to other categories.

Patterson, Elizabeth L. "Hidden Treasures: Bibliographic Control of Microforms, a Public Services Perspective." *Microform Review* 19, 2 (Spring 1990), 76-79.

An eloquent plea from a reference librarian to stop treating microform collections as second-class materials. The article contrasts the eagerness of research libraries to purchase large microform sets with their failure to provide detailed bibliographic records of their contents.

Rütimann, Hans, "The International Project," Commission on Preservation and Access *Annual Report* (July 1, 1989-June 30, 1990,), pp. 21-24.

Reports on the Commission's sponsorship efforts to develop guidelines for the creation of a machine-readable, internationally compatible database of bibliographic records that would enable the efficient and timely exchange of preservation information throughout the world.

Willard, Louise Charles. "Microforms and AACR2, Chapter 11: Is the Cardinal Principle a Peter Principle?" *Microform Review* 10, 2 (Spring 1981), 75-78.

Recounts the AACR2 Chapter 11 controversy, making the case for describing the original publication.

38. Preservation Microforms in an RLIN Environment

Cecilia S. Sercan

Preservation is one of the most widely touted fields in librarianship today. We have all heard about the deteriorating condition of large portions of our country's research library collections. We have heard about the varied ways to overcome this problem. Here I describe one organization's approach to a partial solution to the problem.

Research Libraries Group (RLG) has had a Preservation Program since its very early days. With regard to its plan for microfilming materials held by its member institutions, three goals are paramount:

1. Enhancements to the Research Libraries Information Network (RLIN)
2. Bibliographic control of member-owned microform master negatives
3. Cooperative preservation microfilming projects

As early as 1977, when RLG comprised only four Eastern institutions (Columbia University, Harvard University, New York Public Library, and Yale University), $60,000 was evenly divided among the four members for preservation microfilming. By the time the project was completed, some 61 multivolume titles had been filmed. When Harvard withdrew from RLG, its microfilms from this venture were transferred to Yale. One-sixth of the titles in this project were in Spanish, from Latin America. They are:

Biblioteca histórica de la Iberia. México, 1870–1874, t. 1-20 (NYPL)

Bolivia. Dirección Nacional de Estadística y Censos. *Anuario demográfico*, 1941/42–1949/50, 5 vol. (Columbia)

Cuba. Ministerio de Hacienda. Sección de Estadística. *Comercio exterior*. 1902–03, 1905–37, 1940, 1944–49, 1956–57 (Yale)

Estampa. Bogotá, Oct. 1938–1957 (incomplete) (NYPL)

Havana (City). Universidad. Facultad de Filosofía y Letras. *Revista de la Facultad de Letras y Ciencias*, v. 1–40, 1905–1930 (NYPL)

Perú. Ministerio de Educación Pública. *Memoria*. Lima, 1868–1952. 9 vol. (incomplete) (Columbia)

Pica-pica: periódico satírico, literario, crónica imparcial de teatros, sports, etc. San Juan, 1907–1942 (incomplete) (NYPL)

Revista parlamentaria. Buenos Aires, año 1–18, 1932–1949 (NYPL)

Sociedad Geográfica de Colombia. *Boletín*. Bogotá, v. 12–29 (Columbia)

Sociedad Geográfica de Lima. *Boletín*. Lima, 1891–1915, vol. 1–31 and index (Columbia)

We can see that the preservation of Latin American materials was not irrelevant to the early members of RLG.

After this early effort, the preservation component of RLG was not very active until 1980. At that time, the Preservation Committee was reconstituted with a formal charge; the goals of the Program as stated in the RLG *Preservation Manual* (2d ed.) are:

To develop a plan for sharing preservation responsibilities and thus to ensure continuing availability of research resources in all appropriate fields.

To develop a means to exchange information regularly about items preserved at member institutions.

To define policy issues governing preservation responsibilities of RLG members that correspond to their collecting responsibilities.

To outline systems development work required to use RLIN effectively for preservation purposes, e.g., information about preservation decisions, management reports, etc.

To evaluate available technologies related to preservation to determine RLG's potential role as a site for pilot projects, testing, and experimentation.

To identify special databases or retrospective conversion projects that would expand coverage of information within RLIN and assist in supporting rational cooperative preservation policies. [1]

The primary technology that has been used to accomplish these goals is microfilming. This method can capture the intellectual content of endangered materials when the original object does not have artifactual or intrinsic value. Newspapers usually fall into this category; the originals are filmed and then discarded, leaving the microfilm as the repository of the intellectual content of the originals.

In 1981, the RLG Preservation Committee developed design requirements for enhancements to the RLIN system that would include data about microforms that supported the preservation aims of RLG. Also in 1981, the US MARC 007 field, which describes microforms in great detail, became available. By including this field, a record on-line would tell a user what generation of microfilm a member held, separating microform master negatives from service copies, and preservation master negatives from printing masters.

In October 1982 and March 1983, several new features were added to RLIN to improve communication about microforms. Funds from New York Public Library (NYPL) supported the systems development work required. During this same period, in September 1982, RLG received a grant from the National Endowment for the Humanities to improve accessibility of information about member-owned microform master negatives. Eleven RLG members entered records on RLIN for the master negatives they owned. These were: the American Antiquarian Society, Columbia, Cornell, New York University, Princeton, Rutgers, Stanford, Temple, University of California, Berkeley, University of Michigan, and Yale. When the project was completed in April 1985, about 21,000 records had been added to the database; this was complemented by a similar effort undertaken by NYPL, with funding from the Andrew W. Mellon Foundation.

There is a continued effort on the part of the members of RLG to enter records into the utility for newly produced master negatives. Two union lists for these materials have been produced for records entered in RLIN since October 1982.

This commitment was reinforced by a resolution of RLG's Board of Governors in March 1984, stating: "be it resolved that the members of the Research Libraries Group commit themselves to enter titles queued for filming into RLIN, and to catalog their newly created master negatives on RLIN in a timely fashion."[2] The institutions involved have worked out a series of guidelines, specifications, and forms for use in this ongoing project. RLG also leases a vault at National Underground Storage, Inc., in Boyers, PA, to store its members' preservation-quality master negatives.

The RLIN system highlights the presence of microforms in clustered and unclustered files, showing also if an item is a service copy, printing master negative, or preservation master negative. The MULtiple or PRImary display would show:

```
BKS / PROD  Books       MUL           Ret Maintenance NYCX-LDS
FIN TP SARWACASTRA# - 1 cluster
1) Hadiwikjana, R. D. S. SARWA_C_ASTRA. (Jogja, Indonesia
[1952?-54])
NYCX (c-9124 NIC)   NYCX-1 (c-9124 NIC *cba*)
```

This translates as a fully cataloged record for a title held by Cornell University Library: c-9124, the first part of the information in parenthesis; * * in microform; cba, 3 generations: c, a service (positive) copy; b, a printing master; a, a first generation preservation master.

In searching for microforms specifically, there is not usually any problem in the clustered files. With a small number of clusters, the distinguishing asterisks are easily seen. However, if the user wants to make the search more precise, the ALSo command may be used. This is an option only when the search result brings up fewer than 1000 records. The initial search can be input with a searching string such as:

> fin tw boletin sociedad/als gen a or gen b

which translates as *find title words*, meaning a word in the title, subtitle, or added title, *boletin sociedad*, which *also* has the *generation* field *a*, noting a preservation master microform, *or generation* field *b*, noting a printing master negative. The result of this search contains 8 clusters:

PROD   Serials   MUL   Search   NYCX-CAT
FIN TW BOLETIN SOCIEDAD ALS GEN A OR GEN B - 8 clusters
+
1) REVISTA DE GEOGRAF_IA COLONIAL Y MERCANTIL (MICROFORM)
: T. 1 (1897)–t. 21, no. 11/12 (Nov./Dec. 1924). (Madrid : Impr. de Fortanet,
1897–1924.)
DCLC (c-9120 DLC *ca*)

2) BOLET_IN DE LA SOCIEDAD IB_ERICA DE CIENCIAS NATURALES.
Tomo 18, no. 1 (enero 1918)– (Zaragoza : Librer_ia Editorial de Cecilio Gasca,
1918–)
OHLG (c-9662 OCoLC *a*)

3) BOLET_IN DE LA SOCIEDAD ARAGONESA DE CIENCIAS
NATURALES. (Zaragoza : Librer_ia Editorial de Cecilio Gasca,)
OHLG (c-9662 OCoLC *a*)

4) BOLETIN DE LA SOCIEDAD GEOGR_AFICA DE LIMA (MICROFORM).
(Lima : [La Sociedad])
DCLC (c-9550 DLC *ca*)

5) BOLET_IN DE LA SOCIEDAD GEOGR_AFICA DE LIMA (MICROFORM).
Tomo 1, Num. 1 (15 de abr. 1891)– (Lima : [s.n.],)
DCLC (c-9110 DLC *a*)   CTYG (c-9114 CtY *b*)

PROD   Serials   MUL   Search   NYCX-CAT
FIN TW BOLETIN SOCIEDAD ALS GEN A OR GEN B - 8 clusters

6) Sociedad Geogr_afica de Colombia. BOLET_IN DE LA SOCIEDAD
GEOGR_AFICA DE COLOMBIA [MICROFORM]. a ~ no 1, no. 1, nov. 1924;
2. _epoca, a ~ no 1– junio 1934– (Bogot_a, La Sociedad.)
CTYG (C-9914 CtY *cb*)   NYCG (c-9924 NNC *a*)

```
┌─────────────────────────────────────────────────────────────────────┐
│ 7) Sociedad Geogr_afica de Lima.  BOLET_IN. t. 1-  a~no 1-  abril 1891- (Lima.) │
│ MIUG (c-9110 MiU)   ILNG (c-9665 IEN)   NYCG (c-9924 NNC *a*)       │
│                                                                     │
│ 8) Sociedad Geogr_afica de Lima.  BOLET_IN DE LA SOCIEDAD           │
│ GEOGR_AFICA DE LIMA. t. 1-  abril 1891- (Lima.)                    │
│ DCLC (c-9110 DLC)   CTYG (c-9110 CtY)   CUBG-1 (c-9115 CU)          │
│ CUBG-2 (c-9114 CU *b*)   CUBG-3 (c-9114 CU *c*)   FLUG (c-9665 FU)  │
│ MNUG (c-9110 MnU)   NYCX (c-9665 N1C)                               │
└─────────────────────────────────────────────────────────────────────┘
```

The user can then specify number 6 of the MULtiple display:

dis 6

and the resulting PARtial screen shows information in the form of a catalog card through the collation, with copy information below the broken line:

```
┌─────────────────────────────────────────────────────────────────────┐
│ PROD    Serials    PAR    CTYG0619-S       Search         NYCX-CAT  │
│ FIN TW BOLETIN SOCIEDAD ALS GEN A OR GEN B - Cluster 6 of 8         │
│ +B                                                                  │
│ Sociedad Geogr_afica de Colombia.                                   │
│   Bolet_in de la Sociedad Geogr_afica de Colombia [microform].      │
│ a~no 1, no. 1, nov. 1924; 2. _epoca, a~no 1-  junio 1934-           │
│ Bogot_a, La Sociedad.                                               │
│   v. ill. 24 cm.                                                    │
│                                                                     │
│   ID: CTYG0619-S              CC: 9914         DCF:                 │
│ - - - - - - - - - - - - - - - - - - - - - - - - - - - - - - - - - - │
│                                                                     │
│ Film S1459                                                          │
│                                                                     │
│ MIC                                                                 │
│   \NEGATIVE FILM AVAILABLE FOR REPRODUCTION.\.                      │
│   c.1   (CAT 04/18/84)                                              │
│    ead.                                                             │
│                                                                     │
│ NEG    Film NS164                                                   │
│   \Master negative.\.                                               │
│   c.1   (CAT 04/18/84)                                              │
│    ead.                                                             │
└─────────────────────────────────────────────────────────────────────┘
```

Yale does have a printing master negative and a service copy. If more information about the filming were wanted or needed, a FUL1 or BIBliographic screen could be requested, complete with MARC tags:

```
PROD    Serials   FUL/BIB       CTYG0619-S      Search      NYCX-CAT
FIN TW BOLETIN SOCIEDAD ALS GEN A OR GEN B - Cluster 6 of 8
+
  ID:CTYG0619-S   RTYP:c     ST:P.   FRN:    MS:n      EL:    AD:08-06-80
  CC:9914  BLT:as    DCF:     CSC:d  MOD:   SNR:     ATC:    UD:04-18-84
  CP:ck  L:spa  SL:0  GPC:      CPI:0   IDX:u  CMI:u  ALPH:  ISDS:  TYP:p
  PSC:c  D:1924/9999 FRQ:    REG:x   PHY:   REP:a   CNC:    IS:    TP:u
  MMD:d  OR:r   POL:a    DM:f   RR:a??   COL:b  EML:a  GEN:c   BSE:a
  MMD:d  OR:r   POL:b    DM:f   RR:a??   COL:b  EML:a  GEN:b   BSE:a
  040     CtY‡cCtY‡dCtY
  043     s-ck——
  110 20 Sociedad Geogr_afica de Colombia.
  245 00 Bolet_in de la Sociedad Geogr_afica de Colombia‡h[microform].
  260 00 Bogot_a,‡bLa Sociedad.
  300     v.‡bill.‡c24 cm.
  362 0   a~no 1, no. 1, nov. 1924; 2. _epoca, a~no 1- junio 1934-
  515     Vol. 1, no. 1 for June 1924 preceded by "n_umero extraordinario" dated
          Apr. 1907.
  515     Issues for 1955- also called no. <45/45>-
  500     Microfilm. New York, Columbia University Libraries, filmed for the
          Research Libraries Group. reels. 35 mm.
  500     Microfilm. Washington, Library of Congress, Photoduplication Service.
          reels. 35 mm.

PROD    Serials   FULL/BIB    CTYG0619-S        Search   NYCX-CAT
Cluster 6 of 8
+
  533     Microfilm.‡bNew Haven :‡cYale University Photographic Services,
          ‡d1981.‡e microfilm reels ; 4 in., 35 mm.
  650  0  Geography‡xSocieties‡xPeriodicals.
```

Another of the features present in RLIN is the QD, queuing date, which informs RLIN users of a member's intent to film an item they own. The BIBliographic screen for the original hard copy has as its final field QD with a date in the form MM–DD–YY. The Preservation Committee has suggested that no dates be entered in the QD field for items that will not be filmed within a year, except for serials or series where filming is ongoing. The form of the date of ongoing filming is QD 01–01–01.

The users at a member library can search their own records with this index; it is a local field index. This makes it available to preservation departments as a check for materials returned and processed from outside laboratories. What other members can see as a result of a library's inserting a QD is a signal, in the same location as the *cba* we saw earlier on the MULtiple and PRImary screens, a + (plus sign).

```
PROD    Books    PRI    NYCX91–B2510        Search         NYCX-CAT
FIN QD 1991 ALS LG SPA OR LG ENG - Record 1 of 1

Zambrano Palacios, Germ_an.
  Arrivo, poes_ia. Quito, 1959.
  26 p. 21 cm.

  ID: NYCX91–B2510              CC: 9124        DCF:
- - - - - - - - - - - - - - - - - - - - - - - - - - - - - - - - - - - - - - - -
NYCX (c–9124 NIC +)
```

When we request the BIB screen for this item, we see the QD
01–15–91 indicating Cornell's intention, as of January 15, 1991, to
create a microform copy of this item.

```
PROD    Books    FUL/BIB    NYCX91–B2510      Search      NYCX-CAT
FIN QD 1991 ALS LG SPA OR LG ENG - Record 1 of 1
+
  ID:NYCX91–B2510 RTYP:c   ST:p   FRN:    MS:      EL:1   AD:01–16–91
  CC:9124; BLT:am   DCF:   CSC:d  MOD:    SNR:   ATC:    UD:01–16–91
  CP:ec   L:spa      INT:   GPC:    BIO:    FIC:0 CON:
  PC:s    PD:1959/          REP:    CPI:0   FSI:0 ILC:   MEI:0    II:0
  MMD:    OR:      POL: DM:   RR:      COL:   EML:     GEN:   BSE:
  040     NIC‡cNIC
  100 20  Zambrano Palacios, Germ_an.
  245 10  Arrivo,‡bpoes_ia.
  260 1   Quito,‡c1959.
  300     26 p.‡c21 cm.
  QD      01–15–91
```

When an institution that has used a queuing date receives the film(s)
and storage number for the preservation master negative, two tasks are
required: (1) the removal of the QD field from the record for the hard
copy, and (2) cataloging the microform copies, using the cre* command,
adding as many 007 lines as necessary for the generations produced.

Cornell is working on filming materials from its Southeast Asian
collection, a level 5 or comprehensive collection. First, the QD is
added to records for materials that are prepared to be shipped out for
filming. Often this entails creating an on-line record for titles cataloged
before 1973. Next is the dropping of the QD and creation of the film
record. This step can be greatly delayed because of the time involved
in the processes that go on elsewhere, including the assignment of a
location at the National Underground Storage facility.

When we search the title now, the result is:

```
PROD    Books    MUL              Search            NYCX-MGT
FIN TP SARWACASTRA# - 1 cluster

1) Hadiwikjana, R. D. S. SARWA_C_ASTRA.  (Jogja, Indonesia [1952?-54])
NYCX (c-9124 NIC)  NYCX-1 (c-9124 NIC *cba*)
```

There are two Cornell records in the cluster, both cataloged items, one
for the hard copy, and one for the microform reproduction. When we
request the record:

dis nycx-1

we see the "card catalog" display with the three separate film locations
below the broken line:

```
BKS/PROD  Books  PAR  NYCX91-B17807    Ret Maintenance NYCX-LDS
FIN TP SARWACASTRA# - Cluster 1 of 1 - SAVE record
+
Hadiwikjana, R. D. S.
  Sarwa_c_astra [microform]. Kitab peladjaran dan latihan bahasa Djawa-Kuna =
Kawi, untuk S.M.A./A dan S.G.A Disiapkan oleh Ki Hadiwidjana R.D.S. Jogja,
Indonesia [1952?-54])
  v. 20 cm.

  035: (NIC)SN00754.04
  ID: NYCX91-B17807          CC: 9124        DCF:
- - - - - - - - - - - - - - - - - - - - - - - - - - - - - - - - - - - - -

OLIAX \Wason\Film\N10336\Reel 498\no. 4
  v.2-3
  c.1  v.2
  c.1  v.3

MICRO \Wason\Film\10336\Reel 498\no. 4
  v.2-3
  c.1  v.2
  c.1  v.3

NUS   \Vault 49\Sec.41\Drawer 11
  v.2-3

BKS/PROD  Books  PAR  NYCX91-B17807    Ret Maintenance NYCX-LDS
Cluster 1 of 1 - SAVE record
UPD
  c.1  v.2
  c.1  v.3
```

To see more specific information, we can request the BIBliographic screen:

```
BKS/PROD  Books INP/BIB  NYCX91–B17807    RET MAI/Update  NYCX-LDS

   ID:NYCX91–B17807  RTYP:c  ST:P.    FRN:      MS:      EL:1    AD:05–15–91
   CC:9124  BLT:am    DCF:    CSC:d  MOD:      SNR:    ATC:     UD:05–20–91
   CP:io  L:kaw       INT:    GPC:    BI0:      FIC:0  CON:
   PC:m  PD:1952/1954           REP:a    CPI:0    FSI:0  ILC:     MEI:0    II:0
   MMD:d   OR:?   POL:a   DM:f   RR:a012   COL:b  EML:a  GEN:c   BSE:a
   MMD:d   OR:?   POL:b   DM:f   RR:a012   COL:b  EML:a  GEN:b   BSE:a
   MMD:d   OR:?   POL:b   DM:f   RR:a012   COL:b  EML:a  GEN:a   BSE:a
   035    (NIC)SN00754.04
   040    NIC∔cNIC
   100 10 Hadiwikjana, R. D. S.
   245 10 Sarwa_c_astra∔h[microform].∔bKitab peladjaran dan latihan bahasa
          Djawa-Kuna = Kawi, untuk S.M.A./A dan S.G.A∔cDisiapkan oleh Ki
          Hadiwidjana R.D.S.
   260 0  Jogja,∔bIndonesia∔c[1952?–54])
   300    v.∔c20 cm.
   500    Vol. 2, 3d ed.
   533    Microfilm.∔bIthaca, NY :∔cCornell University,∔d1991.∔eon part of 1
          microfilm reel : 35 mm. Low reduction.
   533    Microfilm.∔bIthaca, NY :∔cCornell University,∔d1991.∔eon part of 1
          microfilm reel : negative ; 35 mm. Low reduction.
   650 0  Kawi language∔xChrestomathies and readers.

BKS/PROD  Books  INP/BIB  NYCX91–B17807   RET MAI/Update     NYCX-LDS

HOL
   650 0  Javanese literature (Selections: Extracts, etc.)
```

Here we find all the technical information relevant to the microfilm copies in the three repeated lines for the three generations described. The two 533 fields in the body of the record tell who produced the film and when.

The combination of the QD (queuing date) feature and the highlighted information in the MULtiple and PRImary displays makes the RLIN system especially valuable to preservation officers, collection development staff, and interlibrary loan departments at all the member institutions.

NOTES

1. *RLG Preservation Manual*, 2d ed. (Stanford, CA: Research Libraries Group, 1986), p. 8.

2. Ibid., p. 17.

BIBLIOGRAPHY

Gwinn, Nancy E., ed. *Preservation Microfilming: A Guide for Librarians and Archivists.* Chicago and London: American Library Association, 1987.

RLG Preservation Manual, 2d ed. Stanford, CA: Research Libraries Group, 1986.

39. OCLC and the Bibliographic Control of Preservation Microform Masters

Thomas H. Marshall

Bibliographic control of preservation microform masters is a very important component of OCLC's overall preservation program. As library preservation activities increase, it is imperative that librarians share information about items to be preserved in order to avoid duplication of effort. OCLC hopes that its major resource, a 23 million record database, will assist in that exchange of information. To this end OCLC is about to publish a document entitled *Guidelines for Recording Preservation Data in the OCLC Online Union Catalog.* If the information that they have made available so far is accurate, three options for providing access and use of preservation information will be available in the Online Union Catalog: (1) the use of Local Data Records (LDRs) in the Union List Subsystem; (2) the inputting of preservation data in the bibliographic record itself; and (3) the tape-loading of preservation microform master records, either from local systems or from other bibliographic utilities, into the OCLC Online Union Catalog.

Before any of these methods are applied, several steps must be taken. Once a decision has been made to preserve an item, the Online Union Catalog should be searched in either the Cataloging Subsystem or the Union List Subsystem to determine whether a bibliographic description for the work exists. If a bibliographic record exists, then it must be determined whether anyone has preserved or is in the process of preserving the item. If no preservation record exists, then one needs to be created using the options described below. By creating such a record before the item has been filmed you reduce the chance that another institution will duplicate your efforts.

LDRs in the Union List Subsystem

As of July 1, 1990, LDRs can be created in the Union List Subsystem for all bibliographic formats. At about this same time a new field appeared in the LDR workform. This field, called PRES, is where a library can input preservation information. The use of this field is defined in chapter 8, "Preservation Data," of OCLC's *Union List: User Manual.* The data elements in this field parallel those found in the 583

Action Note of the *USMARC Format for Holdings Data*. *Standard Terminology for USMARC Field 583* and *Glossary of Selected Preservation Terms* can be found in appendixes D and E of the union list manual, as well. OCLC envisions that libraries will use this capability to provide preservation information such as intent to film, condition of item, and so forth. Until filming is complete, other OCLC users would be able to access preservation information in the same way that holdings and location information can be retrieved from the union list now. Once the filming is complete, OCLC anticipates that the union list record will be removed and replaced by a full bibliographic record for the microform negative. Optionally, the institution could choose to maintain separate LDRs attached to a bibliographic description for each format in the collection. This method of recording preservation data might prove most useful with serial titles—it is serials catalogers who are used to the vagaries of the Union List Subsystem and LDRs. Of course, one drawback to the use of this method is that union listing is not currently available in OCLC's PRISM Service.

Preservation Data in the Bibliographic Record

The other method of recording preservation data is to create a bibliographic record that contains the data in the Cataloging Subsystem. OCLC recommends two techniques for recording these data, and they provide a great amount of flexibility. If filming an item will take an indeterminate amount of time, OCLC recommends, in a technique that they call "commitment to film," that a K level record be created from the record for the hard copy by using the "New" command. If no record exists online, a record can be created based on local cataloging copy, being sure to input at least the 1XX, 245, 260, and 300 fields. This record should include the mandatory elements of the 007 field with the $i set to "a." The record should also include a 533 note similar to the following:

533 Microfilm. $b Tucson, Ariz. : $c University of Arizona Library, $d to be filmed 1991.

Once the completed negative is in hand the library can then go back into the K level record, complete the appropriate information for the film, and upgrade the record to full level. In creating a preservation microform record in this way, you should keep in mind that ARL's *Guidelines for Bibliographic Records for Preservation Microform Masters* do not require that these records be in AACR2 form, or even that headings be upgraded to AACR2 form. OCLC does recommend that headings, at least, be verified in the OCLC Authority File.

The other technique that can be used is called "prospective cataloging." If the library knows that the turnaround time for the film will be relatively short, and if the characteristics of the completed film are already known (in order to complete the 007 field and the 533 note), then the library can create a full level record in advance of the filming. The University of California, San Diego combines these two methods by creating a full level record before filming, but adding the "to be filmed" phrase to the reproduction note.

These preservation records should also include other information, as well. OCLC recommends that if the library is willing to provide copies of the film to other institutions that this information be provided in the 037 field. This field provides stock number, institution name, format of material, and price information. If appropriate, libraries should also make use of the 265 field, which will provide an address for those wanting to order a copy.

OCLC's new PRISM service will add a level of efficiency to this process that was not available with the First System. With PRISM, the cataloger can use the "constant data" feature to create a template of recurring data. Thus, any fields appropriate for preservation records, such as the 007, 037, 265, 533, and any 500 notes, can be added at one time with a few simple keystrokes.

For further information about creating these types of records, see appendix F, "Creating Bibliographic Records for Preservation Data," in the *Union List: User Manual.*

Tape-loading of Preservation Microform Master Records

Lastly, OCLC will provide access to bibliographic records and help prevent unnecessary duplication of effort by tape-loading preservation records created on local systems and exchanging preservation microform records with RLG. OCLC is loading preservation records generated by projects at Harvard and the University of Chicago. By mid-1990, OCLC had processed almost 200,000 preservation microform records from RLIN, of which more than 80,000 were new to the OCLC database. OCLC, in return, sends tapes of records input by their members to RLG for loading into RLIN.

Additional Considerations

There are issues other than how to record preservation data that libraries need to consider when instituting a preservation program. Libraries need to verify that their ILL policies relating to this type of microform product are established accurately in order to avoid receiving requests for material that they are not willing to loan. Also, if "commitment to film" records are loaded into a local system, patrons will somehow have to be made aware that the material is not yet available for use.

Conclusion

OCLC has given its users a variety of mechanisms for creating and providing access to bibliographic records for preservation microform masters. It is now up to the users to make full use of these capabilities in order to reduce duplication of effort and promote cooperation in preservation activities.

BIBLIOGRAPHY

Clareson, Tom. "OCLC's Preservation Program." *Conservation Preservation News* 44 (January 1991), 6-7, 25.

Jenny, Kriss, and Tom Clareson. "OCLC Announces Bibliographic Capabilities for Preservation." *OCLC Newsletter* (July/August 1990), 16-18.

OCLC Online Computer Center. *Union List: User Manual*. Dublin, OH: OCLC, 1989. Loose leaf.

The Bookdealer Connection: Access to Information

40. Serials and Government Documents from the States of Mexico

George F. Elmendorf and Joan A. Quillen

At the time Mexico Sur began, in the fall of 1988, the current bibliography of the states of Mexico was little known. No Mexican state issues a formal annual bibliography. Various state bibliographies exist, but all of them are dated and seriously incomplete.

BorderLine, a recently published regional bibliography from the UCLA Latin American Center, existed, but its organization made us believe that our work would be complementary to it, rather than duplicative. *BorderLine* cites approximately 9,000 entries, primarily published between 1960 and 1985. It includes both articles and books in about a 50–50 ratio. Approximately 70 percent of their citations are U.S. publications. Mexico Sur intended to cover 1980 and all subsequent years, only Mexican titles, and no articles, but to cover serials exhaustively. *BorderLine* was not strong on government documents, and we intended to cover state government documents exhaustively. Also, we began in the South, which *BorderLine* did not cover, though we have now expanded coverage to every state in Mexico.

Mexico Sur, now Mexico Sur/Norte, began as a business, but it also had a dual purpose, and that was as a bibliographic investigation. A number of research librarians encouraged the effort with their belief that a significant number of publications existed that were not reaching their libraries, but they had no more idea than we did of the number of publications or scope of the task. This paper summarizes the results of two and one half years of investigation with an emphasis on serials and government documents.

Mexico Sur has now issued 31 lists totaling approximately 8,000 titles. Ninety percent or more of these titles were issued in a Mexican state. The date parameters are 1980 to present. As would be expected, the coverage in the early 1980s is spotty; the coverage from 1988 to 1991 is virtually complete.

We can now say that 70 percent or more of the titles printed in Mexico that deal with aspects of the states of Mexico are published in those states, as opposed to being published in Mexico City. This is a considerable percentage of the total current Mexican bibliography.

Almost every title published in any state concerns that state or, at most, a region.

We use the Library of Congress as a base to calculate collecting level from our perspective. From 1988 to the present, the Library of Congress has added between 3,500 and 4,000 titles, both monographs and serials, to its collection from the states of Mexico, excluding *Periódicos Oficiales*, which would add perhaps 1,000 pieces. I have appended to this paper a chart of statistics provided by the Library of Congress which indicates the direction and costs of the Library of Congress's collecting efforts for the last decade. Recent years are on a definite trend upward, which should continue.

According to our records, there are a number of very strong collections of Mexican material in the United States. It is probable that these strong U.S. collections are getting stronger than most collections in Mexico, an opinion based on conversations with librarians, archivists, and government employees in the states of Mexico. In fact, many of the Mexican librarians and government employees solicit our lists for bibliographic information on their own states and regions.

Some of the strongest collections in the United States, aside from the Library of Congress, are Harvard, Virginia, Princeton, Yale, Florida at Gainesville, and Texas at Austin. In the West, the University of Arizona and the Bancroft Library at the University of California, Berkeley are collecting in all the states of Mexico. Other institutions are collecting regionally: San Diego State University, Southern Methodist University, and the University of Colorado at Boulder are collecting northern border states. The New York Public Library and Tulane are collecting primarily southern states. Other institutions are collecting special interests. The Stanford Government Documents Library is collecting government documents from all states; the Los Angeles County Law Library is collecting *Periódicos Oficiales* and laws from all states. The University of New Mexico is concentrating on adding to its already large collection of Oaxacan materials. This list by no means exhausts the institutions collecting state publications, but it does give some indication of the interest in Mexican state publications. I would expect this interest to grow as the United States, Mexico, and Canada draw closer together in commercial and other ways.

In a sense, almost all state publications are government documents, as the financing and even printing of these publications is subsidized by the state governments and sometimes by agencies of the federal government. But we deal primarily with those publications traditionally considered by most librarians as government documents and/or serials.

Each state publishes what we generically call *Periódicos Oficiales*, though the names vary widely. This serial and government document publishes all the state laws. The periodicity is most often twice a week. It is virtually impossible to receive a complete run over years by mail subscription, and claims are often not answered. We use the state of Coahuila as an example, as we visited that state in March 1991. We had lists of missing issues wanted by the Library of Congress and the Los Angeles County Law Library, which are the only libraries we know in the United States that are collecting all Mexican states retrospectively to 1980 as well as on a continuing basis.

The first hurdle always is to locate where the *periódico oficial* is sold. In many cases it is at the Palacio de Gobierno; in Coahuila it is not. The Press Office of the state government did not know for sure where it was sold and directed us to the Recinto Juárez, another state archive. That was not the right place, so we went to the Archivo Municipal, which is a well-organized research library. They did not know either, but they got out a recent copy of the *periódico oficial*, and we called and discovered the address.

One of the young researchers at the Archivo Municipal offered to accompany us, and it was a good thing he did. When we arrived, the woman in charge told me it was the beginning of Semana Santa and many employees were on vacation, but she would do the best she could. I showed her the lists of needed numbers and she said she could provide 1990 and 1991 issues, but could not provide issues for previous years as they were in a different archive and she did not have the key. The researcher who had accompanied us offered to be responsible for collecting the needed earlier issues and for sending them to us in a few weeks. We gave him one hundred thousand pesos for postage and photocopying if necessary. The woman asked us to return in three hours to retrieve the 1990-1991 issues.

When we returned in three hours, the needed issues were in two neatly tied bundles. We unwrapped and collated them on the spot. This step is mandatory, as there will almost always be a mistake or an anomaly that needs explaining, and the information will almost never be volunteered. In this case number 94 of 1990 was missing and she said she did not have access to an archival copy. She promised to have the older numbers ready in two weeks for our colleague to retrieve. This took longer than usual because of Semana Santa, but even so several days are often required by a state office to get together the right numbers, so it is vital to go early on the first day of a visit.

We returned to the Archivo Municipal to finish arrangements for the older numbers and to see if they had a copy of the missing number.

They did not, but they thought Planeación had an archive. We had a good contact in that office and decided to go over there. We talked with the man in charge of the library, but he could not initially locate a copy of the needed number. He assured us he would keep looking as he was sure they had a full collection. We left our hotel address and went on to other offices. About an hour later we returned to our hotel and discovered the librarian in the lobby trying to call us on the house phone. He had located a copy of number 94. It turned out the number was the Código Municipal of over 200 pages and had been filed elsewhere in a place for codes. We went back to Planeación and photocopied the piece. We then called the Archivo Municipal again to leave word that we had located a copy of 94 and there was no need for our helpful colleague to locate a copy.

We will not say that all states present problems as difficult as those in Coahuila, but all states require multiple visits and collating in the *periódico oficial* offices. Most of the offices do not have photo-copying facilities. They will usually let you take their archival copy out of the building to photocopy commercially, if they have a copy. The final difficulty in Coahuila is a catch-22 law published in January 1991 that a subscription does not cover any issue over 24 pages. This is unclearly stated on the back page of each issue after January 1, 1991. The net result is that a subscription is not a full subscription, and the subscriber cannot know in advance which issues or how many issues in a given year will be over 24 pages and thus will have to be purchased separately. The woman allowed as how this made subscriptions somewhat useless, and we "ni modo'd" as we paid her.

Every state in Mexico publishes an annual *Informe*. This is the governor's report to the state. It is usually presented to the state congress on the anniversary of the day office was taken. This date varies by state. It is an important document, which in the 1980s often is a multivolume set that includes budget and other statistical information. There is no office in each state where copies of the *Informe* are consistently available. Each state gives the copies away rather rapidly to government officials and offices. You can almost always obtain the most recent *Informe* in some way or other. *Informes* of previous years of the same *sexenio* are usually available, though you sometimes have to photocopy one volume or another. Previous *sexenios* are often difficult to obtain, as not all states have well-organized state archives. Many libraries in the United States collect these *Informes*, and they are always offered in photocopy, as more than one copy is difficult to obtain. In the case of Coahuila, we only needed the most recent *Informe* and were given a copy by the office of Recursos Humanos. The director of that office was very helpful and went to some effort to get us various other state publications.

Every municipal government, at least in the state capitals, publishes an annual *Informe*. These are much less elaborate than state *Informes* and can usually be obtained from the office of the mayor or his assistant. Municipal government periods are usually for three years. It is very difficult to locate copies of *Informes* from earlier administrations. Fortunately, few libraries in the United States collect at this level, as the material is so hard to obtain. Municipal governments also publish archival studies. They sometimes publish fiction and nonfiction. Most often they are not for sale and thus difficult to get, and they go out of print rapidly.

Every state publishes a *Plan de Desarrollo* for the current *sexenio*. We believe this has been mandated by the federal government. It is sometimes issued in multivolume sets. The state offices of planning and development usually can provide these Plans. In addition, some states have annual statistical analyses of the results for that year of the Plan. Coahuila is one of those states and has publications for 1987 to 1990.

Another important government publication which some states have completed is a set of basic developmental studies for each *municipio* of the state. As far as we know, this is the first time such detailed studies have been published in Mexico. These sets may contain over 100 volumes. Coahuila is one of the states that have published these studies, and all 38 of the *municipios* of Coahuila have been done. These studies are almost entirely statistical and include demographic, economic, and physical data.

Some states publish an annual *Agenda Estadística*. Coahuila is one of these states. These statistics are more detailed than the so-called Anuarios published by INEGI. In fact, these INEGI Anuarios are never true Anuarios, and many states have only had one year published in the decade.

State governments publish two other types of publications that are not serials. Government agencies publish monographs describing their operations and/or the situation of their areas of responsibility within the state. Examples of this would be mining, ecology, manufacturing, directories of maquiladoras, and the like. The existence of this type of publication varies widely from state to state. They are almost always given away and rapidly become unavailable. In every state the agency with the responsibility described also handles the distribution. In addition, state agency offices are always scattered around the capital city, so finding these publications becomes a real treasure hunt. Other common state publications are fiction or nonfiction that in the United States would normally be published by commercial houses or university presses. This type of publication varies greatly in volume from state to state and year to year. They may be sold, given away, or distributed through bookstores. Casas de la Cultura or Institutos de la Cultura are often government publishers and/or distributors. Sometimes revistas or journals are published by the state government. These may include fiction or nonfiction and sometimes are mixed. They often are quality publications.

Another category of serials is journals and magazines which are not published by state governments. State universities always publish magazines and journals. Often they are published by faculties. State universities also publish annual *Informes*. These are not consistently published and are more difficult to obtain than state *Informes*. Magazines and journals are also published by groups of researchers and by professional societies. Another type of publisher of magazines and journals is commercial, often with a business orientation. Overall, it can be said that in each state at least five publications of this type are available that are of merit for a research library. There are probably 200 to 250 different magazines or journals available from the Mexican states at any given time.

Similar problems exist in obtaining magazines or journals as exist in collecting *periódicos oficiales*. Since any given serial of magazine or journal type publishes fewer numbers per year, the difficulties are fewer. Periodicity is also a problem; it is seldom as stated, if it is stated at all. Mexico Sur has been working with the Library of Congress and the University of Texas at Austin to gain bibliographic control of these materials. This work consists of reporting to the Library of Congress and the University of Texas at Austin after each buying trip concerning new titles, name changes, terminations, and numbering anomalies.

Another type of serial that is very important for research libraries is conference reports. Some of these reports contain the most scholarly information available in their field in the state or region covered. They can and do cover both fiction and nonfiction. They are most often annual publications. These conference proceedings are sponsored and published by universities, by state governments, by festival committees, or by professional organizations. Offices of the federal government sometimes co-sponsor the conferences and the publications.

Examples of conference publications currently available in Chihuahua and Coahuila include the following: *V Encuentro Nacional de Escritores en la Frontera Norte*, published by the Universidad Autónoma de Ciudad Juárez, but co-sponsored by several other institutions; *II Foro de Actualización del Código Penal. Memorias* was also published by UACJ, but associated with the law faculty; *VI Encuentro Estatal de Presidentes Municipales de Coahuila* was published by the state government of Coahuila; *Actas del Primer Congreso de Historia Regional Comparada, 1989,* also was published by UACJ. It should be noted that titles often change slightly, which creates certain technical bibliographic difficulties. Some of these conferences have been going on for fifteen or twenty years. As is common in all countries, publication is often delayed. In Mexico it is usually a problem of funding. An example of confusion that can occur beyond delay is presented by the recently published *VI Congreso de Historia Regional. Memorias.* The confusion is that Part 2 of the IV Congreso and the V Congreso in 2 volumes have not been published. The Instituto de Investigaciones Económicas y Sociales of the Universidad Autónoma de Sinaloa had the 7th conference coming up and only had funds to publish one volume. They intend to publish 4 and 5 as soon as they have the money.

The legislature and the judiciary of the states are also publishers. They publish journals and monographs. These are almost never distributed commercially, even within the state, and must be gotten with a visit to the appropriate office, the location of which is not always easy to determine.

Another source of state publications is the regional office of some federal institutions. Examples of these are INAH, SEDUE, and SARH. Each has multiple offices in each state, and they sometimes publish material pertaining to the state as Centro de Coahuila or Entidad de Zacatecas. These publications are only available in the publishing offices and almost never make it to the federal headquarters for distribution.

This presentation is representative of government and serial publications of the states of Mexico, not exhaustive. As a percentage of all publications from the states of Mexico, our most recent list from Chihuahua and Coahuila is probably a normal range in showing 10 percent of the titles as serials and an additional 20 percent as government documents which are not serials.

In conclusion, I think we can now have more confidence that bibliographic control is being established over current publications from the states of Mexico. It is hoped that with this information, research libraries can deepen and strengthen their collections.

41. LATBOOK en CD-ROM: Una respuesta profesional de libreros latinoamericanos a las necesidades de los bibliotecarios

Marcelo García Cambeiro

Presentar a LATBOOK como una herramienta de gran utilidad para los bibliotecarios y para las personas que estudian Latinoamérica no es una tarea difícil, puesto que la tecnología en CD-ROM (Disco Compacto Láser) se está imponiendo en el mercado como una solución para el manejo de grandes volúmenes de información a un bajo costo, permitiendo el acceso a la misma con gran facilidad y a velocidades sorprendentes, por casi todos los campos de nuestro registro bibliográfico (autor, palabras dentro del título, país de edición, editorial, descriptores, etc.).

La posibilidad de saber lo que se está editando en Latinoamérica hace de LATBOOK un recurso bibliográfico de notables características. Por otra parte, el mismo es además un catálogo vivo de lo que el profesional que busca información necesita, en el momento que lo necesita.

Con esto quiero decir que cuando un librero confeccionaba, tomemos como ejemplo un catálogo de "Sindicalismo" o sobre "La mujer en Latinoamérica", tal vez no existía esa necesidad específica por parte de quien lo recibía, y por lo tanto el esfuerzo hecho por el librero resultaba no del todo eficaz. Con LATBOOK, el usuario tiene la posibilidad de confeccionar el catálogo de acuerdo a la necesidad que tenga en cada momento, con la certeza de que constantemente se ingresan todos los temas que hacen a la problemática latinoamericana.

Por estos motivos, en el año 1987, pensamos que debíamos dar una respuesta profesional de los libreros a las necesidades de la actualidad. Teníamos entonces la idea de que disponíamos de centros de manejo de información, que eran las librerías colegas de todos los países, y que si lográbamos normalizar los registros de los mismos en emprendimiento podía ser una realidad.

Lo que le pedimos fue que contrataran un bibliotecario que, coordinado desde Buenos Aires, enviara la información estandarizada de todos los libros nuevos que se fueran editando. De esta manera, comenzamos a incorporar países a LATBOOK hasta la actualidad en que cubrimos casi el 90% de Latinoamérica.

Participan en el proyecto librerías de prestigio como es el caso de SEREC (Chile), Luis A. Retta (Uruguay), Iturriaga (Perú), Fernando García Cambeiro (Argentina), Comuneros (Paraguay), Editora Taller (República Dominicana), Scripta (México), Piedra Santa (Guatemala), Gisbert (Bolivia), Brasil (con personal de nuestra empresa) y la posible inclusión de Inca (Ecuador, Venezuela).

La combinación de estas librerías con el trabajo de bibliotecarios hace de la bibliografía "LATBOOK–Libros latinoamericanos" una base de datos única ya que todos los libros allí registrados pueden ser adquiridos a través de los libreros antes mencionados con la certeza que existen, ya que cada asiento bibliográfico se realiza con el libro en la mano. Además, la cobertura está asegurada ya que hay un interés en vender libros, por el cual cuanto más información se ingresa más posibilidades de vender existen. Así como también, cuanto mejor es la información que se ingresa, mayor es la posibilidad de recuperar esa información.

Me gustaría ahora contestar algunas preguntas que me han formulado reiteradamente, pues creo que pueden servir para aclarar alguna duda. Por ejemplo:

1. ¿Qué diferencia existe entre Fichero Bibliográfico Latino-americano y LATBOOK?

Existen varias diferencias. La primera es el medio. Mientras Fichero se edita en papel, LATBOOK se edita en CD-ROM, con las ventajas que esta tecnología posee. Sin embargo, también tenemos como proyecto imprimir un boletín LATBOOK mensual y un anuario a partir de 1992.

La segunda diferencia es que mientras Fichero solicita que le envíen información, nosotros la buscamos. Con la metodología que nosotros implementamos, logramos que casi el 50% de los libros que se registran en LATBOOK no son de distribución comercial. Entiéndase por esto publicaciones gubernamentales, de universidades, institutos, fundaciones, etc., de tiradas reducidas y que casi en ningún caso se encuentran fácilmente.

2. ¿Para qué le puede ser útil LATBOOK existiendo bases como OCLC en los Estados Unidos?

Sabemos de la demora que se tiene para obtener los nuevos libros online a través la OCLC, mientras que LATBOOK cuenta con actualizaciones cuatrimestrales, permitiendo saber qué se publicó al poco tiempo de editado. De cualquier forma LATBOOK es, como toda bibliografía, una ayuda más y debe considerarse como un recurso complementario de otros.

Me gustaría destacar que este emprendimiento cuenta con diez librerías y más de catorce bibliotecarios trabajando en el, empresas que creyeron y creen que LATBOOK es la respuesta profesional que los libreros latinoamericanos deben dar a los bibliotecarios de todo el mundo.

42. Publicaciones uruguayas incluidas en LATBOOK

Luis A. Retta

Hace poco tiempo atrás, la firma Fernando García Cambeiro de Buenos Aires, Argentina, nos informó de su inquietud acerca de realizar una bibliografía latinoamericana en CD-ROM. Luego de algunas conversaciones, logramos un acuerdo para que los libros nuevos uruguayos estuvieran incluidos en LATBOOK, con el fin que las bibliotecas e instituciones especializadas en estudios latinoamericanos tuvieran una nueva fuente de información bibliográfica.

Nuestro servicio a la base de datos de Fernando García Cambeiro consiste en una amplia información bibliográfica de publicaciones nuevas de Uruguay, ya sean folletos o monografías. Incluye también ahora reediciones y traducciones, pero no incluye publicaciones periódicas.

La contribución uruguaya a LATBOOK abarca lo siguiente:

1. *Editoriales comerciales.* Por ejemplo, Ediciones de la Banda Oriental, Arca, Librosur, Proyección, Fundación de Cultura Universitaria, Barreiro y Ramos, Tae, etc.

2. *Ediciones de centros de investigación y organizaciones no gubernamentales.* Por ejemplo: CLAEH (Centro Latinoamericano de Economía Humana), CIEDUR (Centro Interdisciplinario de Estudios sobre el Desarrollo, Uruguay), GRECMU (Grupo de Estudios sobre la Condición de la Mujer en el Uruguay), etc.

3. *Ediciones universitarias.* Incluye la estatal Universidad de la República Oriental del Uruguay, y en este caso de cada una de sus facultades (derecho y ciencias sociales, agronomía, arquitectura, humanidades y ciencias, etc.). También incluye publicaciones de la recientemente formada Universidad Católica Dámaso Antonio Larrañaga.

4. *Publicaciones oficiales.* Por ejemplo: Poder Ejecutivo, siendo incluidas las distintas reparticiones que este Poder agrupa, desde la Presidencia de la República hasta Ministerios y cada una de sus dependencias, como lo es, por ejemplo, la Dirección General de Estadística y Censos o la Biblioteca Nacional. Poder

Legislativo, Intendencias Departamentales, Entes Autónomos y Servicios Descentralizados.

5. *Publicaciones de organismos internacionales con sede o filiales en Uruguay.* Ejemplos: ALADI (Asociación Latinoamericana de Integración), CINTERFOR (Centro Interamericano de Investigación y Documentación sobre Educación Profesional), Instituto Interamericano del Niño, etc.

6. *Folletos, proclamas y programas de partidos y organizaciones políticas.* En este caso en particular es digno destacar que estas publicaciones, que en su gran mayoría no son comercializables, son algunas de ellas difíciles de conseguir. Un ejemplo concreto y claro son algunas de las publicaciones del Movimiento de Liberación Nacional, Tupamaros, que son exclusivamente de uso interno de la organización, de un tiraje limitado. Podemos asegurar que el costo que implica conseguir una de estas publicaciones no justificaría su inclusión en LATBOOK, si no fuera por el solo fin de poder brindar una bibliografía de Uruguay lo más completa posible. Por ejemplo: Documentos y Antecedentes del M.L.N.; Conferencia de Ejércitos Americanos, etc.

7. *Ediciones del autor o "subterráneas".* Aquí existen gran cantidad de ediciones, sobre todo en el área de la literatura, y más aún en el interior del país. Ediciones de grupos literarios que muchas veces no cuentan con sedes, locales o responsables. Por ejemplo: Taller de Escritores Asociados de Maldonado.

Procesamiento de la información bibliográfica

La información bibliográfica vertida a LATBOOK es procesada directamente de la fuente, es decir, que las profesionales encargadas de esta tarea la realizan con la obra en su poder. Este trabajo es realizado por dos bibliotecarias egresadas de la Universidad de la República, Escuela Universitaria de Bibliotecología y Ciencias Afines del Uruguay.

Los pasos que se siguen con cada obra son las siguientes:

1. Catalogación de acuerdo a las Reglas Angloamericanas;

2. Clasificación de acuerdo a la Clasificación Decimal Universal (CDU).

3. Asignación de hasta diez descriptores o key-words por libro, utilizando para ello la Lista de Encabezamientos de Materia de Sears.

4. Preparación de un pequeño comentario acerca del libro, a fin que ilustre mejor el contenido del mismo y así como también se incluyen datos biográficos y/o curriculares del autor, cuando esto es posible.

5. Categorización de la obra de acuerdo a la importancia del autor, editor o tema.

Nuestro servicio a LATBOOK finaliza con el envío de esta información a Fernando García Cambeiro, para su inclusión en el CD-ROM.

Reflexiones para el desarrollo

Cabe mencionar el esfuerzo que significa para la organización Luis A. Retta–Libros la incorporación de nuevos bibliotecarios, con el fin de aportar desde Uruguay la información para una nueva obra de referencia.   La confección de esta información implica muchas horas–hombre de trabajo exclusivamente para este fin, pero tenemos la convicción de que LATBOOK ya es hoy una fuente de información bibliográfica, pero que en el futuro será una herramienta mucho más importante para los usuarios de fuentes bibliográficas latinoamericanas. Esto lo decimos porque LATBOOK hoy cuenta con 1,707 libros de Uruguay, pero sabemos que el caudal de información aumentará enormemente en breve plazo.   Según nuestros registros, desde 1987 a 1990, hemos procesado 5,622 libros, folletos, panfletos y/o monografías publicados en Uruguay.   Todos ellos aún no están incorporados a LATBOOK, pero aquellos que estén en *stock* o que no estén agotados irán siendo introducidos al CD-ROM.

A título de información, nuestra librería catalogó en los últimos años la siguiente cantidad de libros, monografías, folletos o panfletos editados en Uruguay: 1,542 (1987); 1,264 (1988); 1,465 (1989); 1,351 (1990, no es cifra definitiva).

La firma Luis A. Retta–Libros apoya a LATBOOK porque es y será una importante fuente bibliográfica latinoamericana. El trabajo aportado no implica otros compromisos con Fernando García Cambeiro, ya que Luis A. Retta–Libros tiene la absoluta libertad de continuar con su misma política de venta directa a sus clientes, y con su misma política de vender todos los libros uruguayos y a los mejores precios.

Notes from Round Tables

43. La carrera de bibliotecología en El Salvador: Su nueva orientación curricular

Helen Guardado de del Cid

Breve resumen histórico de la capacitación de los bibliotecarios

Antes de 1973, la capacitación de los bibliotecarios en El Salvador se daba a nivel nacional e internacional. A nivel nacional eran impartidos cursos de corta duración por la Biblioteca Nacional, el Ministerio de Educación y la Universidad de El Salvador.

Cada una de estas instituciones contaba con asesores extranjeros en forma esporádica, los cuales impartían cursos a los empleados de esas instituciones y a otros bibliotecarios invitados. También impartieron cursos a nivel nacional los bibliotecarios más destacados en dichas instituciones. Estos cursos eran de corta duración y estaban encaminados a capacitar a los empleados que se encontraban trabajando en sus instituciones ya que no existía otra forma de capacitarlos.

A nivel internacional, en la década de los 60, también se contó con el apoyo de algunos países quienes a través de sus embajadas, concedieron becas para cursos de capacitación. Es de esta manera que algunos de los bibliotecarios salvadoreños fueron seleccionados para optar a este tipo de capacitación y estudiaron en diferentes países latinoamericanos, y en los Estados Unidos de América.

También la Universidad de El Salvador aprovechó estas becas y solicitó ayuda a organismos internacionales como la OEA a través de los cuales se enviaron a cuatro personas a estudiar a la Universidad de Antioquia en Medellín, Colombia, en la que se impartía el grado de licenciado en bibliotecología. Es de notar que éste fue el primer grupo que efectuó estudios de bibliotecología a nivel universitario y que obtuvo el grado antes mencionado. A su regreso estas personas se incorporaron a trabajar en la Universidad de El Salvador, pero en la actualidad ninguno de ellos se encuentra en el país debido a la situación política imperante. También tuvimos una persona que estudió en Londres y otra en Puerto Rico. Esta última obtuvo su maestría en bibliotecología. Todo esto corresponde a la capacitación nacional e internacional y a la formación de bibliotecarios a nivel internacional.

La intervención del ejército en el Campus Universitario

El 19 de julio de 1972 se lleva a cabo la intervención contra la Universidad de El Salvador, la cual es efectuada por la Policía Nacional, Policía de Hacienda, tropas regulares del ejército y Guardia Nacional. En la Asamblea Legislativa del 19 de julio de 1972 se aprobó y emitió el Decreto No. 41 por medio del cual se ordena el cese de las autoridades universitarias, la derogación de la Ley Orgánica de la Universidad y la creación de una Comisión Normalizadora que administraría la Universidad hasta que iniciaran sus funciones las nuevas autoridades universitarias. Dicha Comisión Normalizadora funcionó desde el 20 de julio de 1972 al 31 de mayo de 1973. Entre sus actividades sobresalientes podemos mencionar: promulgar una nueva Ley Orgánica; nombrar el nuevo personal docente y administrativo; y elegir a las nuevas autoridades universitarias.

Debido a la intervención militar, la Universidad permaneció cerrada por espacio de un año con lo cual se tuvo una gran demanda estudiantil en su reapertura. Las autoridades de la Universidad de El Salvador que fungían en 1973 trataron de resolver la demanda estudiantil y acordaron el 10 de mayo de 1973 admitir a la Universidad a todos los estudiantes que solicitaron y llenaron los requisitos de ingreso. Esta resolución se ha conocido como "Política de Puertas Abiertas".

Para esta época el país contaba únicamente con técnicos a nivel medio; pero también se necesitaba un técnico de alto nivel que sólo se podía formar en la universidad; de tal manera que la Universidad de El Salvador formaría los profesionales académicos clásicos que siempre ha formado y de ahora en delante formará también a los técnicos de nivel superior para tratar de acelerar el proceso de desarrollo socio-económico del país.

Creación de las carreras intermedias o técnicas

La Comisión Normalizadora de la Universidad de El Salvador en su sesión No. 150 del 23 de febrero de 1973 acordó que cada facultad nombraría una subcomisión para que estudie la posibilidad de establecer nuevas carreras cortas. Esto debido a que las carreras clásicas tradicionales ya no cumplen con las necesidades del país. Se argumentó que el establecimiento de "carreras cortas" es una idea que se tomó de una solución ofrecida en varias partes del mundo al problema de la superpoblación estudiantil, más la necesidad grande que tiene el país de otro tipo de profesionales que no sean las carreras clásicas. Por lo tanto el Consejo Superior Universitario, en el punto 4° del acta No. 7 del 13 de agosto de 1973 acordó establecer las carreras técnicas. Específicamente en la Facultad de Ciencias y Humanidades se propusieron diez carreras: (1) programador, (2) sociógrafo, (3) comunicación audiovisual, (4) bibliotecología, (5) profesor en filosofía, (6) técnico en educación parvularia, (7) periodismo impreso, (8) medios electrónicos, (9) relaciones públicas y (10) fotografía y filmación. De todas ellas la única que se aprobó fue la de bibliotecología.

Y tal como dijimos anteriormente al inicio de los años 70 no existía en el país ninguna institución educativa que formara bibliotecarios a través de una educación sistemática o formal. Solamente se contaba con instituciones que dictaban pequeños cursos para la capacitación de sus empleados.

Fue a partir de 1973 que personeros de la Biblioteca Central y el Departamento de Letras de la Universidad se dieron a la tarea de institucionalizar la enseñanza de la bibliotecología en la Universidad, y es así como elaboran un proyecto de creación de la carrera para ser presentado al Consejo Superior Universitario, el cual fue aprobado después de muchas discusiones. El acuerdo emitido por el Consejo Superior Universitario fue publicado en el Diario Oficial del 13 de agosto de 1973 en el tomo 24° con lo cual queda legalmente instituida la carrera de bibliotecología en la Universidad de El Salvador.

Este trabajo de creación de la carrera estuvo a cargo de la Lic. Ana Aurora Manzano de Kapsalis, en ese entonces directora de la Biblioteca Central que había realizado estudios en Londres, y de la Lic. Marina Flores de Díaz, sub-directora de la Biblioteca Central que estudió en la Universidad de Antioquia, Medellín, Colombia, y que obtuvo el grado de licenciada en bibliotecología. De parte del Departamento de Letras de la Facultad de Ciencias y Humanidades colaboró con la creación de la carrera la Lic. Rosa Victoria Serrano de López, jefe del Departamento de Letras, ya que la carrera de bibliotecología estaba adscrita al Departamento de Letras por ser el que más ventajas ofrecía para albergar a esta naciente carrera. Esta idea de creación de la carrera también fue apoyada por el Sr. Bernardo Melero, director del programa USIS de libros. Es así como se prepara el pensum de la carrera y se somete a consideración del Consejo Superior Universitario y es aprobada la carrera para que inicie sus labores de inmediato.

Luego se procedió a la contratación de profesores, para lo cual ya se contaba con la Lic. de Kapsalis y la Lic. de Díaz, profesoras nacionales con las cuales se inicia el ciclo I del año 1973-1974. Las profesoras antes mencionadas fueron las que elaboraron el pensum de la carrera partiendo de los estudios que habían realizado, de programas de otras universidades centroamericanas y tomando en cuenta la realidad salvadoreña que hasta esa fecha no contaba con profesionales

en bibliotecología.   El pensum quedó establecido de la siguiente
manera:

Nombre de la asignatura	Unidades valorativas	Pre-requisitos
Primer Año		
Ciclo I		
Organización del conocimiento	3	no tiene
Historia del libro y las bibliotecas	3	no tiene
Materiales bibliográficos	3	no tiene
Inglés I	4	no tiene
Ciclo II		
Bcas. universitarias y nacionales	3	no tiene
Bcas. públicas y especiales	3	no tiene
Bcas. escolares e infantiles	3	no tiene
Inglés II	4	Inglés I
Segundo Año		
Ciclo I		
Administración de bibliotecas	3	no tiene
Selección y adquisición	3	Materiales bibliográficos
Circulación y diferentes métodos de préstamo	3	no tiene
Inglés III	4	Inglés II
Ciclo II		
Teoría de la catalogación	3	Organización del conocimiento
Teoría de la clasificación	3	Organización del conocimiento
Control bibliográfico	3	Selección y adquisición
Inglés técnico	4	Inglés III
Tercer Año		
Ciclo I		
Prácticas de catalogación I	3	Teoría de la catalogación
Prácticas de clasificación I	3	Teoría de la clasificación
Bibliotecología y bibliografía	3	Control bibliográfico
Referencia	3	no tiene
Ciclo II		
Prácticas de catalogación II	3	Prácticas de catalogación I
Prácticas de clasificación II	3	Prácticas de clasificación I
Archivo	3	no tiene
Elaboración de índices y abstracts	3	Bibliotecología y bibliografía

Al finalizar los seis semestres (24 asignaturas) el estudiante deberá presentar un trabajo final que le cubre un semestre más.

La carrera inicia clases en el mes de agosto de 1973. La mayoría de los alumnos eran empleados de la Biblioteca Central con lo cual se quería formar los cuadros básicos necesarios para contar con bibliotecarios académicos que contribuyeran a mejorar la calidad de la educación universitaria a través de los servicios que se prestan en las bibliotecas universitarias.

El ciclo I dio inicio con 35 alumnos de los cuales se graduaron 14 en la primera promoción y 4 en la segunda promoción o sea que se graduó el 51.4% de los alumnos que iniciaron. Esto se debió a diferentes circunstancias tales como cambio de carrera, viaje fuera del país o deficiente situación económica. Es de hacer notar que al inicio de la carrera se contó con el apoyo de las autoridades de la Facultad, pues se compró una bibliografía básica para iniciar las clases. También la Biblioteca Central colaboró en este sentido ya que destinó una pequeña cantidad de su presupuesto para la compra de bibliografía de bibliotecología.

Al iniciarse las clases tuvimos algunas limitaciones tales como el espacio físico, lo cual fue solucionado al determinar que la Biblioteca Central sería el laboratorio de aprendizaje. Dicha biblioteca nos dio todas las comodidades para recibir clases y hacer nuestras prácticas y también nos permitió utilizar sus herramientas de catalogación y clasificación. Con respecto al presupuesto, esto era una situación muy delicada pues después de la compra inicial de bibliografía, únicamente contábamos con el salario de los docentes y de esa manera nos hemos mantenido hasta la fecha (1991). Esta falta de presupuesto ha sido general para todas las carreras de la Universidad, debido a la asfixia económica implantada por el gobierno de El Salvador, el cual solamente asigna presupuesto para salarios y necesidades mínimas como agua, luz, teléfono y otros gastos muy limitados. Con respecto a los docentes, iniciamos con dos nacionales, pero luego se contrató a una portorriqueña con maestría en bibliotecología que residía temporalmente en el país y también a una chilena por un período de dos años aproximadamente.

Evolución de la carrera de 1973 a 1990

Tal como lo mencioné anteriormente, la carrera dio inicio en agosto de 1973 con 35 alumnos, la mayoría de ellos empleados de la Biblioteca Central. Casi todas sus actividades académicas giraban en torno a dicha biblioteca ya que en ella se llevaban a cabo las prácticas o laboratorios asignados a los alumnos.

La primera promoción se llevó a cabo en 1978 (cinco años después de iniciada la carrera); esto se debió a limitantes de profesores, ya que durante dos ciclos no se contó con suficientes profesores. El trabajo de graduación de dicha promoción se titula "Catálogo colectivo de publicaciones periódicas existentes en El Salvador". Este catálogo de 601 páginas se distribuyó a nivel centroamericano, a nivel nacional y se envió un ejemplar a la Biblioteca del Congreso de Estados Unidos. Fueron 14 los graduados en esa primera promoción; 10 eran empleados de la Biblioteca Central y 4 de otras instituciones de la universidad.

Posteriormente han existido 10 promociones con una graduación total de 50 bibliotecarios, los cuales se encuentran trabajando en bibliotecas universitarias, estatales, privadas, etc., y se ha detectado que existe mucho campo de trabajo para este nuevo tipo de profesional formado en la Universidad. Además se ha constatado que los graduados han tenido una buena acogida, especialmente en la empresa privada. También es notorio que un 20% de los graduados se han retirado del país por las condiciones político-sociales imperantes en la última década y se ha tenido noticias que dos de ellos se encuentran trabajando en bibliotecas en los Estados Unidos y Canadá. Al respecto deseo aclarar que nuestro profesional es un técnico de nivel superior capacitado para administrar bibliotecas de cualquier tipo: escolares, universitarias, especializadas, públicas, etc. ya que en su preparación se les imparten conocimientos básicos para la administración de tales tipos de bibliotecas. No tenemos ningún tipo de especialización debido a que la cantidad de años de estudio no permite llevar a cabo una especialización, pero se considera que el personal formado está respondiendo a las necesidades del país, excepto en lo que automatización se refiere, ya que el pensum actual no contempla materias relacionadas con la automatización. Más adelante notarán como el nuevo diseño del pensum, sí contempla asignaturas relativas a la automatización. Pero a pesar de esta limitante, el bibliotecario tiene buena acogida, debido a que ya cuenta con estudios formales de bibliotecología, ya no trabaja en forma autodidacta o en forma empírica, ya no obtiene sus conocimientos sólo de la experiencia, sino que su conocimiento está basado en un estudio sistemático que ha realizado a nivel universitario. Además se vale de la educación continua para aprovechar los cursos de capacitación o de actualización que se imparten a nivel nacional y en algunos casos a nivel internacional.

Es de hacer notar que la carrera de bibliotecología recibe a menudo peticiones de instituciones para que se les suministre candidatos para nuevas plazas de bibliotecario o para que se elaboren exámenes de conocimientos para sus plazas de bibliotecario.

Veamos ahora los factores que han influenciado negativamente en la carrera. La carrera de bibliotecología en la Universidad de El Salvador, al igual que muchas otras carreras, ha tenido serias limitantes que han influenciado negativamente en su desarrollo. Detallaré las más sobresalientes.

Desde la fecha de fundación de la carrera (1973) se han tenido dos intervenciones que han limitado el desarrollo de la carrera, ya que cada intervención significa en la mayoría de los casos un retroceso en el avance alcanzado.

El 26 de julio de 1980, nuevamente se da una intervención militar la cual tiene una duración de cuatro años. Durante esos años se contó con el apoyo de la Biblioteca Nacional en el sentido de darnos albergue para poder impartir nuestras clases y permitirnos utilizar sus colecciones para efectuar los laboratorios. Esto se hizo con el objeto de que los estudiantes no perdieran su año escolar ya que la carrera de bibliotecología únicamente es impartida en la Universidad de El Salvador. Además, otro de los objetivos era que la Universidad no cesara en sus actividades académicas.

A esta situación de impartir las clases fuera del campus, provocado por la intervención, se le conoció como "exilio", ya que se había sacado a alumnos y docentes fuera de su propio territorio, fuera de sus instalaciones; pero la Universidad (alumnos, docentes y autoridades) deseaba continuar con las clases, de ahí la necesidad de alquilar locales o conseguir algún espacio físico donde poder impartir las clases y evitar la frustración de los estudiantes al suspender sus estudios. La Universidad hizo propio el slogan "La Universidad de El Salvador se niega a morir", esto debido a que el gobierno con el cierre estaba impidiendo la continuación de las actividades académicas en la Universidad. Para poder trabajar en el "exilio" se solicitó un aporte económico voluntario al estudiante. Esto se conoce con el nombre de "cuota de funcionamiento" pues servía para cancelar los alquileres de los locales en los cuales se impartían las clases, para gastos de papelería, compra de equipo mínimo y gastos varios. La cantidad solicitada es de ₡50.00 en cada ciclo. Esta cuota se ha seguido solicitando aunque no se esté en el "exilio" debido a que el presupuesto que el gobierno asigna a la universidad no es suficiente para su funcionamiento y este fondo se utiliza para diferentes actividades tales como: mantenimiento del mobiliario, equipo, compras de material mínimo (papel, yeso, borradores, etc.).

Además con la intervención se produjo un cruel saqueo de las instalaciones de la Universidad, específicamente el saqueo de las bibliotecas. De éstas fueron sustraídos muchos materiales bibliográficos que se tenían, con lo cual se disminuye la disponibilidad de materiales para estudiar e investigar. Además en la carrera de bibliotecología se contaba con material básico para clases: 5 Dewey, 20 Reglas de Catalogación Angloamericanas 1a. edición, 20 Listas de encabezamientos de materia de Carmen Rovira y otros, los cuales fueron rescatados en un número de 15, cuatro años después de la intervención; actualmente se encuentran en la biblioteca de la Facultad de Ciencias y Humanidades.

Otra situación desastrosa lo constituyó la destrucción de libros considerados contrarios al sistema imperante. Estos fueron quemados en una hoguera. Es así como en el Campus se encontraron restos de estas hogueras con libros semi-quemados y otros reducidos a cenizas.

Para colmar todo este cúmulo de factores negativos, la naturaleza se ensaña con el país, al sufrir el fatídico terremoto del 10 de octubre de 1986 (*La Prensa Gráfica* y el *Diario de Hoy* 1986). Con este terremoto se dañan las instalaciones de la universidad, el edificio de la Facultad de Ciencias Económicas queda completamente dañado, inhabitable; otros edificios tienen daños de gran consideración y se limita su uso a ciertas áreas y la Biblioteca Central presenta sus columnas muy dañadas y se declara un edificio parcialmente habitable con lo cual pierde gran parte del espacio físico utilizable para albergar las colecciones de materiales.

Y como si todo lo descrito anteriormente fuera poco, el país sufre una ofensiva lanzada por la guerrilla la cual da inicio en sus acciones armadas el día sábado 11 de noviembre de 1989 al anochecer. Esta acción armada paraliza gran parte del país por varios días; en algunos lugares duró de una a tres semanas de combates.

A continuación haré una narración de lo ocurrido el 11 de noviembre de 1989. Para la carrera de bibliotecología fue frustrante, ya que habíamos logrado planificar un curso sobre "Redes y Sistemas" con la Lic. Zaida Sequeira, en ese entonces directora de la Escuela de Bibliotecología de la Universidad de Costa Rica quien aceptó venir a El Salvador a impartir dicho curso. Esta actividad había sido planificada con el apoyo de la Secretaría de Relaciones Internacionales, el Consejo Superior Universitario Centroamericano (CSUCA) y la Facultad de Ciencias y Humanidades. A tal efecto se aprobó el proyecto y un presupuesto mínimo para cubrir los gastos de hospedaje y alimentación de la conferenciante. El curso contó con una gran demanda, ya que se llenó el cupo total de 30 participantes. Para el día sábado 11 de noviembre de 1989, la ponente fue a recoger al aeropuerto a la conferenciante. El vuelo estaba supuesto llegar a las 7.00 P.M. pero llegó retrasado a las 9.00 P.M. Pero desde las 8.00 P.M. se percibía en el ambiente del aeropuerto mucha inquietud y comentarios de que "algo" estaba pasando en la ciudad de San Salvador. No me alteró la noticia ya en la ciudad era muy común cierto tipo de ataque que duraba poco tiempo. La conferenciante, Lic. Sequeira, apareció sonriente a las 9.00 P.M. y el grupo de 10 personas que habíamos ido a recibirla estábamos un poco nerviosos; yo le expliqué que había problemas en la ciudad y que teníamos que esperar a que desaparecieran los problemas. Pero mi sorpresa fue mayor cuando las autoridades del aeropuerto dispusieron, a las 10.00 P.M., que todos deberíamos concentrarnos en la segunda planta del edificio y nos explicaron que ningún vehículo o persona podía abandonar la terminal aérea hasta nuevas órdenes. Durante la madrugada del día domingo 12 de noviembre el aeropuerto fue atacado con fuego de morteros cayendo uno de ellos en el área de estacionamiento y otro en una pista secundaria de aterrizaje. Todas las personas que nos encontrábamos en el aeropuerto sólo teníamos conocimiento de que habían fuertes combates en la ciudad y en otras ciudades en el resto del país, pero desconocíamos la magnitud del ataque. Además nos comunicamos por teléfono con nuestros familiares en la ciudad quienes nos manifestaron que no nos acercáramos a la ciudad pues habían encendidos combates en diferentes puntos.

La noche que vivimos en el aeropuerto fue de grandes especulaciones y de terror al momento del ataque. Todos nos tiramos al suelo mientras duró el ataque; prácticamente puedo decir que intentábamos dormir dentro de tal situación. Lo único que nos acompañaba era el calor humano de cada uno de nosotros, el cual se hacía más intenso en esos momentos. Esa noche pernoctamos en el aeropuerto más de 500 personas, incluyendo a niños. Al amanecer dieron la orden de que podíamos iniciar nuestro viaje de retorno a la ciudad "a cuenta y riesgo de cada quien" por lo cual decidimos hacer una caravana con nuestros vehículos. El camino fue difícil ya que tuvimos que detenernos en varias ocasiones por diversos motivos: barricadas de ladrillos, de troncos de árboles, vehículos quemados, o porque se consideraba que algunos de los vehículos que estaban en medio de la carretera contenían cargas de dinamita. El recorrido que debió durar una hora como máximo fue hecho en más de dos horas. Como a las 10.30 A.M. del domingo 12 de noviembre arribamos a la ciudad, la cual lucía con muy poca gente en sus calles. Llevé a la conferenciante a mi casa materna en las cercanías de la Universidad en donde la noche del domingo se libraron serios combates entre la guerrilla y el ejército. Al amanecer del día lunes 13 de noviembre me di por enterada de la magnitud de la situación y que ya no iba a ser posible llevar a cabo el curso. Por lo tanto, en medio de esa situación, inicié los trámites, con la ayuda de varias personas, para ver la posibilidad de que la Lic. Sequeira se retirara del país, tratando de resguardar su bienestar. Es así como el día lunes por la tarde, en el primer vuelo de TACA (la aerolínea nacional), los cuales estuvieron suspendidos desde el domingo, fue factible obtener un espacio para la conferenciante. Con el apoyo de otra persona logré enviarla de nuevo al aeropuerto y luego cerciorarme de que había arribado sana y salva a su país de origen: Costa Rica. Todo el esfuerzo que habíamos realizado para llevar a cabo el curso se frustró debido a la ofensiva ya que todo estaba preparado. La conferenciante arribó a nuestro país pero no fue factible llevar a cabo el evento. La carrera de bibliotecología había realizado mucho esfuerzo para llevar a cabo este evento y todos nos sentimos impotentes al no salir adelante con lo planificado. Pero al igual que nuestro caso sucedieron con decenas de actividades académicas que debieron ser suspendidas debido a la ofensiva.

Otro aspecto que ha influido negativamente en el desarrollo de la carrera ha sido el poco apoyo que las autoridades universitarias han proporcionado a la carrera de bibliotecología, específicamente la Facultad de Ciencias y Humanidades. Esto debido a la limitación presupuestaria que se le ha impuesto a la Universidad ya que desde 1973, año en que se inició la carrera, no se ha contado con fondos para la compra de materiales bibliográficos. Casi todos los materiales que posee se han adquirido a través de contactos personales hechos con otros bibliotecólogos, los cuales han sido contactados por algunos bibliotecarios nacionales que han asistido a eventos internacionales. Las donaciones más representativas las ha efectuado USIS de México, el Centro Universitario de Investigaciones Bibliotecológicas (CUIB) de la UNAM, la Universidad de Costa Rica y la Universidad de Panamá. Asimismo el programa USIS de libros coordinado por el Sr. Bernardo Melero ha colaborado de diferentes maneras con la supervivencia de la carrera.

Además la carrera de bibliotecología, a pesar de tener un reconocimiento oficial, no se le reconoce en la práctica debido a cuestiones burocráticas, ya que no se contrata a personal especializado en bibliotecología para las bibliotecas, sino que se prefiere a otro tipo de profesional o estudiantes de otras carreras para ocupar cargos en las bibliotecas universitarias. Las autoridades universitarias no están conscientes del trabajo de un bibliotecario profesional y consideran que esos cargos pueden ser desempeñados por personas con profesiones afines.

Por lo tanto el status profesional de los bibliotecarios graduados se ve limitado por este desconocimiento de nuestras autoridades a tal grado que para 1975 la Universidad contaba con 12 bibliotecarios graduados y en la actualidad únicamente cuenta con 6. Asimismo se ve como de los 50 graduados que la Universidad ha formado, solamente 6 laboran en ella. Además, los que han egresado en otras promociones se encuentran laborando en la empresa privada o fuera del país.

Propuesta de cambio curricular

Para dar solución a la crisis que vive la Universidad de El Salvador, se lleva a cabo un "Taller de reactivación académica" de la Facultad de Ciencias y Humanidades, los días 15-19, 26 de enero de 1991, cuyo objetivo principal es que los docentes adquieran las orientaciones pedagógicas para elaborar un programa alternativo según las experiencias curriculares expuestas a fin de desarrollarlo en el ciclo II del año 1989-1990. Este taller proporcionará la fundamentación pedagógica para la planificación integrada de cada una de las carreras. Asimismo se plantearon las experiencias de trabajo realizadas en algunos departamentos y que servirían de base que los equipos docentes seleccionen la alternativa metodológica que responda tanto al objetivo de estudio de la carrera como a mejorar la calidad del aprendizaje de los estudiantes. En este seminario se presentaron diferentes diseños de integración para dar a conocer este intento de ensayar una nueva estrategia curricular, la cual tiene por objeto crear las condiciones reales para formular un nuevo programa en condiciones críticas. Los objetivos generales de este seminario taller son:

1. Promover alternativas curriculares que superen los problemas de la desarticulación de las áreas y conocimientos de los planes de estudio;

2. Elevar el nivel académico-científico de la formación del profesional de la universidad para contribuir a la solución de los problemas nacionales;

3. Desarrollar la aplicación teórico-práctica de los conocimientos científicos de cada asignatura en el marco conceptual de problemas concretos de la realidad nacional;

4. Formular diseños específicos de investigación que permitan integrar los diferentes enfoques que las asignaturas aportan a la formación del futuro profesional.

De este taller, la carrera de bibliotecología tomó las bases para iniciar las integraciones, las cuales fueron puestas en práctica durante el ciclo II, año 1989-1990. Se hicieron las siguientes integraciones, las cuales resultaron ser unas integraciones muy adecuadas.

1. Nombre de la integración: Diferentes tipos de bibliotecas
   Asignaturas integradas: Bibliotecas universitarias y nacionales
   Bibliotecas públicas y especiales
   Bibliotecas escolares e infantiles
2. Nombre de la integración: Teoría de la catalogación y clasificación
   Asignaturas integradas: Teoría de la catalogación
   Teoría de la clasificación
3. Nombre de la integración: Prácticas de catalogación y
   clasificación II
   Asignaturas integradas: Prácticas de catalogación II
   Prácticas de clasificación II

Posteriormente se llevó a cabo el seminario taller "Introducción a la planificación educativa" en mayo de 1990 organizado por la Unidad de Planeamiento Académico de la Facultad de Ciencias y Humanidades en el cual se dieron nuevos lineamientos para el cambio curricular.

El ciclo I del año 1991-1992 se inicia el 2 de abril de 1991 y para esa fecha se presenta un plan piloto de prueba, buscando evaluar la propuesta del cambio curricular que se propone. Esta situación la viven únicamente los estudiantes de nuevo ingreso a quienes se les presenta un nuevo pensum estructurado en áreas de conocimiento, los cuales son:

Fundamentos bibliotecológicos I
Fundamentos filosóficos y sociológicos
Metodología de la investigación
Inglés I

Esta propuesta surgió del grupo de profesores del área con la idea de someterlo a consideración de los alumnos para evaluar los objetivos, metodología, contenidos, evaluación y la bibliografía.

Para poder llevar a cabo esta integración se ha decidido trabajar en base a la solución de problemas, buscando integrar la teoría con la práctica, el recurso humano, el tiempo disponible, el uso de aulas y demás espacios físicos, uso de materiales y equipo disponibles, la administración educativa, la administración académica y las grandes misiones de la Universidad: investigación, docencia y proyección social.

Debo hacer notar que este cambio curricular se encuentra en proceso experimental y que la carrera está preparando un nuevo pensum para formar un bibliotecólogo generalista con tres años de estudio y un licenciado en bibliotecología y ciencias de la información con cinco años de estudio.

A continuación presentaré el nuevo modelo curricular, el cual puede ser considerado como una primera aproximación al nuevo plan de estudios.

Ciclo I
Fundamentos bibliotecológicos I
Metodología de la investigación
Fundamentos filosóficos y sociológicos
Inglés I

Ciclo II
Fundamentos bibliotecológicos II
Investigación documental
Diferentes unidades de
    información
Inglés II

Ciclo III
Administración de bibliotecas
Pedagogía general
Historia de la cultura
Inglés III

Ciclo IV
Teoría de catalogación y
    clasificación
Didáctica general
Psicología general
Técnicas de redacción

Ciclo V
Prácticas de catalogación y
    clasificación I
Archivo
Matemática I
Referencia

Ciclo VI
Prácticas de catalogación y
    clasificación II
Ayudas audiovisuales
Introducción a la informática
Optativa de ciencias

Ciclo VII
Problemas especiales de catalogación
    y clasificación
Hemeroteca y secciones especiales
Programación I
Estadística aplicada a educación

Ciclo VIII
Etica profesional
Teoría de la comunicación
Programación II
Bibliometría

Ciclo IX
Estudio de usuarios
Educación y realidad
Programación III
Seminario de la especialidad

Ciclo X
Bibliografía
Base de datos
Seminario de graduación

Para concluir podemos decir que la Universidad de El Salvador se encamina a un cambio curricular total para 1991 en el cual todas las carreras habrán modificado sus planes de estudio tomando como base la política de solución de problemas.

En cuanto a bibliotecología se modificará el plan vigente para actualizarlo a las necesidades del país y además se propondrá la creación de la licenciatura en bibliotecología y ciencias de la información con el objeto de elevar el status del profesional actual, el cual es marginado por los demás profesionales debido al nivel de estudios que posee en la actualidad.

Asimismo va a ser necesario contar con la colaboración de organismos internacionales con el objeto de que nos puedan proporcionar ayuda para solucionar el problema de la carencia de docentes para el nivel de la licenciatura, ya que en el país no contamos con profesional capacitado a ese nivel para impartir clases con el nuevo curriculum.

También será necesaria la adquisición de computadoras, pues en la actualidad no contamos con ningún equipo mecanizado para impartir las asignaturas relativas a la automatización. Además será necesario ampliar la bibliografía para que el estudiante cuente con los elementos necesarios para sus investigaciones.

Para finalizar, agradezco la oportunidad que se me brinda de dar a conocer nuestra carrera y sus necesidades con el fin de poder obtener algún tipo de ayuda para la carrera en El Salvador, y de esta manera mejorar las condiciones de los bibliotecarios salvadoreños.

BIBLIOGRAFIA

Castro H., Pablo de Jesús. *El currículo universitario y su problemática conceptual en la Universidad de El Salvador: Elementos teóricos para la construcción de su objeto de estudio.* San Salvador, El Salvador, 1989.

_____. *El papel de las ciencias sociales, la investigación científica y la docencia en la organización del proyecto educativo de la Facultad de Ciencias y Humanidades, Universidad de El Salvador.* San Salvador, El Salvador, 1990.

López R., Guillermo F. *Investigación sobre política de puertas abiertas y creación de carreras técnicas en la Universidad de El Salvador.* San Salvador, El Salvador: Facultad de Ciencias y Humanidades, 1974.

Seminario taller: Introducción a la planificación educativa. San Salvador, El Salvador, mayo 1990.

Seminario taller sobre investigación. San Salvador, El Salvador, enero 15-19, 1990.

Seminario de reactivación académica. San Salvador, El Salvador, enero 15-19, 26, 1990.

About the Authors

IRATÍ ANTONIO is a consultant, researcher, and lecturer in documentation and Brazilian music. She is also a student of Library and Information Science at the University of São Paulo, Brazil, where she is writing a thesis on Brazilian music information.

CLAUDIA NEGRAO BALBY is a graduate student of Library and Information Science at the University of São Paulo, Brazil, and a librarian at the São Paulo Children's Library.

ALAN BIGGINS is Librarian at the Institute of Latin American Studies, University of London, England.

COLE BLASIER is Senior Research Associate at the North-South Center of the University of Miami. Until January of 1993 he was Chief of the Hispanic Division, the Library of Congress.

DAVID BLOCK is Latin American Librarian, Cornell University, Ithaca, New York.

THOMAS M. DAVIES, JR. is Director of the Center for Latin American Studies and Professor of History at San Diego State University.

CARL DEAL is Director of Library Collections, University Library, the University of Illinois at Champaign–Urbana.

DANIEL DIVINSKY is Director, Ediciones de la Flor, Buenos Aires, Argentina.

MARTA DOMÍNGUEZ DÍAZ is owner of SEREC–Servicio de Extensión Cultural al Mundo, Santiago de Chile.

ARIEL DORFMAN is an author and Research Professor of Literature and Latin American Studies at Duke University, Durham, North Carolina.

GEORGE F. ELMENDORF is co-owner, Mexico Norte, Redlands, California.

MARCELO GARCÍA CAMBEIRO is a bookseller based in Argentina with the Librería Fernando García Cambeiro.

JEFFREY GARDNER is Director, Information Resources Department of the Radio Free Europe/Radio Liberty Research Institute in Munich, Germany, and formerly Director of the Office of Research Services of the Association of Research Libraries in Washington, DC.

NELLY S. GONZÁLEZ is Director, Latin American Library Services, University Library, University of Illinois at Champaign-Urbana.

CRYSTAL GRAHAM is Latin American Studies Cataloger, Central Library, University of California, San Diego.

HELEN GUARDADO DE DEL CID is Presidenta, Asociación de Bibliotecarios en El Salvador, and Docente de Biblotecología, Universidad de El Salvador.

DAN C. HAZEN is Selector for Latin America, Spain, and Portugal at Harvard College Library, Cambridge, Massachusetts.

LUIS HERRERA is Deputy Director, San Diego Public Library.

SUZANNE HODGMAN is Bibliographer for Ibero-American Studies at the University of Wisconsin at Madison, and past Executive Secretary of SALALM.

DEBORAH JAKUBS, President of SALALM during 1990-91, is Ibero-American Bibliographer and Head, International and Area Studies Department, Perkins Library, Duke University, Durham, North Carolina.

CAVAN M. MCCARTHY is Professor, Departamento de Biblioteconomia, Centro de Artes e Comunicação, Universidade Federal de Pernambuco, Recife, Brazil.

BEATRÍZ MANZ is Professor in the Department of Geography and Ethnic Studies and Director of the Center for Latin American Studies at the University of California, Berkeley.

THOMAS H. MARSHALL is Assistant Head Catalog Librarian and Latin American Cataloger at the University of Arizona Library.

PAULO TARCÍSIO MAYRINK is Professor of Library Science at the Universidade Estadual Paulista, Marília Campus, Marília, Brazil.

CONNY MÉNDEZ ROJAS is Directora, Biblioteca Central, Universidad Centroamericana, Managua, Nicaragua.

GILBERT MERKX is Director of the Latin American Institute at the University of New Mexico, in Albuquerque, and Editor of the *Latin American Research Review*.

FRED G. MORGNER is co-owner, Literatura de Vientos Tropicales, Chapel Hill, North Carolina.

CARMEN M. MURICY has for many years served as a selecting and acquisitions librarian for Brazilian imprints in the Library of Congress office in Rio de Janeiro. She oversees the identification and collection of materials on Brazil's popular groups that the Rio office microfilms.

PATRICIA NOBLE is Subject Librarian, Latin American Studies, University of London Library, and SALALM President, 1992-93.

JOAN A. QUILLEN is owner of Mexico Sur, Redlands, California.

LUIS RETTA is owner, Luis Retta Libros, Montevideo, Uruguay.

LYNNE RIENNER is President and Editorial Director of Lynne Rienner Publishers.

RAÚL P. SABA is Assistant Director of the Latin American Studies Center at the University of Arizona, Tucson.

CECILIA S. SERCAN is Ibero-American Cataloger at the John M. Olin Library, Cornell University, Ithaca, New York.

PETER H. SMITH is Director of the Center for Iberian and Latin American Studies, University of California, San Diego and the Simón Bolívar Professor of Latin American Studies.

GEORGE J. SOETE is Associate University Librarian at the University of California, San Diego.

PETER STERN is Social Sciences Librarian/Latin American Specialist at Rutgers University, New Brunswick, New Jersey.

SCOTT VAN JACOB is Serials Librarian, Boyd Lee Sphar Library, Dickinson College, Carlisle, Pennsylvania.

ANN WADE is half-time curator in the Hispanic Section of the British Library and half-time National Conspectus Officer. In the latter capacity she also acts as Secretary of the LIBER Conspectus Group.

XU WENYUAN is Deputy Director of the Institute of Latin American Studies at the Chinese Academy of Social Sciences, Beijing, People's Republic of China.

LAWRENCE WESCHLER writes for *The New Yorker* and is the author of *A Miracle, A Universe: Settling Accounts with Torturers*, among other books.

ALEXANDER WILDE is Executive Director of the Washington Office on Latin America.

ALEJANDRO WINOGRAD is an Argentine biologist and researcher at the Centro de Estudios para Políticas Públicas Aplicadas, Buenos Aires, Argentina. His fieldwork in Patagonia and Tierra del Fuego has been devoted primarily to sea and land fauna. He has been particularly interested in the utilization of technologies and public policies for ensuring the preservation of national parks and reserves throughout Argentina.

Program of Substantive Panels, Round Tables, and Field Trips

Saturday, June 1

1:00–5:30   Committee Meetings

7:00–10:00 LAMP

Sunday, June 2

8:30–5:30   Committee Meetings

10:00–11:30 New Members' Orientation

7:00–10:00 Executive Board

Monday, June 3

9:30–9:45   Opening Session and Welcome

Deborah Jakubs, SALALM President, Duke University

George Soete, Associate University Librarian, University of California, San Diego

Don Bosseau, University Librarian, San Diego State University

Peter H. Smith, Director, Center for Iberian and Latin American Studies, University of California, San Diego

Thomas M. Davies, Jr., Director, Center for Latin American Studies, San Diego State University

Karen Lindvall-Larson, UCSD; *Iliana Sonntag,* SDSU; Local Arrangements Co-Chairs

10:15–12:15 Theme Panel 1

A New Order in the Old World: The Impact of Recent Events on Latin America

Moderator, *Robert McNeil,* Bodleian Library

Rapporteur, *Shelley J. Miller,* University of Kansas

Cole Blasier, Hispanic Division, The Library of Congress: "The Impact of Perestroika on Soviet Latin Americanists"

459

> *Peter H. Smith,* University of California, San Diego: "Latin America and the New World Order"
>
> *Xu Wenyuan,* Institute of Latin American Studies, Chinese Academy of Social Sciences, Beijing, People's Republic of China: "El enfoque chino sobre los estudios latinoamericanos"
>
> *Alan Biggins,* Institute of Latin American studies, University of London: "Libraries *sans frontières*: REDIAL, Bibliographic Cooperation, and 1992"

1:30–3:00   Theme Panel 2. Sponsored by the SALALM Membership Committee and the SALALM Enlace/Outreach Committee

Challenge 500: Focus on Membership

Moderators, *Laura Shedenhelm,* University of Georgia, and *Sheila Milam*, University of Arizona

Rapporteur, *Susan M. Shaw,* Texas A&M University

Suzanne Hodgman, University of Wisconsin: "The Historical Perspective"

Joan Quillen, Mexico Sur: "The Bookdealers' Perspective"

Luis Herrera, San Diego Public Library: "The Public Librarians' Perspective"

Conny Méndez Rojas, Biblioteca Central, Universidad Centroamericana, Managua, Nicaragua: "The Foreign Librarians' Perspective"

4:00–5:00   Tour, International Relations and Pacific Studies Library and Central Library, University of California, San Diego

5:00–7:30   Reception, Institute of the Americas, University of California, San Diego

Tuesday, June 4

8:30–10:00   Panel

The Contemporary Peruvian Crisis

Moderator, *Peter Stern,* University of Florida

Rapporteur, *Angela Carreño,* New York University

Raúl Saba, University of Arizona: "Peru's Informal Sector: Hope in the Midst of Crisis"

Thomas M. Davies, Jr., San Diego State University: "Disintegration of a Culture: Peru into the Nineties"

Peter Stern, University of Florida: "The Literature of Shining Path"

8:30–10:00 Panel

Analyzing Latin American Library Materials Price Indexes

Moderator, *Scott Van Jacob,* Dickinson College

Rapporteur, *Thomas M. Marshall,* University of Arizona

David Block, Cornell University: "Latin American Book Prices: The Trends of Two Decades"

Carl Deal, University of Illinois: "Survey and Analysis of Support of Latin American Collections"

Nelly González, University of Illinois: "Stretching the Budget: Developing the Latin American Serials Collections for University Libraries"

Scott Van Jacob, Dickinson College: "The Latin American Periodical Price Index Revisited"

10:30–12:30 Theme Panel 3

Latin American Studies, Information Resources, and Library Collections: Whither and How?

Moderator, *Dan C. Hazen,* Harvard University

Rapporteur, *Sara M. Sánchez,* University of Miami

George Soete, University of California, San Diego: "Resource Sharing: The Only Reasonable Whither"

Jeffrey Gardner, Association of Research Libraries: "What They Have and How We Might Get It: Son of Farmington?"

Gilbert Merkx, University of New Mexico: "The Progress of Alliance: An Agenda for Confronting the Crisis in Resources for Foreign Area Studies in the United States"

1:15– 3:15 Workshop

Using New Technologies to Provide Computerized Information on Latin America to End Users: Approaches and Implications

Moderator, *Harold Colson,* University of California, San Diego

Ana María Cobos, Stanford University: "Internet Access to Library Catalogs with Strong Latin American Holdings"

Peter Johnson, Princeton University: "Princeton's Electronic Latin Americana"

Karen Lindvall-Larson, University of California, San Diego: "Enhanced Campus Access to Electronic Newsletters and INFO-SOUTH"

Harold Colson, University of California, San Diego: "A Customized News Update Service Using Reuter Textline"

1:15– 3:15 Panel

Librarianship and Library Collections in Brazil

Moderator, *Mark Grover,* Brigham Young University

Rapporteur, *Cecilia S. Sercan,* Cornell University

Claudia Balby and Iratí Antonio, Universidade de São Paulo: "Computer Education in Brazilian Library Schools"

Cavan McCarthy, Universidade Federal de Pernambuco: "A Regional Database for the Brazilian Northeast"

Paulo Tarcísio Mayrink, Universidade Estadual Paulista, Marília: "School Libraries in Brazil Facing the Twenty-First Century: New Formats"

Victor Torres, University of New Mexico: "The Canudos Collection at the University of New Mexico"

4:00– 5:30 Workshop

LATBOOK en CD-ROM: Una respuesta profesional de libreros latinoamericanos a las necesidades bibliográficas de todo el mundo.

Moderator, *Martín García Cambeiro,* Fernando García Cambeiro, Buenos Aires

Rapporteur, *Gabriela Sonntag-Grigera*, CSU San Marcos
Luis A. Retta, Retta Libros, Montevideo
Marta Domínguez, SEREC, Santiago
Roberto Vergaray, E. Iturriaga, Lima
Ivette Gómez Carrión, SCRIPTA, México

4:00– 5:30   Round Table

La Carrera de Bibliotecología en El Salvador: Su Nueva Orientación Curricular

Helen Guardado de del Cid, Presidenta, Asociación de Bibliotecarios de El Salvador

6:00– 7:00   Latin American Information On Line

Planning Meeting (Open)

Coordinator, *Dolores Moyano Martin*

9:00–10:30   **Rio Street Art**

An illustrated discussion on political and other street in Rio de Janeiro
Richard Phillips, University of Colorado, Boulder
Judith Place, State University of New York, Albany

Videos on Environmental Issues in Brazil

Ilha das Flores, Directed by Jorge Furtado
Reforestation in Brazil, Produced by TV Globo Ciencia. Focus on Tijuca Forest, the world's largest urban forest.

Wednesday, June 5
8:30–10:00   Panel

East Asian Economic Relations with Latin America: Research Findings and Research Challenges

Moderator, *Harold Colson*, University of California, San Diego

Rapporteur, *Laura D. Shedenhelm*, University of Georgia

Gabriel Szekely, University of California, San Diego: "Japan and Latin America"

Sharon Flynn, University of California, San Diego: "Taiwan and Mexico and Costa Rica"

Ron Pettis, Gray, Cary, Ames & Frye: "East Asia and the Mexican Maquiladora Industry"

8:30–10:00 Panel

The ABCs of Preservation Microform Masters: Access and Bibliographic Control

Moderator, *Nancy L. Hallock*, University of Pittsburgh

Rapporteur, *Claire-Lise Bénaud*, University of New Mexico

Crystal Graham, University of California, San Diego

Dan C. Hazen, Harvard University

Cecilia S. Sercan, Cornell University

Thomas H. Marshall, University of Arizona

9:00–10:00 Round Table

How Do You Start a Formal Bibliographic Instruction Program?

Sponsored by the Bibliographic Instruction Subcommittee

Moderator, *Mina Jane Grothey*, University of New Mexico

10:30–12:00 Theme Panel 4

Man and Environment: A Battle for Survival in Latin America

Sponsored by the Subcommittee on Marginalized Peoples and Ideas

Moderator, *Carmen Meurer Muricy*, Library of Congress Office, Rio de Janeiro

Rapporteur, *Patricia Cárdenas*, University of Illinois

Fred G. Morgner, Literatura de Vientos Tropicales: "Poisoning the Garden: Costa Rica's Ecological Crisis"

Carmen Meurer Muricy, Library of Congress Office, Rio de Janeiro: "The Environmental Movement in Brazil: Present and Future"

Marta Domínguez D., SEREC, Chile: "Medio ambiente en Chile, hoy: Informe y bibliografía"

George F. Elmendorf, Mexico Sur/Norte: "Mexico's Environmental and Ecological Organizations and Movements"

Alejandro Winograd, Centro de Estudios para Políticas Públicas Aplicadas, Buenos Aires: "Areas naturales protegidas y desarrollo: Perspectivas y restricciones para el manejo de parques y reservas en la Argentina"

1:00– 2:45 Theme Panel 5

Liberty and Justice for All: Human Rights and Democratization in Latin America

Moderator, *Deborah Jakubs*, Duke University

Rapporteur, *Nancy L. Hallock*, University of Pittsburgh

Alex Wilde, Washington Office on Latin America: "Do Human Rights Exist in Latin American Democracies?"

Lawrence Weschler, *The New Yorker*: "A Miracle, A Universe: Settling Accounts with Torturers"

Beatriz Manz, University of California, Berkeley: "Elections without Change: The Human Rights Record of Guatemala"

Commentator, *Ariel Dorfman*, Duke University and Santiago, Chile

3:00– 4:30 Theme Panel 6

450 Years of Publishing in the Americas: What Lies Ahead?

Moderator, *James Breedlove*, Stanford University

Rapporteur, *Rafael E. Tarragó*, University of Notre Dame

Daniel Divinsky, Ediciones de la Flor, Buenos Aires: "Acerca de la inexistencia de América Latina como uno de los inconvenientes para adquirir material literario a su respecto"

Conny Méndez Rojas, Universidad Centroamericana, Managua: "La situación de la producción bibliográfica nicaragüense"

Grant Barnes, Stanford University Press: "How to Lose Money Publishing Prize Winning Books"

Lynne Rienner, Lynne Rienner Publishers: "Is the Sky Falling? Scholarly Publishing in the 1990s"

4:30– 5:30 Round Table

Latin American Reference Services

Sponsored by the Reference Services Subcommittee

Moderator, *Tony Harvell*, University of Miami

Benita Weber Vassallo, Inter-American Development Bank Library

Gayle Williams, University of Georgia Library

Bruce Harley, San Diego State University Library

Ted Reidinger, Ohio State University Library

Carolyn Mountain, Parish Business Library, University of New Mexico

Tony Harvell, University of Miami Library

4:30– 5:30   Round Table

Electronic Imaging and Latin American Materials: How and When Will We Feel an Impact?

Moderator, *Grete Pasch*, University of Texas, Austin

4:30– 5:30   Round Table

Transborder Maps

Moderator, *Larry Cruse*, University of California, San Diego

Charlene Baldwin, University of Arizona

Heather Rex, University of New Mexico

Rodrigo Quintanilla C., Universidad Autónoma de Baja California

7:00– 9:45   Bookdealers' Reception, Harbor House, Seaport Village

A reading by writer Ariel Dorfman from *Memoria*, a murder-mystery-in-progress.

Thursday, June 6

8:30–10:30   Panel

The Conspectus Ten Years On: Achievements and Future Prospects

Moderator, *Ann Wade,* The British Library

Rapporteur, *Peter S. Bushnell,* University of Florida

Dan C. Hazen, Harvard College Library: "The Latin American Conspectus: Panacea or Pig in a Poke?"

Patricia Noble, University of London Library: "Collection Evaluation Techniques: A British Pilot Study"

Ann Wade, The British Library: "European Approaches to the Conspectus"

Jim Coleman, The Research Libraries Group, Inc.: "Collection Assessment in 1992: The Conspectus Future Perfect"

8:30–10:30 Panel

The Book Dealer Connection: Access to Information

Moderator, *Lief Adleson,* Books from Mexico

Rapporteur, *Scott J. Van Jacob,* Dickinson College

Alfredo Montalvo, Editorial Inca: "El Proyecto Biblioteca Andina"

9:30–10:45 Round Table

Cataloging Issues and SALALM: What Have We Done and Where Are We Heading?

Moderators, *Gayle Williams,* University of Georgia, and *Richard Phillips,* University of Colorado